CAPTAINS AND CABINETS

CAPTAINS &
CABINETS

David F. Trask

Anglo-American Naval Relations, 1917-1918

University of Missouri Press

Title page photograph courtesy of United States Naval Institute.

Permission has been granted by Culver Pictures, Inc., for use of the photographs on pages 9 and 17; by the Audio-Visual Records Branch, National Archives and Records Service for use of the U. S. Signal Corps photographs on page 10, 13, 18, 19, 22, and 24, and for the U. S. War Department General Staff photographs on pages 11 and 20; by the Division of Naval History, Department of the Navy, for use of the photographs on pages 12, 15, 16, and 21; by Brown Brothers for the use of the photographs on pages 14 and 23.

FOR
AMANDA RUTH TRASK
NOEL HUGH TRASK

CONTENTS

PREFACE, 25

1 | Naval-Political Aspects of the American Intervention, 29
January–April, 1917

2 | Early Preparations for the Victory at Sea, 61
April–July, 1917

3 | The Abortive Secret Treaty of 1917, 102

4 | Anxious Months, 126
July–September, 1917

5 | Organizing the Sea Battle, 158
September–December, 1917

6 | Victory in the Atlantic, 186
January–September, 1918

7 | Frustration in the Mediterranean, 225
April, 1917–November, 1918

8 | The Geddes Mission, 283
August–October, 1918

9 | The Naval Armistice, 313
November, 1918

10 | Conclusion, 356

BIBLIOGRAPHICAL ESSAY, 366

LIST OF CHARTS AND MAPS, 374

INDEX, 375

Adm. William S. Sims, force commander of the United States Navy in European Waters. This portrait effectively conveys Sims's self-confidence and strength—an important reason why he exercised great influence on Anglo-American naval relations during 1917–1918.

Arrival of the British Mission in Washington, D.C., on April 22,
1917. Foreign Secretary Arthur James Balfour is second from
left. Secretary of State Robert Lansing is third from left.
The British mission was the first to arrive from Europe, and
it conducted by far the most important negotiations of any
such group. The discussions inaugurated high-level contacts
between the American and Entente governments.

*The British Prime Minister David Lloyd George boarding ship
in France prior to a channel crossing. His sound grasp
of the problems caused by the German undersea offensive
contributed greatly to the adoption of convoy and other
decisions that eventually led to the victory at sea.*

*Secretary of the Navy Josephus Daniels greeting Adm.
William W. Benson, the chief of naval operations. Benson
and Daniels often differed from the views of Admiral Sims,
but they lent support to decisions that put the fleet
commander's views into practice.*

The German leaders. Left to right: Gen. Erich Ludendorff; Kaiser Wilhelm II; Gen. Paul von Hindenburg. Note the Kaiser's withered left arm. These men staked all on the outcome of the submarine war and supported the effort to the bitter end.

Adm. Henning von Holtzendorff, one of the leading supporters of Germany's unrestricted submarine warfare against world shipping during 1917–1918.

Four German submarines in the original "U" series. Later types were larger and could stay out for longer time periods, but undersea craft of this type proved quite effective against merchant shipping.

One of the German U-cruisers developed for use against Allied commerce in 1918. Deployment of these vessels caused much concern, but they proved relatively ineffective because they were awkward and slow at sea. Only a few were actually sent out.

Aerial view of the German High Sea Fleet lying at anchor in Kiel Harbor. The High Sea Fleet generally avoided direct combat, but its presence at Kiel and Heligoland tied down the British Grand Fleet, preventing the Admiralty from using it in antisubmarine operations.

American naval vessels creating a smoke screen to protect a convoy from U-boats in the North Atlantic, 1917. The dazzle painting was intended to camouflage the warships.

The American transport Covington *after being torpedoed on July 1, 1918. This vessel was the first lost while under United States convoy. No American transports were sunk while loaded with troops en route to Europe.*

From left to right: Adm. David Beatty, commander of the British Grand Fleet; Adm. Hugh Rodman, commander of the American battleship squadron attached to the Grand Fleet; King George V; the Prince of Wales (later King Edward VIII and Duke of Windsor); Adm. William S. Sims, over-all American naval commander in Europe. This friendly gathering symbolized close Anglo-American accord in the European theater.

Adm. William S. Sims is second from right, and to his left stands Assistant Secretary of the Navy Franklin D. Roosevelt. The occasion was Sims's return from Europe in 1919. Sims often received strong support from Roosevelt in controversies within the Navy Department.

An American mine layer in the North Sea, helping to lay the
great barrage between Scotland and Norway during 1918. The
task was not completed in time to test the effectiveness of
the barrier properly, although German crews apparently
experienced morale problems as the barrier developed during
the final stages of the war.

The American Admiral Hugh Rodman's battleship division returning to the United States after service with the British Grand Fleet. The presence of these ships in European waters as part of the force that blockaded the German fleet allowed the Admiralty to detach some British vessels for other duties.

Woodrow Wilson in France after the armistice. The President supported his naval leadership in almost every critical respect despite his frequent doubts about the soundness of British naval policy.

PREFACE

For many years historians of the United States participation in World War I were more interested in neutrality (1914–1917) and peacemaking (1919–1920) than in belligerency (1917–1918). Environmental influences between the wars and during World War II drew attention principally to the questions of how the United States entered the war in 1917 and why the peace settlement of 1919 failed to accomplish its purposes.

Circumstances of late have altered considerably; events since 1945 have stimulated interest in the conduct of the war itself as against its origins and consequences. A group of historians more detached from the events of the First World War than distinguished predecessors have made important contributions to our understanding of belligerency—among them Victor Mamatey, Lawrence Gelfand, Arno Mayer, Edward Coffman, N. Gordon Levin, Jr., Daniel Beaver, Wilton Fowler, and Mark Gilderhus. All have benefited from massive archival collections not opened until recent years. The government records of the United States and Great Britain are now available; some French naval records can be examined, but the Italian government had not granted access to any of its materials when this research was in progress.

In an earlier work, *The United States in the Supreme War Council* (1961), I examined the connections between President Wilson's international political objectives and American military strategy during 1917–1918 in the context of the western coalition. The present study extends that enterprise in that it considers the relations between Wilsonian policy and American *naval* strategy in an inter-Allied context during 1917–1918. Almost no prior research has been directed specifically to this subject.

This book concentrates on Anglo-American naval-political relations, because the United States Navy operated in 1917–1918 primarily in support of the Royal Navy. In the past much attention has been given to the general correspondence between American and British policy and strategy during World War I, and this study in general supports that interpretation. And yet, within the over-all pattern of cooperation there appear jarring exceptions. In recent years historians of World War II have pointed increasingly to American differences with Great Britain over war aims and grand strategy. Adam Ulam writes in his recent study of the Cold War entitled *The Rivals* that in reading various accounts of wartime diplomacy "one gets a strong impression that to many Americans in responsible positions British imperialism loomed as much of a potential threat to peace as unreconstructed Russian communism." The following pages convey a somewhat parallel impression of numerous American leaders during World War I, who frequently reflected concern not only about German autocracy but also about British postwar intentions. The controversy about freedom of the seas that divided the British and Americans during the pre-Armistice discussions of 1918 provides perhaps the most significant illustration of Anglo-American conflict during World War I. After all, traditional American espousal of freedom of the seas had rested on antipathy toward the British Empire, supported as it was by the power of the Royal Navy. The requirement of close Anglo-American cooperation during World War I by no means eliminated this historic reality, although it certainly tended to obscure it.

The author hopes that his findings will be of value to readers interested in the study of naval-political history during the immediate postwar years, particularly during the Paris Peace Conference (1919–1920) and the Washington Conference (1921–1922). In a broader sense this study may help to put into sharper perspective the course of events during World War II when, once again, the United States and Great Britain found themselves associated in a martial enterprise that entailed both cooperation and conflict.

What follows is by no means a comprehensive study of all naval-political developments during the phase of American belligerency. Little attention is paid to naval tactics. The investigation skirts the tangled subjects of blockade and relations with neutral powers, to which the distinguished student of those subjects, Marion Siney, is now directing her attention. It avoids inquiry into American activity in Pacific waters, a topic preempted by Professor William Braisted in two brilliant volumes. The work does not present a general history of the Navy Department during 1917–1918, also an important subject to which other investigators might turn. It recognizes the vast importance of domestic social, political, and economic influences upon the course of naval-political history, but it leaves that fascinating subject largely to others, with the hope that information contained herein constitutes a useful point of departure.

This work collects and synthesizes prior research on its subject and in addition investigates certain developments to which previous authorities have given little or no attention. In the latter category are the history of the Allied Naval Council, the story of American involvement in the Mediterranean theater of naval operations, and the Anglo-American controversy over naval questions during the pre-Armistice negotiations in October-November, 1918. These subjects are now open to study because important source collections not available until very recent years contain highly useful information about them. Since this work attempts to utilize and to unite the work of both diplomatic and naval historians, it may on occasion create a certain confusion. Naval historians may encounter an unusual amount of commentary on the diplomatic negotiations of the time; historians of foreign relations might well find the details of naval activity somewhat extended. This outcome is an unavoidable consequence of attempting the study of naval-political history, an enterprise that has not been pursued as assiduously in the United States as in some other locations despite the distinguished tradition inaugurated by Adm. Alfred Thayer Mahan.

I am particularly indebted to the directors and staffs of certain libraries and archives, including the Olin Memorial Library of Wesleyan University, the Love Library of the University of Nebraska, the Frank Melville Library of the State University of New York at Stony Brook, the Houghton Library of Harvard University, the Yale University Library, the National Archives of the United States, the Naval Historical Foundation, the Franklin D. Roosevelt Library (Hyde Park, New York), the Public Record Office of Great Britain, the British Museum, the Beaverbrook Library (London), and the Service Historique de la Marine (Paris).

Several distinguished colleagues in the history of American foreign relations have counseled me in various helpful ways, among them Lawrence Gelfand of the University of Iowa; Ernest R. May of Harvard University; Raymond G. O'Connor of the University of Miami; Walter V. and Marie V. Scholes of the University of Missouri; Samuel Wells, Jr., of the University of North Carolina at Chapel Hill. My colleagues at Stony Brook lent constant stimulus by the simple devices of friendship and counsel, particularly John W. Pratt and Bernard Semmel.

My first intellectual debt is to Dr. Holger H. Herwig, Assistant Professor of History at Vanderbilt University, with whom I have collaborated in certain specialized researches on German-American naval conflict. Dr. Herwig unselfishly shared aspects of his own research on the German Navy during World War I.

The research foundations of the University of Nebraska and the State University of New York supported this study by extending summer fellowships and grants-in-aid.

My wife, Elizabeth Brooks Trask, shared the tribulations of travel and undertook the typing of this text, for which I am once again most grateful.

D. F. T.
Setauket, New York
June, 1972

CHAPTER 1

NAVAL-POLITICAL ASPECTS OF THE AMERICAN INTERVENTION
January–April, 1917

The strategy of warfare at sea, like that involved in land formations, must reflect the political circumstances of the conflict itself, particularly the aims of the contending powers. In short, those who plan and direct naval operations must bear in mind a broad range of political as well as strictly naval considerations. The task of coordinating strategy and policy often becomes especially complicated when coalitions wage warfare, simply because nations who fight together are rarely in complete accord either on the aims of the war or on the means of engaging the enemy. The lack of unanimity on these matters may place notable restraints on the options of individual powers, even those with the most imposing forces.

Despite these rather obvious realities, historians of the American intervention in World War I have given little attention to the relations between naval policy and strategy during the months from April, 1917, to November, 1918, when the United States was a belligerent power in the western coalition. There are useful studies of naval tactics and some enlightening biographies and memoirs of naval leaders, but there exist no extended accounts of the connections between the war at sea and the foreign relations of the United States as they evolved within the context of the western coalition.

Among a broad range of questions that might be raised about the naval-political history of 1917–1918, certain ones are emphasized in the following pages. Above all, what constituted the naval strategy of the United States, and what factors affected its formulation? Those who conducted naval policy had to take into consideration the relationship between American naval actions and those of their European associates—particularly those of Great Britain, but also to an important degree those of France and Italy. In addition, the general diplomatic relations between the principal members of the western coalition impinged upon the conduct of the naval war in many significant ways.

Secondly, how did the United States organize the deployment of its naval forces? In this context, two sets of relationships require extensive analysis, namely, associations between American political and naval leadership, and communications between the naval forces in the field and the naval staff in Washington, D.C. Finally, to what degree did the United States and its partners secure their over-all naval objectives? Needless to say, perfect understanding and harmony did not always obtain between the British, French, Italians, and Americans. The narrative, which provides information from which to derive some answers to these interesting and complicated questions, aims to enlarge our understanding of the ways in which allies enter into both cooperation and conflict as they attempt to impose their collective will upon the enemy.

I

The leaders of Imperial Germany boldly resumed unrestricted submarine warfare in February, 1917, although they were fully aware of the probable consequences. In late December, 1916, Adm. Henning von Holtzendorff, Chief of the Naval Staff, told Field Marshal Paul von Hindenburg, Chief of the General Staff of the Army, that although "war with America is such a serious matter, that everything must be done in order to avoid it," nevertheless, nothing should preclude Germany from utilizing the weapon "that will bring us victory at the right moment." In the event of war with the United States, he continued, that nation would not be able to reinforce the Entente powers effectively, because its shipping would be destroyed by the German U-boats. American troops could not be sent to Europe because the Atlantic would become unsafe for transports. American capital would not countervail lack of access to the principal theater of war. Holtzendorff concluded that the unrestricted submarine campaign should commence by February 1, 1917, in order to force a peace before August 1, "even if it brings America into the war, since we have no other choice."[1] On January 9, 1917,

1. Holtzendorff to Hindenburg, December 22, 1916, Auswaertiges Amt. Abteilung A. Akten. Krieg 1914, "Unterseebooten Krieg gegen England und andere feindliche Staaten." Der Weltkrieg No. 18 Geheim, Records of the German Foreign Office Received by the Department of State from St.

at General Headquarters in Pless, Chancellor Theobald von Bethmann-Hollweg met with the Emperor William II, Holtzendorff, Hindenburg, and Erich Ludendorff, the first quartermaster general of the Army, and agreed to unrestricted submarine warfare. Actually much opposed to the decision, the Chancellor promised to do what was possible to avoid American belligerency, but he made it clear that "It was necessary for us to anticipate . . . the entry of America into the war."[2]

Military and naval leaders in Germany were more confident of success than were political leaders. The initiative pleased Ludendorff; submarine warfare would interdict the enemy's supply of ammunition and thus spare Germany a second battle of the Marne.[3] Count Johann Bernstorff, the German Ambassador in Washington, strongly opposed the decision. On January 14, he told Bethmann-Hollweg that unrestricted submarine attacks would ensure a break with the United States.[4] The Chancellor replied sharply: "I am well aware that with this step we are running in danger of bringing about a break and possibly war with the United States. We are decided to accept this risk."[5] The Emperor unhesitatingly supported the naval initiative. An aide informed the German Foreign Office that the monarch placed no weight on President Wilson's peace moves. "In case a break with America is unavoidable, 'it cannot be changed! We will proceed.' "[6] Bernstorff continued to urge restraint, arguing

Antony's College, reel 8, frame 52/2. This collection is cited hereafter as St. Antony's Papers. Translations from German texts are by Holger H. Herwig.

2. Adolphe Laurens, *Histoire de la Guerre Sous-marine Allemande* (*1914–1918*) (Paris, 1930), 244. Translations from French texts are by David F. Trask. For an account of the Pless conference, see Henry Newbolt, *Naval Operations*, 5 vols. (London, 1928), 4:229–75. This volume is part of the British official history of World War I: *History of the Great War Based on Official Documents*. For a German account, see Arno Spindler, *Wie es zu dem Entschluss zum uneingeschraenkten U-Boots-Krieg 1917 gekommen ist* (Göttingen, 1961), 37–43.

3. Erich Ludendorff, *Urkunden der Obersten Heeresleitung ueber Ihre Taetigkeit, 1916/18* (Berlin, 1922), 21.

4. Bernstorff to Bethmann-Hollweg, January 14, 1917, St. Antony's Papers, reel 8, Geheime Akten, frame 104.

5. Bethmann-Hollweg to Bernstorff, January 16, 1917, St. Antony's Papers, reel 8, Geheime Akten, frames 206–8.

6. Lersner to Foreign Office, January 16, 1917, St. Antony's Papers, reel 8, Geheime Akten, frame 189.

that Wilson's peace initiative was sincere, but the home government ignored his pleas.[7] The parliamentarian Matthias Erzberger, clearly alarmed by the boldness of the decision, suggested to Bethmann-Hollweg that unrestricted submarine warfare should not be announced formally. In that case, should Admiralty expectations not materialize and the United States threaten war, undersea attacks could be stopped without major repercussions.[8]

The lesser partners in the central coalition accepted the decision made in Germany: Count Ottokar Czernin, the Austro-Hungarian foreign minister, disapproved of the decision, but the Emperor Karl concurred in it, and the King of Bulgaria proved willing to support the policy even if it meant a break with the United States;[9] the Turks were apprehensive. Nonetheless, nothing deterred the German Government.[10]

On January 31, 1917, the German foreign minister, Arthur Zimmermann, called in the American ambassador James W. Gerard to present a note announcing the new policy. Hoping to deter precipitate American action, Zimmermann told Gerard that a German-American conflict would weaken the white race and give aid and comfort to the yellow race.[11] The next day Adm. Eduard von Capelle appeared before the Budget Commission of the Reichstag to justify unrestricted submarine war. Should the United States enter the war, he proclaimed, it would add nothing to the strength of the enemy. Even if volunteers could be found to come to Europe, the United States would encounter great difficulties. "The example that the Americans gave us in 1898 in the Spanish-American War, where they suffered wretched fiascos with the armies that they wanted to create, gives us a sense of calm, knowing that the American volunteer battalions will not be able to change the situation to

7. Bernstorff to Foreign Office, January 19, 1917, St. Antony's Papers, reel 9, Geheime Akten, vol. 25, frame 31.

8. Klaus Epstein, *Matthias Erzberger and the Dilemma of German Democracy* (Princeton, 1959), 161–62.

9. Wedel (Ambassador to Austria) to Gruenau, January 20, 1917, St. Antony's Papers, reel 9, Geheime Akten, vol. 25, frame 4; Wedel to Foreign Office, January 23, 1917, St. Antony's Papers, reel 9, Geheime Akten, vol. 25, frame 50.

10. Kuehlmann to Foreign Office, January 31, 1917, St. Antony's Papers, reel 9, Geheime Akten, vol. 26, frame 103.

11. Zimmermann to Gruenau, January 31, 1917, St. Antony's Papers, reel 9, Geheime Akten, vol. 26, frame 26.

our disadvantage." (The old Rough Rider, Theodore Roosevelt, who was soon to contemplate leading another volunteer regiment to France, would not have appreciated this view.) For Capelle the critical reality was that, even with troops in existence, the United States could not get them past the submarines to Europe.[12]

Nothing altered Germany's resolution, despite pressures from various sources. The Austrians expressed continuing concern and planned to keep their ambassador in Washington, but the German envoy in Vienna was instructed to inform them that unrestricted warfare would cease only when Wilson guaranteed an acceptable peace; Germany would not permit "a peace without victors and vanquished."[13] An American advocate of peace, Louis P. Lochner, sent an impassioned telegram to Berlin: "For God's sake rescind submarine order state your terms instead," but Germany remained unmoved.[14] The German industrialist Walther Rathenau, unconvinced by the official optimism of Ludendorff and his circle, opposed unrestricted submarine warfare because he believed that U-boats could not altogether prevent American supplies from reaching Europe. Assured that the strategy was a leap in the dark, he doubted that Germany was either psychologically or economically prepared for the sacrifices that would stem from indefinite total warfare.[15]

General Ludendorff hailed the decision for unrestricted submarine warfare because it engaged the German Navy in operations directly supportive of the effort on the land, the naval mission being defined simply as war on those merchant ships bringing succor to the Entente powers. The alternative to this policy, he argued later, was defeat in 1917.[16] Surely Ludendorff was desperate. His formations were in difficult straits on the Western Front; his allies were unreliable; his troops were critically short of munitions.[17] He gambled everything on the as-

12. St. Antony's Papers, reel 14, Geheime Akten, vol. 65, frame 162.
13. Wedel to Foreign Office, February 6, 1917, St. Antony's Papers, reel 9, Geheime Akten, vol. 27, frame 181.
14. Lochner to Zimmermann, St. Antony's Papers, reel 9, Geheime Akten, vol. 28, frame 81.
15. Walther Rathenau, *Tagebuch, 1907–1922* (Duesseldorf, 1967), 210; Walther Rathenau, *Briefe*, 2 vols. (Dresden, 1926), 1:239.
16. Erich Ludendorff, *Kriegsfuehrung und Politik* (Berlin, 1922), 175, 331.
17. Gerald D. Feldman, *Army, Industry, and Labor in Germany, 1914–1918* (Princeton, 1966), 271.

sumption that Germany could achieve decisions against Russia
and Rumania in 1917 and then attack successfully in the West
before the Americans could reinforce the embattled Anglo-
French armies.[18]

The first month of the new policy surpassed German expectations.[19] This outcome emboldened Ludendorff to recommend
that hospital ships be sunk without warning, since he believed
that the enemy was using them for other than noncombatant
purposes.[20] The naval staff became annoyed at civilian attempts
to vitiate its measures. Holtzendorff informed Zimmermann
roundly that, "The point of the matter is that the success of the
war at sea will be *hampered* if diplomacy is not working parallel
with it." All political and economic effort must be attuned to the
one goal of bringing Great Britain to its knees by effective use
of the submarine against world commerce.[21] The submarine en-
thusiasts must have been annoyed at the Austrians, who maintained their pessimism about U-boat warfare and continually
asked whether Berlin was thinking of suspending the effort.[22]
Holtzendorff, unmoved by American proposals to ease the blockade, thought President Wilson the real scoundrel, since he was
playing "a frivolous game with the future of great states and
peoples," a sentiment to which the Kaiser subscribed heartily.[23]
Encouraged by early success, the naval staff decided to extend
the blockade to the Murmansk Coast in order to inhibit shipments to Russia.[24] By April 1, Holtzendorff felt able to estimate
that every tenth ship entering the blockade areas was being sunk.

18. Ludendorff, *Kriegsfuehrung*, 178.
19. Holtzendorff to Foreign Office, March 8, 1917, St. Antony's Papers,
reel 10, Geheime Akten, vol. 33, frame 219.
20. Lersner to Foreign Office, February 25, 1917, St. Antony's Papers,
reel 10, Geheime Akten, vol. 31, frame 189.
21. The *Praesident des Kriegsnaehrungsamt*—Adolf Tortilowicz von
Batocki-Bledau—had already proposed indemnities for the Dutch, who had
lost some food ships, since the food supply for the Rhineland and West-
phalia was of critical importance. Batocki to Bethmann-Hollweg, St.
Antony's Papers, reel 10, Geheime Akten, vol. 35, frame 56. The quotation
is from Holtzendorff to Zimmermann, March 13, 1917, St. Antony's Papers,
reel 10, Geheime Akten, vol. 34, frame 143.
22. Wedel to Foreign Office, March 14, 1917, St. Antony's Papers, reel
10, Geheime Akten, vol. 35, frame 34.
23. Holtzendorff to the Kaiser, March 18, 1917, St. Antony's Papers,
reel 10, Geheime Akten, vol. 35, frames 14–25.
24. Holtzendorff to Zimmermann, March 21, 1917, St. Antony's Papers,
reel 10, Geheime Akten, vol. 35, frame 144.

At that rate the U-boat warfare would achieve its goal—a victor's peace—by August 1, 1917. He once again reminded Zimmermann that the diplomats, in accordance with the Kaiser's instructions, must adjust all their actions to support the submarine effort.[25]

For all their purposefulness and optimism, Germany's leaders had placed the destiny of the Empire in the hands of a remarkably small force. On February 1, 1917, just over 100 U-boats were in operation, less than half of which were at sea at any given time. A German student of the submarine war says that only 36 boats were ready for combat duty at the resumption of unrestricted submarine warfare. In addition, the U-boats were broadly distributed. Some 48 were based on German ports leading to the North Sea. Another 23 operated from captured Belgian ports on the English Channel, 19 in the Mediterranean, and ten in the Baltic.[26] The U-boats were organized in five flotillas attached to the German High Sea Fleet. A group of U-cruisers (mostly converted merchant submarines) was based on Kiel. Two flotillas of conventional submarines were located at Bremerhaven and Zeebrugge. The two remaining flotillas were in the Adriatic, at Pola and Cattaro.[27]

The flotillas never appreciated very greatly in strength during 1917–1918. Robert M. Grant shows that 133 boats were on hand January 1, 1917, and 144 on January 1, 1918. In the interim 87 had been built, but 63 had been sunk and 15 others lost in other ways.[28] Given the importance attached to the submarine in 1917, the haphazard nature of the German building program is most surprising. No systematic procedure for managing construction was ever established, and orders came sporadically according to the immediate extent of losses incurred by the submarine flotillas. Andreas Michelsen, Commander of U-boats, notes that

25. Ibid., April 1, 1917, St. Antony's Papers, reel 11, Geheime Akten, vol. 37, frame 1.

26. Karl Galster, *England, Deutsche Flotte und Weltkrieg* (Kiel, 1925), 144. Estimates of submarines available on February 1, 1917, vary to some degree. Michelsen's figure is 111. Andreas Michelsen, *Der U-Bootskrieg, 1914–1918* (Leipzig, 1925), 125. The most recent estimate is 105. Robert M. Grant, *U-Boats Destroyed: The Effect of Anti-Submarine Warfare, 1914–1918* (London, 1964), 41. This is the figure given in Arno Spindler, *Der Handelskrieg mit U-Booten*, 4 vols. (Berlin, 1941), 4:1.

27. Michelsen, *Der U-Bootskrieg*, 48–49.

28. Grant, *U-Boats Destroyed*, 72.

only five shipyards were used to build undersea craft, although there was no logical reason for denying contracts to other yards.[29] No submarines ordered after June, 1917, were ever completed.[30]

After February 1, 1917, the German High Sea Fleet pursued two primary missions: it protected the egress and return of the submarines operating in the North Sea and the Atlantic, and it maintained command of the Baltic Sea. This latter achievement kept open the sea lanes to Sweden, a prime source of iron ore and other vital products, and lines of supply to the Eastern Front.[31] The emphasis placed on the submarine forces during 1917–1918 robbed the High Sea Fleet of its most experienced leadership as the more competent officers and men were reassigned to U-boat duty.[32] Surface forces that lost their supporting submarines could operate freely only in the Baltic and could not venture successfully into the North Sea. As a result, three squadrons of the fleet were retired during 1917–1918.[33]

Critics of the German naval effort maintain that the High Sea Fleet should have eschewed its raiding policy in the Baltic and emphasized "tip and run" operations in the North Sea in support of the submarines. Gen. Wilhelm Groener, Ludendorff's successor as first quartermaster general, argued that Ludendorff should have been content with an honorable peace in 1917, since an annexationist settlement was unattainable.[34] Whatever the merit of these views, the fact remains that on February 1, 1917, Germany irrevocably charted a course that would almost certainly force conflict with the United States. To wage the naval war Germany depended upon an astonishingly small force, and its leaders manifested remarkable disregard for the naval and military potential of the probable adversary.

29. Michelsen, *Der U-Bootskrieg*, 128–30.

30. R. H. Gibson and Maurice Prendergast, *The German Submarine War, 1914–1918* (London, 1931), 362.

31. Ludendorff, *Kriegsfuehrung*, 175, 331.

32. Reinhard Scheer, *Germany's High Sea Fleet in the World War* (London, 1920), 280; Erich Ludendorff, *Meine Kriegserinnerungen, 1914–1918* (Berlin, 1919), 404.

33. Galster, *England, Deutsche Flotte und Weltkrieg*, 121; Walther Hubatsch, *Der Admiralstab und die Obersten Marinebehoerden in Deutschland, 1848–1945* (Frankfurt, 1958), 171; Kurt Assmann, *Deutsche Seestrategie in zwei Weltkriegen* (Heidelberg, 1957), 42–43.

34. Otto Groos, *Seekriegslehre im Lichte des Weltkrieges* (Berlin, 1929), 140; Wilhelm Groener, *Lebenserinnerungen: Jugend; Generalstab; Weltkrieg* (Göttingen, 1957), 422–24.

II

The main target of Germany's submarine effort was Great Britain. This island nation, locked for three prior decades in a mortal economic and maritime struggle with Imperial Germany, depended for survival on imports of vital foodstuffs and raw materials. During 1917–1918 Britain had to import annually products valued at between a billion and 1.3 billion pounds. Germany sought to sever the enemy's lifelines with its U-boats. Defense not only of its own but also of all neutral shipping was essential to Britain's survival. As submarine destruction of world commerce rose astronomically during the spring of 1917, British naval experts worked ever more desperately to counter the U-boat threat. Wheat on hand dwindled to six weeks' supply, and coal shortages threatened to immobilize the Grand Fleet. Britain anxiously contemplated two conceivable developments: Admiralty officials hoped for a gradual improvement of anti-submarine measures while the War Cabinet looked forward to American belligerency. The likelihood of the second event increased in direct proportion to German attacks on American shipping. Of immediate interest was the possibility that the United States might protect vital sea lanes even without declaring war.

Prime Minister David Lloyd George bespoke the extreme trepidation of the British Government about the submarine when he opened an allied naval conference in London on January 23, 1917. "The Germans, without inflicting a military defeat upon us, could win the war by destroying our mercantile marine, and therefore this Conference I regard as one of the most serious and most important conferences which has been held since the war began." To counteract the German effort he called for the arming of merchant ships, construction of additional antisubmarine craft and merchant vessels, restriction of imports, improved turn-around speed of ships in port, and rearrangement of the naval command in the Mediterranean. He concluded with an urgent plea for inter-Allied cooperation. "Unless we show a disposition to pool our resources, and to regard not merely our aims as common but our resources as common, we shall not achieve the victory."[35]

35. "Report of Allied Naval Conference," January 23–24, 1917, in the

Lloyd George could not count upon unity of view among his naval leaders. The Commander of the Grand Fleet, Admiral Sir David Beatty, wanted to inhibit the German submarines by close-in mining operations in the Heligoland Bight. He put his views succinctly to Admiral Sir John Jellicoe, the First Sea Lord of the British Admiralty. "Our Armies might advance a mile a day and slay the Huns in thousands, but the real crux lies in whether we blockade the enemy to his knees, or whether he does the same to us."[36] Jellicoe strongly demurred. He thought that Beatty exaggerated the prospects of close-in mining, noting the ease with which German U-boats avoided the mines in the Straits of Dover, as well as the difficulty of producing mines in sufficient quantity. He strongly defended his policy of escorting transports and watching interned shipping:

We may cause them [the Germans] a great deal of suffering and discomfort by the blockade, but we will not win the war by it. The war will not be won until the enemy's armed forces are defeated—certainly on land, and probably at sea—and therefore it is essential to get our troops to France and keep our communications open.[37]

When news of Germany's resumption of unrestricted submarine warfare reached London, the British Foreign Secretary, Arthur James Balfour, conferred with Walter Hines Page, the Anglophile American Ambassador. Afterward Balfour told Lloyd George that Page himself wanted the United States to intervene in the war, but "he has not heard a word from the State Department or any one in touch with the President." Balfour then summarized his conception of British policy in the circumstances. "It would, I take it, be bad policy to say anything which might be twisted in America as a desire on the part of the British Government to force the U.S.A. into war; but this is a point on which you are quite as good a judge as I."[38] The Foreign Office antici-

Records of the French Ministry of Marine, Archives Centrales de la Marine, Paris, Es file, box 13. These records are cited hereafter as MM. This report is also found in the Records of the British Admiralty, Public Record Office, London, ADM 137, book 1796. The Admiralty files are cited hereafter as ADM.

36. Beatty to Jellicoe, January 27, 1917, Papers of Admiral John Jellicoe, British Museum, London, book 49008, vol. 20. Hereafter this collection is cited as Jellicoe Papers.

37. Jellicoe to Beatty, February 4, 1917, Jellicoe Papers, book 49008, vol. 20.

38. Balfour to Lloyd George, February 2, 1917, Records of the British

pated a break in diplomatic relations between the United States and Germany, but at least one highly placed official—Lord Hardinge—doubted that President Wilson would go further.[39] Lloyd George sounded Page on the prospects for consultation, expressing hope that shipments of ammunition to Europe would not be curtailed. The Prime Minister inquired about the extent of merchant shipping in the United States and stated that in the event the United States entered the war he would be glad to have the President at the peace conference. "Your President's cool and patient and humane counsel . . . will be wholesome for us all." Lloyd George also offered, through Admiral Jellicoe and the Chief of the Imperial General Staff, General Sir William Robertson, to "give all possible information." Page asked Washington for instructions on this question but received none.[40]

Sir Cecil Spring Rice, the British Ambassador in Washington, became the focal point in these initial British-American contacts. He was suspicious of the United States—a consequence of President Wilson's abortive attempts to end the war by mediation—and on January 16, 1917, he informed the Foreign Office that a "high official" had told him that "neither President nor Secretary of Navy would consent to any naval agreement with the Allies in anticipation of joint defensive measures." Nevertheless, he proposed to make unofficial suggestions for patrol through his naval attaché. The suspicious Spring Rice was on his guard. He ruled out "too intimate confidences" because "Germans are entrenched in Navy Department and no secrets are kept, but an understanding on general lines might be useful and would save time if crisis arrives."[41] Always on the alert for espionage, Spring Rice reiterated his warning two weeks later.

Foreign Office, Papers of Sir Eric Drummond, Public Record Office, London, Foreign Office file 800, book 329. Hereafter collections held within the Foreign Office Records are referred to as FO. The Papers of Sir Eric are referred to hereafter as the Drummond Papers.

39. Hardinge to Lord Bertie (Ambassador to France), February 2, 1917, Papers of Lord Bertie of Thame, FO 800, book 181. Hereafter this collection is referred to as Bertie Papers.

40. Page to Secretary of State Robert Lansing and Wilson, February 6, 1917, National Archives Microfilm Publications, *Records of the Department of State Relating to World War I and Its Termination, 1914–29* (Washington, D.C.). Microcopy No. 367, decimal file 763.72, document no. 3234. Hereafter this collection is referred to as USDSM 367.

41. Spring Rice to Foreign Office, January 16, 1917, ADM 137, book 1416, 14.

"Information received at the Embassy from time to time points to the fact that military and naval secrets in the possession of the United States Government Departments are imparted to the German authorities by agents employed in this country."[42]

After the beginning of unrestricted submarine warfare, the British Ambassador marked time, reporting the reluctance of the United States to move definitely toward belligerency. He detected a general American feeling that Germany intended to force a war, "But there can be no doubt that the United States would enter most unwillingly into such a conflict. If a conflict does take place it will not be the fault of the President." According to Spring Rice, Wilson was playing for time. "He evidently still hopes that there will be no conflict. With this point of view he has most carefully avoided giving any just ground of offence." No American official had approached him or any other British representative with "a general scheme of co-ordination and organisation of all industries for common defence, or of submarine measures for the protection of life and property at sea." Wilson had his reasons: "It is the evident desire of the President to avoid any appearance of preparation in view of a war with Germany, especially of a war conducted in co-operation with the Allies."[43] A week later Spring Rice noted what he called an "American nightmare . . . an alliance between the belligerent powers of Japan and Germany perhaps, in conjunction with Russia." Japan showed no indication of moving in this direction, but "the fear of it however is an important element in American policy." German intransigence regarding unrestricted submarine warfare increasingly exasperated the Americans, but the government persisted in its effort to give no cause for hostilities. The President and his Cabinet were "determined to take no action until the country insists with practical unanimity that action must be taken. This is far from being the case at present."[44]

Spring Rice found the President intensely frustrating, but,

42. Spring Rice to Balfour, January 31, 1917, ADM 137, book 1436, 23.
43. Ibid., February 9, 1917, ADM 137, book 1436, 19. This letter is also available in the Cabinet Papers, no. 91 (1917), FO 899, book 12. The British Ambassador continued to report in this vein. See Spring Rice to Balfour, February 16, 1917, Papers of Arthur James Balfour, British Museum, London, book 49740. Hereafter this collection is referred to as Balfour Papers.
44. Ibid., February 16, 1917, book 49740.

fascinated by the man, he issued a veritable barrage of commentary on the American leader. On March 1, 1917, he dispatched a prescient analysis to Balfour. Wilson was

an unknown force and the movements of his mind are so mysterious that no one seems to be able to prophecy [sic] with certainty what decision he will arrive at. We may however be pretty certain that no action will be taken which is not felt by the people at large to be absolutely and imperatively necessary. This is his strength. The result is that numbers of people in the East criticise him for being backward and unwilling to face the issue. The result of this criticism is that when he does move forward he has an almost irresistible weight of public opinion which moves with him.[45]

All that the British could do was to maintain dignity and patience, hoping that events would ultimately force the hand of the reluctant President.

It was a difficult game for London to play, especially since the fortunes of the Entente seemed on the wane. Some British leaders seriously considered the possibility of a negotiated peace. On March 23, Gen. Jan Smuts of South Africa initiated a discussion in the Imperial War Cabinet concerning prospects for a settlement in 1917. Smuts wondered whether Britain ought to take advantage of whatever moderate successes it might gain during the summer of 1917 to make a "reasonable peace," even if forced to recede from some of its announced war aims. "The submarine campaign and the possibility of deflection among our Allies might render the situation very uncertain after this year, while Germany would fight with desperate resolution against any policy which could be represented to her people—as some of our public statements had been—as a policy of the destruction of the German nation." The Imperial War Cabinet, however, noted some counterarguments. Germany had staked everything in 1917, and would have few reserves left for 1918. The other Central Powers were already in serious straits, "whereas the resources of the *Entente* Powers, even leaving America out of account, had not reached their fullest development." It was ultimately agreed to seek peace in 1917 but in the event of failure to prepare a great effort for 1918.[46]

45. Ibid., March 1, 1917, book 48740.
46. Minutes of the Imperial War Cabinet, no. 3, March 23, 1917, Rec-

There were still abundant troubles for Britain—lack of money, man power, ammunition, and reliable allies—but no problem loomed larger than the German U-boat campaign. On March 24, 1917, the Admiralty issued "A General Review of the Naval Situation" for the information of the Imperial War Cabinet. The most important issue concerned was the submarine war on shipping. "On the success or failure of this method of attack will depend the capacity of the Allies to continue the war. It is, therefore, not possible to overestimate the seriousness of the view which should be taken of this attempt on the part of the Central Powers to defeat us." The availability of more submarines and the onset of longer daylight hours meant that the Allies and neutrals must expect to lose perhaps 500,000 tons of shipping in March, with an increase to about 700,000 tons in June, after which the situation could be expected to improve. Wheat reserves were very low in Britain, as were coal supplies in France and Italy. The Grand Fleet maintained command of the surface sea, but an effective antidote to the submarine menace was still not available.[47]

The onset of unrestricted submarine warfare produced in London an atmosphere compounded of fear and anticipation— dread of the undersea boats but hope for a possible, indeed probable, declaration of war by the United States. Until the situation matured, as it did during March, 1917, the British could only stand and wait. Initiative for possible future cooperation had now to come from Washington.

III

In America the political climate was shrouded in a mantle of uncertainty. Aggravated by unrestricted submarine warfare but

---

ords of the Imperial War Cabinet, Public Record Office, London, CAB 23, book 40. The Minutes of the Imperial War Cabinet are cited as CAB 23 hereafter.

47. "A General Review of the Naval Situation," March 24, 1917, ADM 137, book 1937, 68–81. A document indicative of the relations between the weaknesses of Britain's allies and the naval war, prepared at about the same time, designated the probable consequences of the withdrawal of each major ally—Italy, Russia, France, and Japan. "Effects of Withdrawal from the War from Naval Aspect," (G. 145), April 3, 1917, Records of the Supreme War Council, Public Record Office, London, CAB 24. Hereafter this collection is referred to as CAB 24.

without clear direction from their President, Americans were be-
wildered by the climactic developments of the opening months
of 1917. Neutral sentiment on one hand and war fever on the
other sharply divided the nation. Surely Wilson was not in an
enviable position: Should he impose an aggressive foreign policy
upon a confused country? How long could he allow German
U-boats to sink American shipping with relative impunity? Despite growing pressure from various sources, Wilson refused to
abandon his neutral stance and instead chose to let the Germans
force his hand. Perhaps the U-boats would help rally the nation
behind him. Indeed, German intransigence, coupled with mounting American losses, might prove more effective than presidential pressure.

The German declaration of unrestricted submarine warfare
as of February 1, 1917, shocked Washington, although it was not
a complete surprise. During January a few reports on this topic
accumulated in the United States. Early in January the American military attaché in Constantinople heard rumors from German officers that Berlin was contemplating a *démarche*. The
American Ambassador to Turkey noted that "the Germans state
[this action] will be a breach of all their promises to such an
extent that it will certainly bring about a rupture of diplomatic
relations between the United States and Germany, if not war."[48]
At the same time Secretary of State Robert Lansing grew pes-
simistic about relations with Germany. One of his visitors reported him as saying that "the situation was becoming intolerable."[49] And on January 29, 1917, Ambassador Gerard in Berlin
reported "fairly reliable information that orders have been given
for reckless submarine warfare."[50]

Two days later the German foreign minister Arthur Zimmermann informed Gerard of Germany's decision to proceed with
unrestricted submarine warfare. Zimmermann claimed that "the
military and naval people had forced this [act] and said that
America could do nothing. . . . The Foreign Office had warned
them and done what it could and was on record against the
step." The submarine was his country's last chance, nor could

48. Elkus to Lansing, January 8, 1917, USDSM 367, 763.72/3117.
49. Diary of Chandler P. Anderson, Papers of Chandler P. Anderson,
Library of Congress, Washington, D.C. Hereafter this collection is referred to as Anderson Papers.
50. Gerard to Lansing, January 29, 1917, USDSM 367, 763.72/3157.

Germany ignore its food problem. "He realized that it was a very serious step and would probably bring the whole world into the war but . . . Germany had this weapon and must use it no matter what the consequences were." Gerard opined that Germany thought the Americans "a fat, rich race without sense of humor and ready to stand for anything in order to keep out of war." He believed that the decision had come because the Germans wished to torpedo grain ships destined for Entente ports from Argentina; they feared the impending Allied offensive; they lacked sufficient food supply at home; their people were demanding use of the submarine; and they had "contempt and hate for America."[51]

President Wilson was in a dilemma. As soon as the news arrived in Washington, Secretary Lansing advised the President to hand Bernstorff his passports and to recall Gerard from Berlin. In addition, the United States could either warn its citizenry to avoid belligerent zones or go to war. Lansing implied support for the second course, since it would give the United States a seat at the postwar peace conference.[52] On the same day Secretary of the Navy Josephus Daniels reported to Wilson the attitude of the Chief of Naval Operations, Adm. William S. Benson. "He had the same abhorrence of becoming enlisted with either side of combatants that you expressed. His view is that if we lose our equipoise, the world will be in darkness. He expressed the hope that you would find a way to avert the calamity."[53] The President steered a course between the clear alternatives recommended by Lansing and Benson. He broke diplomatic relations with Germany almost immediately, but he spent a number of weeks exploring the possibility of armed neutrality. It was a step beyond strict neutrality but short of full belligerency.

The United States was by no means prepared for war. On February 1, 1917, the only plan available in case of war with Germany was the so-called Germany (Black) War Plan developed by the Naval War College. It assumed that only Germany and the United States were at war, that Britain would remain neutral, and that Japan would pose a threat to the rear. The

51. Ibid., January 31, 1917, USDSM 367, 763.72/3170.
52. Lansing to Wilson, Papers of President Woodrow Wilson, Library of Congress, Washington, D.C., box 113. Hereafter this collection is referred to as Wilson Papers.
53. Daniels to Wilson, February 2, 1917, Wilson Papers, box 113.

Black Plan specified methods of defeating a German naval assault in the Caribbean aimed at the Panama Canal and designed to acquire territory in Latin America.[54] Since this document was obviously inappropriate in the present situation, on February 4 the General Board of the Navy produced a series of emergency recommendations: the fleet was to be brought to readiness; recruiting spurred; coastal defense measures inaugurated; and intelligence services organized. Vessels owned by the Central Powers but interned in American ports were to be seized and merchant ships armed for defensive purposes. The Navy Department would arrange, "as soon as possible, plans of cooperation with the naval forces of the Allies for the joint protection of trans-Atlantic commerce and for defensive naval operations against the common enemy."[55] However, most of these measures were not executed because of the President's desire to maintain a public posture of complete impartiality.[56] No immediate contact was made with the Entente navies.

Although Secretary Daniels refrained from overt acts, he did consider the problems that would arise in the event of war. On February 10 he asked the General Board of the Navy to provide detailed recommendations of actions to take in case of war with Germany.[57] The Board defined the Navy's mission as "to guarantee to our citizens and ships their rights under international law on the high seas." Under "Grand Strategy" the Board pro-

54. War Portfolio no. 1, Reference no. 5–Y, Records of the General Board, Archives of the Naval History Division, The Naval Historical Foundation, Washington, D.C., General Board War Portfolios. This collection is referred to hereafter as Records of the General Board. For a detailed discussion of this plan, see Warner R. Schilling, "Admirals and Foreign Policy, 1913–1919," Ph.D. diss., Yale University, 1953, chaps. 1–2. See also Holger H. Herwig and David F. Trask, "Naval Operations Plans between Germany and the United States of America, 1898–1913: A Study of Strategic Planning in the Age of Imperialism," *Militärgeschichtliche Mitteilungen*, February 1970, 5–32.

55. Captain Charles R. Badger, Jr., to Daniels, February 4, 1917, Records of the Department of the Navy, Naval Records Collection of the Office of Naval Records and Library (Record Group 45), Subject File 1911–1927, National Archives, Washington, D.C. UP file: "General Matters Relating to the Operations, Plans, and Policies of the Navy as a Whole." This collection is cited hereafter as USNSF.

56. Frank Freidel, *Franklin D. Roosevelt: The Apprenticeship* (Boston, 1952), 293–94. Freidel insists that "There was no lack of plans; there was a deliberate refusal to execute them because of instructions from the White House."

57. Daniels to General Board, February 10, 1917, USNSF, UP file.

posed to deploy naval forces in order to protect shipping against undersea and surface raiders. It wanted to provide for the defense of home ports and waters and to protect the resources of all the Americas, e.g., the Mexican oil fields. It proposed a patrol of American waters in order to release Allied naval forces for service in European waters, and to mobilize the fleet it suggested a concentration in the lower Chesapeake Bay. Daniels had asked for recommendations concerning means of maintaining communications with Europe and assisting the Allies. The General Board suggested patrols, convoys when practicable, arming of merchant vessels, and training of crews to man guns mounted on merchant vessels. In order specifically to combat the submarine the Board proposed patrols, convoys, guards on points likely to serve as centers of submarine action, guards on unfrequented bays on the American coast that might serve as temporary bases for submarines, and searches to ensure against the use of other places in the Americas that might be available to enemy submarines.[58] Like the Board's earlier recommendations, these steps were held in abeyance while the President deliberated his course.

The prospect of armed neutrality faded in late February and early March as Congress proved uncooperative, and the impracticality of the measure became apparent. Despite this development the Secretary of the Navy loyally supported the President's desire, telling him on February 26 that armed neutrality would be authorized by the Congress. "The people," Daniels thought, "will rejoice in the spirit which marked your address and the moderation which marked your actions. The hysterical talk one hears in Washington and New York does not represent the true public opinion any more than the expressions of those who are for peace at any price."[59] The Secretary's diary reveals that the President took a direct interest in the details of naval planning at this time, in particular the preparation of instructions for the officers on armed ships and the protection of the vessels themselves.[60] As late as March 8, Wilson told Daniels that he still

58. Badger to Daniels, February 17, 1917, USNSF, UP file.
59. Daniels to Wilson, February 26, 1917, Wilson Papers.
60. See the diary entries for March 6 and March 12 in E. David Cronon, ed., *The Cabinet Diaries of Josephus Daniels, 1913–1921* (Lincoln, 1963), 109, 112.

hoped to avoid war and that he wanted to spare no cost or effort to protect shipping.[61] Col. Edward M. House, the President's most trusted counselor, noted that "the President is actively backing up Navy affairs, and is pushing Daniels to an activity that did not seem possible a week or ten days ago." The Colonel attributed Wilson's behavior to pressures that had been exerted by, among others, himself and Assistant Secretary of the Navy Franklin D. Roosevelt.[62] In the same period Roosevelt lunched with Elihu Root, Gen. Leonard Wood, and other conservative militants of like mind, seizing the opportunity to make known his support of former President Theodore Roosevelt's demands for a vigorous policy. His memorandum on these events concluded: "Told J. D. [Daniels] things not satisfactory Boston & worse N.Y. He said nothing."[63] Inaction in the Navy Department increasingly disgusted the energetic F.D.R.

The Chief of Naval Operations developed his own views in a significant memorandum on the naval situation; recognizing the possibility of imminent war, Admiral Benson emphasized that the United States should fight not simply to protect commerce, "but mainly to secure guarantees for the future." Since there was "no guarantee for the future except superiority of fighting power," it was necessary to realize that "the possible combinations, of powers and circumstances, are too numerous and too pregnant with possibilities adverse to our interest to permit us to consider any plan other than one which will permit us to exercise eventually the full naval and military strength of the United States in the defense of our interests." This consideration meant that "we have not only to act quickly but to act with a full realization that we may eventually have to act alone." In other words, the Central Powers might defeat the Allies. To ensure a secure future the nation required a clear statement of purpose and the will to pursue it unfalteringly. Given these considerations, Benson detected three great general missions: to develop the full military and naval strength of the United States as fast as pos-

61. Ibid., 117.

62. Diary of Edward M. House, March 10, 1917, Papers of Edward M. House, Yale University Library, New Haven, Conn. See also the entry for March 6, 1917. Hereafter this collection is referred to as House Papers.

63. Freidel, *Roosevelt: The Apprenticeship*, 298–99. The memorandum was dated March 11, 1917.

sible; to employ its forces in war so as best to build up its fighting power as an independent nation; and to render the maximum possible support immediately to the enemies of the Central Powers.

Benson regarded the third mission as first in priority, but he considered the others as essential to future security. In executing the third mission, therefore, the United States should retain full strategic, tactical, and administrative control of all its forces. It should operate in areas exclusively assigned to the United States —those waters closest geographically to the nation. The principal mode of assisting the Entente powers was "to make war on enemy submarines within the areas assigned and to deflect sufficient commerce to the transatlantic trade to ensure the full support of the entente powers." He believed that antisubmarine vessels were required in the present situation: "Vessels of these classes can be built quickly and may have a deciding influence on the present war." On the other hand, "I submit without argument that vessels should be built not only to meet present conditions but conditions that may come after the present phase of the world war." In other words, the United States should not discontinue its program of capital-ship construction. In the future, Benson continued, the United States must have sufficient sea power to "dispute the freedom of the seas with potential enemies. . . . We may expect the future to give us more potential enemies than potential friends so that our safety must lie in our own resources."[64] Did he refer to Great Britain as well as to the most obvious "potential enemy," Japan?

If this memorandum was both veiled and confused, perhaps based on the opinion that Germany might soon defeat the Entente powers, it is difficult to escape the conclusion that the Chief of Naval Operations was no idealistic dreamer. He was concerned primarily with the interests of the United States. He hoped to adopt mobilization policies and plans of cooperation with the Entente powers that entailed the least possible degree of entanglement. If he would provide sufficient assistance to guarantee victory over the Central Powers, he was unwilling to countenance building programs and naval operations that did

64. Benson to Daniels, February, 1917, Papers of Josephus Daniels, Library of Congress, Washington, D.C. Hereafter this collection is referred to as Daniels Papers.

not relate directly to the postwar security of the nation as well as to its wartime effort. The memorandum attributed no altruistic motivations to the European Allies, but on grounds of national interest Benson was prepared to make an imposing naval effort. It was also clear that the principal mode of naval assistance during wartime must be an effective contribution to the struggle against the submarine.[65]

Throughout this period the activities of the Navy Department constantly reflected intense preoccupation with the defense of the United States and the other Americas as against offensive operations in European waters.[66] This concern reflected in part the President's desire to avoid provocation of Germany, but it also demonstrated a general lack of accurate information about the true nature and extent of the submarine emergency and the measures required to cope with it. More deeply, it represented the continuing impact of the national tradition of preserving isolation from Europe and Europe's ways.[67]

Events during March, 1917, finally forced the President's hand. His more militant advisers became increasingly energetic

65. This point is stressed in an unsigned memorandum in the records of the Navy Department dealing with the use of emergency funds allocated by Congress. "[We] must prepare ourselves to render futile and destroy the immediate menace of the German submarine campaign in order to destroy the ultimate menace of her full strength used against us, but at the same time we must prepare ourselves *to meet the ultimate menace* if it comes, for unless we are prepared to meet it the very life of our nation is endangered." The memorandum concluded with recommendations concerning methods of coping with submarines and also a rush naval building program. Unsigned memorandum on use of emergency funds, March 13, 1917, USNSF, UP file.

66. See, for example, Benson to Commandants of Naval Districts 1–8 and 15, "Defense in Home Waters," March 19, 1917, USNSF, UP file. But see a memorandum by Captain T. P. Magruder entitled "General Situation," in Papers of Franklin D. Roosevelt, Franklin D. Roosevelt Library, Hyde Park, N.Y., Naval Affairs file, group 10, box 27, cited hereafter as Roosevelt Papers. This document assumes a war with Germany and advocates close cooperation with the British fleet.

67. Secretary Daniels's diary for February and March, 1917, mentions concerns about German activities in the Caribbean. On February 27, the Cabinet decided to send ships to support the Cuban Government against revolutionary action. "W[ilson] said I am very free from G[erman] suspicions but so many things are happening we cannot afford to let Cuba be involved by G[erman] plots." Daniels also worried about protecting the Virgin Islands, just recently acquired from Denmark, against German attack. Cronon, ed., *Cabinet Diaries*, 6, 10.

as Germany's design became evident. Secretary of State Lansing made no secret of his desire for war.[68] On March 19, he wrote to Wilson arguing that war was inevitable and that speedy action was imperative, and one by one, he listed the reasons for supporting intervention: American belligerency would encourage Russia, just then in the throes of the early revolution; it would hearten democratic elements inside Germany; it would vastly encourage the Entente powers while discouraging the German militarists; it would curb restlessness at home; finally, continued neutrality would mean a loss of "future influence in world affairs."[69] These arguments all carried weight with the President, but Lansing's last consideration probably was the primary reason for the ultimate decision. During the period of neutrality Wilson had tried desperately by mediation to bring about a peaceful settlement. Having failed in this endeavor, and having been presented with overt acts of violence by Germany that could not be ignored, he found himself with no honorable alternative except to wage war. To do otherwise would have been to sacrifice all influence in the determination of the future, something he was not in good conscience prepared to do.[70]

The President reached his fateful decision about March 20, the day of a climactic meeting in which he indicated his general intentions to the members of his Cabinet. His advisers were ready with suggestions for immediate cooperation with the European Allies. House had already urged him to consider the United States "a huge reservoir to supply the Allies with the things they most need. No one looks with favor upon our raising a large army at the moment, believing it would be better if we would permit volunteers to enlist in the Allied armies."[71] Secretary of Agriculture David F. Houston was of like mind. On March 20, he told the President to find out what the Allies needed. He thought that the idea of providing an army was "crude." It would have to come, but it was far in the future. For the present, it was necessary to emphasize that the Allies needed supplies, credit, and maritime transport, along with naval assistance against the enemy's submarine offensive. Jules Jusser-

68. Anderson diary, March 10, 1917, Anderson Papers.
69. Lansing to Wilson, March 19, 1917, USDSM 367, 763.72/3577½.
70. For an extended argument in support of this general view, see David F. Trask, *Victory Without Peace: American Foreign Relations in the Twentieth Century* (New York, 1968), 57–66.
71. House to Wilson, March 19, 1917, Wilson Papers.

and, the French Ambassador, had stressed just these matters in conversation with him, ignoring the need for land forces.[72]

Naval activity now rapidly increased. On March 23, Wilson ordered Daniels to add 87,000 men to the Navy.[73] The next day the Secretary of the Navy formally requested that Lansing obtain intelligence regarding enemy submarines and cruisers from American consuls.[74] Most important, the United States began to establish direct contact with Great Britain and France regarding modes of assistance, especially immediate naval support. These consultations were well advanced by April 2, when the President went to Congress and asked for a declaration of war. When the ordeal was past, he wrote poignantly to an old friend:

Your letter is just what my heart desired and I am delighted that you now have the opportunity of pointing out to your friends in New York the truth of what you have all along been telling them, that it was necessary for me by slow stages indeed and with the most genuine purpose to avoid war to lead the country on to a single way of thinking. I thank God for the evidences that the task has been accomplished. I think I never felt the responsibilities of office more profoundly than I feel them now, and yet there is a certain relief in having the task made more concrete and definite.[75]

After two anxious months, Wilson finally decided for war. Spring Rice, for all his crotchety and perverse ways, had been fully accurate in his description of Wilson's approach to public opinion; Ambassador Page had been entirely wrong. At one point the Anglophile envoy had decided that Wilson would not go to war because he was "constitutionally unable to come to such a point of action. . . . He has no quality of *real* leadership." Spring Rice sensed what Page could not grasp, i.e., the President's tactic of letting delay work to his advantage. In the Navy Department the energetic yachtsman Franklin D. Roosevelt was emboldened to go full speed ahead on his pet project—the construction of miniscule submarine chasers, fifty feet in length.[76] On April 6,

72. David F. Houston, *Eight Years with Wilson's Cabinet: 1913 to 1920: with a Personal Estimate of the President*, 2 vols. (Garden City, N.Y.), 1:242–43.
73. Cronon, ed., *Cabinet Diaries*, 121.
74. Daniels to Lansing, March 24, 1917, USDSM 367, 763.72/3599.
75. Wilson to Cleveland Dodge, April 4, 1917, Wilson Papers.
76. Diary of Ambassador Walter Hines Page, February 19, 1917, Papers of Walter Hines Page, Houghton Library of Harvard University,

1917, the United States committed itself to indefinite total warfare. The next task was to perfect its contacts with the European
Allies, in particular with Great Britain and France.

IV

Strict American neutrality precluded detailed Anglo-American
discussions of joint naval strategy before the declaration of war.
President Wilson himself was the main obstacle to preparatory
discussions. During the early months of 1917 enormous doubt
and tension pervaded the atmosphere of London. The British
War Cabinet had been irritated, in the wake of the German declaration of unrestricted submarine warfare, by lack of a sound
general appreciation of the situation by America. On February
5, it authorized the Foreign Secretary, Arthur James Balfour, to
explore a whole range of possible areas of cooperation with the
United States—finance, steel production, merchant shipbuilding, and intelligence on German naval activity—and had further
instructed various responsible officials including the First Sea
Lord (Sir John Jellicoe) and the Chief of the Imperial General
Staff (Sir William Robertson) to prepare memoranda "showing
the manner in which the United States of America could best
render assistance in the event of their entry into the war."[77]
Nothing came of these early efforts, given President Wilson's insistence upon restraint and the British respect for that desire.
The only exception to the rule of restraint was a vague expression
of interest in consultations conveyed from the Navy Department
to the British naval attaché, Captain Guy Gaunt, on February 17.[78] When informed, the Foreign Office responded simply with the statement that naval cooperation would be discussed through diplomatic channels if a German-American war
materialized.[79]

Anglo-American consideration of possible cooperation did

Cambridge, Mass. This collection is hereafter cited as Page Papers. Carroll
Kilpatrick, ed., *Roosevelt and Daniels: A Friendship in Politics* (Chapel
Hill, N.C., 1952), 33.

77. Minutes of the War Cabinet (WC 54), February 5, 1917, CAB 23,
book 1.

78. Spring Rice to Foreign Office, February 17, 1917, FO 371, book
3112.

79. W. Graham Greene to Spring Rice, February 22, 1917, FO 371,
book 3112.

not begin seriously until about March 20, when the President reached his fateful decision for war.[80] On that very day the naval secretary of the Admiralty recorded that "there does not at present appear to be any indication (but rather the reverse) of the American Navy being employed outside their own waters," but initial discussions were about to develop. Franklin D. Roosevelt and the Director of Naval Intelligence secretly approached Captain Gaunt with a request for British views. The two Americans, Gaunt reported, were "most anxious that some scheme of co-operation should be communicated to them at once"; they hoped to influence the attitude of the General Board. Once its members reach decisions, observed Gaunt, "there is a danger that it would be difficult to make them change their minds without exciting jealousy and anti-British sentiment which pervades United States Navy."[81] Roosevelt's impetuous and indiscreet initiative, clearly without the slightest official sanction in Washington, did not precipitate action in Britain. The Foreign Office thought it "most desirable that such schemes should be formulated: but United States of America should call us into counsel." The Admiralty expressed the same view, but authorized Gaunt to treat the matter privately if consulted again.[82] Such contacts were imminent. On March 22, the French naval attaché reported an American desire to discuss naval cooperation, a sign of growing activism in Washington.[83] Three days later Gaunt reported another discussion with Roosevelt, this time in the company of Frank L. Polk, an important official in the State Department. The two emissaries told Gaunt that they knew the initiative should come from the United States, but "until actual state of war is proclaimed they are unable to approach us officially." Roosevelt urged the dispatch of British naval officers to advise the United States on antisubmarine measures and coastal patrol.[84]

80. Exponents of intervention, such as Franklin D. Roosevelt, strained at the bit. The Assistant Secretary of the Navy, on March 19, 1917, expressed to Daniels his belief that the French and British should be consulted. Cronon, ed., *Cabinet Diaries*, 117.

81. Barclay to Foreign Office, March 20, 1917, FO 371, book 3112.

82. Foreign Office to Barclay, March 22, 1917, FO 371, book 3112; Admiralty to Gaunt, March 22, 1917, ADM 137, book 1436, 134.

83. Adolphe Laurens, *La Guerre Sous-marine: La Protection des Navires de Commerce*, 2 vols. (n.p., n.d.), 1:327.

84. Barclay to Foreign Office, March 25, 1917, FO 371, book 3112. A copy is also in ADM 137, book 1436, 147.

In London Ambassador Page could no longer contain himself. Obsessed with a sense of the most extreme urgency he discussed naval cooperation with Balfour and other British leaders. The Foreign Secretary was interested but determined to be correct. He wished to receive a request "through the ordinary diplomatic channels to consider how the two Navies could best assist each other in the present crisis. We were most anxious to help and be helped, but had no desire to intervene unasked in other people's affairs." Page replied that he had urged the dispatch of a high-ranking American admiral, and Balfour expressed eagerness to receive him.[85] On that very day the French Admiralty ordered one of its officers, Adm. R. A. Grasset, to proceed to the United States for naval consultations.[86] Page reported his conversation with Balfour accurately, and then added an appeal for action. The British hoped for extensive cooperation, and he urged that Washington send an admiral immediately to inaugurate this effort.[87]

President Wilson, in his glacial way, finally decided to take preliminary action, although not for love of Page, who was suspected in Washington of being entirely too Anglophile for comfort.[88] On March 24, Wilson told Daniels that "The main thing is no doubt to get into immediate communication with the Admiralty on the other side (through confidential channels until

85. Balfour to Barclay, March 23, 1917, FO 371, book 3112.
86. Page to Lansing, March 23, 1917, USDSM 367, 763.72/3579. At about this date Captain McDougall—the American naval attaché in London—approached the Admiralty about informal discussions, but there is no information about the response of the British. See ADM 137, book 1436, 32–42. A copy of the Page telegram is in the Papers of Admiral William Sowden Sims, Archives of the Naval History Division, The Naval Historical Foundation, Washington, D.C. Hereafter this collection is cited as Sims Papers. On March 25, 1917, Page wrote to his son Arthur concerning the views of Admiral Jellicoe. "More ships, merchant ships, any kind of ships, and take over patrol of the American side of the Atlantic and release the British cruisers there." Burton J. Hendrick, *The Life and Letters of Walter Hines Page*, 3 vols. (New York, 1922), 2:218.
87. Grasset's orders are in MM, Es file, box 13.
88. A comment by Wilson to Daniels about Page is typical of the prevailing attitude in Washington. "Page meddles in things outside his domain. I do not mind this if he gave us his own opinions but he is giving him [sic] English opinions." Daniels diary, March 28, 1917, Cronon, ed., *Cabinet Diaries*, 123. For examples of Page's tendency to offer Anglophile advice, see his reactions to the "peace without victory" speech in the Page diary, January 16, 1917, and Page to Wilson, January 20, 1917, Page Papers.

the Congress has acted) and work out the scheme of coopera-tion."[89] The next day Richard Barclay, a British functionary in the United States, reported to the Foreign Office that the United States was beginning to stir, mentioning that Roosevelt had told him of the impending dispatch of an admiral.[90] On March 28, Rear Adm. William Sowden Sims, the commandant of the Naval War College, was called to Washington and ordered to Great Britain to establish direct contact with the British Admiralty. In 1920, before a committee of the Congress investigating the naval conduct of the war, Sims testified that on his departure Admiral Benson had given him some stern advice. "Don't let the British pull the wool over your eyes. It is none of our business pulling their chestnuts out of the fire. We would as soon fight the British as the Germans." Benson defended himself rather lamely before the same panel:

Well, I might put it this way. I thought that there were certain things going on that we ought to be prepared for in an emergency. Our ships were being held up and certain things were going on that might make it necessary for us to take a definite stand. I never had any idea that we would have to fight any other country; no.[91]

Whatever the truth of the matter, Benson was certainly not overly enamored of the British, whereas Sims was a well-known exponent of close Anglo-American relations. In 1910 he had suf-fered a presidential reprimand for proclaiming publicly in a speech at the Guildhall in London that in the event of war the United States would fight with the British.

As Sims began his wartime mission, Great Britain prepared to send delegates of its own to the United States. On March 26, the War Cabinet noted the need for the dispatch of a high British official to inaugurate effective Anglo-American cooperation.[92] The next day Admiral Sir Montague E. Browning, the British officer commanding in the West Indies, was ordered to prepare for a visit to Washington in order to discuss cooperation.[93] On

89. Wilson to Daniels, March 24, 1917, Daniels Papers. See also Cronon, ed., *Cabinet Diaries*, 121.

90. Barclay to Foreign Office, March 25, 1917, FO 371, book 3112.

91. Quoted in Schilling, "Admirals and Foreign Policy," 77–78.

92. Minutes of the War Cabinet (WC 104), March 26, 1917, CAB 23, book 2.

93. Admiralty to Browning, March 27, 1917, ADM 137, book 1436, 152.

April 3, the Imperial War Cabinet decided that Balfour should consult Page about a mission to the United States.[94] Page rapidly relayed the suggestion to Secretary Lansing,[95] and the next day the War Cabinet decided to send Balfour at the head of the British mission.[96]

During these days the British Government groped toward a general policy for Anglo-American naval cooperation. On March 24, an Admiralty memorandum proposed four types of immediate assistance. The United States should dispatch flying squadrons to both the North and South Atlantic to counteract German commerce raiders; it should send destroyers to participate in the war against the submarine, based on Ireland; American ships should patrol the eastern and western coasts of the Americas; and finally, the United States should retain naval forces in the Far East because the British had been compelled to recall their ships from that area.[97]

By April 5, Balfour was in possession of a relatively well developed program of American assistance. This scheme, modified and expanded as the situation clarified in the late spring of 1917, guided his conversations in Washington during April and May. The first priority was shipping. "It is evident," he wrote in a memorandum given to Page and sent on to Spring Rice for the information of President Wilson, "not merely from the point of view of Great Britain, but from that of the Allies generally, that the tonnage problem is the one most urgently in need of solution." The United States could assist by seizing enemy ships interned in its harbors, chartering neutral shipping for use in safe waters, releasing ships employed on the Great Lakes and the coastwise trade for ocean transport, and expanding ship construction. A second concern was money: the United States could help by providing additional foreign exchange. A third requirement in Europe was rolling stock, especially for Russia. Next, elements of the United States Navy were required in force in European waters. There was no apparent need for the battle

94. Minutes of the Imperial War Cabinet (IWC 7), April 3, 1917, CAB 23, book 40.
95. Page to Lansing, April 5, 1917, USDSM 367, 763.72/3644.
96. Minutes of the War Cabinet (WC 115), April 6, 1917, CAB 23, book 2.
97. Admiralty memorandum on American cooperation, March 24, 1917, ADM 137, book 1436, 119–20. This memorandum was forwarded to Gaunt on March 28 and to Barclay on March 29. It was also given to Admiral de Chair, assigned to accompany the Balfour mission.

fleet, but "the share which American cruisers could take in policing the Atlantic is of the greatest importance; and all craft from destroyers downwards, capable of dealing with submarines would be absolutely invaluable." Finally, the Foreign Secretary noted that the provision of manpower would be "vital," should the war continue for an extended period.[98]

In Washington the Government was slowly bestirring itself. The Secretary of the Navy began to consider the possible impact of belligerency on the naval building program, although he continued to emphasize defensive arrangements in American waters.[99] Secretary of the Interior Franklin K. Lane informed his son of the American preparations. The Navy would "make a line across the sea and hunt submarines"; the Army would enroll a million recruits, "and as many more as necessary as soon as they can be got ready."[100] Ambassador Page did what he could by correspondence to energize his friends in the United States, emphasizing naval assistance.[101] Throughout this period the Government was disinclined to mobilize a huge army. One unidentified observer caught the mood in Washington very well: "As far as this country is concerned, this should be a war of finance, supplies, and transportation, and the best protection which we have against foreign aggression, are the soldiers of France and England and the navies of the Allies, and the latter can be ably assisted by our navy."[102] These assumptions reflected

98. Balfour to Spring Rice, April 5, 1917, FO 371, book 3112. A copy of this message is in ADM 137, book 1436, 305–9.

99. Daniels diary, March 28 and 29, 1917, Cronon, ed., *Cabinet Diaries*, 123–24. But see, for an early suggestion that capital-ship construction be dropped in favor of antisubmarine vessels, Captain T. P. Magruder to Daniels, March 18, 1917, Roosevelt Papers, Assistant Secretary file, group 10, box 27.

100. Lane to George W. Lane, April 1, 1917, in Anne Wintermute Lane and Louise Herrick Wall, eds., *The Letters of Franklin K. Lane: Personal and Political* (Boston, 1922), 244.

101. See letters to Frank N. Doubleday and David F. Houston, April 1, 1917, in Hendrick, *Page*, 2:224, 226–27. To Houston, the Secretary of Agriculture, he wrote: "We must work out with the British Navy a programme whereby we can best help; and we must carry it without hesitancy or delay."

102. Memorandum by unidentified author forwarded by President Wilson to Newton D. Baker, April 4, 1917, Papers of Newton D. Baker, Library of Congress, Washington, D.C. Hereafter this collection is cited as Baker Papers. See also on this belief David F. Trask, *The United States in the Supreme War Council: American War Aims and Inter-Allied Strategy, 1917–1918* (Middletown, Conn., 1961), 9.

an awareness of the need to frustrate Germany's attempt to end the war before the United States could bring its power effectively to bear.

On April 5, the day before Congress voted for war, the General Board of the Navy presented a memorandum to Secretary Daniels indicating its views on the forthcoming naval effort. The United States should, first, "obtain from the Allied Powers their views as to how we can best be of assistance to them and as far as possible conform our preparations and acts to their present needs." The Government nonetheless should bear in mind "that should peace be made by the powers now at war we must also be prepared to meet our enemies single handed. We should not depend upon the defensive but prepare for and conduct a vigorous offensive." Recognizing the necessity of concentrating for the moment on construction and employment of antisubmarine craft, the Board nevertheless stressed again the need to "keep constantly in view the possibility of the United States being in the not too distant future compelled to conduct a war single handed against some of the present belligerents." It must therefore "steadily increase the strength of the fighting line, large as well as small vessels." The memorandum also specified a number of concrete steps to be taken immediately, most of which had been proposed earlier.[103] The Board's preoccupation with the possibility of having to continue the war alone reflected a persistent belief among many naval officers that Germany was likely to emerge victorious in Europe. Admiral Benson, of course, had already expressed comparable views. These notions were bound to conflict with British recommendations that the United States build antisubmarine craft and merchant ships as opposed to capital ships.

By the time the United States officially entered the war some thought had been given both in London and in Washington to the ways by which the United States could provide assistance to the embattled Entente Powers, but detailed plans had not been agreed upon. The Admiralty remained painfully conscious of anti-British sentiment in some quarters of the Navy Department. On the American side, neither Benson's interest in American "guarantees for the future" nor the overt Anglophilism of Page and Roosevelt boded well for future naval cooperation. Balfour

103. Badger to Daniels, April 5, 1917, USNSF, WV file: "Value of the United States in the War."

and Daniels, the Imperial War Cabinet, and the General Board had, by April 5, come independently to some general agreement, all recognizing that the navies must concentrate on the defeat of the German undersea offensive against merchant commerce. Fears, prejudices, and suspicions had slowly receded in face of the mounting U-boat threat, a circumstance that at least cleared the way for direct negotiations as soon as the United States became a belligerent.

❋ ❋ ❋ ❋

Germany's decision to launch unrestricted submarine warfare on February 1, 1917, reflected the counsel of a naval pressure group headed by Admiral Holtzendorff. It carried along an eager Kaiser, a willing General Staff, a reluctant Chancellor, and a reticent Foreign Office, claiming that military necessity and determined public opinion required this fateful step. Germany's leaders thus rejected a negotiated settlement of the war in favor of a victor's peace. They purposefully opted for a massive undersea attack on commerce in order to end the war before the United States could intervene with sufficient force to affect the outcome decisively.[104] Shackled to this policy, Berlin surrendered the diplomatic initiative to London and Washington.

After February 1, Great Britain adopted a policy of patience and studied restraint. Seeking to avoid alienating America's reluctant President, yet exceedingly interested in American belligerence, British leaders allowed events to force the United States into the conflict. Some sense of skepticism and even of rivalry often tinged the British attitude, as Wilson continually rebuffed suggestions of various kinds that the United States immediately enter into extensive consultations with London, particularly about naval cooperation. Yet, in the end, Britain's stoic policy of dignified patience served it well.

In Washington, President Wilson delayed his decision for war as long as possible, exploring all alternatives to full belligerency. He took action only after he became convinced that the United States could hope to dominate the peace settlement only by making a truly important contribution to victory over the Central Powers and when he felt certain that public opinion had ma-

104. This interpretation of Germany's decision appears clearly in Sims to Benson, October 2, 1918, Sims Papers.

tured sufficiently to ensure national approbation for a declaration of war. German actions played into his hand. By April 6, when the President led the American people into what he called "the most terrible and disastrous of all wars," the United States had barely begun to assess the full import of the decision for belligerency. There was no Anglo-American conspiracy in early 1917, just as there was no real preparation for conflict in the United States. All manner of inherited attitudes militated against any other state of affairs in Washington—chief among which were powerful emotions and ideas associated with the age-old tradition of abstinence from European politics.

President Wilson's policy of delay precluded real energies in the Navy Department, but the confused situation in that quarter also reflected many lost years of miscalculation. Preliminary efforts to organize for the victory at sea were begun, but no mature plans were concerted and no real consultation had taken place with the European Allies before April 6. These circumstances would soon alter, given the iron will of a remarkable President who did not accept battle until he discerned no other reasonable course, but who, when committed, would dedicate himself single-mindedly to the pursuit of victory.

CHAPTER 2

EARLY PREPARATIONS
FOR THE VICTORY AT SEA
April–July, 1917

Sir Maurice Hankey, the indefatigable secretary of the British War Cabinet, caught quite well the quintessential importance of command of the sea in 1917. "At this stage," he wrote, "nearly every decision which the Supreme Command had to make was found to depend in some way on shipping."[1] Germany sought to force defeat upon the western coalition by interdicting the maritime supply of its enemies. The Allies and their American associate must contain this German naval offensive against merchant shipping or accept defeat. The American Ambassador in Paris, William G. Sharp, graphically illustrated the extent of maritime losses during World War I: suppose a train passed by the "resurrected hulks of these lost ships"; the journey "would require ten hours of constant riding at the pace of fifty miles an hour before the last boat had been passed."[2] Germany had acted on the "unswerving conviction" of its naval leadership that unrestricted submarine warfare would end the war in a few months,[3] and the Allies realized that the German estimate would come true unless means of controlling the submarine materialized in the immediate future. The outcome of the war hung in the balance during the spring and summer of 1917. No problem created more anxiety in Washington as the United States launched upon its massive reinforcement of the Allies.[4]

Some Europeans privately expressed doubt that the American intervention would be either timely or extensive. Lord Bertie of Thame, the British Ambassador to France, discussed this ques-

1. Lord (Maurice) Hankey, *The Supreme Command: 1914–1918*, 2 vols. (London, 1961), 2:632–33.
2. William Graves Sharp, *The War Memoirs of William Graves Sharp: American Ambassador to France, 1914–1918*, Warrington Davison, ed. (London, 1931), 169.
3. Henry Newbolt, *Naval Operations*, 5 vols. (London, 1928), 4.
4. This generalization is a commonplace among practically all authorities on the naval history of the war. See for example, Thomas G. Frothingham, *The United States in the War, 1917–1918*, 3 vols., *The Naval History of the World War* (Cambridge, Mass., 1926), 3:25, 31, 59.

tion with French Premier Alexandre Ribot when news of the American declaration of war reached Paris. Bertie maintained that the United States Navy would be most helpful in dealing with submarines, but that the American contribution to the war on land would not amount to "anything more than a demonstration" for a long time to come. Ribot concurred and also expressed concern about the political intentions of President Wilson. The American might be willing to make peace before the Germans were beaten sufficiently to guarantee acceptance of Allied war aims. Seeking to reassure Ribot, Bertie made a gruesome argument: "When the German submarines have sunk a large number of American ships the blood of the American people will be up and they may insist upon fighting the war to a good finish."[5] Many Europeans quite rightly suspected that the United States might settle for a relatively magnanimous peace, but they erred in another widespread assumption, namely that the American reinforcement would not materially affect the outcome of the war. During the early months of belligerency the problems of the naval war became relatively clear in Washington, as did the requirements for victory at sea. These realities were not easy to grasp, given the atmosphere of crisis that pervaded the spring of 1917 and the chaotic situation that prevailed within the United States Government, unprepared as it was to wage war at the outset of its participation in the greatest conflict in history.

I

Hopeful of inducing an early and imposing American contribution to the naval war, both Britain and France dispatched admirals to the United States as soon as possible after the declaration of war. These emissaries made known the initial desires of their governments. Admiral Browning, the British commander in the Caribbean, represented the British; Admiral R. A. Grasset, the French commander in the same area, expressed the views of France. Their consultations with American officials took place on April 10 at Hampton Roads, Virginia, and on April 11 in Washington.[6] Browning had as instructions a memo-

5. Bertie memorandum, Bertie Papers, April 8, 1917, FO 800, book 181.
6. Secretary Daniels recorded some comments in his diary on the arrival of the Allied representatives. As so often occurs during this period,

randum prepared in the British Admiralty and forwarded to American officials that stressed above all else the need for anti-submarine craft and merchant shipping. The Admiralty discounted the importance of coastal defense against German operations in American waters, because submarine activity in the western Atlantic was unlikely. It saw no immediate necessity for the dispatch of the American battle fleet, because the British Grand Fleet by itself could contain the German High Sea Fleet, although it assumed that some larger American vessels might be helpful later in the English Channel.[7] Admiral Grasset's instructions also stressed the need for antisubmarine craft and merchant shipping, but gave considerable attention to arrangements for receiving American supplies and troops in French ports.[8]

The conference produced a number of concrete arrangements. The United States agreed to maintain flying squadrons in both the northern and southern regions of the Atlantic in order to counteract German surface raiders, and also to patrol American waters off both coasts. Naval units in the Far East would remain on station. Some small patrol boats would be sent as soon as possible to the French coast, along with railway material needed to improve communications from the shore to the Western Front. Perhaps the most important decision was an American agreement to dispatch six destroyers to European waters.[9]

Daniels noted the impetuosity of his Assistant Secretary. "Benson went down on steamer to meet French & British Admirals at Old Point [Comfort] with Mayo and Wilson [two American admirals] to discuss best method of co-operation. Roosevelt wished to go down to meet them as honor. I said no. He did not like it but——." See Daniels diary for April 7 and 9, 1917, E. David Cronon, ed., *The Cabinet Diaries of Josephus Daniels, 1913–1921* (Lincoln, 1963), 130–31.

7. "The Question of the Assistance which Might Be Given by the United States Navy and by the United States Generally from the Naval Point of View," April 4, 1917, USNSF, file TP: "General Plans and Naval Policies, U.S. Naval Forces in Europe, (including those submitted to the Force Commander [Sims] by Allies)." A copy dated April 9, 1917, is in USNSF, WV file. Other matters, including mine laying, action against German surface raiders, employment of American submarines, transport of troops from Australia and New Zealand, and the position of Norway in the war were also discussed.

8. A copy of Grasset's instructions, undated, is in ADM 137, book 1436, 189.

9. Browning to Admiralty, April 13, 1917, ADM 137, book 1436, 179–80. A copy of this document is in USNSF, file WV. Some account of the conferences is in Ray Stannard Baker, *Woodrow Wilson: Life and Letters,*

Participants in the discussions recorded varying reactions. Secretary Daniels was obviously impressed by the danger of the submarine. "O for more destroyers!" he confided to his diary. "I wish we could trade the money in dreadnaughts for destroyers already built." He "Told Grace & Co. [a shipping firm] we would consider buying destroyers [from Latin American countries] but not dreadnaughts."[10] Admiral Browning noted the evident desire of the Americans both to receive counsel and to make a significant naval contribution. He was impressed by Secretary Daniels, but more strongly by the Commander of the Atlantic Fleet, Adm. Henry T. Mayo, and Assistant Secretary of the Navy Franklin Roosevelt.[11] Spring Rice echoed Browning's general attitude toward Secretary Daniels,[12] while Admiral Grasset's appraisal was not as favorable. Although he observed that Daniels and Benson extended "une particulière cordialité," he was struck by American unreadiness. The Navy had no war plans and had made no particular adjustments in the light of the European war. Its leaders generally seemed lethargic, particularly the Chief of Naval Operations. Admiral Benson's "spirit is slow and he does not seem possessed of the moral authority that comports with his rank and functions; he is, besides, . . . a bureaucrat who arrived at the grade of admiral through political changes happening in the ministry." Grasset also detected little ability in other naval officers, but he wrote most enthusiastically about the Assistant Secretary of the Navy. Roosevelt, like his Uncle Theodore, was "a convinced and active partisan of an immediate intervention on our coasts. He does not hide his sympathies in regard to France and I have found in him the best backing to support my requests."[13]

At one point in the discussions Admiral Benson asked why the Allies did not concentrate on a close-in blockade of the German

8 vols. *War Leader* (New York, 1939), 7:11. See also Sir Frederick B. Maurice, *Lessons of Allied Co-operation: Naval, Military, and Air, 1914–1918* (New York, 1942), 95.

10. Daniels diary, April 11, 1917, Cronon, ed., *Cabinet Diaries*, 133.

11. Browning to Admiralty, April 13, 1917, ADM 137, book 1436, 182–88.

12. Spring Rice to Balfour[?], April 13, 1917, Papers of Sir Cecil Spring Rice, FO 800, book 242, cited hereafter as Spring Rice Papers. See also Spring Rice to Foreign Office, April 26, 1917, ADM 137, book 1436, 194.

13. Adolphe Laurens, *La Guerre Sous-marine: Protection de la Navires de Commerce*, 2 vols. (n.p., n.d.), 1:329–31.

coast in order to contain the submarines in their bases. Grasset replied that the British considered it "extremely difficult," given the conditions of modern warfare, but Benson persisted in his advocacy of a close-in blockade.[14]

II

Just as these meetings took place in the United States, Admiral Sims made his initial contacts with British leaders in London. A full report on the naval situation from Admiral Jellicoe deeply alarmed the American sailor, who had thought the submarine danger well in hand. The First Sea Lord reported to the War Cabinet that Sims proposed sending a telegram to Washington that would lead to "every possible effort being made by the Americans to assist us in every possible way to combat the submarine menace, more especially as the Government of the United States held very strong views relative to the 'freedom of the seas.' "[15] Sims was as good as his word. On April 14, he began a series of alarmist cables to Washington describing the extent of the submarine crisis and urging all-out American assistance. The submarine problem had been underestimated in the American press, as had some broader difficulties of the Entente powers, particularly in regard to faltering Russia. Submarines had sunk over 500,000 tons in February and March; over 200,000 tons had gone to the bottom during the first ten days of April. Sims concluded grimly: "The issue is and must inevitably be decided at the locus of all lines of communications in the Eastern Atlantic." Therefore he recommended immediate dispatch of destroyers to Queenstown, in Ireland, and contributions of merchant tonnage to help frustrate the U-boat campaign. Although Sims discounted the immediate importance of the United States Atlantic Fleet, he conceded that "two divisions of dreadnoughts might be based on Brest for moral effect against anticipated raids by heavy enemy ships in the channel out of reach of the British main fleet." He observed that some enemy submarines might make minelaying visits to the American East Coast, but that such forays would be of minor importance because of the difficulties

14. Memorandum, April 16, 1917, MM, Es file, box 13.
15. Minutes of the War Cabinet (WC 117), April 11, 1917, CAB 23, book 2.

of maintaining extensive undersea operations across the great expanse of the Atlantic.[16]

In this message Admiral Sims adumbrated the general position he was to maintain with utter consistency throughout the course of the war: the naval resources of the United States should be utilized to combat the submarine, and the United States should employ its merchant shipping in support of the home populations of the Allies and their armies on the Western Front. "I early took the stand," he wrote later, "that our forces should be considered chiefly in the light of reinforcements to the Allied navies, and that, ignoring all questions of national pride and even what at first might superficially seem to be national interest, we should exert such offensive power as we possessed in a way that would best assist the Allies in defeating the submarine." He was opposed to independent American fleet operations. "If we had adopted this course, we should have been constructing naval bases and perfecting an organization when the armistice was signed; indeed, the idea of operating independently of the Allied fleet was not for a moment to be considered." Sims was contemptuous of those who worried about defensive arrangements in American waters. "The best way to fight Germany was not to wait until she had vanquished the Allies, but to join hands with them in a combined effort to annihilate her military power on land and sea."[17]

Sims rapidly cultivated the closest possible relationship with Walter Hines Page, and the two acted always together in negotiations between London and Washington. Page's cables to the Department of State unfailingly supported those of Sims to the Navy Department in every particular. The Ambassador inaugurated his supportive effort on April 27:

Whatever help the United States may render at any time in the future, or in any theatre of the war, our help is now more seriously needed in this submarine area for the sake of all the Allies than it can ever be needed again, or anywhere else.

After talking over this critical situation with the Prime Minister

16. Sims to Daniels, April 14, 1917, USNSF, TP file. This message is also in USDSM 367, 763.72/3840, and William Sowden Sims, in collaboration with Burton J. Hendrick, *The Victory at Sea* (Garden City, N.Y., 1920), 374–76.

17. *Victory at Sea*, 45, 47.

and other members of the Government, I cannot refrain from most strongly recommending the immediate sending over of every destroyer and other craft that can be of anti-submarine use. This seems to me the sharpest crisis of the war, and the most dangerous situation for the Allies that has arisen or could arise.

If enough submarines can be destroyed in the next two or three months, the war will be won, and if we can contribute effective help immediately, it will be won directly with our aid. I cannot exaggerate the pressing and increasing danger of this situation. Thirty or more destroyers and other similar craft sent by us immediately would very likely be decisive.

There is no time to be lost.[18]

Page's biographer later reported that the Ambassador wrote this message after Sims complained that the Navy Department did not believe either him or the British. "They think I am hopelessly pro-British and that I am being used. But if you'll take it up directly with the President, then they may be convinced."[19]

Almost immediately Sims began to discuss various alternatives and modifications of the naval war against the submarines. On April 16, Secretary Daniels asked him why it was not practicable to blockade the German coast and preclude the movement of submarines.[20] Sims replied immediately and definitely. He thought the blockade concept "quite unfeasible" in the present circumstances; the Admiralty had investigated the matter thoroughly and had concluded that it was out of the question. "To best of my knowledge and experience we should adopt present British methods and base further developments only upon actual experience in cooperation with them."[21] The next day Sims explained to Admiral Benson why the British had not attempted to convoy merchant shipping. "The area is too large; the necessary vessels are not available." He was, however, consulting with the Admiralty on the possibility of convoy opera-

18. Burton F. Hendrick, *The Life and Letters of Walter Hines Page*, 3 vols. (New York, 1922), 2:279. For a discussion of the Sims-Page relationship, see 274–78.

19. Ibid., 278. The cable of April 27 is also in USNSF, WV file.

20. Carroll Fitzpatrick, ed., *Roosevelt and Daniels: A Friendship in Politics* (Chapel Hill, N.C., 1952), 42. See also Cronon, ed., *Cabinet Diaries*, 137.

21. Sims to Daniels, April 18, 1917, USDSM 367, 763.72/3936. This message is also in USNSF, file TT: "Joint Arrangements, U.S. and other Navies, including cooperation and lack of cooperation."

tions if the United States could put in enough ships to override earlier objections.[22]

At this time the Admiralty issued a truly unprecedented order. "In view of the importance of obtaining every possible assistance from the United States in connection with submarine warfare and other important war operations, all information that may be of use to the United States Navy should be communicated by the Departments concerned with operational matters to Admiral Sims, it being understood that the First Sea Lord is to be consulted should there be any doubt as to the expediency of communicating any particular item of secret information."[23] In the desperate circumstances of the day, the Admiralty did not intend to stand on ceremony. Sims's information constantly moved him to send more and more urgent cables homeward. On April 21, he reported that 408,000 tons of shipping had been lost already in April. "Of utmost urgency that we give maximum assistance immediately, every other consideration should be subordinated. I urge the immediate sailing of all available destroyers followed at earliest possible moment by reenforcement of destroyers and all light draft craft available."[24]

Succor was on the way. On April 24, a flotilla of six destroyers —the advance guard of the American Navy in European waters —departed for Queenstown and arrived on May 4.[25] The Navy Department was fully aware that much more effort was required, and Daniels immediately began work on the dispatch of another flotilla.[26]

While naval leaders coped with the problem of curbing the submarines, civilians interested themselves in the problem of replacing lost merchant tonnage. Statistics of sinkings for the first months of unrestricted submarine war were truly alarming. In February some 540,000 tons went to the bottom, an increase

22. Sims to Benson, April 19, 1917, USNFS, file TD; "Admiral Sims' Personal Files." This message is reprinted in Sims, *Victory at Sea*, 376–84.

23. Office memorandum for W. Graham Greene, April 29, 1917, ADM 137, book 1436, 46.

24. Sims to Opnav, April 21, 1917, USDSM 367, 763.72/13451. Lansing, who received the message, thought it important enough to telephone immediately to Daniels. Cronon, ed., *Cabinet Diaries*, 139. For a similar message, see Sims to Daniels, April 24, 1917, USNSF, TT file. This message is also in USDSM 367, 762.73/4031.

25. Baker, *Wilson*, 7:34, 51.

26. See the entries in the Daniels diary for 24 and 27 April, 1917, Cronon, ed., *Cabinet Diaries*, 140, 142.

of about 170,000 tons over January; in March the figure was almost 600,000 tons, and in April the total ballooned to almost 900,000 tons.[27]

The early success of the submarines delighted the German naval staff.[28] Extensive efforts to recruit labor for expanded U-boat production took place in Germany at this time, even though nothing was done to correct the fact that workers engaged in submarine construction complained bitterly because they were paid less than those employed in munitions factories.[29] The Admiralty remained firm in its resolve to pursue unrestricted submarine warfare. Admiral Holtzendorff told Zimmermann on April 15, 1917, that General Hindenburg would overrule the Foreign Office whenever he felt that the civilian leadership was not providing wholehearted support for the Admiralty. After all, war was merely an extension of diplomacy by other means.[30] Holtzendorff estimated that Britain had about 11 million tons of shipping at its disposal, including neutral vessels. He believed that if an average of 600,000 tons per month could be sunk for six months, and if about 1.2 million tons of the available 3 million tons of neutral shipping could be frightened off the seas, then Britain would lose about 39 per cent of its shipping, a "final and irreplaceable" loss.[31] Ludendorff, exultant, was quick to argue that the Russian revolution would allow him to transfer troops to the Western Front, while "at sea, the U-boats are operating more successfully than the Admiralty predicted. The doubts of Count Czernin regarding the fulfillment of Admiral Holtzendorff's predictions are ungrounded; we can expect that a total success of U-boat warfare can be reached in the 5–6 month period suggested by the Admiralty." The combination

27. These figures appear in Hankey, *Supreme Command*, 2:639. Various authorities differ somewhat, but all reflect the same pattern of sharp increase.

28. See the diary entries of Adm. G. A. von Mueller for March 16 and 23, 1917, in Walter Goerlitz, ed., *The Kaiser and His Court: The Diaries, Note Books, and Letters of Admiral Georg Alexander von Mueller, Chief of the Naval Cabinet, 1914–1918* (London, 1961), 248, 250.

29. Gerhard Ritter, *Staatskunst und Kriegshandwerk: Das Problem des "Militarismus" in Deutschland*, 4 vols. (Munich, 1964), 3:450; Gerald D. Feldman, *Army, Industry, and Labor in Germany, 1914–1918* (Princeton, 1966), 310.

30. Holtzendorff to Zimmermann, April 15, 1917, St. Antony's Papers, reel 11, Geheime Akten, vol. 39, frame 1.

31. Newbolt, *Naval Operations*, 4:345.

of success against Russia and against merchant shipping would permit continuance of the war even without the assistance of that doubtful ally Austria.[32]

Intelligence sources available to Holtzendorff suggested that Britain must sue for peace in a few months, due to a lack of raw materials to maintain industrial production and food to sustain the civilian population.[33] Despite this optimism the Kaiser was as yet unwilling to authorize submarine warfare off the American coast. He did not want to arouse what he considered the less militant regions of the United States, particularly the Midwest and the West. The Admiralty thought that sinkings on the American coast might inhibit assistance to Britain, but the foreign minister, Zimmermann, opposed any unnecessary provocation of the United States.[34]

In Washington, President Wilson was doing what he could to stimulate construction of merchant shipping. He established the Emergency Fleet Corporation with Gen. George Goethals as its general manager and authorized the repair and use of German ships interned in American harbors.[35] One great problem was the adverse effect of extensive merchant ship construction on the naval building program. Daniels posed the question to himself feverishly. "Ships? Shall we build battle cruisers or postpone them & build only destroyers and merchant ships? Will wait to see Shipping Board &c."[36] While the United States deliberated, British officialdom became increasingly disturbed at the lack of concrete results in America. Sir Leo Chiozza Money, representing the Ministry of Shipping, complained to Sir Robert Cecil at the Foreign Office about delays. It seemed quite apparent to him

32. Gruenau to Foreign Office, St. Antony's Papers, reel 11, Geheime Akten, vol. 39, frames 140–41.

33. Holtzendorff to the Kaiser, April 24, 1917, St. Antony's Papers, reel 11, Geheime Akten, vol. 40, frame 23.

34. Zimmermann to Gruenau, April 18, 1917, St. Antony's Papers, reel 11, Geheime Akten, vol. 39, frames 80–81.

35. Baker, Wilson, 7:15, 22, 55–56; Cronon, ed., Cabinet Diaries, 133.

36. Daniels diary, April 18, 1917, Cronon, ed., Cabinet Diaries, 137. See also the comment of Secretary of the Interior Franklin K. Lane, Lane to George W. Lane, April 15, 1917, Anne Wintermute Lane and Louise Herrick Wall, eds., Letters of Franklin K. Lane: Personal and Political (Boston, 1922), 246. Lane noted the shortage of steel plate and shipyards. He favored postponing battleship construction. "Whether we will succeed in getting the Secretary of the Navy to agree to this is a question, but I am going to try."

that "the seriousness of the situation is not yet realised on the other side of the Atlantic." He thought Wilson's interest in building wooden ships a sign of American insufficiency. If America hoped to take a leading role in the war, it must build millions of tons of ships per year, utilizing "a considerable part of the engineering skill and labour of the country."[37]

III

At just this moment Great Britain reached a decision of the greatest import for the future, one that was to deeply affect the conduct of the naval war and ultimately help to bring some order to decision making about naval and merchant ship construction. The Admiralty, convinced that dispersion of shipping rather than its concentration on the high seas was the appropriate response to the submarine danger, believed that ships in convoy would present a more desirable target than ships by themselves. Convoys would have to proceed at a low speed, since no ship could exceed the pace of the slowest vessel. Zigzagging would be impossible; merchant captains would have great difficulty merely maintaining station in a convoy formation. Fog and other weather conditions would also cause great confusion. The Admiralty did not believe that enough escort vessels were available to protect convoys, and, finally, there was fear that convoys would cause impossible congestion in already overtaxed ports.[38]

Some British leaders, among them the Prime Minister himself, became increasingly restive at what they considered unimaginative policy at the Admiralty. Lord Hankey maintains that his memorandum of February, 1917, about the possibility of convoy finally convinced Lloyd George that a change in policy should take place,[39] although Lloyd George did not take immediate action. He waited until the United States had entered the war, until certain difficulties associated with the military command in France had been disposed of, and until Admirals Beatty and Sims approved of the concept.

37. Chiozza Money to Cecil, April 27, 1917, papers of Lord (Robert) Cecil, FO 800, book 198, hereafter cited as Cecil Papers.

38. Hankey, *Supreme Command*, 2:698; Elting E. Morison, *Admiral Sims and the Modern American Navy* (Boston, 1942), 345.

39. Hankey, *Supreme Command*, 2:645–48, 673–74.

On April 25, the War Cabinet authorized the Prime Minister to "visit the Admiralty with a view to investigating all the means at present in use in regard to anti-submarine warfare."[40] On the next day Admiral Sir Alexander L. Duff, the responsible Admiralty officer, recommended that the Admiralty adopt the convoy system. The skeptical Admiral Jellicoe wisely decided to support this change.[41] The First Sea Lord was himself concerned primarily at this time with pressing for reductions in Britain's overseas commitments, particularly in the Balkans, to release more vessels for service in the danger area. Like everyone else in London, he was convinced that "we shall be very hard put to it unless the United States help to the utmost of their ability."[42] On April 26, Sir Robert Cecil notified Balfour, then visiting Washington, of Lloyd George's decision to experiment with the convoy system, repeating a familiar refrain: "This system cannot possibly be put into force without more destroyers. Will you impress with great force upon U.S. authorities very urgent need for more destroyers being sent to assist us?"[43] Sims eagerly notified the Navy Department of the decision and made his usual plea for immediate assistance.[44] Lord Beaverbrook, a close associate of the Prime Minister, reports that Lloyd George forced an official decision at the Admiralty on April 30. He alienated Jellicoe and First Lord of the Admiralty Sir Edward Carson, but boldness had its rewards.[45]

The convoy system employed cruisers or armed merchantmen

40. Minutes of the War Cabinet (WC 126), April 25, 1917, CAB 23, book 3.

41. Newbolt, *Naval Operations*, 4:19–21; Hankey, *Supreme Command*, 2:650.

42. Jellicoe to Carson, April 27, 1917, Newbolt, *Naval Operations*, 4:24. See also Jellicoe's statement in the Minutes of the Imperial War Cabinet (IWC 12), April 26, 1917, CAB 23, book 40.

43. Cecil to Balfour, Papers of Arthur James Balfour, April 26, 1917, FO 800, book 208; hereafter this collection is cited as Balfour Papers, FO 800.

44. Sims to Daniels, April 30 and May 1, 1917, USNSF, TT file. These cables are also in USDSM 367, 763.72/4189 and 4216.

45. Lord Beaverbrook, *Men and Power, 1917–1918* (London, 1956), 155–56. See also Sims to Palmer, May 1, 1917, USNSF, TD file. For a recent thorough account, see Arthur J. Marder, *From the Dreadnought to Scapa Flow: The Royal Navy in the Fisher Era*, 5 vols., *1917: Year of Crisis* (London, 1969), 4:152–67. Marder is more sympathetic to the Admiralty than other authorities.

as escorts for commercial shipping on the high seas, and destroyers provided protection when the convoy passed through the submarine danger zone.[46] This system ultimately proved quite successful. Convoys were difficult to locate and difficult to attack because of their protective shield of escorts. Submarines were ultimately forced to operate primarily in narrow seas, where other means of antisubmarine warfare—mines, depth charges, aircraft, hydrophones, nets, and the like—were most effective. The result was increased security for merchant shipping and decreased safety for submarines.[47] The German Admiralty estimated that the convoy system decreased the volume of Allied shipping in actual use by about 30 per cent because of reduced speed on the high seas and added turn-around time in port, but the net gain for the Allies was imposing indeed.[48]

The decision to inaugurate convoy must have aroused satisfaction in Washington. Admiral Sims's biographer does not believe that President Wilson had much to do with the change in policy, but certainly the President favored the initiative. As early as February 25, he had asked Daniels why the British had not adopted the convoy system. Daniels explained that the Admiralty thought dispersion a sounder principle, but Wilson persisted in the opinion that the British "ought to convoy."[49] Shortly after the British change of front, Daniels once again recorded the President's opinion "that merchant ships should be convoyed by naval ships, but expressed his view, as he said, without confidence as he is no expert. He also outlined his views as to changing course & ports on trips to England of our ships."[50] The President was reluctant to interfere in naval affairs, but he maintained a constant interest in them, and he nursed growing suspicions of British competence.

46. "Naval Weekly Appreciation 1," May 1917, ADM 137, book 511, 341.
47. "Summary of Activities of U.S. Naval Forces Operating in European Waters," ca. November, 1918, USNSF, WV file.
48. Groos, *Seekriegslehren im Lichte des Weltkrieges* (Berlin, 1929), 187.
49. Daniels diary, February 25, 1917, Cronon, ed., *Cabinet Diaries*, 105. Franklin K. Lane was another advocate of convoy in the early months of the crisis. See Lane and Wall, eds., *Letters of Franklin K. Lane*, 236–40. For Morison's view, see *Admiral Sims*, 362–63.
50. Daniels diary, May 4, 1917, Cronon, ed., *Cabinet Diaries*, 146. It is not clear whether Wilson knew of the British initiative at this time.

IV

By late April the General Board of the Navy had finally begun to concern itself with the severe U-boat crisis and was ready to recommend what Admiral Sims and British statesmen had been urging for several weeks, a major reinforcement of the anti-submarine effort in British waters.[51] This growing receptivity to British suggestions meant a great deal to Balfour, the British foreign secretary, who had arrived in the United States at the head of an emergency mission. Balfour later told Sims: "Things were dark when I took that trip to America. . . . The submarines were constantly on my mind. I could think of nothing but the number of ships which they were sinking. At that time it certainly looked as though we were going to lose the war."[52] Secretary of Agriculture Houston remembered that "Mr. Balfour and his colleagues reflected in their appearance, manner, and conversation the gloom that hung over their country and the Allies: the submarines were playing havoc with shipping and it did not seem impossible that Great Britain might be cut off— horrible thought."[53] When the Balfour mission was first broached the United States did not seem receptive, but Colonel House made a cogent argument for its dispatch. He informed the President that a conversation with Sir William Wiseman, the head of British intelligence in the United States, had led to an agreement that it would alienate the British if Balfour were not encouraged to come. They advised that military and naval participants should be "of minor reputation so that their coming would not be heralded." Balfour's mission "could be interpreted as having to do with trade, blockade and other matters connected with the Foreign Office."[54] On April 8, the day that House wrote to the President, Secretary Lansing communicated the

---

51. Badger to Daniels, April 18, 1917, Records of the General Board. See also Badger to Daniels, May 3, 1917, Records of the General Board; Daniels diary, May 2, 1917, Cronon, ed., Cabinet Diaries, 145.

52. Sims, Victory at Sea, 14.

53. David F. Houston, Eight Years with Wilson's Cabinet: 1913 to 1920: with a Personal Estimate of the President, 2 vols. (Garden City, N.Y.), 1:277–78. See also a similar observation in Lane and Wall, eds., Letters of Franklin K. Lane, 252.

54. House to Wilson, April 8, 1917, Wilson Papers, box 116. See also House to Wilson, April 5, 1917, Wilson Papers, box 116.

willingness of the United States to receive the British mission and informed Ambassador Sharp in Paris that a French mission would also be welcome.[55]

Balfour's approach in the United States was a logical extension of his tactfulness before the American declaration of war. When he arrived in Washington he told members of the State Department that his mission had come "to put themselves at the service of this country. They did not want to suggest but to answer questions and give, if it is wanted, the benefit of their experience that we might profit by their mistakes."[56] Balfour's charm and the restraint of his associates helped greatly to ensure the success of the visit. After a conversation with the President he informed Lloyd George that the United States had as yet done little to prepare for the war. Washington leaders were "indeed fully acquainted with character of these problems and . . . determined to cope with them in large and useful spirit but mechanism for effectually carrying out this policy is still in large measure lacking."[57]

Naval questions immediately arose. Balfour received urgent cables from London requesting immediate naval reinforcement and merchant shipping.[58] Daniels recorded that the British naval adviser, Admiral Sir Dudley R. de Chair, thought "the allies would win but regarded the German submarine warfare as very serious and were not unmindful of the terrible struggle before victory."[59] In a series of conferences Admiral de Chair and a

55. Lansing to Page, April 8, 1917, Wilson Papers, box 116. The delay disgusted Ambassador Page, who later wrote to Frank Polk about the matter. "Not a word at all came from the President. If he [Mr. Balfour] had seen the telegrams that I sent and the answers I got, he wd never have gone." Page to Polk, May 3, 1917, Page Papers, folder 1069.

56. Diary, April 21, 1917, Papers of Breckinridge Long, Library of Congress, Washington, D.C., hereafter cited as Long Papers. Long was the third assistant secretary of state.

57. Balfour to Lloyd George, April 26, 1917, FO 371, book 3119, file 86512.

58. Cecil to Balfour, April 22, 1917, Balfour Papers, BM, book 49692; Cecil to Balfour, April 25, 1917, Balfour Papers, FO 800, book 208; Cecil to Balfour, April 26, 1917, Balfour Papers, book 49692. The latter cable was specifically ordered sent by the Imperial War Cabinet, which resolved that Cecil send a telegram to Balfour "impressing upon him as a matter of the utmost urgency the importance of inducing President Wilson to exercise his personal authority in order to secure the dispatch of all available destroyers." Minutes of the Imperial War Cabinet (IWC 12), April 26, 1917, CAB 23, book 40.

59. Daniels diary, April 22, 1917, Cronon, ed., *Cabinet Diaries*, 139.

colleague from the French commission, Admiral Chocheprat, worked out a number of concrete agreements with their American counterparts. The European sailors constantly expressed "extreme and unconcealed anxiety" along with the view that the Entente powers must find relief in the United States "not only as to the ultimate outcome of the war, but to avert immediate disaster," an opinion that deeply impressed the Navy Department.[60] De Chair reported successful efforts to bring about the dispatch of destroyers and the provision of merchant shipping.[61] Chocheprat reacted less optimistically, doubting that the United States Navy would be able to take a great part in the war, but he too reported success in obtaining commitments to provide naval assistance and shipping and took special note of a desire in Washington to seize the offensive against the submarines.[62]

Balfour's mission was certainly a triumph. Despite his advanced age the Foreign Secretary worked most assiduously to communicate the needs of the Allies and to elicit agreements on a wide variety of questions from the United States. The visit had a marked effect on American attitudes toward the war and Great Britain as well. Balfour himself noted that Admiral Benson "was supposed to be anti-British, and [Daniels] . . . to be incapable of taking wide view of Naval policy. But no sign of these shortcomings [was] visible in the policy actually adopted."[63] The Foreign Secretary had gained his initial impression of American leaders from Spring Rice, one of the reasons why he began to consider replacing the Ambassador with the former British Foreign Secretary, Lord Grey.[64] Even the acerbic Spring Rice conceded that the mission had accomplished a great deal, but he was still worried about the degree of American commitment.

60. Badger to Daniels, February 25, 1921, Daniels Papers.

61. De Chair to Admiralty, May 15, 1917, Cabinet Papers, no. 293 (1917), FO 899, box 13.

62. Report of Admiral Chocheprat, May 20, 1917, MM, Es file, box 12. See also Laurens, La Guerre Sous-marine, 1:332–33. Daniels noted that when Chocheprat called to take leave, the French Admiral "bluntly through Naval attaché expressed hope that our good sentiments would be followed according to their claims for practical help." Daniels diary, May 1, 1917, Cronon, ed., Cabinet Diaries, 144.

63. Balfour to Lloyd George[?], April 30, 1917, FO 371, book 3113.

64. Balfour to Foreign Office, May 6, 1917, Balfour Papers, book 49692. Ultimately Lloyd George rejected Lord Grey because his mind was "too much fixed on peace and too little on the active prosecution of the war." Minutes of the War Cabinet (WC 140a), May 16, 1917, CAB 23, book 13.

"The realities of war have not yet reached this country and it will take them some time to realise the true significance of the struggle as it affects America."[65]

During his visit Balfour initiated discussions with Colonel House concerning a secret naval agreement between the United States and Great Britain, a subject of sufficient enough importance to require a separate account in Chapter 3. These extremely delicate negotiations contemplated a change in the building plans of the United States Navy in order to allow construction of antisubmarine craft and merchant shipping. In return Great Britain was to enter into certain engagements, particularly the lending of capital ships under certain contingencies.

V

During May and June, 1917, Admiral Sims worked furiously in London to attune the American naval effort to the problem of the submarine. With the dedicated cooperation of Ambassador Page he maintained a constant barrage of cablegrams and letters to the Navy Department in Washington, calling ever more insistently for almost complete concentration on one prime wartime mission—the dispatch of sufficient antisubmarine craft to frustrate the German undersea offensive against commerce. Some assistance began to materialize, although it was much too modest to satisfy the impatient Admiral and the anxious Ambassador. No American destroyers had appeared in Europe by May 1, the first flotilla of six reaching the Irish coast at Queenstown on May 4. By June 1, however, some 24 had arrived, and by the first of July, 28 of the 52 available American destroyers were on station.[66] Various considerations influenced the Navy Department to withhold dispatch of the remaining destroyers. Some were in need of repair; others were deemed necessary for coast defense. The President kept in mind the need to reserve some as escorts for American troop transports.[67]

Sims and Page found themselves frustrated to a degree by indecision in the British Government as well as at home. No one

65. Spring Rice to Governor General of Canada, May 18, 1917, Balfour Papers, book 49692.

66. Warner R. Schilling, "Admirals and Foreign Policy, 1913–1919," Ph.D. diss., Yale University, 1953, p. 89.

67. Daniels diary, May 1, 1917, Cronon, ed., *Cabinet Diaries*, 145.

was as yet fully decided on the proper over-all approach to the antisubmarine war, despite the adoption of the convoy system. Some experts advocated attacking the submarine bases on the coast of Flanders or perhaps undertaking close-in mining to inhibit movement to and from bases at Zeebrugge and Ostend on the Belgian coast. Page noted that to the best of his knowledge "all naval men among the Allies agree that these things can't be done," but he could not resist wondering whether this attitude was "merely routine professional opinion—a merely traditional opinion—or is it a lack of imagination? . . . What are the limits of the practicable?"[68] The Ambassador was convinced that the solution to the submarine war was the key to victory; if the submarine remained free to continue its depredations, "the Germans may use this success to keep their spirits up and go on till next year."[69] If it could be contained, he thought the "whole Teutonic military structure would soon tumble."[70] Sims and Page succeeded in convincing Americans visiting London that their views were correct.[71] From France Ambassador Sharp also called for reinforcements against the submarine.[72] Converts to the cause of antisubmarine warfare increasingly lent support to the pleas of Sims and Page.

The initial success of the convoy system in June strengthened the hand of Sims, as did growing recognition in Washington that the tonnage question was of paramount importance. On June 14, he proposed "adopting the convoy system for all traffic and particularly from our North Atlantic ports."[73] A few days later Ambassador Page dispatched a particularly insistent plea to the President and the Secretary of State summarizing the argument for emergency action in its mature form:

This critical situation demands the fullest and most prompt action possible. It seems to me to be the key to any possible early end of the war. It may well be that the issue of the war itself is involved unless aid come. The fighting power of the allies will inevitably be lowered

68. Hendrick, *Page*, 2:246.
69. Page to Frank N. Doubleday, May 3, 1917, ibid., 241.
70. Page to Wilson, May 4, 1917, ibid., 261.
71. See R. C. Grady to Sims, May 16, 1917, USNSF, TP file. Grady had been in Europe on a tour of inspection and was to report his findings to the Navy Department.
72. Sharp, *War Memoirs*, 174.
73. Sims to Daniels, June 14, 1917, USNSF, TP file. A copy is also in TT file.

within a few months and be very seriously impaired before we have an army to come and to be maintained in the face of constantly increasing dangers. The Germans are making such positive gains by submarines that they can afford to withdraw gradually in France and to hold on until the Allied fighting power is thus weakened. It is the most serious situation that has confronted the Allies since the battle of the Marne.[74]

Sims cabled in equally apocalyptic terms to the Navy Department: "If we cannot offer more immediate actual assistance even to the extent of sending the majority of the vessels patrolling our own coast lines which cannot materially affect the general situation we will fail to render the service to the Allied cause which future history will show to have been necessary."[75]

The alarm was also out in Britain. On June 18, the Ministry of Shipping calculated that Britain would have only about 12.5 million tons of shipping available at the outset of 1918; the earlier estimate of 17 million tons was incorrect. Since 8 million tons would be needed to supply the fighting fronts, only 4.5 million tons would remain for trade. The Ministry of Shipping recommended that Great Britain plan to produce at least 3 million tons during the coming year.[76] At this time the War Cabinet made plans to concentrate the naval building program on destroyers; on June 26, it voted to build 24 destroyers during the coming year along with 8 light cruisers, 18 submarines, and some lesser craft, all of which were needed in the war against the submarine.[77] Clearly the British were willing to devote almost all of their energies to immediate wartime necessities, the policy they were urging upon the Americans.

By late June and July Sims had strengthened his own understanding of the convoy system and had completely convinced himself of its practicality. The enemy was concentrating its naval

74. Page to Lansing and Wilson, June 20, 1917, Wilson Papers, box 121. A copy is in USDSM 367, 763.72/13317.
75. Sims to Daniels, June 21, 1917, USNSF, TT file. A paraphrase of this message was apparently obtained by the Admiralty and read to a meeting of the War Cabinet. Minutes of the War Cabinet (WC 168), June 22, 1917, CAB 23, book 3. Sims probably passed it to Jellicoe.
76. Maclay to Lloyd George, June 18, 1917, Papers of Prime Minister David Lloyd George, Beaverbrook Library, London, F file/35/2/15. Hereafter this collection is referred to as Lloyd George Papers. See also Maclay to Lloyd George, June 27, 1917, Lloyd George Papers, file F/35/2/17.
77. Minutes of the War Cabinet (WC 168 and 169), June 22 and 26, 1917, CAB 23, book 3.

forces in a relatively small area; the Allies were not. "If we concentrate our shipping into convoys and protect it with our naval forces we will thereby force the enemy, in order to carry out his mission, to encounter naval forces which are not embarrassed with valuable cargoes, and which are a great danger to the submarine." The naval consequences would be of the utmost significance. "The handicaps we now labor under will be shifted to the enemy; we will have adopted the essential principal [sic] of concentration while the enemy will lose it."[78] Sims put his argument in quite detailed language to a friend in the Navy Department:

What we seek is offensive actions against the submarine. The objective of the submarine is the contrary. He avoids all contact with armed forces—destroyers, submarines, and other anti-submarine craft and devotes his attention to sinking merchant vessels. He is perfectly correct in his objective. It is found exceedingly difficult to bring him to action. It is for this reason that I have always advocated interposing our armed forces directly between the submarine and the submarine's objective. This is why I have strenuously advocated the convoy system and I am glad to say that it is now being put into operation as rapidly as possible. . . . It may well be that this will be the solution to the submarine question. That is, it is believed that it will reduce the losses considerably below the rate of the building, and this will mean that the submarine campaign will be defeated.[79]

Sims's optimism proved justified. Word of the convoy system began to filter into Germany and immediately produced concern. The German Embassy in Switzerland reported on May 20 that only one ship of sixty-nine in a wheat-carrying convoy from America had been sunk and that the English now believed that the U-boat could no longer interdict traffic from the United States.[80] The German Ambassador in Sweden reported a few days later "that England could survive only a few more months of U-boat warfare" because of growing industrial unrest,[81] but the German envoy in Switzerland reported again that an informant in London reported a gloomy prospect. The American fleet would join the British in protecting convoys; consequently,

78. Sims to Daniels, June 29, 1917, printed in Sims, Victory at Sea, 388.
79. Sims to Captain Dudley W. Knox, July 9, 1917, USNSF, TD file.
80. Embassy in Switzerland to Bethmann-Hollweg, May 20, 1917, St. Antony's Papers, reel 12, Geheime Akten, vol. 43, frame 182.
81. Ambassador in Stockholm to Foreign Office, May 24, 1917, St. Antony's Papers, reel 12, Geheime Akten, vol. 44, frame 7.

the U-boat campaign would not succeed in forcing peace negotiations.[82] By June Hindenburg's headquarters began to reflect concern.[83] The Commander himself warned Bethmann-Hollweg of the dangers of publicizing the fall deadline for the U-boat victory. He still thought that the U-boat would eventually bring Britain to its knees, but to establish a public date for the victory would lead to dejection in Germany if the deadline was not met.[84] The Chancellor replied rather pessimistically. Austria-Hungary would probably not last out the year; Britain would not be defeated by the fall of 1917; the German victory in Russia would not counteract failure in the West; the French would not collapse, given the onset of American assistance.[85] Other civilian leaders were becoming restive. Matthias Erzberger now concluded that military victory was no longer within the grasp of Germany and that a negotiated peace was the only means of surviving the war intact.[86] Walther Rathenau remained critical of the U-boat command, pointing out to Ludendorff that the United States and Great Britain together could produce enough merchant shipping to replace what was being sunk by Germany.[87] Sinkings in May had fallen off by almost 300,000 tons from the high figure of nearly 900,000 in April. In June the total spurted to almost 700,000 tons, but in July only about 550,000 tons went to the bottom, and from that time on the sinkings per month were almost always below 350,000 tons. The German Admiralty first admitted that sinkings were rapidly declining in July when the U-boats reported sighting convoys.[88] U-boat losses also began to increase. Only 20 were sunk during the first half of 1917, but the total rose to 43 during the second half of that year.[89] Germany tried to counteract the convoy by retraining its sub-

82. Ambassador in Bern to Foreign Office, May 29, 1917, St. Antony's Papers, reel 12, Geheime Akten, vol. 44, frame 143.

83. See Feldman, *Army, Industry, and Labor in Germany*, 362.

84. Hindenburg to Bethmann-Hollweg, June 29, 1917, St. Antony's Papers, reel 12, Geheime Akten, vol. 48, frame 183.

85. Bethmann-Hollweg to Hindenburg, June 25, 1917, St. Antony's Papers, reel 12, Geheime Akten, vol. 48, frames 187–91.

86. Klaus Epstein, *Matthias Erzberger and the Dilemma of German Democracy* (Princeton, 1959), 186.

87. Walther Rathenau, *Tagebuch, 1907–1922* (Duesseldorf, 1967), 220–21.

88. Goerlitz, ed., *The Kaiser and His Court*, 285; Arno Spindler, *Der Handelskrieg mid U-Booten*, 4 vols. (Berlin, 1941), 4:224.

89. Robert M. Grant, *U-Boats Destroyed: The Effect of Anti-Submarine Warfare, 1914–1918* (London, 1964), 41.

marine commanders and by offering incentives to sustain the morale of the submarine crews, but the zenith of submarine success had been reached in April, 1917.[90]

When the German Reichstag debated its famous peace resolution during the summer of 1917, Bethmann-Hollweg and Ludendorff did their best to defend the policy they had inaugurated in February. The Chancellor maintained on July 7 that Germany should combine the submarine offensive with an effective defensive in the West and an energetic attack against Russia in order to force Britain to the peace table, rather than to try to achieve total victory.[91] Ludendorff explained to a parliamentary delegation on July 13 that unrestricted U-boat warfare would stem the tide of supplies from the United States and destroy the war economy of the Entente powers by denying them raw materials and other necessities. He had recognized from the start, he said, that the U-boat attacks would force the United States into the war, but this consideration did not matter because of the absolute need to halt the flow of material to England.[92] Nevertheless, despite disturbing signs and portents indicating that the U-boats would not achieve their objectives, Germany sustained its resolve during the summer of 1917.

In London Sims began to interest himself in the question of continuing relations with the Allies. His first problem in inter-Allied relations was British Admiral Sir Lewis Bayly, commanding at Queenstown where the American destroyers were based. Bayly was a notoriously difficult, if competent, man. Sims recognized the situation immediately and set about assiduously courting Bayly's favor, at the same time enjoining his subordinates to show the most complete desire to cooperate with the salty seadog at Queenstown.[93] The endeavor proved successful —Sims and Bayly became fast friends.[94] The American admiral was also careful to cultivate good relations with the French Navy.[95] Although he recognized the likelihood of future diffi-

90. R. H. Gibson and Maurice Prendergast, *The German Submarine War, 1914–1918* (London, 1931), 186, 191.

91. Herbert Michaelis, et al., eds., *Ursachen und Folgen vom Deutschen Zusammenbruch 1918 und 1945 bis zur staatlichen Neuordnung Deutschlands in der Gegenwart*, 8 vols. (Berlin, n.d.), 2:14–15, 17.

92. Ibid., 27; Erich Ludendorff, *Urkunden der Obersten Heeresleitung ueber Ihre Tactigkeit 1916/18* (Berlin, 1922), 413.

93. Sims to Taussig, April 29, 1917, USNSF, TD file.

94. Sims to [?], June 1, 1917, USNSF, TP file.

95. Sims to Pratt, June 6, 1917, USNSF, TD file.

culties, he was reasonably assured that friendly inter-Allied relations at the outset of cooperation would prove invaluable in the long run. He wrote in this vein to Capt. William V. Pratt, his principal confidant in the Navy Department:

I believe there is no case on record where Allies have cooperated together for any considerable length of time without more or less serious friction. I am out to make an exception. . . . There has been to date material for any amount of friction, due to peculiar personalities, but I believe that they [disputes] have been successfully overcome. That other causes [of tension] will arise is perfectly certain. . . . If we can get by these for a certain length of time, so as to really get into the game with these people, all danger of friction will disappear.[96]

Ambassador Page approved heartily of this approach, one that he himself had utilized for a long time, and he was fulsome in his reports on the extent of good Anglo-American feeling and the striking impression made by Admiral Sims in London.[97] He admitted to Wilson, however, that the emergency had a great deal to do with the general feelings of good will, discerning in British gratitude "a confession of the Allies' dire need of our help—a far more urgent need than anybody confesses or than anybody realizes but the man who knows the inside facts. . . . In fact nothing [could] keep these nations all together a week but dire necessity; it's another case of all hanging together or all hanging separately."[98]

Sims was as good as his word; throughout the anxious months of his service in London, he persisted in his resolve to sustain good personal relations with the Allies. On July 3, 1917, he informed all personnel under his command that everyone in the American service must be concerned with relations between the United States and the Entente powers. The "paramount purpose" of American activity must be to achieve maximum cooperation with the Allies. "Our attitudes and efforts," he held, "must be on the assumption that Allied and U.S. Services are one and the same service."[99] This was unprecedented doctrine

96. Sims to Pratt, June 7, 1917, USNSF, TD file.
97. See, for example, Page to Wilson, June 8, 1917, Wilson Papers, box 120. Page to A. W. Page, July 8, 1918, in Hendrick, *Page*, 2:290.
98. Page to Wilson, June 22, 1917, Wilson Papers, box 121.
99. Instructions to American personnel, July 3, 1917, USNSF, TT file. Of course, the British assiduously courted good relations with Sims. On July 3, the War Cabinet reiterated its earlier decision to give Sims full access to Admiralty information. Minutes of the War Cabinet (WC 174), July 3, 1917, CAB 23, book 3.

indeed. It was clearly required by the circumstances of the time, but it was bound to create difficulties between Sims and those in the American Government who were not as imbued as he with the virtues and potentials of Anglo-American accord.

If Sims became intensely popular in London, his relations with the Navy Department were not very smooth. During the early months in Europe he and his associates in Washington moved slowly and sometimes acrimoniously toward a workable association. Very often commanders in the field discover that the home forces begin to feel left out of the war. Captain Pratt gave early indication of this tendency. "I feel," he reported, "from what Ad. Benson says, that he feels we, meaning the U.S. ought to be taken in pretty closely to the Allies plan of water strategy and tactics."[100] Just as frequently, commanders in the field begin to believe, sometimes correctly, that they are not being properly supported at home. On May 31, Sims began a series of messages to Washington urging expansion of his staff. He wanted officers to perform liaison functions and enlisted men to cope with clerical duties.[101] In particular, Sims sought the services of his close friend Pratt, but the Captain was soon made Assistant Chief of Naval Operations and was never allowed to serve overseas.[102] Sims recognized that his command in Europe should function as a "co-ordinating link between the [Navy] Department and the British and French Admiralties," and this circumstance required full and free communications between the field command and the home staff.[103] He rapidly became convinced that the Navy Department was improperly organized and operated and that this circumstance prejudiced success at sea.[104]

Sims soon received confirmation of disarray in Washington. On June 22, one of his subordinates, R. R. M. Emmet, presented a long report on conditions in the Navy Department that he had

100. Pratt to Sims, May 15, 1917, USNSF, TD file.

101. Sims to Daniels, May 31, 1917, USNSF, TP file. See also Sims to Daniels, June 2, 1917, USNSF, TP file.

102. Sims to Pratt, June 7, 1917, USNSF, TD file.

103. Sims to Daniels, June 8, 1917, USNSF, TP file.

104. In Washington others shared Sims's opinion, particularly Ambassador Spring Rice and Assistant Secretary of the Navy Roosevelt. See House diary, May 22, 1917, House Papers; Spring Rice to [?], June 14, 1917, Spring Rice Papers, FO 800, book 242. For further information about F.D.R.'s attitude, see Kilpatrick, *Roosevelt and Daniels*, 36.

recently observed in Washington. Admiral Benson had been particularly irritating. He "seemed to think Admiral Sims and our officers abroad in danger of becoming [obsessed] with all things British to detriment of clear judgment." Emmet believed that Benson had no clear conception of the magnitude of the tasks facing Sims, that Benson doubted the ability of the British Navy to perform its tasks properly, that he was unwilling to send additional personnel to Sims, and that he was overwhelmed by the growth of the Navy Department. In addition, Secretary Daniels was "a slow decider." The Paymaster of the Navy Department, Captain McGowan, had told Emmet that Daniels thought he and Roosevelt "dangerous war mad lunatics." McGowan believed that President Wilson was largely unaware of what was taking place in the Navy Department and that the Government generally was not alert to the extent of the crisis. The report also maintained that the Navy Department did not fully understand the problems it faced and that Benson and Daniels were convinced that Sims's judgment was warped because of his undue confidence in Great Britain.[105]

Despite these developments Sims pressed his views ever more strongly on the Navy Department. He became increasingly prone to criticize its operations as experience confirmed his views of the proper way to further the American naval effort. He believed that, unless there was incontrovertible evidence to the contrary, the United States should seek to improve rather than change British methods, and he was quick to cite the importance of close inter-Allied cooperation in supporting various requests and recommendations.[106] As his concern about Washington's failures mounted, Sims became increasingly involved in strengthening his own organization in London[107] and slowly

105. Emmet to Sims, June 22, 1917, USNSF, TD file. Colonel House also complained of Daniels's tendency to procrastinate. House diary, May 22, 1917, House Papers.

106. See, for example, Sims to Daniels, July 3, 1917, USNSF, TT file. This cable dealt with Sims's support of British methods of shipping control as against proposals emanating from the Navy Department. His cable ended sharply: "It is impossible to present this case [that shipping control should center in London] by cable and it is therefore urged that Department will accept these recommendations based on one consideration only, namely, our interests in the one cause against common enemy (stop)." Sims's anger was stimulated by Daniels to Sims, July 1, 1917, USNSF, TT file.

107. Sims to Pratt, July 6, 1917, USNSF, TD file.

but surely built up a large staff. Whatever the other shortcomings of Daniels, he was willing to concentrate naval authority in Europe in the hands of Sims.[108]

Like most theater commanders, Sims found it difficult to appreciate the obstacles faced by the home staff, but others shared his general doubts about the competence of the Navy Department. British officials in Washington encountered frustrations in their approaches to the Navy Department, although its administration seems to have improved after Captain Pratt became assistant chief. Captain Gaunt, the British naval attaché, reported that when Pratt took office "the result was at once cruisers for convoy work, release of destroyers, and I hope, several other items; but the great point is that it is done immediately." The attaché remained disquieted; he wanted the Admiralty to forward "some settled policy" to him:

Admiral Benson does not exactly complain, but points out that all we do is ask for things as they come along, but there is no settled policy that we can set forward and say we are working along those lines. . . . I think that he [Benson] has a sort of feeling that he should be taken closer into the general scheme of the Allies' sea policy, instead of, as at present, just being asked from time to time to supply units which have no connection with one another.[109]

The lack of an effective British organization in Washington had already attracted the attention of the War Cabinet.[110] After an approach by Balfour, Page approved the dispatch of a special British naval mission to Washington, and Admiral de Chair was proposed to head it.[111] De Chair actually prepared a plan of operations for the projected mission, reflecting British desires clearly in his rationale for it. The Admiralty should maintain control of inter-Allied naval operations, and because the United

108. In May, 1917, Admiral Benson had wanted to send another admiral to represent the United States in France. Daniels characteristically delayed his decision. His diary entry summarized his policy. "I waited. After cablegram from Sims it was clear that there ought to be only one command abroad." Daniels diary, May 7, 1917, Cronon, ed., *Cabinet Diaries*, 148.
109. Gaunt to Secretary of the Admiralty, July 5, 1917, ADM 137, book 1437, 13–15.
110. Minutes of the War Cabinet (WC 160), June 11, 1917, CAB 23, book 3.
111. Balfour to Spring Rice, June 21, 1917, FO 371, book 3119 (file 110899); Page to Lansing, June 22, 1917, USNSF, TT file.

States was capable of expanding its navy more than any other, "it is of greatest importance that the development of their Sea Forces should proceed along lines dictated by British war experience and be co-ordinated with British policy in order that the utmost value may be obtained by British-American combination on the sea."[112] A few days later Jellicoe told the War Cabinet that the United States would welcome a naval mission. Balfour was instructed to settle the matter through Page, but on July 18, Spring Rice recommended delay, noting that the United States was now satisfied with the present arrangements and that "the French have been thought rather too insistent and there is some anxiety as to possible crisis in Congress."[113]

During May, June, and July, 1917, Sims engaged in a number of exchanges with the Navy Department concerning various plans and proposals advanced in Washington to which he took strong objection. These discussions probably added to the growing tension between London and Washington, but they ultimately helped clear the air. The most important discussions concerned the feasibility of close-in mining operations near German bases, the possibility of establishing a mine barrage across the North Sea to contain the submarines, the question of arming merchant ships, the likelihood of German submarine operations on the American coast, and the possibility of dispatching the American battle fleet to European waters. In all these matters Sims took the view of the British Admiralty, a tendency that probably strengthened the conviction of Benson and others that he was hopelessly pro-British and unable to exercise independent judgment.

On May 6, Pratt had advised Sims of the Navy Department's interest in mining operations close to the German coast in order to bottle up the submarines.[114] Sims was adamantly opposed to this tactic and informed Pratt that the mine fields would have to bar all openings in order to be effective—an unattainable object. Mines were in short supply, and it was impossible to maintain constant patrol on a mine field. Without such patrols

112. De Chair recommendation, June 25, 1917, ADM 137, book 1436, 258–63.
113. Minutes of the War Cabinet (WC 173), July 2, 1917, CAB 23, book 3; Spring Rice to Foreign Office, July 18, 1917, ADM 137, book 1436, 276.
114. Pratt to Sims, May 6, 1917, USNSF, TD file.

the Germans could easily sweep away enough mines to permit free movement of submarines. Sims insisted that since submarines could not be contained in their bases, the only proper approach was to attack them with antisubmarine craft in the open sea. "Do not forget in all this business the extreme value of the element of time. Whatever is done must be done as soon as possible. . . . The presence of our [destroyer] flotillas on this side is of more value than five hundred thousand mines four months from now."[115]

Sims responded in similar terms to a proposal to mine the North Sea. The Bureau of Ordnance had suggested this enterprise as early as April 15, 1917, and Daniels asked the Admiral to comment on its feasibility.[116] Sims argued that neither sufficient mines nor the proper types were available and that the problem of patrolling several hundred miles of mine barrages was insurmountable. He insisted once again that the proper response to the submarine threat was the provision of antisubmarine craft.[117] Sims later stoutly defended his early opposition to the North Sea barrage: "In 1917 the idea was not among the possibilities—there were not mines enough in the world to build such a barrage, nor had a mine then been invented that was suitable for the purpose."[118]

The Navy Department believed that the submarine could be countered to a considerable degree by placing adequate guns and trained gun crews on merchant ships.[119] Sims, heartily contemptuous of this view, considered merchant ships lacking in

115. Sims to Pratt, June 6, 1917, USNSF, TD file.
116. Baker, *Wilson*, 7:21, 65. The idea was discussed in the Cabinet meeting of May 4, 1917. Cronon, ed., *Cabinet Diaries*, 146. Admiral de Chair reported this interest to the Admiralty, in de Chair to Admiralty, May 10, 1917, ADM 137, book 1436, 352. The Admiralty reported back that the project had been previously considered but rejected as impracticable. Admiralty to Gaunt for de Chair, May[?], 1917, ADM 137, 1436, 355.
117. Sims to Daniels, May 14, 1917, USNSF, TP file. See also—for a report on British views given to Sims—R. C. Grady to Sims, May 16, 1917, USNSF, TP file. Grady reported that the British had considered the project before and had rejected it. "The objections are given as lack of necessary patrols, impossibility to maintain nets, impracticability to mine in water over 50 fathoms with anchored mines, and the undesirability of floating mines on account of possible danger to their fleet." For another criticism of the North Sea barrage, more fully developed than in earlier reports, see Sims to Earle, July 11, 1917, USNSF, TD file.
118. Sims, *Victory at Sea*, 191.
119. Daniels to Sims, received June 24, 1917, USNSF, TP file.

speed and protection. Guns on board would not preclude attack without warning. He told Daniels that some thirty armed ships had been sunk in six weeks without ever sighting a submarine and reiterated a familiar theme: "The mission of the Allies must be to force submarines to give battle." Arming merchant ships accomplished one purpose; it forced submarines to utilize torpedoes instead of gunfire to sink merchant shipping.[120] Sims hoped that the Navy would not divert men and material needed for antisubmarine craft to the task of arming merchant ships.

Nothing annoyed Sims more than persistent concern in Washington about coast defense in the Western Hemisphere. He was convinced that "Defensive measures on our own coast or in any other locality and in fact all defensive considerations should be subordinated to the offensive against the submarines where they are operating." He argued that German submarines were unlikely to operate on the American coasts because of the distance from their bases and the undue strain such activities would impose on submarine personnel. Any such operations would diminish the effect of the submarine campaign because U-boats could be much more effective in other waters. Any ships employed in coastal protection would be more valuable in European waters.[121] On April 4, 1917, Admiral Benson heard that German submarines were on the American coast, and he then took all manner of actions to guard against sinkings.[122] Actually, the German Admiralty had been slow to permit unrestricted submarine operations outside of the formal blockade areas, which did not extend into American waters; it did not authorize attacks on American ships within the blockade areas around the British Isles and elsewhere until May 22.[123] Sims thought that the Germans were chary of submarine attacks on the American coast because restraint would "strengthen the peace propaganda in America."[124]

120. Sims to Daniels, June 28 and June 29, 1917, in Sims, *Victory at Sea*, 386, 390.

121. Sims to Daniels, May 14, 1917, USNSF, TP file; Sims to Daniels, June 21, 1917, USNSF, TT file; Sims to Earle, July 11, 1917, USNSF, TD file.

122. Daniels diary, April 14, 1917, Cronon, ed., *Cabinet Diaries*, 135.

123. Holtzendorff to Bethmann-Hollweg, May 10, 1917, St. Antony's Papers, reel 12, Geheime Akten, vol. 42, frame 82; Holtzendorff to Foreign Office, May 22, 1917, St. Antony's Papers, Geheime Akten, vol. 43, frame 155.

124. Sims to Daniels, June 21, 1917, USNSF, TT file; Sims to Pratt, July 16, 1917, USNSF, TD file.

He was correct. On July 14, Hindenburg's headquarters decided that U-boat warfare on the United States coast should not be undertaken until a "continuous" campaign could be mounted. Single actions would only drive neutrals into the arms of America.[125] Sims derided the possibility considered early in the war that Germany might seek to establish submarine bases in unfrequented bays and harbors because such bases could not be properly supported.[126]

Sims exploded when the Navy Department persisted in maintaining patrols along the eastern coast. To his friend Pratt he wrote in high dudgeon:

It would be very funny, if it were not so tragic, the spectacle of many dozens of ships, destroyers, yachts and so forth parading up and down the American coast three thousand miles away from where the vital battle of the war was going on. How is it that they cannot see that this is as wrong as it possibly can be from a military point of view[?] In other words, why does not America send her forces to the front instead of keeping them three thousand miles in the rear[?] If there were any danger off our coast or if dangers should develope, later you could send the forces back again, or such as were needed, before any considerable number of the enemy could get over there.[127]

These appeals had some effect, but Sims never reconciled himself to the retention of any important vessels on the American coast.

No real controversy developed over another of Sims's convictions—that there was little use for the American battle fleet as an independent unit in Europe. He was willing to condone the dispatch of a few capital ships for duty in the English Channel, but he did not discern a use for the entire panoply of American naval power. He wanted to be kept informed of fleet policy and preparations, should a need for dreadnoughts and other large vessels develop, but he argued in this context as in all others that the only real necessity, overpowering in importance, was the dispatch of antisubmarine craft for patrol and convoy duties.[128]

125. Memorandum on U-boat warfare on the American coast, July 14, 1917, St. Antony's Papers, reel 12, Geheime Akten, vol. 50, frames 35d to 35g.
126. Sims to Pratt, July 26, 1917, USNSF, TD file.
127. Ibid., July 3, 1917, USNSF, TP file.
128. Sims to Navy Department, June 7, 1917, USDSM 367, 763.72/5196. See also a memorandum drawn up in London discussing arguments in favor of dispatching the fleet. "Co-operation of British and American Battle Fleet," June, 1917, USNSF, TT file.

All these discussions figured in a crisis over American naval policy that transpired at the end of June and continued into early July, when President Wilson suddenly intervened in the activities of the Navy Department. This episode fixed the course of American activity for many months to come.

VI

President Wilson largely refrained from direct intervention in naval affairs during the anxious early months of the war. On occasion he interested himself in various questions such as armed neutrality and convoy, and at times he urged action upon Secretary Daniels, responding to the advice of close associates like Colonel House, but he left matters largely to the Navy Department. By late June, however, he had become irritated at the seeming failure to curb the submarine. Lloyd George had sent one of his principal political associates, the publisher Lord Northcliffe, to the United States, to expedite American assistance. Northcliffe soon became aware of the President's growing annoyance and informed one of his associates that Wilson "complained of a lack of submarine news, as did [Houston, Lane, and Hoover] . . . all used the same argument—'We cannot expect sacrifices from our people unless they know that Great Britain is suffering too.'" Northcliffe attributed this attitude to the confused state of affairs in the United States. "Unfortunately, the cross-currents here are many. Millions of Americans are most enthusiastic in our cause. There are many millions of others who do not believe a word of the English news; and who think we are lying about the submarines."[129] Northcliffe was not alone in observing the President's growing impatience with British naval policy at this time. Secretary Daniels noted the Chief Executive's belief that Britain utilized its battleships too conservatively.[130]

At just this time, Sims and Page in London prepared a major effort to force adoption of their views about the proper utilization of American naval power. On June 25, Sims once again sent information to Page from Queenstown that indicated the seriousness of the submarine crisis. He wondered whether "it would not be well to send another telegram to Mr. Lansing and the

129. Northcliffe to J. T. Davis, June 20, 1917, Lloyd George Papers, file F/41/7/8.
130. Daniels diary, June 27, 1917, Cronon, ed., *Cabinet Diaries*, 169.

President, and also send them the enclosed correspondence?"[131] Page responded quickly, writing in the most sensational tone he had yet assumed:

Sims . . . says that the war will be won or lost in this submarine zone within a few months. Time is the essence of the problem and anti-submarine craft which cannot be assembled in the submarine zone almost immediately may come too late. There is therefore a possibility that the war may become a war between Germany and the United States alone. Help is far more urgently needed in this submarine zone than anywhere else in the whole war area.[132]

Secretary Lansing responded by recommending to the President that he dispatch a commissioner to Europe in order to analyze the submarine crisis. His justification reflected the general confusion in Washington. "I feel that our regular representatives are so imbued with the British point of view that we are getting reports which exaggerate the difficulties of the situation, and yet, of course, I cannot be sure that this is so." He thought, therefore, that it might be useful to dispatch someone to London who possessed "a hard head and full judgment."[133] Did the Secretary have himself in mind? In any event he was among those who tended to dismiss the counsel of Page and Sims because of their real or presumed Anglophilia. The two men in London gradually realized that their pleas were to a great extent ineffective because of their pro-British reputations. Sims even suspected Daniels and Benson of believing that the British hoped to lure American ships into dangerous waters to fight while they kept their own warships safely in harbor. Page now launched his supreme effort to legitimize his views—he made application for support to Arthur James Balfour. The Foreign Secretary duly dispatched a message to Washington on June 30 that reviewed the crisis and called for the dispatch of all available antisubmarine vessels as soon as possible.[134]

All this activity probably conditioned the President's action on July 2, when he sent a message to Daniels calling for independent exertions by the United States. "As you and I concluded yesterday, the British Admiralty had done practically nothing

131. Sims to Page, June 25, 1917, in Hendrick, *Page*, 2:283.
132. Page to Lansing and Wilson, June 27, 1917, ibid. A copy of this message is in USDSM 367, 763.72/5552.
133. Lansing to Wilson, June 28, 1917, USDSM 367, 763.72/13407b.
134. Hendrick, *Page*, 2:285–86. See also Baker, *Wilson*, 7:138–39.

constructive in the use of their navy and I think it is time we were making and insisting upon plans of our own, even if we render some of the more conservative of our own naval advisers uncomfortable."[135] Wilson may have had in hand a report on the Navy Department prepared for him by the American author, Winston Churchill, which was relatively friendly to Daniels and highly favorable to Sims, but generally critical of the American naval bureaucracy and particularly of the General Board.[136] On July 3, Daniels received a draft of a dispatch to Sims in which the President, according to the Secretary, "wanted offensive in submarine warfare & merchant ships to be convoyed. I wrote that England had decided to convoy."[137] If the President, at this date, was unaware that the convoy system had been adopted on an experimental basis, it is a sad commentary on the communication between his office and the Navy Department.

Wilson's draft cablegram to Sims reflected both the President's irritation with the British and his desire for effective new departures. Implicit in it was also some criticism of Sims:

From the beginning of the war I have been surprised by nothing so much as the failure of the British Admiralty to use Great Britain's great naval superiority in any effective way. In the presence of the present submarine emergency they are helpless to the point of panic. Every plan we suggest they reject for some reason of prudence. In my view this is not a time for prudence but for boldness even at the risk of great losses. . . . I would be very much obliged to you if you would report to me, confidentially of course, exactly what the Admiralty have been doing and what they have accomplished and add to this report your own independent judgments already arrived at on that side of the water. . . . I beg that you will keep these instructions absolutely to yourself and that you will give me such advice as you would give if you were handling an independent navy of your own.

Included in the message was a strong endorsement of the convoy system, along with criticism of what the President deemed

135. Wilson to Daniels, July 2, 1917, Wilson Papers, box 122. This message is quoted in Frank Freidel, *Franklin D. Roosevelt: The Apprenticeship* (Boston, 1952), 304–5.
136. A copy of this report, undated, is in USNSF, TD file. It is discussed in Freidel, *Roosevelt: The Apprenticeship*, 309–10. The author was not related to his English namesake.
137. Daniels diary, July 3, 1917, Cronon, ed., *Cabinet Diaries*, 172. See Daniels to Wilson, July 6, 1917, Daniels Papers. This letter explained the convoy system in some detail.

slow and halfhearted policy by the Admiralty.[138] This message, slightly revised by Daniels, went out to Sims on July 4.[139] Page soon reported that Sims had received it and was "greatly pleased." He was careful also to state that the American sailor did not "always nor wholly agree with the British Admiralty. In fact, they have made considerable reorganizations after seeking his advice. They defer to him greatly."[140] The implied criticism in Wilson's cable had not passed unnoticed in London.

These events probably had something to do with the timing of various decisions made within the Navy Department. On July 3, Secretary Daniels forwarded to Lansing a comprehensive statement of American naval policy in connection with the war. The document listed six basic principles:

1. A desire to cooperate fully with the Allies against the submarine.

2. A desire to cooperate fully in order to cope with any future wartime problem.

3. A commitment to the termination of the war as the first object without jeopardizing the future of the American fleet by its "disintegration."

4. A recognition that the main wartime mission of the Navy was to safeguard lines of communication to the Entente powers.

5. Endorsement of offensive policy within the limits imposed by a general commitment to support joint actions proposed by the Allies.

6. Willingness to take certain specific actions, including (a) dispatch of all antisubmarine craft not needed at home; (b) readiness to send the entire fleet if necessary; and (c) receptivity to discussions of joint plans of operation with the Allies.[141]

138. This draft message, written on the President's personal typewriter, dated July 4, 1917, is in the Wilson Papers, box 122.

139. Wilson to Sims, July 4, 1917, USNSF, TD file. See also Baker, *Wilson*, 7:146–47. The message is reproduced in full in several places. See United States Department of State, *Papers Relating to the Foreign Relations of the United States: 1917*, supp. 2, *The World War*, 2 vols. (Washington, D.C., 1932), 1:117–18. See also Josephus Daniels, *The Wilson Era: Years of War and After, 1917–1923* (Chapel Hill, N.C., 1946), 84–86. Daniels maintains that the message was sent because Sims said that the North Sea barrage would not work.

140. Page to Wilson, July 6, 1917, Wilson Papers, box 122.

141. Daniels to Lansing, July 3, 1917, USDSM 367, 763.72/6268. See also Morison, *Sims*, 359. The letter is reprinted in Department of State, *1917*, supp. 2, vol. 1, *The World War*, 116–17.

These commitments were hardly as openhanded as Sims might have desired, since they implied something less than full confidence in the naval capabilities and the long-range intentions of the Entente, but they were certainly sufficient to ensure a considerable naval contribution by the United States.

On July 5, Lord Northcliffe reported to Lloyd George the results of his efforts to uncover the state of American opinion on naval matters. The American view that the British Navy was inactive against submarines was as great a hindrance to Anglo-American relations as the problem of Ireland. The American Navy, he thought, favored three specific lines of activity, all to be pursued with the utmost vigor: offensives against the German fleet and its ports such as the base at Zeebrugge; closure of the North Sea with nets and mines; and convoy through the submarine danger zone. Admiral Benson was reluctant to concentrate on the production of antisubmarine craft because it would delay the capital-ship building program. Northcliffe reported Benson as believing that "if war ends in compromise that leaves German Fleet intact or in defeat of Allies, danger to U.S. [is] so great that utmost battleship and battlecruiser strength would be necessary in view of possible S. Atlantic and Pacific developments." Benson thought, however, that the difficulty might be met "by British offering latest type of battleships or battle-cruisers in exchange . . . against anti-submarine product of labour, etc., so displaced from capital ship programme here." Comments followed on the American views. Attacks on German bases were impractical; so was the North Sea mining project because of sea conditions and lack of patrol craft. And finally, Britain could not "exchange modern battle ships or battle cruisers for anti-submarine craft while the German Fleet remains intact." The proper policy was "to guarantee naval assistance to the U.S. after the war."[142] Perhaps Northcliffe was unaware of an extremely secret discussion of this very question between the United States and Britain, a matter discussed at length in the next chapter.

The statements of Daniels and Northcliffe both reflect the tendency to make a "halfway covenant" with the war that characterized the Navy Department during the early months of American belligerency. Daniels and Benson clearly wanted to

142. Northcliffe to Lloyd George, July 5, 1917, USNSF, TP file. This document is a paraphrase; how it fell into American hands is not known.

provide quick and effective assistance against the submarine, but not at the expense of certain long-range naval interests, most of them related to postwar considerations. Sims, on the other hand, was convinced that the first and only consideration should be the defeat of the submarine offensive. Sims would have taken comfort in an important recommendation just being made by a special committee in the Navy Department headed by his friend, Captain Pratt. This group proposed that the United States undertake the building of 200 destroyers beyond those already authorized to be used during the war. Daniels immediately approved this recommendation. It meant that the United States would be forced, if involuntarily, to postpone much of its program for the construction of capital ships. The acceptance of the Pratt report forced the hand of skeptics such as Admiral Benson. Advocates of Sims's views in the Navy Department could now press destroyer construction effectively.[143]

Sims made his response to the President's urgent message on July 7. He reacted directly to the implication that he was not reporting his own opinions. "I wish to make it perfectly clear that my reports and dispatches have been in all cases an independent opinion based upon specific facts and data which I have collected in the various Admiralty and other Government Departments. They constitute my own conviction and hence comply with your request for an independent opinion." After reiterating his arguments against close-in mining operations and the like, he took his familiar stance. "It is my opinion that the War will be decided by the success or failure of the submarine campaign." Operations on land would depend upon maintenance of lines of communication. Given this circumstance, he continued, if he "had complete control of our Sea Force, with the success of the Allied cause solely in view," he would adopt seven basic policies:

1. Send as much of the American fleet as possible into European waters.

2. Use the advance force, before the main fleet arrived, for antisubmarine and convoy operations.

3. Prepare supply and fuel ships to support the effort in Europe, developing communications to France immediately.

143. A discussion of the report, submitted July 6, 1917, is in Schilling, "Admirals and Foreign Policy," 101–3. See Kilpatrick, *Roosevelt and Daniels*, 36–37.

4. Concentrate naval construction on destroyers and light craft, depending "on the fact which I believe to be true that regardless of any future developments we can always count upon the support of the British Navy."

5. Concentrate all other construction on the provision of merchant shipping.

6. Emphasize convoy operations above all else.

7. Develop an organization in London near the actual fighting fronts sufficient to ensure effective naval performance.[144]

In these terms Sims definitely stuck to his guns, adopting the ancient military premise that the best defense is a good offense. He dismissed the principal consideration in Washington against all-out concentration on the immediate problem of the submarine—concern for the future—by contending that Great Britain would certainly support the United States in any possible postwar contingency. This faith, of course, was just what Benson and Daniels did not possess.

In Washington the reaction was relatively calm, although Sims's message was interpreted as further proof that he was a pawn of the Admiralty. On July 13, the President had a conversation with Sir William Wiseman and seized the opportunity to urge a definitive commitment to the convoy system. This decision by Britain, he argued, would make it easier for him to obtain funds from Congress for the construction of destroyers.[145] The next day Daniels wrote the President that the United States was already doing all that Sims suggested except dispatching the main fleet. To this possibility Daniels reacted negatively, an indication that the caution so often imputed to Great Britain was not absent in Washington. The Secretary's comment on the convoy question, while factually correct, was hardly an accurate reflection of the situation in London as reported by Sims. Drawing attention to the decision to escort ships, he recalled that it had been almost universally opposed at first. "All wisdom does

144. Sims to Wilson, July 7, 1917, USNSF, TP file. There is some confusion as to the exact date of this message. The copy in the Wilson Papers is dated July 11, 1917, with the indication that it was received on July 12. This date is also given in Department of State, *1917*, supp. 2, vol. 1, *The World War*, 124–26. The most likely explanation is that Sims prepared his reply by July 7, but did not send it until July 11.

145. Charles Seymour, ed., *The Intimate Papers of Colonel House*, 4 vols., *Into the World War* (Boston, 1928), 3:71.

not come from trained naval officers and your point of view is now accepted."[146] Daniels failed to mention that Sims had also been an early advocate of convoy.

Much later, Daniels claimed that the President had a personal motive in writing as he had to Admiral Sims. The President told him that he

was more foxy in my letter to Sims than you may think. His friends would later say, if I had not written, that Sims is original and that if he had been given his way he would have proceeded along lines of such vigor as to win success. Now in his reply he has advised nothing except what the British have planned and has shown that instead of being original he follows the British slavishly.[147]

It is entirely conceivable that the President spoke to Daniels along these lines. In any event, he did not take steps to relieve Sims or to compromise activities in London seriously. He did retain for a long time his belief that the British were thoroughly unimaginative. During a visit to the Atlantic Fleet on August 11, 1917, he made a speech to the assembled officers in which he made an emotional plea for new and bold ideas. "Every time we have suggested anything to the British Admiralty," he maintained, "the reply has come back that virtually amounted to this, that it had never been done that way, and I felt like saying, 'Well, nothing has ever been done so systematically as nothing is being done now.'" He hoped for innovative ideas from his own officers. "There is no other way to win," he concluded, "and the whole principle of this war is the kind of thing that ought to hearten and stimulate America."[148] Despite his positive views, the President did not impose upon his naval adviser. In fact, the President resumed for the most part the laissez-faire attitude about naval questions that he had manifested before his activities of June and July.

Undaunted by his brush with the President, Sims continued to promote his views in the Navy Department. On July 16, he dispatched a definitive comment "Concerning Policy of U.S. Naval co-operation in war, and allied subjects," in which he explained and justified British naval policy as well as his own ideas. This effort was his response to Daniels's letter of July 3

146. Daniels to Wilson, July 14, 1917, Wilson Papers, box 122.
147. This comment was made on July 16, 1917. Daniels, *Wilson Era: Years of War and After*, 623.
148. Quoted ibid., 43–44.

to Lansing concerning fundamental naval principles. Sims began with the assumption that his mission was "maximum co-operation with the Allies in defeating a common enemy." He thought other considerations mischievous:

All of my despatches and recommendations have been based on the firm conviction that the above mission could and would be accomplished, and that hence such questions as the possibility of post-war situations, or of all or part of the Allies being defeated and America being left alone, were not given consideration—in fact I cannot see how we could enter into this war wholeheartedly if such considerations were allowed to diminish in any way the chances of allied success.

Here was a direct repudiation of Admiral Benson's perspective. Sims was anxious to dispel the notion that his recommendations would force "disintegration" of the American fleet. Would the dispatch of supporting elements have this effect? He thought not. The principal role of the American fleet was as a reserve for the British Grand Fleet, which was deployed to contain the German High Seas Fleet in its bases. The submarine effort of Germany was designed to force the Allies to disperse their forces. Sims wished to counteract this effort by concentrating all available naval craft useful against submarines in the relatively small area within which the submarines congregated for attacks on merchant shipping—the sea approaches to the British Isles. Since American destroyers, submarines, and other light craft usually employed as screens for the movements of capital ships would be detached from the main American fleet for service *between* their own fleet and that of the enemy, the American fleet was not actually "disintegrated." In case of need, auxiliary units on distant stations could easily be regrouped to provide screens for capital ships.

Sims capped his recommendations with a plea to augment the staff in London. Reiterating one of his favorite views, that "one of the greatest military difficulties of this war, and perhaps of all Allied Wars, has been the difficulty of co-ordinating and co-operation in military effort," he presented detailed proposals for what he called the "Advance Branch of our Naval Council," which ought to be located in London because of its proximity to the fighting front and to other admiralties. Recognizing that his position in London rendered him vulnerable to the charge of undue British influence, he nevertheless insisted that he was his own man. "I have done everything within my ability to maintain a broad viewpoint."[149]

Despite the lively suspicions of both Sims and the Admiralty current in Washington, Sims ultimately built an organization in London that approximated the one he had proposed to Daniels, and he utilized it to accomplish the naval mission he had in mind. The Navy Department was not always receptive to the Admiral's recommendations, but Sims gradually managed to gain his ends. Differences of view between the force commander in London and his superiors in Washington reflected not only the inherent tendency to disagreement between a theater commander and general headquarters at home but also the massive anxiety and confusion so rife during the spring and summer of 1917. The outcome of the war hung in the balance. Russia was about to collapse completely. A great Anglo-French offensive in France had failed to achieve its object. The Italian front was unstable. German submarines continued to sink thousands of tons of indispensable merchant shipping. Small wonder, then, that tempers became short and that sometimes even the strongest men wilted under the pressure.

If President Wilson was dissatisfied with the British Admiralty, so was Prime Minister David Lloyd George, who had earlier forced a reluctant Admiralty Board to adopt the convoy system. In July he finally achieved another object. Sir Eric Geddes, a dynamic administrator who had earlier reorganized British transport in France and who was then serving as Controller of the Admiralty, became First Lord of the Admiralty in succession to Sir Edward Carson.[150] The British Admiralty soon began to change its ways. In a few months Lloyd George would achieve another object—the removal of Admiral Jellicoe as the First Sea Lord.

By July the initial shock of belligerency had been absorbed and the United States had begun to make a measurable contribution to the war at sea. It had dispatched a talented and energetic

149. Sims to Daniels, July 16, 1917, Sims Papers. A copy is also in USNSF, TP file.
150. Lloyd George apparently hoped to reform the Admiralty without relieving Sir Edward Carson. Lloyd George to Carson, July 7, 1917, Lloyd George Papers, file F/6/2/37. Hankey describes the changes in the Admiralty in *Supreme Command*, 2:655–56. For a thorough and accurate summation of this affair, see Marder, *1917: Year of Crisis*, 192–209.

commander to Europe in the person of Admiral Sims. At home
the Navy Department had cleared its decks for an extraordinary
effort to expand American naval activity. Above all else the basic
outlines of inter-Allied naval strategy for the rest of the war
had become visible to both captains and cabinets. That strategy
rested on the frustration of the German submarine campaign.
If the Allies solved the puzzle of the submarine, they would encounter no real difficulty in sustaining a tight blockade of the
Central Powers while preserving their own lines of communication. The key to success was the tactical device of convoy,
adopted by the British Admiralty after prolonged hesitation
only a few short weeks after the American declaration of war.

In Germany the military leadership had survived the parliamentary crisis associated with the ill-starred peace resolutions.
The naval leadership remained firmly wedded to the practice of
unrestricted submarine warfare as the key to victory. It became
evident that victory would not come as soon as had been anticipated in February, but the thought of failure did not trouble the
military and naval leadership, still secure against civilian criticism such as that emanating from the Reichstag.

All the engaged navies now settled down to a protracted tug
of war, but before turning to that extended conflict, it is convenient to consider at some length an abortive effort to arrange
a secret naval alliance between the United States and Great
Britain, which transpired during the early months of the American intervention. These highly secret negotiations reflected not
only the extreme anxieties of 1917 but also the extent to which
long-range political considerations impinged upon naval policy
even at the moment of utmost emergency at sea.

CHAPTER 3

THE ABORTIVE
SECRET TREATY OF 1917

As soon as the United States intervened in the war, the Navy Department interested itself in many types of ship construction. One aspect of this question was the fate of the capital ships then being built or projected that were intended to augment the American battle fleet. Leaders as diverse as Navy Secretary Daniels and Interior Secretary Lane wondered whether the capital-ship program should be postponed. Lane favored setting aside the planned schedule, arguing that none of these vessels could be put into service for three years, but Daniels characteristically reserved judgment.[1]

On April 20, the General Board of the Navy presented its views on the capital-ship question. The Board thought it necessary to consider not only the present emergency but also the possibility of "a war resulting from the present one in which the United States may be confronted by Germany and Japan operating conjointly in the Atlantic and Pacific; it is also possible that we may have to meet these two powerful navies without allies to restrict the operations of the German fleet." This statement was a delicate means of broaching the possibility that Germany might soon defeat the Entente powers, a catastrophe already entertained seriously by Admiral Benson. The General Board was impressed by the significance of the "time element" as it had revealed itself during the present war. It was imperative to decide on "the necessary protective measures" and to prosecute them vigorously. To ensure readiness the United States "must hasten the development of a symmetrical fleet equipped with fighting units in the proportions which experience in this and other wars has proved to be imperatively necessary . . . even if the construction facilities of the country have to be increased several fold to accomplish this purpose." In specific terms the

1. Lane to G. W. Lane, April 15, 1917, Anne Wintermute Lane and Louise Herrick Wall, eds., *The Letters of Franklin K. Lane: Personal and Political* (Boston, 1922), 246; Daniels diary, April 18, 1917, E. David Cronon, ed., *The Cabinet Diaries of Josephus Daniels, 1913–1921* (Lincoln, 1963), 137.

General Board considered as most urgent the provision of screening forces. "Every possible effort should be made, beginning now, to increase (1) scouts and cruisers, (2) destroyers, (3) battle cruisers, . . . and . . . further, the construction of battleships and submarines should be continued and expedited, using the full resources of the nation to do so." The Board had in mind a two-power standard, advocating a building program to create an American fleet equal to that of the combined German and Japanese fleets. This standard would require an enormous number of ships not yet authorized: 13 dreadnoughts; 10 battle cruisers; 6 armored cruisers; 16 light cruisers; 86 destroyers; and 108 submarines.[2]

Throughout this recommendation the doctrine of the revered naval theorist Adm. Alfred Thayer Mahan was unmistakably in evidence. For Mahan, apostle of *Realpolitik*, the battle fleet was the final locus of national power. All naval considerations ought to be subordinated to the development and maintenance of the battle fleet in full panoply.[3] The proposal of the General Board was clearly an application of that general doctrine so dear to the hearts of naval officers imbued with the views of Mahan during training at the Naval War College, the Naval Academy at Annapolis, and other centers of naval education. If one considered this doctrine in the light of a distinct possibility that the Entente powers might be defeated and the United States might then face a naval challenge from a German-Japanese combination, it was logical that the General Board would urge its observance despite the submarine crisis. That crisis, however, was a condition, whereas a war against a combination of Japan and Germany was only a theory. What would the United States decide to do?

I

When the Balfour mission arrived in Washington, one of its most important objectives was to secure an American commitment to limit its wartime maritime construction to antisubmarine craft and merchant shipping. This policy would, of

2. Badger to Daniels, April 20, 1917, Records of the General Board.
3. For a discussion of Mahan's views on this question, see Paul Y. Hammond, *Organizing for Defense: The American Military Establishment in the Twentieth Century* (Princeton, 1961), 62–64.

course, require postponing all or part of the American capital-ship building program. These ideas were not received enthu-siastically in the Navy Department, although its officers grew rapidly in their understanding of the reasons for British concern, as did other American leaders. Franklin K. Lane informed Frank Cobb of the *New York World* that, "We have been carrying on a ship-building program with reference to conditions *after the war*. It is only within ten days that we have realized that the end of the war will be one of defeat unless we build twice as fast as we proposed to build."[4]

On May 10, 1917, Captain Gaunt, the British naval attaché in Washington, sent a message on the capital-ship question to the Admiralty:

United States Navy have not yet dropped capital ship programme as they fear superiority of Japanese Navy after the war. The suggestion has been made though not by responsible heads of Departments that if capital ship programme is dropped British Government should guarantee assistance to United States after the war in case of trouble with Japan. Can any information be given as to the extent and progress of new construction for Japanese Navy as I am continually being asked if Japan is continuing work on new capital ships.[5]

This message antedated by three days the first informal discus-sions of this question. Colonel House broached the topic to a responsible official of the British mission, Sir Eric Drummond, who was Balfour's personal secretary.

House summarized his conversation with Drummond care-fully in a diary entry for May 13, 1917:

In talking with Drummond, I called attention to the Allied demand that we build submarine destroyers at the expense of our major battle

4. Lane to Cobb, May 5, 1917, Lane and Wall, eds., *Letters of Franklin K. Lane*, 253.
5. Gaunt to Admiralty, May 10, 1917, ADM 137, book 1436, 210. The Admiralty replied that it was considering the naval agreement. It reported that the Japanese planned to maintain a fleet of eight battleships and four battle cruisers not more than eight years old. Admiralty to Gaunt, May 16, 1917, ADM 137, book 1436, 211. On May 11, Ambassador Page recorded in his diary some remarks of Admiral Sims in which the latter expressed the view that fear of Japan was a prime barrier to changes in the Ameri-can building program. Sims proposed as a solution a promise of British assistance in the event of difficulties with Japan. Page diary, May 11, 1917, Page Papers.

ship program. To do this would leave us at the end of the war where we are now, and in the event of trouble with Japan or Germany, we would be more or less helpless at sea. I thought if Great Britain would agree to give us an option on some of her major ships in the event of trouble with Japan, we would go ahead with our destroyers without fear of subsequent events.

Drummond replied that Germany's navy might be left intact after the war and Great Britain might have need of all her fleet in a further war with Germany. In this event I suggested we give Great Britain an option to read that in case of war with Germany we would return the battle ships which we had taken over, and would give her in addition an option on some of our major ships. He thought this an excellent arrangement and is to take it up with Mr. Balfour and let me know the result.[6]

House had no authorization to sound the British on such an audacious proposal, one that was totally out of keeping with over 100 years of national tradition. However logical, given the conditions of the war, it was bound to arouse deep reservations in minds other than that of the flexible presidential adviser.

Balfour reacted immediately, reporting the Drummond conversation to London the next day. He explained that he had not obtained an American agreement to postpone capital-ship construction in favor of destroyers and merchant ships because of "fear of Japan." He then explained the House proposal, observing that "I doubt whether this is consistent with United States constitution, and, in any case it is a violent departure from United States practice." Nevertheless, if he received authority he would continue the discussions. He had a consideration in mind quite apart from the provision of destroyers. "There would be a great advantage in obtaining anything in the nature of a defensive alliance with United States. Of course, Japan's susceptibilities will have to be spared, but this should not be difficult to manage."[7]

In mentioning the difficulties in the way of such an arrangement Balfour might have recalled a conversation on the ques-

6. House diary, May 13, 1917, House Papers. See also Charles Seymour, ed., *The Intimate Papers of Colonel House*, 4 vols., *Into the World War* (Boston, 1928), 3:66–67.

7. Balfour to Lloyd George, May 14, 1917, ADM 137, book 1436, 217. A copy is also in FO 371, book 3119. It is reprinted as Appendix 2 to the Minutes of the War Cabinet (WC 142), May 22, 1917, CAB 23, book 2.

tion of secret treaties with the President on April 23. Wilson had frankly expressed a desire to avoid obligations like those that already bound together the Entente powers, although he intended to "throw himself wholeheartedly into it [the war] and see it through to a finish." He gave two reasons for opposing such arrangements: that the country would oppose a secret treaty with any European country, and of "utmost importance" was his wish to "exercise a powerful and valuable influence" in the event that one of the Allies showed itself "uncompromising and unpractical" over some aspect of a wartime engagement. Balfour thought this view quite appropriate. "Were I in his place," he told Lloyd George, "I should have decided as he has done."[8] The Foreign Secretary must have been surprised when House later approached him with the proposal for a secret naval agreement. He did not know, of course, that House had acted on his own initiative; he must have presumed that House had been asked to raise the matter unofficially and confidentially because of its extreme delicacy.

The news from Balfour stimulated an immediate study at the Foreign Office, led during Balfour's absence by Sir Robert Cecil. On May 18, its Far Eastern Department produced a remarkably detailed memorandum considering the question from four points of view. Would the arrangement contradict the letter and spirit of the Anglo-Japanese Alliance? Would it antagonize Japan to the extent of leading that nation to abrogate the Anglo-Japanese Alliance? If so, how could Japan injure Great Britain? Should the matter be discussed with Japan?

Regarding the relationship between the agreement and the Anglo-Japanese Alliance, Article 4 of the alliance expressly excluded the United States from its scope. Therefore the proposed arrangement did not formally contravene its letter, but it would certainly violate its spirit. The United States was

an important factor in that sphere [East Asia] and is potentially the main Far Eastern antagonist of our Japanese Ally. An Alliance between Great Britain and the United States is therefore bound to qualify the solidarity and effectiveness of the Anglo-Japanese Alliance—all the more, as, since its conclusion, the Far Eastern interests of Great Britain and America have become increasingly identified and those of Great Britain and Japan have become correspondingly

8. Balfour to Lloyd George, April 26, 1917, FO 371, book 3119 (file 86512).

estranged. The new proposal would set a formal seal on this new orientation of British policy and would to that extent be contrary to the spirit of the Anglo-Japanese Alliance.

Article 4 would allow the British to stand aside if Japan and the United States went to war, but "the proposed Anglo-American Alliance would oblige us to side with America in the event of Japan attacking her."

Japan could hardly fail to interpret such an arrangement as opposed to its interests. The proposed treaty would deliver "the most decisive blow at what has become Japan's traditional policy in the Far East, namely Japanese penetration of China in the Pacific (involving incidentally a menace to the Philippines) under the protection of the Anglo-Japanese Alliance." In the circumstances the Anglo-American accord would be interpreted as "sounding the death knell of her more predatory ambitions."

Japan had a number of options in response to an Anglo-American combination: it could "declare openly against the Allies and could combine with Mexico against the United States"; it could attack Manchuria; it could support revolutionaries in India; it might also "create chaos in China for purposes of intervention to abet a Manchu restoration under her aegis and so provoke a Far Eastern crisis which would enable her in a German-Japanese interest to divert attention from the war and seriously embarrass us"; or, finally, it could withdraw naval reinforcements sent to assist the Allies in the Mediterranean and elsewhere. If the arrangement with America materialized, it would certainly provoke a great sensation in Japan, undermining support for the Anglo-Japanese Alliance and the "present insecure Government."

Despite these considerations the Far Eastern Department discerned certain advantages in the proposed treaty. Events in the Far East demonstrated that British interests were incompatible with the aspirations of Japan. Any settlement with the United States could "hardly fail to constitute the first rift in Anglo-Japanese relations," but it would have many political and strategic benefits:

The Alliance with America would safeguard our Imperial interests from Wei Hai Wei to Australia and back to Singapore, Columbo and Suez, while, should it mature into a formal "Entente" for purposes of our joint China policy, we shall have laid the foundations of a future entirely favourable to ensure . . . our position in the East and Far East against a danger which we have every interest to believe is a real one.

Lord Hardinge appended to the document some views of his own that suggested a possible modification of the arrangement proposed by House in order to mitigate Japanese opposition. The United States might frankly acknowledge Japan's spheres of interest in Manchuria and the Shantung peninsula, and also its acquisition of the German islands in the Pacific north of the equator—a step that would "go far to remove any suspicion of American hostility towards moderate Japanese ambitions." Might it not be possible to arrange a tripartite defensive alliance between the United States, Great Britain, and Japan? Japan would gain American recognition of its sphere of influence in China. The United States would obtain a "guarantee of the security of the Philippines and Honolulu against attack." Both countries would benefit from a relaxation of mutual distrust. As to Great Britain, "The advantages of such a policy . . . are obvious." Lord Hardinge thought it not impossible to work out such an arrangement, but he recognized that negotiations must be handled most carefully. "Otherwise we run the risk of driving the Japanese into the enemy's camp."[9]

Here was a truly far-reaching analysis, one that would certainly have created the most extraordinary sensation both in Washington and Tokyo, had it been available in either place. Cecil recognized its import and notified Balfour of the need to inform Japan of any such arrangement with America. Probably reflecting his reading of Lord Hardinge's commentary, he speculated that "it might be necessary to recast the [Anglo-Japanese] alliance altogether." The matter would have to be very carefully considered by the War Cabinet, but it offered certain real advantages, chief among which was the prospect of obtaining destroyers and a defensive alliance from the United States. The great difficulty, of course, was to reconcile Japan to the arrangement. He concluded with an interesting observation. "With or without a guarantee popular opinion here would undoubtedly force us to go to the assistance of America if she were attacked by Japan. It would therefore be perfectly safe as a matter of

9. Memorandum on the proposed naval alliance, May 18, 1917, FO 371, box 3119 (file 97867).

practical politics for the United States to forego building capital ships at the present time."[10]

On May 22, Cecil brought the matter to the War Cabinet, and a searching discussion took place, once again concentrating on the implications of the proposed naval agreement for Anglo-Japanese relations. Balfour's proposition was that the naval guarantee would permit the United States to concentrate its shipbuilding on destroyers, "and that this guarantee might eventually be developed into a general defensive Naval Alliance between the two Powers." How could Japan be disposed of without undue difficulty? Cecil had three alternatives in mind. One possibility was to give Japan a free hand in China, but Cecil deprecated this approach because it would involve "serious dangers in future to India and our position generally." A second option was to permit Japan a definite sphere of influence in Manchuria or the Shantung. Finally, "It might also be possible to induce Japan to come into a Triple Alliance with ourselves and the United States, on the basis of American assent to the suggested Japanese sphere of influence in China." Cecil was inclined to explain to Japan that the guarantee was being given simply to obtain needed destroyers, "reassuring them that we would certainly not lend . . . [capital ships] to the United States for the purpose of an attack on Japan." The difficulty was that "the Japanese would not be content with such an explanation, and would regard the agreement as involving in fact a general Anglo-American Alliance affecting the situation in the Far East, and interfering with Japan's ambitions in China."

The outcome of the discussion was a general agreement that it would be "very inadvisable to do anything at the present stage of the war that would give the Japanese any justifiable ground for alarm or suspicion, and so upset the general position in the Pacific." Walter Long, the Secretary of State for the Colonies, thought that Australia and New Zealand were generally satisfied with the arrangements recently made with Japan concerning the Pacific Islands and would be disturbed at any major alteration in the *status quo*. It was also asserted that there was no assurance that the United States Senate would agree to anything approaching a naval alliance. "There was a danger of our upsetting existing relations with Japan, without securing anything

10. Cecil to Balfour, May 19, 1917, FO 371, book 3119. A copy is in the Balfour Papers, FO 800, box 208.

tangible from the United States." Admiral Jellicoe then pointed out that a guarantee might be unnecessary, because what the United States would require in the event of a war with Japan was not capital ships but destroyers. The War Cabinet authorized Jellicoe to inquire into the probable American naval requirements during a war with Japan "in order to convince the United States Government that destroyers would be of more use to them than capital ships in any war with Japan."[11] The War Cabinet was obviously intrigued by the Balfour proposal, but much concerned about the possibility of serious difficulties with Japan.

Admiral Jellicoe soon produced a memorandum comparing the naval strength of the United States and Japan. His research showed that the United States had 14 dreadnoughts in hand with 9 building, whereas Japan had only 3 in use with 4 building. In predreadnoughts the United States held a marked edge—23 to 9. Only in battle cruisers did Japan enjoy a margin: the United States was building 4 and had projected 6 more, but Japan had 7 afloat. The United States had 17 large cruisers to Japan's 10. The two countries, however, were about even in light cruisers— 20 for the United States and 17 for Japan. The First Sea Lord then drew his conclusion:

It is evident from this comparison that as against Japan only, the most urgent requirements were for light cruisers, Destroyers, and antisubmarine craft, and that with the exception of Battle Cruisers, it would be a waste of resources to build more capital ships. The same requirements apply to the present war, and it seems essential to press the United States Government to concentrate on building the classes of vessels required even at the cost of postponing the completion of Dreadnought Battleships.[12]

Of course, the difficulty not mentioned by Jellicoe was that the

11. Minutes of the War Cabinet (WC 142), May 22, 1917, CAB 23, book 2. In February, 1917, the British had made an arrangement with Japan, prompted by the prospect of the American intervention, in which Britain promised to support Japan's claims concerning the Shantung and former German insular possessions north of the equator in return for Japanese support of British claims to German islands south of the equator. See Minutes of the War Cabinet (WC 54), February 5, 1917, CAB 23, book 1; for the official Anglo-Japanese exchanges, see copies of Greene to Ichiro Motono, February 16, 1917, and Motono to Greene, February 21, 1917, Wilson Papers, box 114.

12. Jellicoe memorandum (G.T. 855), May 27, 1917, FO 371, book 3119.

United States entertained not simply a one-power standard, but a two-power standard—an intention to build a fleet comparable to the combined forces of Germany and Japan.

Balfour left the United States before the negotiations could continue further. Upon his departure he presented a memorandum to Secretary Lansing in which he drew attention to the proposed naval guarantee, concluding that he thought it not impossible to work out a scheme "to give the United States some kind of call upon Allied capital ships should the need for them arise," a project to be given consideration later by the two governments.[13] Meanwhile, Admiral de Chair reported that the Navy Department had recently placed orders for antisubmarine craft. "If these [orders] are carried out expeditiously some of our requirements will be met."[14]

As of early June the position of the War Cabinet was largely that arrived at tentatively on May 22. Great Britain wished to proceed with the matter, but it had to consider the consequences for its relations with Japan. The United States should be aware that in case of need the British Navy would certainly come to its assistance. The United States ought to postpone its capital-ship program, not only because destroyers were needed to hunt the German submarines but also because its principal requirements in any war with Japan would be light cruisers and destroyers.[15] The proposed naval agreement was held in abeyance until Balfour returned to London; meanwhile Spring Rice continued to report indecision in the United States concerning the building program.[16]

II

If Japanese questions aroused the most serious deliberations in London, they were also of great moment in Washington.

13. Balfour memorandum, May 23, 1917, Cabinet Papers, no. 243 (1917), FO 899, box 12. A copy is dated May 24, 1917, in the Wilson Papers, box 119.

14. De Chair to Gaunt, May 22, 1917, Cabinet Papers, no. 293 (1917), FO 899, book 13. See also de Chair to Secretary of the Admiralty, June 7, 1917, ADM 137, book 1436, 244–45.

15. Cecil to Balfour, June 4, 1917, FO 371, book 3119. A copy of this message in the Admiralty records indicates that it is from Lloyd George to Spring Rice, but the Foreign Office copy is probably correct. ADM 137, book 1436, 224–26.

16. Spring Rice to[?], June 9, 1917, Spring Rice Papers, FO 800, book 242.

American leaders were unanimous in their distrust and fear of Japan. On February 2, 1917, when the Cabinet considered Germany's resumption of unrestricted submarine warfare, President Wilson startled the group by suggesting that racial considerations might be of great import in deciding the American response. According to Secretary of Agriculture Houston, the President said "frankly that, if he felt that, in order to keep the white race or part of it strong to meet the yellow race—Japan, for instance, in alliance with Russia, dominating China—it was wise to do nothing, and would submit to anything and any imputation of weakness or cowardice."[17] Breckinridge Long, an official in the State Department charged with surveillance of Far Eastern affairs, shared the general suspicions of Japan and mentioned to Balfour the prospect of difficulty with that nation during the latter's visit to Washington. Balfour naturally dismissed Long's concerns.[18] Colonel House also feared the Japanese. On May 11, he wrote mordantly to the President, trying to estimate the consequences of Russia's political instability. "If Russia swings back to autocratic government, I think a close alignment between Germany, Japan and Russia is certain."[19]

At the outset of American belligerency, naval opinion was definitely anti-Japanese, but divided on the extent of the threat. One general feeling was that if the Japanese could be more deeply engaged in the European war, the danger of anti-American activity would be minimized.[20] Up to this point the Japanese fleet had contributed only marginally to the war effort, supplying some thirteen old cruisers and destroyers for escort duty in the Mediterranean.[21] On May 19, the General Board commented in some detail on "Japanese Cooperation with the Allies." After suggesting the dispatch of about twenty-five addi-

17. David F. Houston, *Eight Years with Wilson's Cabinet: 1913 to 1920: with a Personal Estimate of the President*, 2 vols. (Garden City, N.Y.), 1:229–30.
18. Long diary, April 22, 1917, Long Papers.
19. House to Wilson, May 11, 1917, Wilson Papers, box 118.
20. Pratt to Sims, May 15, 1917, USNSF, TD file. Pratt felt that if the European victory was complete Japan would not be able to acquire any support in the region.
21. Edwin Denby to Bainbridge Colby, September 23, 1921, USDSM 367, 763.72/13545. This letter was in response to a request from Colby about the extent of Japanese naval activity during the war. Denby thought that the Japanese vessels had performed capably in the Mediterranean, but "in all probability, however, their participation did not materially affect the final outcome of the war."

tional Japanese destroyers to European waters, the Board proposed that the Japanese Army be put into the battle on the Eastern Front. Some 750,000 troops could be transported in two months across the Trans-Caucasian Railroad to that critical theater of war in order to bolster the Russian Army. The Board gave a political justification for its suggestions, in addition to citing military and naval benefits: "The possibility of an ultimate alliance between Japan and Germany to the detriment of the United States has recently received much attention, but if Japan is persuaded to take the field and continue active warfare against Germany until the end of the war, the danger of such an alliance will be minimized on account of the resulting antagonism."[22] Nothing came of this proposal, but it indicated a lively interest in the problem. Pratt and Sims both came to the conclusion that fears of Japan should not militate against strenuous production of antisubmarine craft. Sims summarized his views succinctly: "I do not think we will have anything to fear from them after this war is over for many years to come. Of course, the war itself is going to strengthen us immensely in a military sense and our battle fleet must soon hopelessly outstrip theirs."[23] These opinions did not lessen American distrust of Japan. The Navy Department was reluctant to turn over certain inventions to the British Admiralty, notably the Ford range finder, because of fear that it might fall into Japanese hands. Sims was disturbed by the constant presence of Japanese naval officers at the Admiralty.[24]

In Washington, Secretary Lansing and Breckinridge Long began to explore various methods of dealing with the Japanese threat to China. They considered reviving the railway consortium in China that had been repudiated by Wilson in 1913.[25]

22. Badger to Daniels, May 19, 1917, Records of the General Board. Daniels sent a copy of this letter to Secretary Lansing on July 2, 1917. USDSM 367, 763.72/6082.

23. Sims to Pratt, June 7, 1917, USNSF, TD file. For Pratt's views, see Pratt to Sims, May 15, 1917, USNSF, TD file; Pratt to Sims, June 7, 1917, Sims Papers.

24. Emmet to Sims, June 22, 1917, USNSF, TD file; Sims to Pratt, July 6, 1917, USNSF, TD file.

25. Long diary, June 24 and 25, 1917, Long Papers; Lansing to Wilson, June 25, 1917, Wilson Papers, box 121. Lansing made an interesting comment: "My own view is that the whole question, being of so much importance to our future relations in the Far East, ought to be considered with little regard to the past."

Very soon they launched preparations for a special Japanese mission comparable to that sent early by Britain, France, and other Entente powers, a visit that led ultimately to the Lansing-Ishii agreement. These activities reflected continuing distrust of Japanese intentions, but the crisis in Europe had reached such great proportions that Far Eastern questions inevitably receded in importance. Germany was not concerned about Japan. On May 25, 1917, Zimmermann informed Hindenburg's headquarters that the Japanese would do nothing more than send a few antisubmarine craft to the Mediterranean and remain relatively inactive in the Indian Ocean, because Japan "does not wish to see its ships fight on the side of the Americans."[26]

During this period President Wilson determined the basic diplomatic posture he would sustain throughout the period of belligerency. He decided to make the most imposing contribution possible to the military and naval defeat of the Central Powers, but he was determined to avoid diplomatic engagements that might lessen his ability to influence the postwar peace settlement. On May 29, the Cabinet discussed the question of whether the United States should make a public declaration of war aims. Wilson was opposed. Daniels noted his words: "I have not permitted myself to think of plans & policies when war ends. We trust our allies but make no alliances & this country will be ready to see that right settlement is made when all sit at the peace table." He was confident that "America would have its way when it proposed what is right."[27] These considerations had precluded extensive discussion of secret treaties and war aims during Balfour's visit. They would continue to have this effect until 1918, because the President was assiduous in his commitment to a policy of restraint.[28] The prospects for the secret project of House and Balfour were hardly bright. The President was determined to maintain freedom of action—something that secret understandings might well diminish.

26. Zimmermann to Gruenau, May 25, 1917, St. Antony's Papers, reel 12, Geheime Akten, vol. 44, frame 16.

27. Daniels diary, May 29, 1917, Cronon, ed., *Cabinet Diaries*, 159. See also the entry for June 1, 1917, ibid., 160.

28. David F. Trask, *United States in the Supreme War Council: American War Aims and Inter-Allied Strategy, 1917–1918* (Middletown, Conn., 1961), 6–8.

III

When Arthur Balfour returned to Britain, he began work immediately on the proposed naval agreement. On June 19, he presented a draft treaty to the War Cabinet, asking that it be given early consideration. Bowing to the objections that had been raised to a bilateral arrangement with the United States, the Balfour formula contemplated an understanding among all the leading members of the western coalition. Its wording was brief and intentionally broad:

That, in view of the diversion of Government shipbuilding in the naval yards of the United States of America from the construction of capital ships to that of vessels suitable for anti-submarine warfare, the Governments of the United States of America, Great Britain, France, Italy, Russia, and Japan engage singly and severally to assist each other against any maritime attack for a period of four years after the present war.[29]

Balfour took note of the important considerations raised by the proposal and indicated that "diplomatic instruments" would have to be devised if the War Cabinet accepted the idea and it proved acceptable to the other concerned nations.[30] Meanwhile the War Cabinet proceeded with revisions of British building plans for the next year that stressed the production of light craft (8 light cruisers, 24 destroyers, and 18 submarines), an indication that it was willing to impose upon itself the same policy it urged upon the United States.[31]

In Washington the Navy Department finally reached a unilateral decision largely to postpone the capital-ship program for the duration of the war. On July 2, Pratt informed Sims of this development:

We all feel that this must be done, though we realize that such a policy may leave us with our guard down in case of future complica-

29. Minutes of the War Cabinet (WC 165), Appendix 2, June 19, 1917, CAB 23, book 3. A copy in Balfour's own handwriting is in Balfour Papers, book 49748.

30. Minutes of the War Cabinet (WC 165), June 19, 1917, CAB 23, book 3.

31. Minutes of the War Cabinet (WC 168 and 169), June 22 and 26, 1917, CAB 23, book 3.

tions. There, however, is where you come in, and we must trust to your good offices, in your diplomatic way, to make the situation safe for the future. That is the happy solution, and it is a solution which I hope from the bottom of my heart may be accomplished for the future well being of the Anglo-Saxon race. Whatever might be the outcome, even were a forced peace to result, England's fleet must never go elsewhere except to join our own, and such portion of it as we might need in future contingencies ought to be at our disposal. There must be no mistake about that. But willy-nilly we of us here who may have an iota of say in directing our policies, are turning every effort in the direction of a successful solution of this problem, leaving the future to take care of itself.[32]

On July 6, a committee headed by Pratt proposed to Daniels that the United States proceed to build some 200 destroyers in addition to those already authorized; Daniels's acquiescence was a clear commitment to the general policy that had been urged upon the Department by Sims and various British officials since the outset of American belligerency. Objections to this policy raised by Benson and others now faded away.[33]

In London Balfour prepared his final effort to obtain American acceptance of his proposed naval understanding, but its prospects were now distinctly poor. The President was firmly opposed to any secret arrangements during the period of belligerency, and the Navy Department had finally decided to postpone much of its capital-ship construction in deference to the immediate need for antisubmarine craft. Colonel House retained his devotion to his private initiative, but he was to encounter determined opposition from his friend in the White House.

On July 3, the War Cabinet received Balfour's finished thoughts on the proposed naval agreement. He discerned two prime reasons for America's reluctance to commit herself definitively to the production of antisubmarine craft, and neither related to the immediate naval situation. One was the German fleet, "which will still be powerful because it does not come out to fight its enemy," and the other was the Japanese fleet, "which has no enemy to fight." He put his proposition sharply. "My sug-

32. Pratt to Sims, June 22, 1917, Sims Papers.
33. Schilling, "Admirals and Foreign Policy," 101–3. Jellicoe reported word of changed views in Washington soon after. Minutes of the War Cabinet (WC 181), July 11, 1917, CAB 23, book 3. See also Sims's recognition of changing attitudes in Washington, in Sims to Bayly, July 11, 1917, Sims Papers.

gestion is that for four years, i.e., for the time required to build
new capital ships, America should have the right to call other
fleets to her assistance, in case of maritime attack." He remained
of the opinion that the most desirable arrangement would be a
treaty of "mutual maritime defence between America and Great
Britain alone." Such an arrangement would be both simple and
adequate. He had another compelling reason for desiring an
agreement of this nature. "I confess that, for reasons of high
policy, there is nothing I should like more than a defensive
Alliance with America, even for four years, as would be capable of extension and development, should circumstances prove
auspicious."

Balfour realized that he could not hope to accomplish this
immediate objective because of the Anglo-Japanese Alliance.
There was no logical incompatibility between the two alliances,
because both were defensive in nature, but he knew that any
such agreement "might produce a very unpleasant feeling in
Tokyo. It would be regarded . . . as the beginning of the end of
an Alliance which has already lasted twenty years, and has, on
the whole, conduced to stability in international relations in the
Far East." The alternative approach, then, was "to try to associate Japan from the beginning with the new arrangement."
It would "have the triple effect of allaying Japanese fears, of
engaging Japanese support, and of advertising the Treaty as a
protection against Germany." However, if Germany were named
as the object of the agreement, it would also be necessary to
engage the participation of France and Italy, although Russia
might possibly be excluded "on the ground that her geographical
position would prevent her navy taking any important part in
the struggle."[34] The War Cabinet authorized Balfour to open
negotiations, noting that the dispatch of a Japanese mission to
Washington might help to expedite the consultations.[35]

On July 5, Balfour sent a cablegram to House proposing negotiations. He reviewed the arguments for the arrangement he
had discussed before the War Cabinet, adding the view that the
United States really needed destroyers rather than capital ships
for a war with Japan. In this message he listed the United States,

34. Minutes of the War Cabinet (WC 174), Appendix, G.T.—1138
(dated June 22, 1917), July 3, 1917, CAB 23, book 3.
35. Minutes of the War Cabinet (WC 174), July 3, 1917, CAB 23,
book 3.

Great Britain, France, Italy, Japan, and Russia as appropriate signatories. He concluded simply: "Should President like this scheme I am prepared to take any steps he may desire in bringing it to fruition. If he sees objection to it I would endeavor to find some acceptable alternative."[36]

In London Balfour reviewed his proposal with Ambassador Page, unaware that House had not really explored the matter in detail with President Wilson. Page wrote enthusiastically to Wilson on July 6, outlining the basic attributes of Balfour's proposal, but indicating that the Foreign Secretary had in mind a four-power arrangement between the United States, Great Britain, France, and Japan. Page laid special stress on the point that this agreement would not interfere with a postwar security organization. "This [is] in no way to take the place of, nor in any way to affect, any League to Enforce Peace that may hereafter be made, but only to pledge us now the help of the British fleet during this period, so that we may feel free with regard to Japan or Germany." Balfour naturally did not mention to Page the considerations of "high policy" that also undergirded his project.[37] For Colonel House the fat was now in the fire:

Today brought an important cable from Balfour concerning the proposed naval agreement. It is of such moment, and of such a delicate nature that the greatest care needs be taken. If Japan should learn that these negotiations are in process, there is no telling what the result might be. I shall confine all knowledge of it to the President and the Acting Secretary of State [Frank L. Polk].[38]

The Colonel now set about to consummate his private project.

On July 8, House wrote to the President explaining for the first time his dealings with Balfour in detail. He told Wilson that his original suggestion had been to agree to postpone capital-ship construction in return for "an option on the purchase of such British capital battleships as we might wish to replace those which we discontinued building because of our desire to aid them." He justified the option arrangement as being aimed

36. Balfour to House, July 5, 1917, House Papers.
37. Page to Wilson, July 6, 1917, Wilson Papers, box 122. Page, convinced that Great Britain would enter into the arrangement even if Japan refused its signature, wondered whether it would be approved by the Senate. Page to A. W. Page, July 18, 1917, Page Papers (folder 989).
38. House diary, July 7, 1917, House Papers.

no more against Japan than against France, Italy, Russia, or even Great Britain itself. He also suggested his earlier plan of including a clause allowing Britain to regain possession of its ships in the event of another Anglo-German war.

House sent along a copy of a memorandum from Balfour explaining the multilateral project—largely a paraphrase of the War Cabinet memorandum—but the Colonel was obviously intent upon pursuing his original proposal. "I cannot see that the solution Balfour suggests would be of much service." It would preclude a German-Japanese combination, but "in the event of trouble between Japan and ourselves, or other parties to the agreement, they would be forced to be neutral, or if there was war between any of the signatory powers, the others would necessarily be neutral." He ended with an injunction to maintain close security. "I take it they desire these negotiations to go on unofficially in order that there be no embarrassment with Japan. That is, as soon as they become official, their treaty obligations with Japan might compel them to disclose all negotiations of this nature." Was this statement a delicate method of excusing his earlier activities? As the next step House proposed that the President send his views so that he could discuss the matter with Sir William Wiseman, who was shortly returning to Great Britain.[39]

Instead of adopting this procedure the President decided to discuss the question personally with Wiseman, which he did in detail on July 13.[40] At the outset of the conversation Wilson observed that capital ships were no longer of great value in naval warfare; the future belonged to destroyers and submarines. Therefore, "he did not consider the question of the U.S. delaying the building of capital ships as very important from a strategic point of view." His reservations about altering the capital-ship program had to do with the fact that Congress had authorized a certain building program and he could make changes only by placing the matter before the legislators. Expressing strong ap-

39. House to Wilson, July 8, 1917, Wilson Papers, box 122. The Balfour memorandum is filed with it. A copy is also in the House Papers. For some account of this episode, see Seymour, ed., *Intimate Papers*, 3:67–69.

40. Balfour was pressing Wiseman for action on the naval proposal, noting: "Its importance cannot easily be exaggerated." Balfour to Wiseman, July 13, 1917, Balfour Papers, FO 800, book 209.

probation of the convoy system, he indicated his intention to ask Congress for additional funds to support a new destroyer program. He saw no difficulty in obtaining shipyard space for destroyer construction. The President could not resist adverting critically to Sims, "who is always considered an original man," but who "had done nothing since his arrival in London but repeat the views of the British Admiralty."

With these preliminaries out of the way the President then turned to the proposed naval agreement. Wiseman summarized his remarks cogently in a memorandum prepared for Balfour:

With regard to DAMON'S [Balfour's] suggestion covering the naval shipbuilding difficulty by some species of defensive alliance: AJAX [Wilson] stated that in his opinion the Allies had entered during the stress of war into various undertakings among each other which they would find it very difficult, if not impossible, to carry out when the war is over; and he was not in favor of adding to that difficulty. Moreover, he pointed out that while the U.S. was now ready to take her place as a world-power, the strong feeling throughout the country was to play a "lone hand," and not to commit herself to any alliances with any foreign power. With regard to JAPAN, AJAX said that in his opinion a successful attack on the Pacific Coast was absurd owing to the long distance from the Japanese base and the difficulty they would have in obtaining any suitable base on the Pacific Coast. The possibility of their attacking the Philippines or some outlying possession was, he thought, quite another matter, and presented a possibility which could not be overlooked.

Having delivered himself of these opinions—which constituted a thorough repudiation of House's preliminary conversations—the President concluded gracefully, assuring Wiseman that "it was his intention to co-operate with Great Britain frankly and whole-heartedly in the common object of bringing the war to a successful conclusion as quickly as possible."[41]

The proposed naval agreement was dead, slain by a President who had never authorized the introductory conversations undertaken with Balfour, an enterprise that had led to extensive activity by the War Cabinet and the British Foreign Secretary for

41. Wiseman memorandum, July 13, 1917, Papers of Sir William Wiseman, Yale University Library, New Haven, Conn. Hereafter this collection is cited as Wiseman Papers. Copies are in the House Papers, box 20, and in Balfour Papers, FO 800, book 209. See also Seymour, ed., *Intimate Papers*, 3:70–72.

over a month. House refused to accept defeat immediately. On July 17, after discussing the matter with Wiseman, he wrote to Wilson. His first object was to dispute the President's appraisal of the value of capital ships. "Surely," he began, "the present control of the seas is solely due to the superiority of the British Fleet in capital ships. No amount of smaller craft could take their place." He thought submarine warfare was as distinct from conventional sea warfare as war in the air from conventional conflict on land. He then maintained, in terms that Mahan would have been proud to endorse, that "it is as true today as it was before the war that the . . . nation having the most potential capital battleships in both size and speed . . . [is] the nation that will dominate the sea." House then turned to his real concern—the proposed naval agreement—making another plea for its acceptance. "I hope that you will insist upon some arrangement with England by which this country may obtain some of their capital ships at the end of the war, in the event we should wish them. The arrangement would be a safe one, for they need not be taken if not desired." He had, he said, discussed the question with Lord Fisher and other British naval officials, "and there was no disagreement as far as I can remember."[42]

The Colonel's next step was to authorize Wiseman to report to Balfour that he thought an agreement could be reached that would satisfy both countries. "In the meantime, the United States will proceed as energetically as possible to build Destroyers and use every other means to meet the U Boat menace." Wiseman added that "the next step depends upon the general relations between the two countries, which I propose to discuss with you in London."[43]

Colonel House probably did not know that Balfour had discussed the matter with Ambassador Page and also with Sims. On July 26, the Admiral wrote to Captain Pratt about his connection with the negotiations and his reaction to them. He had been concerned about hesitancy in America "to do everything right now that could be done, because of the fear of the position we might be in after the war was over, no matter how it should be decided." He had then arranged through Page for a conference

42. House to Wilson, July 17, 1917, House Papers.
43. Wiseman to Balfour, July 18, 1917, Balfour Papers, FO 800, book 209.

with the Foreign Secretary, telling him of "the absolute necessity of giving our Government an assurance that, no matter how the war turned out, the British Fleet, or such portion of it as might be desirable, would be at our disposal." Balfour agreed and said that he would take up the matter with the War Cabinet. Later on, Balfour told Sims that he had drawn up a treaty to achieve the object the American had in mind. Sims wanted to know if the guarantee could come before the treaty, which would inevitably require some time to negotiate. He then talked over the matter with Lloyd George, who agreed that such a guarantee should be forthcoming. Because Lloyd George was "overcharged," Sims could not be sure that he would act immediately. He concluded with still another affirmation of his confidence in Anglo-American solidarity:

As far as I am personally concerned, I would never have needed any such assurance, because I cannot imagine a condition of affairs at the conclusion of this war which would not leave the entire British Fleet and the entire British nation behind us in case any enemy became disagreeable. In this connection, I may say that it is very generally recognized over here that America's coming into this war is going to be the salvation of the Allies.[44]

Despite the lack of any encouragement from the White House, Colonel House persisted for several weeks in his hopeless endeavor. He told Wiseman early in August that the ship construction program was moving ahead very well, and that "I am taking up with Washington the capital ship proposal so that discussions may take place while you are in London."[45] This effort came a cropper. On August 24, House informed Wiseman that "capital ship question is lagging because of pressure of matters of immediate urgency. I shall not push it further until I go to Washington in September."[46] He might have given up entirely at this point, because Balfour had written off the project. Ambassador Page, writing to Wilson, reported that Balfour had received the American views on the proposed treaty, presumably from the Wiseman memorandum. The Foreign Secretary agreed with the

44. Sims to Pratt, July 26, 1917, USNSF, TD file.
45. House to Wiseman, August 4, 1917, Balfour Papers, FO 800, book 209.
46. House to Wiseman, August 24, 1917, Balfour Papers, FO 800, book 209.

President that there was no likelihood of a Japanese attack on the United States and that no treaty arrangement was necessary. Page concluded that "there is not a shadow of a doubt but, if such an attack [should] be made, Great Britain [would] come to our rescue." Lloyd George had wanted to send a message to this effect, "but his associates preferred to have the matter reach you in the most informal way possible, at first."[47] Perhaps Lloyd George had indeed thought of fulfilling his promise to Sims, but Balfour and others probably urged alternate methods in deference to House's desire for confidentiality.

Colonel House made one final effort in September to convince Wilson of the need for the naval agreement. In private conversation with the President, House began by recalling their divergence of view about the utility of capital ships. After House made his argument in their behalf,

[the President] refused to discuss it further, declaring that no matter whether I was right or he was right, it was impracticable to make an arrangement with Great Britain at this time looking to our securing some of her capital battleships after the war in consideration of our abandoning our shipbuilding program of capital ships in order to build submarine destroyers. He thought the only thing that could be binding on Great Britain would be a treaty, and a treaty must necessarily go to the Senate for confirmation. He did not believe this country was prepared for a treaty of that sort with Great Britain.

House insisted that some form of treaty could be arrived at that would be acceptable to the people, but Wilson responded that "if the British Government wanted to do this after the war, they would do it anyway, and if they did not want to do it, we had no way of making them short of a treaty."[48] And so it was left.

The Colonel maintained his opinion, but the President had his way. Because House had kept his negotiations on a most confidential and unofficial basis, the President could simply drop the matter without prejudice to anyone. House attributed Wilson's lack of interest in the proposal to the latter's assumption that capital ships had become relatively unimportant in the present conflict, but in fact the most telling motivation was the Presi-

47. Page to Wilson, August 14, 1917, Wilson Papers.
48. House diary, September 9, 1917, House Papers. Others besides the President wondered whether the Senate would accept such a treaty. See, for example, Page to A. W. Page, July 18, 1917, Page Papers (folder 989).

dent's fear of diplomatic entanglements that might prejudice his plans for the peace settlement.

Throughout the period of his close connection at the White House, the Colonel avoided direct disagreements with his friend, realizing that his influence rested to a great extent on his ability to recognize and reinforce presidential viewpoints of interest to him. When the two men did not agree House usually failed to obtain his ends. In dealing with the secret naval accord, the Texan demonstrated his remarkable affinity for the "old diplomacy." President Wilson leaned toward much different methods—toward what Arno Mayer has called the "new diplomacy."

If no general naval treaty was arrived at in 1917, many of the considerations that emerged during the crisis of the naval war reappeared in 1921–1922, when the great naval powers did agree to a number of far-reaching understandings couched in the Four-Power, Five-Power, and Nine-Power treaties of Washington. The episode of 1917 constitutes part of the historical background to those imposing agreements. The abortive discussion is of great interest in another sense. It reveals the extent to which general political considerations sometimes overshadow special naval concerns in the making of policy, even at the height of a crisis universally recognized as likely to settle the outcome of a general war. This episode should interest all students of Woodrow Wilson's wartime diplomacy because it provides additional evidence to support the view that the war leader was bound and determined to avoid entanglements that would lessen his ability to exercise control over the postwar peace settlement. Although the President was willing, indeed anxious, to do all that was possible to pursue the war effectively against the Central Powers, he consistently opposed decisions that might conceivably limit his freedom of action after hostilities came to an end. Those who persist in denying to Woodrow Wilson a deserved reputation as a disciple of Clausewitz will discover in his naval policies further discomfiting evidence to disprove their views.

At the end of the affair everybody was minimally satisfied, with the exception of Colonel House. Balfour could point to the ultimate decision of the United States to build destroyers; the President could claim success in avoiding potentially embarrassing treaty engagements. Sims and Jellicoe got what they wanted—a clear American decision to stress the campaign against the submarine. The episode helped to clear away barriers to continuing and effective naval cooperation. The submarine, however, was as yet unconquered. To this task the navies of the Allied and Associated Powers now dedicated all their energies.[49]

49. In 1927, when the British wished to publish some account of the Balfour mission in the official naval history, Sir Esme Howard, the British Ambassador, requested permission from the United States. The excerpt Britain wished to clear for publication noted reasons why the United States was concerned about altering its program of naval construction. The principal difficulty was Japan. The State Department did not wish to veto publication officially, but it made clear its opposition, and the matter was dropped. For relevant correspondence, see USDSM 367, 763.72/13692.

CHAPTER 4

ANXIOUS MONTHS
July–September, 1917

By July, 1917, the United States had weathered the initial shock of belligerency, and President Wilson had defined his fundamental wartime policies. The United States intended to maintain diplomatic independence from the Entente nations, calling itself an "Associated" rather than an "Allied" power. It would make those military and naval contributions necessary to guarantee victory over the Central Powers with effort sufficient to ensure the negotiation—in fact, if necessary, the dictation— of a Wilsonian peace. In his war message of April 2, Wilson made crystal clear his determination to wage war vigorously; the United States would "exert all its power and employ all its resources to bring the Government of the German Empire to terms and end the war."[1] This effort did not mean that the United States fought for the same aims as the Entente powers. In July the President informed House privately that *"England and France have not the same views with regard to peace that we have* by any means." Fortunately, when the war was won, the United States "could force them to our way of thinking because by that time they will, among other things, be financially in our hands."[2] Here was *Realpolitik* in its starkest form. If the United States proposed to make a considerable contribution to the inter-Allied military effort, it would dispose its power not only to achieve coalition objectives but also to secure its own fundamental diplomatic aims, whatever those might turn out to be.

If the President conscientiously avoided public comments on war aims and serenely bypassed entangling agreements with the Allies, he worked furiously throughout the summer and fall of 1917 to perfect a national organization for war, and others throughout the government and nation matched his energy. The task was not easy. The United States had not made extensive prewar preparations, and the emergency in Europe created by setbacks on land and sea precluded a measured mobilization.

1. Woodrow Wilson, *The Public Papers of Woodrow Wilson: War and Peace*, R. S. Baker and W. E. Dodd, eds., 6 vols. (New York, 1917), 1:9.
2. Wilson to House, July 21, 1917, House Papers.

The result was an extremely uncomfortable atmosphere in all branches of the American Government—a jarring situation constantly reinforced by the confusions and anxieties of a truly dangerous year.

The responsible naval leadership of the United States, both at home and abroad, did not escape these adversities, but during the second half of 1917 it took great strides toward full efficiency. The Navy recognized that victory would not come easily or quickly, but most of its personnel set about their tasks with an underlying belief that an effective American reinforcement would ensure the ultimate defeat of the Central Powers. Three distinct but interrelated problems particularly engaged naval leaders during this period: coordination had to be established between the Navy Department in Washington and the headquarters of Admiral Sims in London; general political relations between the United States and Great Britain had to be clarified as a basis for joint strategy (in the nature of things, the naval effort of the Allied and Associated Powers in European waters was primarily Anglo-American in character); and effective means of regulating the over-all naval effort of the Allies had to be brought into existence. Two international naval conferences held during early September and late November contributed to a favorable evolution of all these relationships. By 1918 as the western coalition faced the dangerous prospect of a great German land offensive in France, its naval enterprise was reasonably well organized.

I

Admiral Sims did not alter his basic views of the naval war in the wake of President Wilson's irritating but short-lived intervention. His faith in the convoy system continued undiminished; he was convinced that it would force submarines to accept battle on terms more favorable to the Allies than previously.[3] "This war," he maintained, "is going to be won or lost by one specific feature, and that is the preservation of enough of the world's tonnage to feed the countries at war, and to keep their armies supplied."[4] He was much annoyed when Captain Pratt

3. Sims to Pratt, July 26, 1917, USNSF, TD file.
4. Sims to Pratt, August 11, 1917, USNSF, TD file.

wrote rather insouciantly that Britain could win the war by itself, but that American assistance would hasten the inexorable end. Sims thought differently: "There is not a man in England in a position to know anything about the situation who believes that England can win the war without a great deal of assistance." The Admiral then recapitulated his familiar arithmetic argument, showing that continuing submarine losses at the present

1. Merchant Shipping Losses in Gross Tons,
January, 1917 — November, 1918

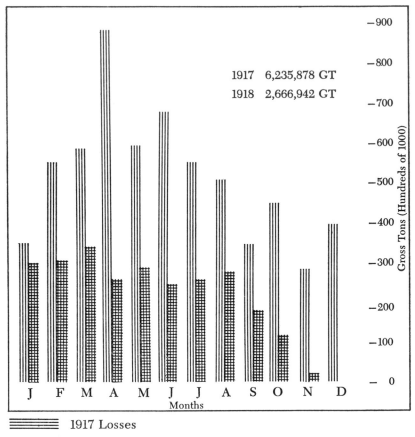

| | 1917 Losses |
| | 1918 Losses |

Source: Adapted from a chart in Arthur J. Marder, *From the Dreadnought to Scapa Flow: The Royal Navy in the Fisher Era, 1904-1919*, vol. 5, *Victory and Aftermath (January 1918-June 1919)* (London, 1970), III.

level would force the British to make peace within a certain limited period.[5]

Sims correctly represented the state of official opinion in Britain. The War Cabinet decided on July 13 that "the submarine is the one menace that might defeat us, and . . . from the point of view of the whole alliance, it is most important to concentrate every possible effort on the protection of trade in the approaches to the United Kingdom."[6] Balfour indicated the lengths to which Britain was prepared to sacrifice national prerogatives in the interest of victory when he informed Spring Rice that he would not quibble over the ownership of ships then building in America originally intended for British registry. "The immediate need was to build ships in the largest number and the shortest time, and to use them in the trade and in the routes most required from the point of view of the war. If these ends could be secured, it was a matter of quite secondary importance under what flag these merchant vessels sailed."[7] The War Cabinet recognized the extreme exigencies of the period, but was convinced that the United States would provide enough destroyers to ensure the success of the convoy and sufficient merchant shipping to maintain tonnage above survival levels.[8] The Admiralty waxed optimistic about the efficacy of the convoy system, although it was not yet viewed as "a final solution to the submarine menace." It had proved effective in early experiments because, as Sims had prophesied, it guaranteed "a concentration of force close to the enemy's objective, ready to take the offensive the moment a submarine is sighted."[9]

New dangers constantly disturbed the naval leadership. At this time Sims began to wonder whether Germany would attempt to counteract the convoy system by utilizing large submarine cruisers of the *Deutschland* class displacing close to

5. Sims to Pratt, July 26, 1917, USNSF, TD file. A copy of this letter in the Sims Papers is dated July 28, 1917.

6. Minutes of the War Cabinet (WC 183), July 13, 1917, CAB 23, book 3.

7. Balfour to Spring Rice, July 18, 1917, Cabinet Papers, no. 291 (1917), FO 899, box 13.

8. "Report of Cabinet Committee on War Policy," G.-176, August 10, 1917, CAB 24, book 4.

9. "Naval Weekly Appreciation, 10," August, 1917, ADM 137, book 511, 363.

2,000 tons that were originally developed as commerce carriers and could mount two guns and carry about thirty torpedoes. These unwieldy craft were sluggish in the water and therefore more vulnerable to attack than the smaller U-boats. Sims had an answer to this problem. Reserve battleships could be used as escorts for convoys in the middle passage until the merchant ships received their highly mobile destroyer escorts in the dangerous waters close to Britain.[10] The danger of the submarine cruisers did not yet materialize because Germany failed to expedite construction of these larger submersibles, but the western coalition had to make its calculations with this danger in mind.

In August Sims began to interest himself in the transport difficulties created by the need to bring a large American army to Europe. The military disasters of the summer in France made is clear that the United States, contrary to some earlier estimates, would have to deploy a large armed force on the Western Front.[11] Where would the shipping be found? Sims summarized the problem for his friend Adm. Lewis Bayly at Queenstown. "If America should send a million troops to France within the next year she could do so only at the expense of diverting shipping which is now wholly necessary to supply the Allies and maintain their armies at the Front."[12] He raised the issue quietly with Pratt, writing that it would be "a radical mistake" if the United States shipped so many troops that it deprived the Allies of supplies essential to the maintenance of their armies. One of his staff had concluded that "no very considerable army can be landed in, and maintained in France during the next year or eighteen months."[13] Sims had some reason for alarm. The French, of course, although also concerned about the shipping question, were more interested in the American Army than the British and had begun to exert pressure for early reinforcements. Gen. Ferdinand Foch had expressed the French desire for American troops late in July. Sims recognized that the French needed "definite assurances, particularly as to the number and charac-

10. Sims to Pratt, July 26, 1917, USNSF, TD file; Sims Report on Allied conference (July 24–27, 1917), July 30, 1917, QF file: "Naval & Military Conference at Paris."

11. David F. Trask, *The United States in the Supreme War Council: American War Aims and Inter-Allied Strategy, 1917–1918* (Middletown, Conn., 1961), 8–15.

12. Sims to Bayly, August 14, 1917, USNSF, TD file.

13. Sims to Pratt, August 14, 1917, USNSF, TD file.

ter of troops and their time of availability"—information "extremely desirable from a standpoint of morale if nothing else."[14]
The concern of France was in part a function of mutinies in its
regiments following the failure of the heavily advertised Nivelle
offensive on the Western Front earlier in the year. Washington
reacted to these pressures in ways that alarmed Sims. On July
28, Daniels sent a somewhat peremptory message declaring that
the "paramount duty of the destroyers in European waters is
principally the proper protection of transports with American
troops. . . . Everything is secondary to having a sufficient number
to insure protection to American troops."[15] This policy directly
contravened Sims's belief that the primary mission of the American destroyers should be escort duty for merchant convoys
approaching the British Isles.

In Washington President Wilson sustained his criticism of
British inaction. He was particularly annoyed at the Admiralty's
failure to launch a close-in offensive against German naval bases.
Hopeful of unearthing new ideas he told Daniels on July 30 of
his desire to "mobilize the initiative of the Navy and ask every
naval officer to send his views of how we ought to fight to win
naval victories. He wanted young men who would be as coura-
geous as Hobson to be called to the front."[16] Hobson, it will be
recalled, was the youthful naval officer who had attempted to
block a Cuban port during the Spanish-American War by sinking a vessel across the harbor mouth under the fire of Spanish
batteries. In a speech to the officers of the Atlantic Fleet on
August 11, Wilson gave vent to his general views:

We are hunting hornets all over the farm and letting the nest alone.
None of us knows how to go to the nest and crush it, and yet I despair
of hunting for hornets all over the sea when I know where the nest
is and know that the nest is breeding hornets as fast as I can find

14. Sims report on Allied conference (July 24–27, 1917) July 30, 1917,
USNSF, QF file. A copy is also in the TT file. See also Sharp to Wilson,
July 18, 1917, in William Graves Sharp, *The War Memoirs of William
Graves Sharp: American Ambassador to France, 1914–1918*, Warrington
Davison, ed. (London, 1931), 175. This message reflected French anxi-
eties at the time.
15. Quoted in Josephus Daniels, *The Wilson Era: Years of War and
After, 1917–1923* (Chapel Hill, N.C., 1946), 95. See also Ray Stannard
Baker, *Woodrow Wilson: Life and Letters*, 8 vols., *War Leader* (New
York, 1939), 7:197.
16. Daniels diary, July 30, 1917, E. David Cronon, ed., *The Cabinet
Diaries of Josephus Daniels, 1913–1921* (Lincoln, 1963), 184.

them. I am willing for my part, and I know you are willing, because I know the stuff you are made of—I am willing to sacrifice half the navy Great Britain and we together have to crush that nest, because if we crush it, the war is won.[17]

Sims had already heard too much of the hornet or rat or wasp nest analogy, and he was anxious to correct what he considered its "error."[18] He still accepted the British arguments about the extreme naval dangers attendant upon such tactics, but he was now also equipped with certain political arguments. An attack on Dutch territory might force that nation into the hands of Germany. The French might be opposed to any major extension of the British presence across the English Channel. Belgium was opposed to operations in its territory because of the damage that would result.[19] The British Navy had restudied this matter and concluded that blocking operations, mine barrages, and other proposals for close-in offensive action were still impractical.[20] Sims informed Pratt that the British studies were "really to arrive at conclusions that can be passed out to the very numerous suggestions that are made in this line. Many of these are by such prominent people, politically, that they cannot be neglected." Sims did not know that on the very day he wrote to Pratt, the President was making a passionate plea for just such a policy to no less an assemblage than the officers of the American fleet. Wilson would not have appreciated his admiral's remark that the British effort was intended to confute the civilian "who thinks that he knows more about naval warfare than the Admiralty."[21]

The President sustained his interest in a naval offensive. On August 16, he discussed naval matters with Daniels and some of his leading officers, dwelling on "the absolute necessity of find-

17. Quoted in Daniels, *Wilson Era: Years of War and After*, 44. For House's report of a conversation with Wilson on this speech, see an excerpt from the House diary, September 9, 1917, in Charles Seymour, ed., *The Intimate Papers of Colonel House*, 4 vols., *Into the World War* (Boston, 1928), 3:176.

18. He sent Ambassador Sharp in Paris an article explaining the "error" with obvious gusto. Sims to Sharp, July 31, 1917, quoted in Sharp, *War Memoirs*, 176–77.

19. Sims to Pratt, July 26, 1917, USNSF, TD file.

20. Beatty to Jellicoe, August 13, 1917, Jellicoe Papers, BM, book 49008.

21. Sims to Pratt, August 11, 1917, USNSF, TD file.

ing & ending the hornet's nest, & destroying the poison or re-
moving the cork. He impressed upon them the need of an
offensive and reiterated his view that we cannot win this war
by merely hunting submarines when they have gotten into the
great ocean." When Admiral Mayo said that he hoped the President did not have undue expectations, Wilson replied: "No,
but he expected plans by which America could lead & be the
senior partner in a successful naval campaign. He was ready to
make great ventures for a chance to win out but of course wished
no policy that would mean suicide."[22] Wilson had a supporter
in Ambassador Sharp. Increasingly influenced by signs of exhaustion in France, he also wanted to find some means of blocking the submarine bases. He thought that the United States
Navy possessed the qualities for this effort. "Ingenuity, boldness,
and dash—which qualities I believe the British Navy, with all
its superiority in ships, has greatly lacked—will be brought to
bear on the problem."[23] The President obviously agreed with
Sharp and apparently preserved his negative view of British
energies for many months to come.[24]

Experience in 1918, when the British valiantly but unsuccessfully undertook to block the harbors at Zeebrugge and Ostend,
seems to support the correctness of the Admiralty view, but the
widespread desire to take the offensive against the submarines in
1917 reflects the pervasive anxiety aroused by the German undersea operations. Sims himself finally began to show some signs
of wear, realizing that his continuing defense of Admiralty ideas
exposed him to criticism and perhaps to mischief at home. On
August 7, he asked Page to send certain clippings to the President through Lansing in order to clarify his views on the submarine danger. Sims told the Ambassador that he had "received
word, practically directly from the President, that he [Wilson]
was much displeased with my reply to his cablegram; that it
did not change his opinion at all; and that he regards me owned

22. Daniels diary, August 16, 1917, Cronon, ed., *Cabinet Diaries*, 191.
23. Sharp to Wilson, August 24, 1917, quoted in Sharp, *War Memoirs*,
201.
24. For indications of this persistence, see the Daniels diary, October 19
and October 26, 1917, Cronon, ed., *Cabinet Diaries, 223, 227.* On the
latter occasion Daniels took Admiral Browning of the British Navy to the
Cabinet meeting. "The President emphasized to him his earnest desire to
do something audacious in the line of offense."

by the Admiralty and so pro-British that he considered the advisability of replacing me by some other officer."[25] (Sims indeed had a well-informed source.) To Pratt he expressed himself most vigorously, defending his sympathies for the Entente:

You must not assume that because I am pro-British and pro-French and pro-all the rest of the allies, that I am necessarily anti-American. I have lived a long time in the United States (46 years). [Sims was born in Canada.] I have shown some interest in the efficiency of our navy. I am 59 years old and have a modest reputation for reasonable independence of thought. So do not assume in the pride of intellect that I am owned by the British or any other Admiralty. If you do not think a pro-ally is the right kind of man for this job, they should have sent a pro-Russian with a trunk full of bombs.[26]

Despite his pique, the Admiral quickly regained his poise, and he diverged not a whit from his initial conception of the proper way to wage the naval war. At the end of August he told Pratt: "The only effective co-operation with the British Fleet would be to use the forces present to make a homogeneous fighting unit."[27] Like President Wilson, Sims was not easily dissuaded from deeply felt opinions. Fortunately for the Admiral, Wilson was imbued with the belief that civilian leaders should not intervene unduly in military and naval affairs, a view that he derived from his study of the Civil War. In addition, growing optimism about the effectiveness of the convoys must have strengthened Sims's hand, although no one thought that victory was near.[28] The Germans had estimated that sinkings of 900,000 tons a month would reduce British shipping by 35 per cent on July 1 and by 50 per cent on October 1.[29] In fact, the reduction was indecisive. Production of merchant ships and increased utilization of neutral shipping compensated for declining monthly losses of about 558,000 tons in July, 512,000 tons in August, and 352,000 tons in September. Nevertheless, anxieties would not down, because the requirements of the war constantly imposed new demands for merchant shipping. Ambassador Page com-

25. Sims to Page, August 7, 1917, USNSF, TD file.
26. Sims to Pratt, August 11, 1917, USNSF, TD file.
27. Sims to Pratt, August 30, 1917, Sims Papers.
28. For favorable estimates by Sir Eric Geddes, see the Minutes of the War Cabinet (WC 223 and 228), August 24 and September 5, 1917, CAB 23, book 3 and book 4.
29. Holtzendorff to Zimmermann, August 3, 1917, St. Antony's Papers, reel 12, Geheime Akten, vol. 51, frames 127–29.

municated the mood of London in a gloomy letter to Secretary Daniels:

Our army in France had bought coal in England, but it can't get ships to carry it. The French & Italians will again suffer for coal this winter —not enough ships. Practically every problem of the war turns on ships. If the Allies had the ships that have gone down, they [could] pretty quickly end the war. The Germans are able to continue only because of their submarines.[30]

2. World Shipbuilding Output in Gross Tons (excluding Central Powers)

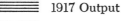

First Quarter	Second Quarter	Third Quarter	Fourth Quarter[1]

1,500,000

1,000,000

500,000

▤ 1917 Output

▦ 1918 Output

Source: Adapted from a chart in Arthur J. Marder, *From the Dreadnought to Scapa Flow: The Royal Navy in the Fisher Era, 1904-1919,* vol. 5, *Victory and Aftermath (January 1918-June 1919)* (London, 1970), 113.

Note: Total output for 1917 was 2,938,000. Total for 1918 was 4,008,000.

[1]The 1918 fourth-quarter figure is based on October.

30. Page to Daniels, September[?], 1917, Daniels Papers.

The bold President Wilson was prepared to commit half of the Anglo-American naval strength to offensives against the Germans, but the Navy Department proved far less militant. During the early months of his mission in London, Sims had occasionally mentioned the prospect of dispatching units of the Atlantic Fleet to Europe. At one point he had even considered a request for the entire formation. In July and August Sims proposed the transfer of four coal-burning dreadnoughts to Europe for service in the Straits of Dover.[31] Daniels was strictly opposed, giving as reasons the lack of personnel and a definite "program" for their employment.[32] Sims protested vigorously, assuming with some accuracy that fear of "disintegration" lay behind the attitude of the Navy Department. To both Pratt and Benson he repeated his view that to interpose detachments of the main American fleet between the main body and the enemy did not violate the Mahanite principle of preserving the integrity of the fleet. He also adduced an additional argument that must have deeply annoyed the proponents of a "symmetrical" fleet. Even if the American battle fleet proceeded to European waters, it would not be deployed as an independent unit, simply because it was by no means a balanced formation. To Pratt he argued that "it could not even cruise in comparative safety because it has not the auxiliary forces that are necessary to protect it." The fleet could be employed only as part of an inter-Allied force. To Benson he pointed out that in all plans for combined operations known to him the Allied naval forces were distributed according to types rather than national units. His final argument was an appeal to national pride and to history. "In my opinion not to comply with the expressed requirements of the Allies in the present situation is to take a very grave and unnecessary risk of our fair reputation among nations." To Pratt he asked: "Can we afford to have history record that the Allies asked for reinforcements and we declined to send them?"[33] These were compelling arguments indeed, but they went unheeded for the moment.

Sims also encountered continued difficulty in efforts to augment his organization in London. He sought additional personnel but none materialized. By the end of July he could express

31. Sims to Pratt, July 26, 1917, USNSF, TD file.
32. Daniels diary, August 18, 1917, Cronon, ed., *Cabinet Diaries*, 192.
33. Sims to Pratt, August 30, 1917, USNSF, TD file; Sims to Benson, September 1, 1917, USNSF, TD file.

his dismay in the strongest language. Responding to a letter
from Pratt requesting that he undertake certain activities, Sims
wrote that he could not comply with such orders without an adequate staff. He assumed the Navy Department must have its
reasons for refusing to send him assistance, but he could not
imagine what they could be. "Can you wonder that things have
happened as they have? Can you wonder that I cannot for the
life of me understand what is behind all this? Can you wonder
at the ASTONISHMENT of the people over here, who see me
carrying out my present work without a staff?" He insisted that
he was in the most important billet in the Navy and that he
needed the best officers to support his work.[34] "I fully realise the
demands made on the naval personnel . . . ," he told Pratt, "but
as the naval staff organization abroad is the one co-ordinating
link between the current allied war situation abroad, and the
Department, I submit that its demands should take precedence
over a large majority of the other demands made for training and
other purposes at home."[35] Sims had recently been promoted
to Vice Admiral and made the Force Commander of the United
States Navy in European waters, but these arrangements, he
insisted to Daniels, were not sufficient to meet his needs.[36]

In Washington the Navy Department began to encounter the
criticism that it had failed to respond rapidly enough to the
demands of the war. The American author Winston Churchill
reported to the President the results of his investigation of the
Department. He wanted to place vigorous young men in positions of power and to reduce the role of the General Board,
which he deemed unduly deliberate and conservative.[37] Franklin Roosevelt sustained his criticism of Daniels and Benson and
continued to advocate early and effective action.[38] These pressures, augmented by those emanating from the White House,

34. Sims to Pratt, July 26, 1917, USNSF, TD file.
35. Sims to Pratt, July 30, 1917, USNSF, TT file. A copy is in the TD
file.
36. Sims to Daniels, July 31, 1917, USNSF, TD file.
37. An unsigned memorandum in the Daniels Papers, dated July 29,
1917, was apparently supplied to him by Churchill. See the entry in the
Daniels diary, August 2, 1917, Cronon, ed., *Cabinet Diaries*, 185. A copy
of the Churchill report to the President, undated, is in USNSF, TD file. A
copy is also in the Roosevelt Papers, Naval Affairs file, group 10, box 157.
38. See the memorandum by Franklin D. Roosevelt, July 26, 1917,
quoted in Frank Freidel, *Franklin D. Roosevelt: The Apprenticeship* (Boston, 1952), 307.

began to stimulate Daniels to greater activity—a development that ultimately benefited Sims.[39] The Secretary of the Navy proved himself a cautious administrator during the war years, generally deferring to the opinions of Admiral Benson. Like most of his colleagues in the Cabinet he was particularly desirous of avoiding conflicts with President Wilson. Sims was to learn that energetic advocacy could sway the Secretary of the Navy in critical situations, provided that it did not require that Daniels contradict the desires of his Chief in the White House. Daniels's diary clearly reveals his distaste for Sims, but it also indicates that usually he did not attempt to forestall necessary actions when Sims made an effective argument for them.

Mindful of information conveyed to him that his command might be in jeopardy, Sims was anxious to clarify his powers and authority in Europe. On August 14, he put this point bluntly to Pratt. His relations with the British were quite good, and he wanted to avoid any interference in his activities. "I should not like this intimate relation to be interfered with by the sending of anybody else to assist me in this command. I do not know that any such measure is contemplated, but it has occured [sic] to me that it might be in the future." He thought it wise "to let well enough alone, particularly in a case which is more or less unique in allied operations."[40] He was also energetic in claiming the prerogatives of his command, complaining extensively when the Navy Department ordered redistribution of his forces despite the understanding that he had the responsibility for such decisions. He was equally assiduous in demanding information from Washington relating to his activities.[41] Slowly but surely the Admiral improved his working relations with the Navy Department, although he was forced to continue his drumfire of criticism for many months. As an antidote to misunderstandings in Washington, Sims urged the dispatch of officials from the Navy Department to observe actual conditions in Europe. This experience would make them much more effective when they resumed their duties at home.[42]

39. For signs of Daniels's growing concern, see the Daniels diary, August 8 and August 14, 1917, Cronon, ed., *Cabinet Diaries*, 189, 190.

40. Sims to Pratt, August 14, 1917, USNSF, TD file. Sims repeated this plea in Sims to Benson, September 1, 1917, USNSF, TD file.

41. Sims to Pratt, August 11, 1917, and August 18, 1917, USNSF, TD file.

42. Sims to Pratt, September 3, 1917, USNSF, TD file.

If these developments seemed to ensure better communication and cooperation between the field command and the naval staff in Washington, there was indication that the Navy Department was far from fully converted to Sims's policy of all-out concentration on the submarine war. On August 29, 1917, the General Board reported to Daniels on its views concerning the naval building program for 1919. The Board recognized that, although the present conflict required certain changes in emphasis, "the battleship remains as heretofore the principal reliance of the sea power of a nation." Fortunately the British Navy was able to contain the German fleet, "thus giving us time for an extensive war preparation which under normal conditions we could not hope to enjoy." It was important to expand shipbuilding facilities so that the United States could continue to develop a balanced fleet. "A new alignment of powers after the present war must not find our fleet in all the types of vessels composing it, unprepared to meet possible enemies in the Atlantic and Pacific at liberty to act singly or jointly with all their naval powers against us." The country should possess sufficient building capacity to produce both merchant ships and men of war at the same time in all the necessary numbers and sizes. Again and again the Board returned to its preoccupation with the future. "After the war, international adjustments that will have to be made [involve] questions of the utmost importance and the Navy of the United States should be steadily increased in size and power to meet the needs of the country in the future."[43] The call for expanded building facilities was an attempt to resolve the dilemma of choosing between naval and mercantile requirements—a problem that engaged Daniels's attention throughout the summer—but it was certainly an unrealistic proposal.[44] Despite the remarkable industrial vigor of the United States, it was unlikely that either capital-ship construction or shipyard construction could be expanded rapidly enough to make a major impact on the war within two or three years.

The British Government remained dissatisfied with the pace of action in Washington. Lord Northcliffe, energetically attempting to stimulate the United States, believed that "both the

43. Badger to Daniels, August 19, 1917, Records of the General Board.
44. See, for example, Daniels diary, August 14, 1917, Cronon, ed., *Cabinet Diaries*, 190.

American Government and public were, probably with some reason, confused as to the actual situation, owing to the contradictory tone of the reports which were current." The War Cabinet decided on July 23 that "some definite statement on the subject was necessary and that it was highly desirable that any such statement should be made direct to the President."[45] Phillip Kerr, the Prime Minister's secretary, produced a message to be transmitted to Wilson by Northcliffe. Once again Britain concluded that the submarine campaign would not force peace, but that it was seriously affecting the war effort. The American effort against the submarine was "absolutely vital to the successful prosecution of the war and the attainment of an early peace." Britain urged two courses of action: the provision of antisubmarine craft and a substantial increase in the output of merchant shipping. Some 350,000 to 400,000 tons must be produced in America per month to maintain tonnage at proper levels. The "period of greatest stress" would be the first six to nine months of 1918. "It is, therefore, of utmost importance that we know as soon as possible the probable American monthly output for the next twelve months."[46] The Cabinet was especially hopeful of early American naval assistance because "many months must elapse before the United States of America could render effective military assistance." It suggested no basic changes in naval policy, but urged consideration of recommendations having to do with offensive actions against submarines.[47]

Britain continued to consider sending a special naval mission to the United States, but this idea encountered strong resistance. Spring Rice was opposed, informing Balfour that "the United States Departments are quite satisfied with the present arrangement and are working in a very satisfactory way with our naval and military representatives." Once again he reminded Balfour that "It cannot be too often insisted that to be useful we must be inconspicuous." Lord Northcliffe subscribed to a similar view, telling Balfour that he could be relied upon "never to use minatory language. I have been dealing with these people [for]

45. Minutes of the War Cabinet (WC 193), July 23, 1917, CAB 23, book 3.
46. Minutes of the War Cabinet (WC 203), Appendix 3, August 2, 1917, CAB 23, book 3.
47. "Report of Cabinet Committee on War Policy," (G.–176), August 10, 1917, CAB 24, book 4.

thirty years. Nothing can be gained here by threats, much by flattering and self-abnegation."[48] Sims also opposed the dispatch of Englishmen to the United States; he had another idea, and after participating in an inter-Allied meeting in Paris near the end of July, he presented it to Pratt:

It was very interesting during my visit to Paris this week, to have a large number of important personages state that the best thing that could happen to the Allies just now would be to have President Wilson do the unprecedented thing of coming over here with a large commission to visit England and France and perhaps Italy; see conditions with his own eyes and leave a very competent commission behind him to keep him informed.[49]

Sims undoubtedly hoped that such a mission would clarify a whole range of misunderstandings of peculiar importance to himself as well as to the Allies at large.

The British Government shared Sims's desire to enhance Washington's grasp of the European situation, every day realizing more clearly than before that the outcome of the war would probably depend upon the effectiveness of the American reinforcement. Leaders in London naturally hoped to establish the best possible associations with their American counterparts. To provide information, Sir William Wiseman was ordered in August to return to London and report on the state of Anglo-American relations.

To the War Cabinet he argued that relations were not in good repair. "There still remains a strong mistrust of Great Britain, inherited from the days of the War of Independence and fostered by the ridiculous history books still used in the national schools of America." On the other hand Americans were sympathetic to France. They had the distinct impression that the Allies wanted a maximum of help, but were providing a minimum of information to support their requests. "There is a feeling that some of the money and material is not needed for strictly war purposes,

48. Spring Rice to Balfour, August 9, 1917, Spring Rice Papers, FO 800, book 242; Northcliffe to Balfour, August 26, 1917, Balfour Papers, FO 800, book 209.

49. Sims to Pratt, July 26, 1917, USNSF, TD file. A copy in the Sims Papers is dated July 28, probably the correct date, since the conference in Paris took place from July 24 to 27. The possibility of a Wilson visit to Europe or a Lloyd George visit to America was discussed by the War Cabinet at this time. Minutes of the War Cabinet (WC 200a), July 31, 1917, CAB 23, book 13 (secret minutes).

but for *post bellum* development. Confusion reigns, not only in the administrative departments, but in the public mind." His solution was to establish an inter-Allied council in Paris to control all requests made of the United States: "If our naval and military leaders want the support of the United States they must be prepared to take the President into their confidence, not only as to their general plans, but as to the situation from day to day." Despite the difficulties, Wiseman was optimistic about improving Anglo-American relations. Although America would never openly accept British leadership, it was "nevertheless true that unconsciously she is holding on to British traditions and would more readily accept the British than any other point of view, always provided no suggestion escaped that England was guiding or leading the foreign policy of the United States." The moment appeared to him of great importance. "It is no exaggeration to say that the foreign policy of America for many years to come is now in process of formation, and very much depends on the full sympathetic and confidential exchange of views between the leaders of the British and American people."[50] Here was an impressive report indeed that confirmed the prior analyses both of Balfour and Spring Rice and came from one high in the confidence of Colonel House.

The War Cabinet reacted by developing a plan to invite a congressional delegation to visit Britain, France, and Italy, "since the American people were not yet fully awake to the gravity of the situation." The Congress could then "be brought personally into touch with the work in progress behind the lines and on the fighting fronts, &c."[51] Nothing came of this gambit. Nor did the British succeed in arranging a commission in Paris to deal with purchasing problems. Spring Rice pointed out one of the reasons for American hesitancy. The President had "a rooted distrust of military and naval advisers, and . . . he has had an extremely disagreeable experience with various special commissioners." The President had just one real confidant. "House turns out to be the only one that he can really trust to,

50. Wiseman apparently prepared two memoranda—one a draft that was later enlarged. This memorandum is reprinted as Cabinet Memorandum no. 738, August, 1917, FO 899, book 4. A second memorandum, dated August 21, 1917, is reprinted as Cabinet Memorandum no. 739, FO 899, book 4. The quotations above are drawn from both versions.
51. Minutes of the War Cabinet (WC 224), August 27, 1917, CAB 23, book 3.

and I suspect that he gets all his information of an unofficial
character through House as General Intelligence Officer and
editor of news."[52]

Spring Rice had a point; the President had shown great reluctance during the summer of 1917 to enter into extended
negotiations on military and naval questions with Allied representatives in Europe. Wilson preferred to avoid entanglements
that might be embarrassing later on, but imperious necessity
forced his hand. He eventually acquiesced in the dispatch of a
special naval mission to Europe in late August, 1917, headed by
Adm. Henry T. Mayo. That mission ultimately made a useful
contribution to the conduct of the naval war.

II

In June, 1917, Balfour and Page collaborated in an effort to
induce the President to send representatives to an inter-Allied
conference scheduled for July. Balfour informed Spring Rice that
"America was already, in the sphere of production and finance,
the most important of the Allied Powers; in the naval and military sphere, her importance was steadily growing." Moreover,
"President Wilson was deeply interested, not merely in the conduct of the war, but in the arrangements to be made at its conclusion, and he would certainly claim to be represented when
important Allied interests were under discussion."[53] Page tried
a somewhat different approach. Telling Wilson that Balfour desired American participation at the upcoming conference, he
noted that such gatherings "bring to light the incredible friction
between the Allies and their apparently irreconcilable differences. It is not a happy family." Therefore "we ought to be represented at these conferences, if for no other reason, [than] to
get clear insight into these strong controversies and differences
under the surface. To judge only from such [conflicts] as have
come, and are constantly coming, to my knowledge, they are
numerous and exceedingly embarrassing."[54]

52. Spring Rice to Balfour, September 7, 1917, in Stephen Gwynne, ed.,
The Letters and Friendships of Sir Cecil Spring Rice, 2 vols. (Boston,
1929), 2:409–10.
53. Balfour to Spring Rice, June 21, 1917, USDSM 367, 763.72/6128.
54. Page to Wilson, June 21, 1917, Wilson Papers, box 121. Page made a
formal request later. See Page to Lansing, July 2, 1917, USDSM 367,
763.72/5646.

The British motive was obvious: Balfour hoped for more effective methods of extorting assistance from the United States. His efforts came to naught. Lansing asked guidance from the President, reporting that Russia as well as Britain had recommended representation,[55] but the President was unresponsive. On July 11, Acting Secretary of State Frank Polk notified Page that "this Government is not ready at the present time to take part in the inter-allied war conferences."[56] Wilson remained convinced that the best policy was to avoid undue entanglement in Entente affairs in order to preserve diplomatic independence for the future. On July 18, Page again requested permission for Sims and Gen. John J. Pershing, the American land commander recently arrived in Europe, to attend the imminent inter-Allied conference.[57] Polk replied immediately, once again denying permission and this time giving cogent reasons. President Wilson did not wish to take part in a conference representing all the Allies, because the United States had not declared war against Austria, Bulgaria, or Turkey. Moreover, he feared that participation "might give the impression to this country that this Government was discussing not only the conduct of the campaign, but also the ultimate purposes having to do with peace aims."[58] At this time Spring Rice believed that the Americans were becoming aware of "the immense power conferred upon them by holding the purse" and the significance of their naval contribution. "They may," the Ambassador concluded, "insist on representation as a consequence of taxation."[59] The acidulous Ambassador in this case was in error.

Despite the President's decision, Sims attended the conference as an unofficial observer. In his correspondence there is an unsigned letter to him stating that the President opposed official representation at the approaching political conference, but that an Allied naval gathering taking place at the same time was "quite a separate matter." Page for his part claimed that participation in the naval discussions "could not in any way be con-

55. Lansing to Wilson, July 3, 1917, Wilson Papers, box 122.
56. Polk to Page, July 11, 1917, USDSM 367, 763.72/5646. For the reaction in London, see Page diary, July 16, 1917, Page Papers.
57. Page to Lansing, July 18, 1917, USDSM 367, 763.72/5896.
58. Polk to Page, July 20, 1917, USDSM 367, 763.72/5896.
59. Spring Rice to Balfour, July 21, 1917, Cabinet Papers no. 306 (1917), FO 899, book 13.

sidered as an attendance or a visit to the Allied Conference."[60]

Sims returned from the conference with additional information to send to the Navy Department about the shipping crisis. In Paris a representative of the British Ministry of Shipping, Graeme Thomson, had presented a detailed report on the effect of the submarine war. The Allies were likely to suffer an average monthly loss of half a million tons. If the Allies could produce 3 million tons of shipping during the first nine months of 1918, ship construction thereafter would balance losses—provided the estimates available concerning American production proved accurate. Thomson called for a full report on tonnage available to the Allies, directing attention in particular to new demands such as transport for American troops to Europe.[61] Sims drew from his participation in the conference the conclusion that "Early steps towards allied coordination of effort in this direction are considered the most vital military necessity of the moment." He recommended that representatives of American shipping and military interests attend a forthcoming conference on transport scheduled for August 10, supporting his suggestion with the information that both French and British naval and military officialdom had urged this course.[62]

After considering his experience in Paris, Sims made a comprehensive report and recommendation to the Navy Department. His principal objective was to urge the need for "closer co-ordination of effort" between the United States and its associates:

All the military future plans are certainly largely dependent upon America's action. Although America's military support is urgently needed, it is nevertheless absolutely necessary that such support should not place any new demands upon the allied shipping situation considered alone. It is also very evident that the general campaign against the enemy, both military and what might be called a "shipping campaign," is really dependent upon America's support, and hence that the efficient prosecution of the war requires a closer co-ordination

60. Unsigned letter to Sims, July 24, 1917, USNSF, QC file, "Records of the Allied Naval Council."

61. "Report of a Joint Naval and Military Conference Held at Paris on July 24, 1917," (G.T.–1534), CAB 28, book 2. Sims, who was present, reported this information in Sims to Daniels, July 28, 1917, USNSF, QF file. For the French minutes of the conference, see MM, Es file, box 13.

62. Sims to Daniels, July 28, 1917, QF file. See also Sims to Pratt, July 28, 1917, Sims Papers.

of effort between the United States and the European Allies than now exists. By this it is meant that the Allied War Councils, both military and in other fields, should be supplied immediately, and should be kept supplied with more definite information of America's plans and intentions.

Sims was convinced that American representatives were needed in Europe; cable communications would not suffice. It was also "vitally important that all branches of war activity should be co-ordinated, and hence that such representatives as we send should be formed into one organization." Unrepentant, Sims concluded with the observation that his experience at the conference confirmed rather than modified views expressed in earlier dispatches.[63]

The United States finally decided to take action. On July 30, Lansing informed Page that the United States was willing to send representatives to the forthcoming conference, recommending that Admiral Mayo lead the American mission with Sims also in attendance.[64] Page immediately indicated the hearty approval of London.[65] Sims was pleased, telling Daniels that the consultations would greatly benefit all concerned and proposing that Mayo's staff arrive a week or so before the conference to undertake preliminary investigations.[66] The mission of Mayo was "exactly in line with the suggestion that I have been making that we send people over here to get the information you require."[67] Page presented similar views in a communication to the President.[68]

This decision to send Admiral Mayo to Europe may well have resulted from the President's annoyance with the British Admiralty as well as from obvious necessity. When Daniels and Mayo visited the President prior to the Admiral's departure, Wilson strongly impressed upon them the importance of taking

63. Sims report on the naval conference (July 24–27, 1917), July 30, 1917, TT file. A copy is in the QF file.

64. Lansing to Page, July 30, 1917, USNSF, TT file. State Department files include a message from Polk to Page, July 28, 1917, with the same information included in the Lansing message cited above. USDSM 367, 763.72/6059.

65. Page to Lansing, July 31, 1917, USNSF, TT file. A copy is in USDSM 367, 763.72/6064.

66. Sims to Daniels, July 31, 1917, USNSF, TT file. A copy is in the QC file.

67. Sims to Pratt, August 14, 1917, USNSF, TD file.

68. Page to Wilson, August 14, 1917, Wilson Papers, box 125.

the offensive. Mayo was somewhat cautious in responding to the President's comments, leading Daniels to muse: "Is Mayo hopeful enough?"[69] The President later informed House of his decision to send the mission, telling the Colonel that he wanted the delegation "to go over and find a way to break up the hornet's nest and not to try to kill individual hornets over a forty-acre lot." House also recorded Wilson's expression of willingness "to risk the loss of half our navy if there was a commensurate gain."[70]

The energetic Assistant Secretary of the Navy Roosevelt wanted to head the mission. To bring effective influence to bear in his behalf he may himself have enlisted the aid of a British newspaperman in the United States, Arthur Willert, who communicated Roosevelt's desire to Sir William Wiseman in London:

Cooperation between Naval Department and Admiralty includes important political problems also technical questions with which officers could not deal. It has been suggested to me that the best way to meet this suggestion would be to send FRANKLIN ROOSEVELT with a small civilian staff as well as officers. FRANKLIN ROOSE-VELT, who is the best man here, has been for some time anxious to get into personal touch with ERIC GEDDES [the First Lord of the Admiralty] in order to arrange for effective joint policy. . . . If you should get GEDDES or BALFOUR to send message that we should appreciate the sending of responsible civilian representatives of Naval Department at the head of the Department's delegation, FRANKLIN ROOSEVELT'S name should not be mentioned, as it has not been suggested to PRESIDENT yet. I cannot answer for the effect of such a message, but it can do no harm if it appears to be spontaneous. Prompt action is necessary as PRESIDENT will make his decision early next week.[71]

On August 13, Roosevelt approached Daniels and told the Secretary that "we would get nothing from the Naval officers who go to Europe. Needed a civiilan commission. Wanted to go

69. Daniels diary, August 16, 1917, Cronon, ed., *Cabinet Diaries*, 191–92.

70. See the excerpt from the House diary for September 9, 1917, in Seymour, ed., *Intimate Papers*, 3:176. The Daniels diary for August 8, 1917, records the views of Arthur Pollen, who strongly favored the dispatch of the Mayo mission and energetic offensive action. He looked "for more vigorous offensive because of change in English Admiralty." Cronon, ed., *Cabinet Diaries*, 189.

71. Willert to Wiseman, August 11, 1917, Balfour papers, FO 800, box 209. A search of various records does not reveal any British response to this plea.

himself. No."[72] Thus ended ingloriously another effort by Roosevelt to make an important impact on American naval policy. The decision to send naval officers rather than civilian negotiators accorded squarely with Wilson's readiness to make important military and naval contributions to victory while avoiding diplomatic commitments that might prove compromising at a later date.

As Mayo's mission departed, Washington received messages from Europe describing the lack of inter-Allied coordination, the necessity of American contributions, and the strong bargaining power of the United States. Page reported to Wilson that American intervention was universally considered the salvation of the Entente cause, but he continued to emphasize the danger of the submarine. "The future of the world seems . . . to hang on the answer to this question: Can the war be won in spite of the submarines? Can a great American army be brought over and its large subsequent supply-fleet be sufficiently safeguarded?" He greatly regretted continuing signs of inter-Allied discord. "The waste in the war caused by the failures of the European Allies to work together with complete unity is one of the most pitiable aspects of the conflict. . . . This jealousy and distrust runs more or less through all the dealings of the continental Allies with each other. It's a sad tale."[73] Ambassador Sharp in Paris shared many of these sentiments. He thought the French would sustain their effort despite the great privations that confronted them, mentioning that the American intervention had been a major factor in sustaining morale. Inter-Allied disunity resulted from failure at "reconciling their interests not alone in plans affecting the prosecution of the war but of final adjustments to be made of their respective claims at the conclusion of peace." He had a suggestion to make; since the war could not be won quickly on the ground, the Allies should augment their aerial arms greatly in order to break the stalemate.[74] General Pershing also contributed his view: "Allies now firmly realize dependence upon our cooperation and we need not hesitate demand both aggressive naval policy and full share of all

72. Daniels diary, August 13, 1917, Cronon, ed., *Cabinet Diaries*, 190. See also Pleadwell to Sims, September 13, 1917, USNSF, TD file.

73. Page to Wilson, August 14, 1917, Wilson Papers, box 125.

74. Sharp to Wilson, August 24, 1917, Wilson Papers, box 125.

commercial shipping."[75] All these reports indicated that Mayo would find an anxious but cooperative audience in Europe.

When Admiral Mayo arrived in Britain late in August he engaged in consultations with British officials preparatory to the naval conference itself, which had been postponed to September 4. He lost no time letting the Admiralty know of President Wilson's desire for boldness. First Lord of the Admiralty Eric Geddes explained the situation to Lloyd George. Admiral Mayo had instructions that "he is not to be too much influenced by the fear of running risks. He told me that President Wilson's words were —that you cannot make omelettes without breaking eggs, and that war is made up of taking risks." Geddes did not appear alarmed by this pronouncement; he too hoped for a more energetic naval policy. "We hope to get more co-operation from them," he concluded, "both now and in the future."[76]

Sims also looked for measurable accomplishment. He saw in the consultations an opportunity to shake the general conviction in Washington that he was "hopelessly British" and therefore "incapable of independent judgment."[77] He told his friend Admiral Bayly at Queenstown that Mayo had been exploring affairs in depth with Admiralty officials and that his visit would be "the means of clearing up the situation in the mind of our people back home."[78] Ambassador Page wrote in optimistic terms to the President, reporting that Mayo's visit had caused "great satisfaction" and that the British were "showing him everything that he cares to see and . . . answering all his questions."[79] Adm. William R. Hall, the extraordinarily competent head of British naval intelligence, informed Lord Bertie in Paris that he hoped for more concrete accomplishment at the approaching conference than had been true of previous meetings, because "this time we have the Americans who also talk our language." He spoke most warmly of American naval officials in London. "The naval officer over here really means business and there is a similar absence of the

75. Pershing to Chief of Staff, August 24, 1917, Wilson Papers, box 125.
76. Geddes to Lloyd George, August 29, 1917, Lloyd George Papers, file F/17/6/8. A copy is in the Papers of Sir Eric Geddes, ADM 116, book 1804.
77. Sims to Whittlesey, August 29, 1917, USNSF, TD file.
78. Sims to Bayly, September 3, 1917, Sims Papers.
79. Page to Wilson, September 3, 1917, Wilson Papers, box 126.

usual talk of the great deeds which the American Eagle is going to perform."[80] Obviously, Sims's businesslike approach to his command had succeeded in gaining the confidence of the British Navy. Sims remained alert to the inevitable stresses and strains of inter-Allied cooperation—the manifold difficulties of "trying to co-ordinate with people who, after all, talk quite a different language and have different view points"—but he remained confident of ultimate success.[81]

Admiral Mayo's concerns largely determined the agenda of the naval conference. He sought information on present as well as future policies and plans, and changes contemplated in the immediate future—all to the end of determining the nature of American cooperation.[82] Measures to counteract the submarine offensive dominated the agenda, which gave opportunities to consider prospects for a close-in offensive in German waters, creation of a mine barrage in the North Sea, offensive measures against submarines, operation of the convoy system, and certain specific requests of the French and Italian navies. The nations represented were the United States, Great Britain, France, Italy, Japan, and Russia.[83]

Jellicoe began proceedings by describing a scheme for a close-in offensive against the Heligoland Bight, in which he proposed to sink some 83 old battleships and cruisers filled with concrete in order to pen up the German fleet. Various reactions resulted. The United States withheld views, but the French and the Japanese thought it possible, and the Russian delegate made a strong plea for the close-in offensive in order to relieve pressure then being exerted by the enemy. Only the Italian delegate demurred: "He thought his Government considered that the Italian ships mentioned were of very great use in their present employment." The conference finally decided to refer the plan to the various governments for official opinions.[84] Mayo's immediate reaction, expressed to Admiral Benson, was: "Personally believe

80. Hall to Bertie, August 31, 1917, Bertie Papers, FO 800, book 181.
81. Sims to Fletcher, August 30, 1917, USNSF, TP file. This letter discussed problems of cooperation with the French off their coast.
82. Mayo to Jellicoe, September, 1917, reproduced in memorandum from Admiralty to Mayo, "Present Naval Policy," September 17, 1917, ADM 137, book 98. See also Mayo to Daniels, September 8, 1918, Papers of Admiral William S. Benson, Library of Congress, Washington, D.C. This report is also in USNSF, QI file, "International Naval Conference."
83. Mayo to Daniels, September 8, 1917, USNSF, QI file.
84. "Report of Naval Conference of Powers United Against Germany,"

nothing will come of this proposition as consider full examination of difficulties will show impossibility of success."[85] He was a sound prophet.

The second item was the question of the North Sea barrage, much favored by certain leaders in Washington. Sims immediately attacked the plan, arguing that a barrage of this nature was an all-or-nothing proposition. "Submarines do not attack fighting vessels; they attacked lines of communication. Submarines would make every effort to get out. Either the barrage is successful or it fails absolutely." He drew attention to the difficulty of patrolling a barrage some 240 miles in length. Geddes argued the point briefly, stating that if the barrage slowed submarines by 50 per cent it would be worth while, but Sims replied that the likelihood of success was so limited that it was not desirable to commit the patrol craft needed to maintain the barrage, because these vessels could be utilized more effectively as convoy escorts. It was decided that the mine barrage was not feasible until the means of constructing it became available, but the various governments were to report on what assistance they could furnish for the project.[86]

The conference then discussed various antisubmarine methods then in use. The British described certain experiments involving listening devices (the hydrophone), aircraft, kite balloons, and torpedo salvos. They believed that the most successful method of attacking submarines was use of the submarine itself. Mystery (Q) ships—armed craft disguised as merchant vessels—were next in effectiveness, although this tactic was in decline because submarines had become wary. Destroyers and patrol vessels were less dangerous, their chief value being that they forced submarines to operate beneath the surface. The participants concluded that the most desirable antisubmarine methods, in order, were to block enemy submarine bases; to attack the submarine at sea; to mine the submarines. All governments agreed to amplify, expand, and improve their antisubmarine methods as rapidly as possible.[87]

September 4–5, 1917, Admiralty document M.00223, USNSF, QI file; Mayo to Daniels, September 8, 1917, USNSF, QI file.

85. Mayo to Benson, September 5, 1917, Benson Papers.

86. "Report of Naval Conference," (M.00223), USNSF, QI file; Mayo to Daniels, September 8, 1917, USNSF, QI file.

87. Mayo to Daniels, September 8, 1917, USNSF, QI file.

The convoy system then came under discussion. Geddes reported initial success, but urged the need for improvements, given the likelihood that the enemy would soon dispose of better submarines. He indicated that the greatest percentage of loss now occurred in the Scandinavian and Mediterranean trades, to which the French admiral present, Ferdinand-Jean-Jacques de Bon, proposed that the United States consider sending older battleships to the Mediterranean for convoy duty. Sims was firm in his advocacy of the convoy as against other antisubmarine tactics and once again insisted on the importance of building destroyers. Large German submarine cruisers, to which Geddes had adverted, could be counteracted by using dreadnoughts as escorts until relieved by destroyers in the most dangerous waters near the European coast. No important decisions emerged from this rather general conversation.[88]

There was also some discussion of Italian and French needs. Representatives of both nations approached the United States privately to press their claims, probably because the United States was not at war with Austria-Hungary. The Austrian fleet contested Allied control of the Mediterranean along with German submarines operating out of Adriatic bases. Italy wanted to explore the possibility of purchasing destroyers from the United States while France expressed anxiety about difficulties associated with the transport, landing, and supply of American troops arriving in Europe. Mayo agreed to take up these matters in Washington.[89]

Mayo was somewhat disappointed in that the conference rarely moved beyond generalities. He attributed this outcome largely to the limited powers of the various national delegations. While some useful things were accomplished, he reported that the various delegations "usually lack authority to make definite arrangements and usually have been furnished with instructions to press matters which affect their own countries particularly." This reality tended "to restrict their appreciation of the broad scope of the matters usually dealt with in conference."[90] Never-

88. "Report of Naval Conference," (M.00223), USNSF, QI file.
89. Mayo to Navy Department, September 6, 1917, USNSF, TP file; Mayo to Daniels, September 8, 1917, USNSF, QI file. Sims also responded helpfully to the French requests. Sims to Minister of Marine, October 3, 1917, USNSF, QC file.
90. Mayo to Daniels, September 8, 1917, USNSF, QI file.

theless the meeting was a useful step toward fuller coordination of the inter-Allied naval effort, and it stimulated more activity in the United States.

Sims had privately expressed some concern that the Mayo mission might make recommendations counter to those that he had sent to Washington, but no such dire outcome material-ized.[91] He had often advocated the dispatch of naval experts to inform themselves on European conditions, assuming that it would strengthen support in Washington for his views. The Mayo mission definitely had that effect. Sims praised Mayo for his contributions to inter-Allied good will, and comparable com-mendations were forthcoming from Spring Rice and Geddes.[92] When Mayo returned to Washington he submitted a detailed report that recorded the decisions made in London and the re-quests presented by the various Allies. He placed heavy stress on the importance of immediate action, responding to the sense of urgency that existed in Europe, and was firm in his opinion that the Navy Department should emphasize production rather than improvement of its equipment.[93]

On October 20, the Navy Department sent a message to Sims announcing its decisions on the recommendations made by the naval conference: it deemed impractical the project to block the Heligoland Bight with old battleships; it would do everything possible to make mines available for distant barrage operations, particularly in the North Sea; it would continue to supply every vessel available for escort; it would also improve its intelligence efforts regarding submarine activities, and base American sub-marines on the Azores in order to augment support of the critical trade route in that part of the Atlantic. The British had asked

91. For expressions of this concern, see Sims to Pratt, September 8 and September 11, 1917, USNSF, TD file. Mayo strongly supported Sims's view that destroyers should be given priority over capital ships. Daniels diary, September 8, 1917, Cronon, ed., Cabinet Diaries, 203.

92. Sims to Mayo, October 10, 1917, USNSF, TD file; Spring Rice to Balfour, October 19 and October 25, 1917, Cabinet Papers, nos. 476 and 494 (1917), FO 899, book 13; Geddes to Daniels, October 13, 1917, Geddes Papers, ADM 116, book 1605.

93. Mayo to Daniels, October 11, 1917, USNSF, UP file, "General Matters Relating to the Operations, Plans, and Policies of the Navy as a Whole." See also Tracy B. Kittredge, Naval Lessons of the Great War: A Review of the Senate Naval Investigation of the Criticisms by Admiral Sims of the Policies and Methods of Josephus Daniels (Garden City, N.Y., 1921), 202–3.

the United States to commandeer certain shipping. This matter was referred to the Shipping Board for decision.[94]

One other proposal particularly intrigued the Navy Department. Sims was told that the "question of proposed mine barrage Scotland to Norway . . . is not definitely concurred in but careful consideration is being given to this particular subject," because it was "considered in principle to promise good results."[95] Indications during the naval conference and after—including a message from no less a figure than Admiral Jellicoe—that the Admiralty was revising its previous attitude toward the project, bolstered interest in this scheme.[96] Earlier opposition, aside from lack of patrol craft, was based primarily on the lack of effective mines, but the United States had developed a model that was both safe and effective and that could be produced in sufficient numbers to arm a massive barrage. It also was planning to build large groups of submarine chasers and other craft that could patrol the barrage effectively. Sims's objection was that the barrage would violate the territorial waters of a neutral country—Norway—but by late 1917 initial trepidations about such incursions had largely dissipated. Roosevelt and Mayo favored the barrage, but Benson and other department officials at first opposed it.[97]

The conflict was finally resolved when the General Board approved the barrage project. That group decided, wrote Daniels, that it was "the only big thing the combined navies could do," but the Secretary was dubious. It was "a stupendous undertaking—perhaps not impossible but to my mind of doubtful practicability. North Sea too rough & will necessitate withdrawing all our ships from other work and then can we destroy the hornets nest or keep the hornets in?"[98] Ironically, Daniels's reservations were compounded of views expressed earlier by the President and Admiral Sims. Once the commitment was made, however, he defended the project to the President and worked

94. Navy Department to Sims, October 20, 1917, USNSF, QI file. A copy is also in the TT file.
95. Navy Department to Sims, October 20, 1917, USNSF, QI file.
96. Jellicoe to Benson, September 22, 1917, USNSF, TT file. See also the Admiralty memorandum given to Mayo entitled "Present Naval Policy," September 17, 1917, ADM, 137, book 1437, 110–14.
97. Daniels diary, October 16, October 17, 1917, Cronon, ed., *Cabinet Diaries*, 221, 222.
98. Daniels diary, October 29, 1917, ibid., 228.

energetically to expedite it.[99] The decision particularly pleased the ebullient Assistant Secretary of the Navy, who by degrees made the barrage his special project, having been foiled in an earlier effort to commit the Navy Department to the production of small submarine chasers fifty feet in length. When Daniels received the report of the General Board, Roosevelt was not above writing "I told you so." He did not conceive the project, an impression he apparently tried to convey later on, but he had indeed interested himself in it from the time of the early French

BRITISH WATERS

SHETLAND ISLANDS

60°

ORKNEY ISLANDS

Scapa Flow

NORTH SEA BARRAGE AREA

Bergen

NORWAY

Skagerrak

SCOTLAND

North Sea

Rosyth

Firth of Forth

Edinburgh

55°

Dogger Bank

Heligoland

Heligoland Bight

Liverpool

IRELAND

ENGLAND

Wilhelmshaven

Queenstown

Hoofden

Rotterdam

London

Dover

Antwerp

Folkestone

Strait of Dover

Zeebrugge

Ostend

Calais

Boulogne

Falmouth

50°

English Channel

Paris

10°   5°   0°   5°

99. Daniels diary, October 30, 1917, ibid., 228–29.

and British missions of April, 1917, and he remained among its most enthusiastic proponents.[100] Sims never became wholly enthusiastic about the barrage, but like Daniels he worked loyally to further the project.

The Mayo mission moved the Admiralty to a redefinition of the grand naval strategy of Great Britain that did not alter during the rest of the war. Since Britain was the most important naval power, its outlook inevitably controlled for the most part the naval contributions of the other coalition partners, including the United States. To contain the German High Sea Fleet, Britain continued to rely primarily on the Grand Fleet:

The Grand Fleet adopts a waiting attitude in the Orkney Islands ready to attack the High Sea Fleet should a favourable opportunity arise, its attendant flotillas and submarines being used as far as possible for trade protection and hunting submarines in the northern area. The Fleet is occasionally based on Rosyth as an alternative.

As for the undersea war, the Admiralty was committed to the convoy system:

The trade outside the North Sea is mainly protected by escorting it with destroyers, etc., through the most dangerous submarine areas, and these areas are also patrolled as far as possible by destroyers, sloops, trawlers, decoy ships, and—in the vicinity of the coast—by aircraft. The efficiency of this system depends upon the number of destroyers, small craft, etc., available for hunting the submarines.[101]

The Admiralty continued to rely on American reinforcements for the expansion of the convoy system. In various requests handed to Admiral Mayo during his London visit it sought large numbers of antisubmarine craft—destroyers, trawlers, submarine chasers, tugboats, and motor launches. It also asked for the dispatch of cruisers as escorts for convoys on the long middle passage and for a squadron of four coal-burning dreadnoughts to augment the patrol of the Straits of Dover.[102]

100. For information on Roosevelt's role and attitude, see Daniels diary, October 29, 1917, ibid., 228; Carroll Kilpatrick, ed., *Roosevelt and Daniels: A Friendship in Politics* (Chapel Hill, N.C., 1952), 39–40; Freidel, *Roosevelt: The Apprenticeship*, 312–17.

101. Admiralty memorandum, "Present Naval Policy," September 17, 1917, ADM 137, book 1437, 103–9.

102. See memoranda dated September 17 and September 22, 1917, ADM 137, book 1437, 179–80, 212–13. See also the memorandum entitled

❀   ❀   ❀   ❀

If the United States had wanted to alter the general outlines of inter-Allied naval strategy, the opportunity presented itself during the early months of American belligerency. Certainly the United States influenced the decision to adopt the convoy system as a basic response to the resumption of unrestricted submarine warfare, but the essential British principles—containment of the German High Sea Fleet and defensive measures against attacks on merchant shipping—did not change. Rumblings had occurred in Washington, but incipient criticism of British practices did not engender important policy proposals because the arguments for the Admiralty principles were sound and because Admiral Sims became a strong supporter of prevailing naval doctrine after his arrival in London. Sims advocated energetic prosecution of the war, but he called for better execution rather than fundamental changes in policy.

The naval conference in London early in September contributed measurably to the improvement of inter-Allied naval coordination, but much remained to be done. This reality became apparent during the difficult fall and early winter of 1917. The submarine war seemed to be turning in favor of the western coalition, but other setbacks—failure on the Western Front, a smashing Italian defeat, and above all the defalcation of Russia in the wake of the November revolution—created a new crisis in the war comparable as a harbinger of impending defeat in 1918 to the initial impact of the war against commerce in early 1917. Indications of continuing Anglo-American differences hardly lightened the mood in Washington and London as the long winter gradually engulfed the opposing armies and navies.

"Form of future Naval assistance desired from the United States of America," September 27, 1917, Geddes Papers, ADM 116, book 1806.

CHAPTER 5

ORGANIZING THE SEA BATTLE
September–December, 1917

Despite the failure of the submarine offensive to end the war in autumn of 1917, Germany sustained its commitment to that naval initiative. Hindenburg was convinced that the undersea campaign greatly supported his efforts on land, and he was assiduous in his efforts to ensure that the Foreign Office did not vitiate its effectiveness.[1] His opponents remained alert to the danger of the submarine. Admiral Sims told the head of the Bureau of Navigation in Washington, Rear Adm. L. C. Palmer, that "the war will be lost or won according to whether we or the Huns win the submarine campaign—whether we maintain the essential lines of communication or they cut them."[2]

The German naval staff experimented with various methods of counteracting the antisubmarine tactics of the Allies. It did not implement a plan to hunt convoys with packs of submarines because U-boats were not available in sufficient numbers to cover all the convoy routes, but it tried to improve its intelligence methods and began to concentrate on operations near the shore where escorts left the convoy.[3] The blockade zones were also expanded to force dispersion of convoy escorts, lessening the threat to the submarine.[4] The High Sea Fleet undertook some surface raids on convoys in the North Sea, an attempt to force additional dispersion of escort craft.[5] Some of these raids succeeded. In October, 2 German cruisers destroyed an Allied convoy of 10 freighters and 2 destroyers on the route between Norway and Great Britain, and in December, 4 destroyers and a light cruiser sank a convoy of 6 freighters and also one of its two destroyer escorts. The German naval staff initially thought well

1. Hindenburg to Michaelis, August 3, 1917, St. Antony's Papers, reel 12, Geheime Akten, vol. 51, frame 150.

2. Sims to Palmer, October 8, 1917, USNSF, TD file.

3. Arno Spindler, *Der Handelskrieg mit U-Booten*, 4 vols. (Berlin, 1941), 4:399–400.

4. Ibid., 396; for notification from the Admiralty, see Holtzendorff to Kuehlmann, October 8 and October 28, 1917, St. Antony's Papers, reel 13, Geheime Akten, vol. 55, frames 45–47.

5. Kurt Assmann, *Deutsche Seestrategie in zwei Weltkriegen* (Heidelberg, 1957), 52–53; Reinhard Scheer, *Germany's High Sea Fleet in the World War* (London, 1920), 310.

of the prospects for additional surface raids on convoys, but the Allies riposted by utilizing larger vessels as escorts. The Germans then decided against employing vessels of their own for attack purposes.[6] The High Sea Fleet also pursued offensive operations in the Baltic Sea in order to maintain its communications with the Eastern Front and to preclude assistance to Russia.[7] All this activity stimulated false optimism. Gen. Wilhelm Groener reported in his diary that "Everyone is placing his hopes on the submarine warfare. Among the troops there is supposed to be a wide-spread hope that there will still be peace by winter."[8] These expectations were disappointed.

Dissension and inadequate organization in the German high command militated against success at sea. In October the Kaiser was forced to mediate conflicts between Holtzendorff, the head of the naval staff, and Reinhard Scheer, the admiral commanding the High Sea Fleet.[9] A separate U-boat office was finally established in December, 1917, headed by Vice Adm. Ritter von Mann-Tiechler.[10] One of its first efforts—ordering the production of many new submarines[11]—collapsed when Ludendorff refused to release labor for submarine yards, arguing that the existing force could achieve at least a 10 per cent rise in its productivity.[12] All this error would ultimately benefit the Allies, but the consequences of these German difficulties became evident only slowly during the late months of 1917 and in 1918. Submarines sank about 460,000 tons of shipping in October. In November the figure declined to 290,000 tons, but in December it jumped again to 400,000 tons. These figures reflected the partial effectiveness of the convoy system, but they also stimulated continuing alarm within the western coalition, especially given

6. For information on the raids of October and December, 1917, see Karl Galster, *England, Deutsche Flotte und Weltkrieg* (Kiel, 1925), 121; Otto Groos, *Seekriegslehren im Lichte des Weltkrieges* (Berlin, 1929), 193; *The Kaiser and His Court: The Diaries, Note Books, and Letters of Admiral Georg Alexander von Mueller, Chief of the Naval Cabinet, 1914–1918*, Walter Goerlitz, ed. (London, 1961), 318.
7. Groos, *Seekriegslehren*, 138, 213–14.
8. Wilhelm Groener, *Lebenserinnerungen: Jugend; Generalstab; Weltkrieg* (Göttingen, 1957), 559.
9. Walther Hubatsch, *Der Admiralstab und die Obersten Marinebehoerden in Deutschland, 1848–1945* (Frankfurt, 1958), 177.
10. Scheer, *Germany's High Sea Fleet*, 328.
11. Ibid., 335; Andreas Michelsen, *Der U-Bootskrieg, 1914–1918* (Leipzig, 1925), 131; Goerlitz, ed., *The Kaiser and His Court*, 318.
12. Gerald D. Feldmann, *Army, Industry, and Labor in Germany, 1914–1918* (Princeton, 1966), 444.

indications that merchant tonnage requirements would increase sharply during 1918.

The German Admiralty continued to refrain from submarine operations in American waters. By September, 1917, Germany had dropped the pretense that it was not at war with the United States, since its armies now faced U.S. troops in France, but no formal declaration of war was forthcoming. The new foreign minister, Richard Kuehlmann, thought that this tactic had helped stem the war fever in certain parts of the United States. To maintain this mood the Admiralty would not send U-boats to the American coast.[13] When the blockade zones were enlarged in October the Germans carefully left American waters open in order to avoid adverse public reactions in the United States.[14] Only in December did the Germans begin to treat maritime commerce moving to the United States as contraband; until this time it had been considered neutral shipping.[15] This policy confirmed the wisdom of Sims's earlier advice to avoid undue concentration on coast defense in home waters.

In London Sims and Page noted the success of antisubmarine measures during the fall and early winter with noticeable satisfaction, but they sustained their drumfire of requests for more and more antisubmarine craft, still convinced that the war would be decided by the outcome of the undersea war.[16] These views found their counterparts among responsible British officials.[17] Sims continued to warn the Navy Department that a refusal to respond to Allied needs might force the Entente powers to an unsatisfactory peace. Postwar investigations might then reveal that "we have not done our utmost to prevent it and that our military decisions in many cases have been unsound."[18]

13. Kuehlmann to Hindenburg, September 7, 1917, St. Antony's Papers, reel 13, Geheime Akten, vol. 53, frames 62–63.

14. Holtzendorff to Foreign Office, October 8, 1917, St. Antony's Papers, reel 13, Geheime Akten, vol. 54, frames 78–84.

15. Holtzendorff to Foreign Office, December 15, 1917, St. Antony's Papers, reel 13, Geheime Akten, vol. 57, frame 200.

16. Sims to Pratt, September 24, 1917, USNSF, TD file; Sims to L. C. Palmer, October 8, 1917, USNSF, TD file; Page to Doubleday, November 9, 1917, quoted in Burton J. Hendrick, *The Life and Letters of Walter Hines Page*, 3 vols. (Chapel Hill, N. C., 1952), 2:327.

17. Minutes of the War Cabinet (WC 247b), October 11, 1917, CAB 23, book 13 (secret minutes); Memorandum by Jellicoe, "The Influence of the Submarine upon Naval Policy and Operations," November 18, 1917, Geddes Papers, ADM 116, book 1806.

18. Sims to Pratt, November 21, 1917, USNSF, TD file.

3. Numbers of Merchant Ships Lost to Submarines in the
Atlantic during the Period of Unrestricted Submarine Warfare,
February, 1917-October, 1918

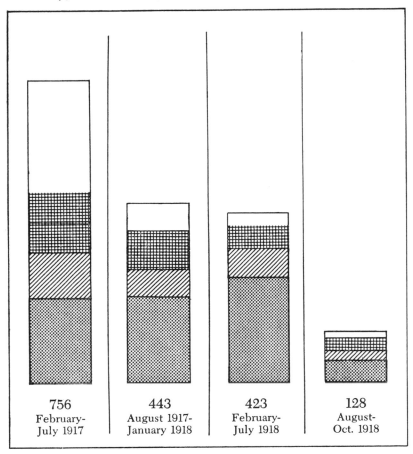

756	443	423	128
February- July 1917	August 1917- January 1918	February- July 1918	August- Oct. 1918

U. K. south and west coastal waters

North Sea and East Coast

Atlantic and Bay

Western Approaches

Source: Adapted from a chart in Arthur J. Marder, *From the Dreadnought to Scapa Flow: The Royal Navy in the Fisher Era, 1904-1919,*
vol. 5, *Victory and Aftermath (January 1918-June 1919)* (London, 1970),
116-17.

This was strong talk indeed, reflecting the fact that Sims had still not established completely satisfactory relations with the Navy Department despite continuing efforts to accomplish that end. Early in September Sims received a curious and highly indiscreet message from Lt. P. H. Bastedo, recently arrived in Europe. Before leaving the United States the young officer had conversed at length about the naval war with Mrs. Cary Grayson, the wife of the President's personal physician. Mrs. Grayson told him that the President had said in her presence that "he would like to see any plan put into effect that Admiral Sims believed would effectively do away with the submarine menace, regardless as to whether the plan were favored by the British Admiralty or the Navy Department." That evening Dr. Grayson himself called on Bastedo to discuss the matter further, apparently to relieve the fears of his wife that she had been indiscreet. The doctor, himself a rear admiral, confirmed the report of his spouse. "He said that the President would like to see the submarine menace done away with speedily; that the President had given him to understand that the British had fallen into a rut." Grayson also claimed that he had urged upon Wilson the appointment of Sims. Bastedo reported further that an arrangement had been made to ensure attention in the Navy Department to Sims's requests. Clearly the general tenor of Bastedo's information was to convey to Sims the message that he would receive support from the highest authority against any opposition.[19]

Sims was much disturbed by this episode, realizing that to act on such information was to fish in extremely troubled waters. He determined ultimately to report the whole matter confidentially to Admiral Benson. After reviewing the information that Bastedo had offered, Sims pointed out that "there was no statement made that the President directed that the above information be conveyed to me, and I of course do not assume that he did so. . . . I have done nothing in connection with this message from Dr. Grayson, and do not propose to do anything." He noted that Bastedo should not have agreed to deliver such a message, but excused the lieutenant because of his youth.[20] In

19. Bastedo to Sims, September 9, 1917, USNSF, TD file. A copy is also in the Sims Papers.
20. Sims to Benson, September 27, 1917, USNSF, TD file. A copy is in the Sims Papers.

this manner, Sims conveyed to the Department his loyalty, despite differences of view between himself and Washington.

As Sims prepared his communication to Benson, the Chief of Naval Operations dispatched one of his own to the Force Commander in Europe. He informed Sims that Pratt had circulated some of his letters, but that he had stopped reading them because of the "constant spirit of criticism and complaint that pervaded them at all times" and the intimation that Pratt and a few others were the only efficient officers in the Navy Department. He expressed appreciation of Sims's work, but also his feeling that Sims did not understand the full dimensions of the difficulties being encountered in Washington. He was surprised that no general plan of operations had come from the Admiralty and complained of the British failure to send full information on mining questions. With these animadversions out of the way Benson told Sims that he was sending authority for the Force Commander to redistribute his forces as he wished in European waters, subject to Admiralty approval. He also told Sims that the Navy Department was unwilling to send over coal-burning dreadnoughts unless definite plans were forthcoming for their employment. At the end he admitted his unusual frankness, but explained that he wanted to clarify the situation in order to guarantee the fullest cooperation between the Navy Department and Sims. "This is the absolute and full intention of this office and will continue to be so under all conditions."[21]

The inauguration of the Sims-Benson correspondence, despite its early subject matter, led by degrees to better coordination. Sims continued to press his requests for additional staff and to improve communications between Washington and London.[22] He sought to define his role as an intermediary between the Navy Department and the Admiralty in ways designed to strengthen the confidence of Benson and others in his good faith:

The organization under Admiral Sims has been established in London with the primary purpose of serving as the co-ordinating link between the Admiralty and the U.S. Navy Department, to keep it informed of the progress of the war, to take up with the Admiralty

21. Benson to Sims, September 24, 1917, USNSF, TD file. The authority to redistribute his forces came in Benson to Sims, October 2, 1917, USNSF, UP file.
22. Sims to Benson, October 9, 1917, USNSF, TD file.

and interpret the Admiralty's views and wishes in all questions of naval activity which may arise.[23]

This description must have been satisfactory to the Navy Department, and Benson made every effort to separate personal feelings from professional considerations.

If Sims slowly but surely imposed many of his desires upon the Navy Department, he did not succeed in all his enterprises. The Department continued to oppose the dispatch of the coal-burning dreadnoughts Sims had been requesting for several months. In October the London headquarters received important and unexpected support from one member of the General Board, who adduced arguments of a much different nature than those offered by Sims. A memorandum by Captain Belknap argued in the first place that a refusal to dispatch capital ships "will be invoked in future against building of large vessels"; but he thought the major consideration one of "prestige." The Navy should seize every possible opportunity to take part in the war. "There should be no possibility of anyone, at home or abroad, hostile, allied, or neutral, forming the opinion that we are performing an auxiliary or secondary part in the military prosecution of the war." The Navy ought to participate actively in all important engagements. "It is of the first importance to our present and future prestige to have the Navy of the United States in a principal role in every prominent event."[24] These arguments did not prevail immediately, but they were indicative of the fact that Sims's requests were by no means uniformly suspect in all quarters of the Navy Department.

Sims managed in late 1917 to make two arrangements that improved his position vis-à-vis the Navy Department. One was a successful campaign to remove the naval attaché in London, Captain McDougall, and have himself appointed in his place. "This [action]," he told Pratt, "will enable us to avoid numerous cross wires and no inconsiderable amount of irritation."[25] A

23. Sims memorandum, October 11, 1917, ADM 137, book 1437, 251. For information on new modes of communication discussed on October 17, 1917, see ADM 137, book 1437, 254–58.

24. Belknap memorandum, October 19, 1917, Records of the General Board.

25. Sims to Pratt, November 21, 1917, USNSF, TD file. For his formal notification of appointment to the Admiralty, see Sims to Secretary of the Admiralty, December 12, 1917, ADM 137, book 1437, 282.

second and vastly more important accomplishment was the establishment of a "Planning Section" in the London headquarters. There had been growing interest in this innovation. The American author Winston Churchill, continuing his interest in naval affairs, on October 22 wrote to President Wilson urging that, "unquestionably the most important, indeed the essential thing still to be achieved is that of partnership between our Service and the British. It must be a full partnership." To accomplish part of this objective he proposed "a combined staff of American and British strategists and material officers to sit constantly together to exert their entire energies upon making plans for the future conduct of the war."[26]

Similar thoughts were developing in London. On October 28, one of Sims's subordinates drafted a memorandum discussing the failure to establish fully effective relations with the Admiralty, despite that organization's open offer of full communication. The will to cooperation was present, but not the way. "The fault lies with the Machinery of carrying out the willingness which seems to be existent on both sides." What could be done? The author suggested American representation "when the various officials of the Admiralty are assembled in confidence with a view of reaching important decisions as to operations or policy."[27] This line of thought culminated in an effort somewhat later to make Admiral Sims an honorary member of the Board of Admiralty. It also was part of the process leading to a recommendation to the President similar to that of Churchill's that officers be sent to improve communications with the Admiralty.[28]

In November Admiral Benson finally bowed to concerted pressure from both Sims and his British colleagues and approved the creation of a planning section that would allow American officers to improve communications with the Admiralty. Despite his support of the proposal Benson remained wary of British purposes. He insisted that "the officers detailed for this duty

26. Churchill to Wilson, October 22, 1917, Daniels Papers.
27. "Hasty Estimate of Situation Concerning Methods of Cooperation Between This Organization [London], Admiralty and Navy Department," October 28, 1917, USNSF, TT file.
28. Sims to Benson, October 18, 1917, USNSF, TD file. Perhaps this message resulted from the memorandum cited in the preceding note.

should come here [London] fully imbued with our national and naval policy and ideas."[29] Sims, much pleased, made considerable use of the planning section in 1918.[30] Its mission was "to make studies of particular problems, to prepare plans for future operations, and also to criticise fully the organization and methods which were already in existence."[31] The planning section, composed of a group of unusually talented officers who were greatly devoted to Admiral Sims, did exactly as desired, working in tandem with Admiralty planners, and made significant contributions to the Anglo-American effort during the decisive stages of the war.[32]

Sims also remained unchallenged in his position as the highest ranking official of the United States Navy in Europe. In September Franklin Roosevelt had contemplated the prospect of establishing himself in Europe as the civilian head of an organization to coordinate the Anglo-American naval effort. One of Sims's correspondents reported that the Assistant Secretary had urged the plan on several occasions, "but I gathered that there was no inclination to accept it on the part of higher authorities." Once again the irrepressible Roosevelt failed to bring off a scheme to promote his more active participation in the war.[33]

These improvements in the relationship between the Navy Department and the headquarters of Admiral Sims in London took place as the United States and Great Britain experienced a depressing phase of their wartime collaboration. The great conflict took its toll on the emotions of the officials of both nations as the year ran its dreary course. Despite the Mayo mission, the Navy Department remained suspicious that the British Admiralty was less than fully responsive to the demands of the war. Information coming to Sims and to the British Government reported these feelings. Daniels was supposed to harbor the belief that Britain was not making a maximum effort.[34] Benson was angry at "being kept in the dark on important matters,"

29. Benson to Navy Department, November 19, 1917, USNSF, UP file.

30. Sims to Pratt, November 21, 1917, USNSF, TD file.

31. William Sowden Sims, in collaboration with Burton J. Hendrick, *The Victory at Sea* (Garden City, N.Y., 1920), 253.

32. For a detailed review of its activities, see Planning Section Memorandum No. 71, "History of Planning Section," December 30, 1918, USNSF, TX file, "Planning Section."

33. Pleadwell to Sims, September 13, 1917, USNSF, TD file.

34. Ibid.

according to the British naval attaché in Washington who talked confidentially with the Chief of Naval Operations. "The conversation was a private one, but he spoke so bitterly I thought I should let you [Jellicoe] know."[35] Spring Rice also caught this mood. Recommending strongly that Captain Gaunt be recalled to Britain for consultations, since he possessed the "full confidence" of the Americans, the Ambassador relayed familiar observations: "They are willing to do anything we ask but hope that Admiralty will be more frank with them as impression prevails that we are reserved as to reasons why we make our requests. There is a suspicion that we are unwilling to take them into full partnership and they believe that Sims is under too much British influence."[36] The Foreign Office approved the Gaunt mission, but angrily denied the truth of the allegations made in Washington. "There is . . . no foundation whatever for the impression which is stated to prevail in the Navy Department that they are not being treated with frankness by the Admiralty. It seems possible that this impression may be produced by credence being given to false rumours which reach the United States."[37] Despite public protestations of pleasure at the activities of the Mayo mission, the British Government was actually somewhat disappointed. On September 17, Admiral Jellicoe and General Robertson both complained of American inaction at a meeting of the War Cabinet. "Admiral Mayo's attitude was mainly one of apology owing to his not having the power to make any decisions." The two officials were ordered to provide information on means of improving cooperation. The Cabinet also considered the possibility of recalling Spring Rice, who was very unpopular in Washington, and extending the stay of the Lord Chief Justice, the Marquess of Reading, who had been dispatched to rationalize British purchasing activities in the United States. This step might lessen confusion stemming from the separate and sometimes conflicting activities of Spring Rice, Northcliffe, and Reading.[38]

35. Gaunt to Jellicoe, September 9, 1917, ADM 137, book 1437, 318.
36. Spring Rice to Foreign Office, received September 13, 1917, ADM 137, book 1437, 319.
37. Foreign Office to Spring Rice, September 18, 1917, ADM 137, book 1437, 321. A similar message went out, in Foreign Office to Spring Rice, September 21, 1917, ADM 137, book 1437, 326.
38. Minutes of the War Cabinet (WC 234), September 17, 1917, CAB 23, book 4.

Balfour, Geddes, and Jellicoe proceeded through Ambassador Page to communicate to the United States the British reaction to reports that they had not been fully cooperative. Page reported: "They assure me that there could be no greater mistake and that they have given all information asked for and volunteered all that has occurred to Admiralty officials as likely to be useful and that everything has been and is open to our Admirals and our Government." Sims and Mayo, he said, would confirm this attitude. Geddes suspected that some troublemaker was causing difficulties. Page believed that "misunderstanding has arisen because personal acquaintance and contact are lacking between naval authorities in Washington and London." The British were anxious for another exchange of views.[39]

Spring Rice continued to report American suspicions. Noting that the Americans considered the British "unnecessarily reserved," the Ambassador gave an explanation for some lack of full consultation. "One reason why reserve is necessary is the German spy system and the want of precautions here." Fortunately Lord Reading's mission would help to improve relations. Having delivered himself of his customary dark suspicions of German intrigue, the Ambassador communicated more useful comments. "Mr. Page, like Admiral Sims, and most American officials on your side, are considered to be too much under your influence. It would be dangerous to take their advice as representing the opinion of their Government unless expressly authorised to do so." Most important, however, was his observation on the President. "He wants to keep his situation of aloofness with a view to the peace negotiations, he wants to convince the American people that he has not entered into any entangling alliance, and he does not trust any representative except one [House]. He has as great an aversion to special commissioners as you have an affection for them."[40]

The episode ended satisfactorily. Spring Rice soon reported that on a visit to the Navy Department both Benson and Daniels expressed full confidence in Great Britain.[41] Daniels's response

39. Page to Lansing and Wilson, September 21, 1917, USDSM 367, 762.73/6955. See also Page to Wilson, September 25, 1917, Wilson Papers, box 127. The "troublemaker" was identified as Arthur Pollen.
40. Spring Rice to Balfour, September 21, 1917, Cabinet Papers, no. 444 (1917), FO 899, book 13.
41. Spring Rice to Balfour, September 27, 1917, Cabinet Papers, no. 454 (1917), FO 899, book 13.

to the Page message was succinct. "I answered that we had no such view and could not imagine how such an impression had been implanted."[42] Acting Secretary of State Frank Polk cabled to Page: "There is absolutely no foundation for any such impression and the Department is at a loss to know where such ideas could have arisen." He stated that all American representatives sent to London "had assured us of perfect freedom in regard to all such matters and of the fullest and heartiest cooperation from the First Lord of the Admiralty down."[43] Daniels repeated this view on October 10, when Spring Rice called upon him to present Lord Reading.[44] In order to avoid another contretemps, Spring Rice continued to counsel caution, particularly in regard to the dispatch of emissaries to Washington without the prior consent of the President.[45] British officials now began to suggest that Admiral Benson make a visit to Europe.[46]

This little incident, unimportant by itself, illustrated the continuing problems of effective Anglo-American coordination, but it also indicated a broad desire in both countries to maintain effective cooperation in matters relating to the naval war.

During the period September–November, 1917, the United States and Great Britain began most seriously to consider the merchant shipping problems with which they were confronted. The depredations of the submarine and the demand for ships to transport the American troops to Europe forced to the surface some hard questions. How much merchant shipping should be constructed in Britain and America? What percentage of the available tonnage should be allocated to carry American troops to Europe? Officials in London and Paris became increasingly concerned. André Tardieu, the French purchasing agent in the United States, complained of the difficulty of obtaining shipping in Washington because of plans to use all available for the

42. Daniels diary, September 27, 1917, E. David Cronon, ed., *The Cabinet Diaries of Josephus Daniels, 1913–1921* (Lincoln, 1963), 212.

43. Polk to Page, September 29, 1917, USDSM 367, 763.72/6955.

44. Daniels diary, October 10, 1917, Cronon, ed., *Cabinet Diaries*, 218. Spring Rice also reported a cordial exchange. Spring Rice to Balfour, October 11, 1917, FO 371, book 3112. See also Benson to Jellicoe, October 22, 1917, USNSF, TT file.

45. Spring Rice to Balfour, October 12, 1917, Cabinet Papers, no. 467 (1917), FO 899, book 13.

46. Page to Wilson, September 25, 1917, Wilson Papers, box 127; Geddes to Daniels, October 13, 1917, Geddes Papers, ADM 116, book 1605.

transport of American troops. Gen. Ferdinand Foch, the French chief of staff at this time, wanted to call an inter-Allied conference to settle the problem.[47] In London the War Cabinet instructed Balfour to communicate the British concern to Wilson through Colonel House.[48] Balfour's message indicated that the coalition would have to produce some 8 million tons of shipping per year in order to meet minimum needs. Of this amount the United States was advised to construct 6 million tons; the British would build about 2.5 million. Like Foch, the Foreign Secretary was also concerned about American troop transport.[49]

Aside from the obvious question of industrial priorities in both nations, each country suspected that the other was developing wartime shipping policy with an eye to international trade in peacetime. Each laid plans to ensure that the other utilized its shipping in terms of immediate military necessities.[50] Needless to say, these suspicions hardly contributed to a constructive negotiating atmosphere. Spring Rice reported ominously that there was, in the United States, "an under current of feeling that, by the end of the war, America will have all the ships and all the gold in the world, and that the hegemony probably of the world, and certainly of the Anglo-Saxon race, will pass across the Atlantic."[51] Controversies at the time over an American decision to commandeer ships building for Britain in the United States, the question of who would pay for facilities being constructed for American forces in Europe, and control of neutral shipping stirred additional misgivings on either side of the Atlantic.[52]

47. *United States Army in the World War*, 17 vols., *Policy-Forming Documents* (Washington, D.C., 1948), 2:51.

48. Minutes of the War Cabinet (WC 246), October 8, 1917, CAB 23, book 4.

49. Balfour to House, October 11, 1917, Charles Seymour, ed., *The Intimate Papers of Colonel House*, 4 vols., *Into the World War* (Boston, 1928), 3:190–93. See also Minutes of the War Cabinet (WC 247b), October 11, 1917, CAB 23, book 13 (secret minutes).

50. Daniels diary, October 11, 1917, Cronon, ed., *Cabinet Diaries*, 219; Minutes of the War Cabinet (WC 253), October 19, 1917, CAB 23, book 4.

51. Spring Rice to Balfour, October 25, 1917, Cabinet Papers, no. 494 (1917), FO 899, book 13. For an example of American suspicions, see Knox to Sims, November 6, 1917, Sims Papers.

52. For information on these matters, see United States Department of State, *Papers Relating to the Foreign Relations of the United States: 1917*, supp. 2, 2 vols., *The World War* (Washington, D.C., 1932), 1:622–40;

Ultimately, these problems were resolved, but the most important immediate issue remained unsettled—that of shipping demands created by the imminent dispatch of many American troops. The British remained doubtful that the American reinforcement on land could become really effective before 1919.[53] Given indications that the United States was contemplating use of its shipping primarily to supply its own army, the War Cabinet became increasingly alarmed,[54] as did British representatives in the United States. Arthur Murray, a British journalist, put the problem concisely to Balfour's private secretary. "If there is sent abroad a larger number of [American] troops than ought, having regard to other urgent requirements, to be sent across, the demands for shipping to keep and maintain them there will grow, and the situation vis-à-vis Allied necessities would become acute."[55]

Admiral Sims was similarly concerned, and he had recourse to Admiral Benson in order to sound warnings. American troop shipments should be considered in relation to the over-all war effort, with a careful eye to the ability of Britain and France to receive them. His solution to the difficulty was also in accord with British thinking—an inter-Allied conference to settle the question.[56] On November 16, he discussed the reasons for the difficulty in a letter to Captain Pratt. Problems of this nature always arose between allies. They were "founded upon a certain measure of distrust as to the intentions of the various countries and [they had] a direct bearing upon the probable condition of their over-sea trade after the war." He thought "the rivalries of great shipping companies also exert a very powerful influence." All in all, the necessary degree of coordination could be antici-

Balfour to Spring Rice, October 26, 1917, Cabinet Papers, no. 408 (1917), FO 899, book 13; Admiralty memorandum, "Responsibility for Cost of Establishing United States Seaplane Stations in England," October 27, 1917, Geddes Papers, ADM 116, book 1806.

53. For the opinion of Lloyd George that "Judging from the precedent of our own Army we ought not to count on any great assistance from the United States of America before 1919," see Minutes of the War Cabinet (WC 247b), October 11, 1917, CAB 23, book 13 (secret minutes).

54. Minutes of the War Cabinet (WC 259), October 29, 1917, CAB 23, book 4.

55. Arthur Murray to Drummond, October 23, 1917, Lloyd George Papers, file F/60/2/34. See also Reading to Lloyd George, November 1, 1917, Lloyd George Papers, file F/60/2/35.

56. Sims to Benson, October 28, 1917, USNSF, TD file.

pated "until we reach the point where all of the Allies are more or less seriously alarmed as to the probable outcome of the war. As this condition has now been reached," he concluded, "I believe we may look for a degree of cooperation in this respect that we have never had before."[57] Sims, as always, reflected not only British viewpoints but his own very considerable inclination to political realism.

The incalculable pressures of the war continued to fray Anglo-American temper and judgment. Secretary Daniels observed that the President was looking "weary—war-torn." Wilson "rather quizzically" told the Secretary: "My mother did not raise her boy to be a War President—but it is a liberal education."[58] The situation moved Spring Rice to new heights of paranoia. To Balfour he wrote: "You will notice that there are three sorts of Universalists who seem an especial danger to the Allies. The Catholics, the Socialists, the Jews. Germany's attitude is that Universalism, as being hostile to the national spirit, is to be suppressed in Germany but encouraged elsewhere."[59]

All these circumstances contributed to a growing realization among the Allied and Associated Powers that improved means of coordinating this over-all political-military effort must be arranged at no very distant time. It became quite apparent that the Central Powers would make a final supreme effort to win the war in 1918—encouraged by their defensive victory in France, offensive success against Italy, and the complete collapse of Russia. The condition predicted by Admiral Sims was coming to pass. The exigencies of the war would force an enhanced degree of coordination in all spheres—in the naval as well as military, political, financial, industrial, and logistical areas. The result was a gradual trend toward a great inter-Allied conclave in order to settle methods of cooperation for the final phase of the war. Lloyd George began this movement in September, 1917, writing

57. Sims to Pratt, November 16, Sims Papers. A copy is in USNSF, TD file. For an early estimate of the question, see Sims to Pratt, September 24, 1917, USNSF, TD file. Dudley Knox informed Sims that "naval circles" questioned the frankness of the British. "They are strongly influenced by fears that after the war we are going to be an uncomfortably strong trade rival." Knox to Sims, November 6, 1917, Sims Papers.

58. Daniels diary, November 26, 1917, Cronon, ed., *Cabinet Diaries*, 242.

59. Spring Rice to Balfour, November 30, 1917, Cabinet Papers, no. 7 (1918), FO 899, book 14.

a remarkable letter to President Wilson in which he argued that "the comparative failure of the Allies in 1917 is . . . in some measure due to defects in their mutual arrangements for conducting the war." He had in mind, in order "to establish effective unity in the direction of the war on the Allied side," to create "some kind of Allied Joint Council, with permanent military and probably naval and economic staffs attached to work out the plans for the Allies, for submission to the several Governments concerned."[60]

The United States Government did not respond quickly to this message, but the idea continued to interest the British. As Anglo-American relations became more complicated, the War Cabinet considered proposing the dispatch to Europe of Colonel House, or perhaps Secretary of War Newton D. Baker, in order to improve communications.[61] Sims dutifully began to consider comparable projects. On October 15, he suggested to Pratt that a visit from Admiral Benson might help to clear the air. "I am sure he would go back enlightened to a degree that I have not been able to accomplish." He also thought that it would be "extremely useful" if Daniels made the trip. His greatest enthusiasm, however, was for a trip by the President himself. "The finest thing of all would be for the world to come to their breakfast tables some fine morning and find that President Wilson had landed in London for a conference with the Allies. There is nothing that I could think of that would have the moral effect that this would have."[62]

By degrees the British proposal that the United States send a mission to an inter-Allied conference became acceptable in Washington. Allied importunities and German successes forced the hand of the President,[63] and he ultimately decided to send Colonel House to Europe at the head of a strong delegation; Admiral Benson was to accompany him as a naval representa-

60. Lloyd George to Wilson, September 3, 1917, Wilson Papers. It is printed in David Lloyd George, *War Memoirs of David Lloyd George*, 6 vols., 1917 (Boston, 1934), 4:518–24. For an account of its drafting and approval, see Lord (Maurice) Hankey, *The Supreme Command: 1914–1918*, 2 vols. (London, 1961), 2:694–96.

61. Minutes of the War Cabinet (WC 241), September 28, 1917, CAB 23, book 4.

62. Sims to Pratt, October 15, 1917, Sims Papers.

63. David F. Trask, *The United States in the Supreme War Council: American War Aims and Inter-Allied Strategy, 1917–1918* (Middletown, Conn., 1961), 15–16. See also Seymour, ed., *Intimate Papers*, 3:203.

tive. Spring Rice summarized the reasons for the American decision quite perspicaciously:

His [Wilson's] change of view with regard to representation on the War Council is very significant. You are aware of the reasons why the President objected. He was a co-belligerent but not an Ally. He had no end in common with the other Allies but an ideal one. There was no practical bond of union, and there was therefore no practical co-operation. But now he realised that before his ideal ends can be obtained, the war must be won, and he feels that this is a practical proposition to be accomplished by practical means, the first and foremost of which is co-operation. I have no doubt that there will be a growing desire to ensure co-operation here.[64]

Wilson carefully circumscribed his acceptance of the invitation to dispatch a mission to the forthcoming inter-Allied conference. He made certain that the gathering was considered a council of war about practical military measures rather than a major diplomatic negotiation dealing with ultimate aims, an approach quite in accord with his desire to help defeat the Central Powers without committing the United States to embarrassing or dangerous political entanglements.[65]

The House mission arrived in Europe on November 7, amidst an atmosphere of crisis. Lloyd George was that day meeting with the premiers of France and Italy in Rapallo, Italy, in order to establish the Supreme War Council, an agency designed to coordinate the complete political-military activities of the western coalition. The British Prime Minister had matured the project outlined to President Wilson in September, assisted by the crisis that followed the great military defeat of Italy at Caporetto in late October. Also on November 7, the Bolsheviks successfully overthrew the Russian provisional government, an event that precipitated an early armistice on the Eastern Front. The American mission had planned to remain in London for only a few days, but its stay was extended for some three weeks. The inter-Allied conference in Paris was postponed until the end of No-

64. Spring Rice to Balfour, Cabinet Papers, no. 494 (1917), FO 899, book 13.
65. Lansing to American Embassy, November 8, 1917, USNSF, VP file, "Diplomatic Policies and Plans, including Peace Plans." This message carefully explained the important but limited purposes of the United States for the information of the Ambassador and his staff.

vember, because of the ominous events in Italy and Russia and political crises in both France and Britain. Georges Clemenceau emerged at just this time as the war leader of France. Lloyd George had to fight hard in Parliament to retain his position, a consequence of political disturbances associated with the creation of the Supreme War Council.[66]

Three days after the mission reached Britain, Admiral Benson took the first step toward general acceptance of the naval viewpoints expressed by the British Admiralty and Admiral Sims. On November 10, Daniels received a message from Benson recommending the dispatch of the four coal-burning dreadnoughts Sims had been requesting since the summer. The ships were sent soon thereafter.[67] Decisions now came more quickly; the crisis would not brook delay. Ambassador Sharp caught the meaning of contemporary events. "Just now the watchword is, concert of action and unity of command. May its importance come soon to be realized to be as great as the unity of the very purpose to win the war itself."[68]

The arrangement for a Supreme War Council included provision for a group of permanent military representatives to offer expert counsel on land warfare. From the first, Lloyd George contemplated a parallel group of naval advisers, but this arrangement did not materialize at the Rapallo conference. On November 15, the matter came up in the British War Cabinet. Jellicoe informed the group that the Italians were about to request naval reinforcements in the Mediterranean. "This raised the question of naval co-operation in the new Supreme War Council. The view was expressed that centralization of naval control was equally desirable to that of military control, but that it should be a separate organisation and have its headquarters in London."[69] The latter proviso balanced the fact that the Supreme

66. For a detailed discussion of the founding of the Supreme War Council and the activities of the American mission, see Trask, *United States in the Supreme War Council*, 20–38. For Sims's comments on these events, see Sims to Pratt, November 16, 1917, Sims Papers. A copy is in USNSF, TD file.

67. Daniels diary, November 10, 1917, Cronon, ed., *Cabinet Diaries*, 235.

68. Sharp to Wilson, November 12, 1917, Wilson Papers, box 129.

69. Minutes of the War Cabinet (WC 274), November 15, 1917, CAB 23, book 4.

War Council and its military representatives were to be established at Versailles, but it also reflected the desire of the British Government to maintain preponderant influence over the conduct of the naval war.

Although Colonel House and others were critical of some aspects of the arrangement for a Supreme War Council, they strongly favored an effective institution to coordinate the war effort of the western coalition. The President made comparable feelings abundantly clear in a message to Colonel House. The time had come for much more active American influence. "Take the whip hand. We not only accede to the plan for a unified conduct of the war but insist upon it. It is not practicable for us to be represented *in the same way* as the other governments on the civil side, but we will be on the military."[70] The Supreme War Council was made up of the head of government and one other representative from Britain, France, Italy, and the United States. The United States did not seat a political representative, hoping by this device to avoid undesirable political entanglements, but Gen. Tasker H. Bliss, the retiring Chief of Staff of the United States Army, was made the American military representative.[71] On November 16, the General Board signified its approval of greater coordination, recommending "appointment of a joint interallied agency to coordinate and direct the military and naval operations of the allies."[72] The stage was set for American participation in the deliberations of a naval coordinating agency, but there was a brief delay while the arrangements were completed for what was to become the Allied Naval Council.[73]

On November 20, Sims and Benson had dinner with Sir Eric Geddes, Admiral Jellicoe, and some other Admiralty officials;

70. Quoted from a draft of a message to House written by the President, ca. November 15, 1917, Wilson Papers, box 129. See also Seymour, ed., *Intimate Papers*, 3:220. See also McAdoo to Wilson, November 15, 1917, Wilson Papers, box 129.

71. Trask, *United States in the Supreme War Council*, 32–34.

72. Badger to Daniels, November 16, 1917, Records of the General Board.

73. When Daniels discovered that Bliss was to become the American military representative, he asked Wilson whether a naval representative would be needed. Wilson thought that one should be appointed, but noted that none had as yet been arranged for. Daniels to Wilson, November 21, 1917, Wilson Papers, box 130; Wilson to Daniels, November 22, 1917, Wilson Papers, box 130.

then and there the final form of the proposed naval group took shape. Sims summarized its composition and procedure for Captain Pratt:

The idea agreed upon was to have a council composed of the Chiefs of Staff of the various Admiralties concerned, except that I would represent our Navy Department. This Council [was] to meet at stated intervals and also as often as the council itself might consider necessary outside the regular meetings. . . . It would be composed of representatives of United States, Great Britain, France, Italy, and Japan.[74]

On November 26, the Board of Admiralty approved the proposal for an Allied Naval Council, defining its mission as "to watch over the general naval conduct of the war and the coordination of naval action." It would "make recommendations for the decision of the Governments, and keep itself informed of their execution, and report thereon to the respective Governments as may be necessary." Each national naval staff would be obligated to communicate its general policies to the Allied Naval Council in order to ensure that it was "kept informed of the general progress of events, and determine upon methods that will ensure complete co-operation and that the best disposition is being made of the forces employed."[75]

A French observer clearly identified the principal motivations of Great Britain in forcing the establishment of the Allied Naval Council. Pressure to coordinate the naval effort had been developing in London. The British also wanted a naval institution in which they would exercise great influence to counterbalance in some degree the French predominance in military planning. It was also a function of the desires of those in the Admiralty who wished to adopt a more active offensive policy as against the defensive orientation of Jellicoe. The makeup of the council was an effort to avoid the complications that had arisen in connection with the arrangement for the permanent military representatives; Lloyd George had opposed appointing the military

74. Sims to Pratt, November 21, 1917, Sims Papers. A copy is in USNSF, TD file.
75. Minutes of the Board of Admiralty, November 26, 1917, ADM 167, book 53; Daniels to Benson, November 26, 1917, USNSF, QC file. See also Daniels diary, November 26, 1917, Cronon, ed., *Cabinet Diaries*, 242.

chiefs of staff to this body because of his dislike for General Robertson.[76]

The preliminaries to the first meeting of the Allied Naval Council, scheduled for Paris during the sessions of the inter-Allied conference, were now completed; while these events took place Admiral Benson in London immersed himself in discussions of inter-Allied naval questions with Admiralty officials. On November 20, the House mission met with Lloyd George in the most important of its preliminary meetings while in London. The Prime Minister observed that the United States should prepare troops as rapidly as possible for service in France, "so as to be able to sustain the brunt of any German attack in the course of the next year." His second point was that the United States must extend its ship production "at an unprecedented rate." Benson indicated that "the principal factor in the whole of American cooperation was that of shipping, and that without ships it was impossible for men or material to be transported from the United States." Bainbridge Colby, the American shipping representative, reported that the United States would provide 4.6 million tons of shipping by the end of 1918, and about 6 million tons by May, 1919. Benson did not neglect to express the traditional American support for freedom of the seas, something that hardly pleased the British. "In order that the various countries of the world may carry on their trade and may be of real assistance to each other," proclaimed the American Admiral, "there must be free communication, and that communication can only be carried on through the freedom of the seas."[77] To raise this issue was to pose a challenge to British imperialism, and certainly Lloyd George, like a famous successor, did not intend to preside over the liquidation of the British Empire. Even in the midst of a great crisis, which imposed upon the western coalition the necessity of the closest possible coordination, Benson could not resist comments on the subject most likely to alienate his coadjutors in London.

Despite his jarring comments on freedom of the seas Benson was obviously impressed by the information he gathered in Lon-

76. Memorandum on the ANC, November 22, 1917, MM, Es file, box 14.

77. Report of Anglo-American discussion, November 20, 1917, CAB 28, book 3. For the American report, see Department of State, 1917, supp. 2, vol. 1, The World War, 366–84.

don. Sims was jubilant, informing Admiral Bayly in Queenstown that the Chief of Naval Operations was "recommending practically all the measures that I have been recommending during the past six months." He thought it a "great pity" that no mission had come to Europe when the United States had entered the war, but he was pleased that Washington would now be sufficiently informed on the needs of the Entente powers. He was also hopeful that "all of the Allies are now sufficiently apprehensive to get down to business."[78] Colonel House impressed Sims. He told Captain Pratt that while the Colonel's habits were "rather peculiar," he had "no doubt that he is doing a very valuable stunt."[79] The Colonel himself altered some of his previous opinions on naval questions. Admiral Jellicoe managed to convince him that American preferences for close-in offensives were unsound, although House reported that Benson had successfully advocated a further attempt to close the Straits of Dover to submarines.[80]

The stage was now set for a preliminary meeting of the Allied Naval Council. Sitting for the first time in Paris on November 29–30, 1917, the council devoted itself largely to a discussion of its constitution. Sir Eric Geddes gained acceptance to his proposal that the council be made up of the naval chiefs of staff with "the object of making their agreement more complete and in order to follow naval warfare in a joint study and to decide together on the manner and conditions of making the best use of all the Allied Resources."[81] Other discussion was less important; before substantive matters could be discussed it was necessary to obtain agreement of the various members to the proposed constitution of the council and to prepare working papers for its first official session in January. Certainly Great Britain manifested far more interest in the formation of the council than did the other powers. Geddes obviously hoped that it would help to energize the Italian Navy and to improve Anglo-American cooperation.

78. Sims to Bayly, November 20, 1917, Sims Papers. See also Daniels diary, November 21, 1917, Cronon, ed., *Cabinet Diaries*, 239.

79. Sims to Pratt, November 21, 1917, Sims Papers.

80. House diary, November 21, 1917, quoted in Seymour, ed., *Intimate Papers*, 3:236.

81. Minutes of the First Session, ANC, November 29–30, 1917, USNSF, QC file. French minutes are available in MM, Es file, box 13.

On December 1, Benson asked Daniels to seek American assent to the proposed constitution for the Allied Naval Council. He reported that House approved it and that no announcement of its existence was to be made until the member governments had reported their concurrence.[82] Public announcement of the formation of the Allied Naval Council was made on December 14, and Sims was officially designated as the American member on January 8, 1918.[83]

Admiral Sims later praised the work of the council, claiming that membership on it became the most important of his assignments during 1918. "Without this council," he wrote, "and without the cooperation for which it stood, our efforts would have been so dispersed and would have so overlapped that their efficiency would have been greatly decreased."[84] Lloyd George was similarly impressed by the Allied Naval Council, considering it amazing that no such institution had been formed before December, 1917. "The sea front was as essential to victory as the Western or any other front, and it was impossible rightly to judge the wisdom or otherwise of the general campaign without understanding thoroughly how the command of the sea would affect the military situation and especially the economic conditions which determined the equipment and morale of the various belligerents."[85] Although the Allied Naval Council by no means accomplished all that was expected of it, it was a useful institution through which the Allied and Associated Powers arranged those over-all naval plans on which they were able to agree. It also helped to clarify the circumstances that precluded effective cooperation on other matters. Its formation was certainly not the least of the accomplishments of the great inter-Allied meeting in Paris.

When the House mission returned to Washington various members submitted formal reports of their activities. The mission leader was greatly disturbed by European conditions, although he believed that the western coalition had taken important forward steps in Paris. "What discourages one most in

82. Benson to Daniels, December 1, 1917, USNSF, QC file.
83. Daniels diary, December 14, 1917, Cronon, ed., *Cabinet Diaries*, 250; Sims to Navy Department, January 4, 1918, USNSF, QC file; Daniels to Sims, January 8, 1917, USNSF, QC file.
84. Sims, *Victory at Sea*, 257.
85. Lloyd George, *War Memoirs*, 4:515.

the whole situation is the lack of unity of control and action. There is but little coordination anywhere between the Allies." Inter-Allied jealousies were at the root of the problem. "None of them at heart like each other, and I doubt whether any of them like us. It is the thought of 'hanging together or separately' that keeps them going. Fortunately a like condition exists in the Central Alliance."[86]

This general attitude pervaded the reports of other participants, including that of Admiral Benson.[87] Like Colonel House, he believed that "all countries opposed to Germany in this war, except ourselves, are jealous and suspicious of one another." Unlike Colonel House, he thought that the Entente powers "believe . . . in the sincerity and unselfishness of the United States; and feeling thus, they are not only willing for the United States to take the lead in matters which affect our common cause; but they are really anxious that we should dominate the entire allied situation." Convinced that no additional naval assistance of real significance could come from France and Italy, Benson reverted to his earlier view that the burden of war might eventually devolve upon an Anglo-American combination standing alone against the Central Powers. These considerations indicated an early and imposing reinforcement. "I believe that no time should be lost nor should any effort be spared to assist all the allies at the earliest possible date and to the utmost extent by any means which will help toward the prosecution of the war."

In his report Benson listed the decisions made in Europe and some recommendations for additional action. It had been decided: to send a division of battleships to the Grand Fleet; to dispatch the entire battle fleet to European waters in the spring if conditions warranted the step; to proceed with the distant mine barrage in the North Sea; to close the Straits of Dover; to undertake a naval offensive with American participation; to make Sims the naval attaché; to invite Sims to the "morning conference" at the Admiralty; to improve naval coordination with France; to create the planning section; and, finally, to form the Allied Naval Council. Benson recommended in addition dispatch

86. House report, December 15, 1917, USDSM 367, 763.72/13416. For printed reports, see Department of State, *1917*, supp. 2, vol. 1, *The World War*, 366ff.

87. For reports of Benson's concern, see the Daniels diary, December 15, 16, and 20, 1917, Cronon, ed., *Cabinet Diaries*, 251, 253.

of more patrol craft, development of naval aviation, establishment of an advanced base in the Azores, and improvement of port facilities on the French coast. He did not fail to include an admonitory comment on merchant shipping. What was required was a logical administration of available tonnage. "It matters not what flag any ship or ships may sail under provided they are engaged in carrying out well defined plans . . . which meet with the approval of the several governments concerned."[88]

Sims had correctly divined the change in Benson's outlook. As confirmatory evidence accumulated, he could not resist noting this change in letters to his favorite correspondents—Admiral Bayly and Captain Pratt. To Bayly he reported that Benson was now prepared to send over every available antisubmarine craft;[89] to Pratt he penned a warning that great difficulties lay ahead: "I assume that . . . all you people now in Washington thoroughly realise that the Allies are really up against it; that the crux of the whole situation is the shipping question and whether the allies will be able to hold their own against Germany until the building program at least equals the present rate of destruction of shipping."[90]

Officials in Washington needed no more convincing; the shipping problem moved insistently to the fore. No question complicated the shipping program more than the demands for transportation to ferry American troops to Europe in great numbers. If the Allies had earlier been somewhat hesitant about requesting the preparation and shipment of American troops, this tendency rapidly dissipated in late 1917 as evidence accumulated to indicate the strong likelihood of an "end-the-war" offensive by Germany during 1918. This effort became possible in great part because of reinforcements transferred from the Eastern Front in the wake of the Russian defalcation. From the time of the House mission the great question was the manner in which the American formations would be utilized on the Western Front. General Pershing was from the very outset firmly committed to the creation and employment of an independent American army under its own command operating in its own

88. Benson report, December 14, 1917, USDSM 367, 763.72/13416. See also Seymour, ed., *Intimate Papers*, 3:269, 299.
89. Sims to Bayly, December 10, 1917, USNSF, TD file.
90. Sims to Pratt, December 21, 1917, USNSF, TD file. A copy of this letter is in the Sims Papers.

sector. This approach would delay considerably the effective date of American activity. Given the extent of the emergency, the Entente powers revived and strengthened their earlier recommendation for the "amalgamation" of American troops by small units into the veteran British and French armies in France in order to reap the benefits of American manpower at the earliest possible moment.[91]

If Pershing was from the first completely opposed to amalgamation, Sims took the opposite view. At the time of the House mission's visit to Europe, the Admiral rehearsed for Pratt various arguments in behalf of amalgamation. He began by stressing the time factor, arguing that the creation of an independent army would delay the impact of American manpower on the Western Front. "Would it not be much more efficient if we supplied these men to strengthen the lines of the western front in the same way that the British would supply a million men of their own if they had them [?]" Sims saw many objections to this course. "Of course I recognise that for us to do what appears to me to be the logical thing would involve considerable sacrifice of national pride, or rather the sacrifice of considerable opportunity for national and personal distinction." And further, "Of course I also recognise that such a scheme would involve more or less powerful political considerations. But if we could reason out what would be the most efficient thing to do, are we not big enough to do it?" Sims favored reinforcing the British Army as against the French Army because common language would expedite effective cooperation. Amalgamation would release shipping otherwise tied up by the needs of an independent army. Sims knew that his thinking was directly opposed to that of Pershing and others. "Don't give me away to the army," he warned Pratt, "as they might assassinate me—and I am not nearly ready to die yet." To negate an expected charge of pro-British sentiment, Sims concluded: "The subject of this letter is being quite extensively discussed by Americans on this side, though I have not heard of any of our Allies mentioning it, and I have not discussed it with any but Americans."[92] In this fashion the opposing viewpoints concerning amalgamation took shape, and the topic be-

91. For the background of the "amalgamation" question, see Trask, *United States in the Supreme War Council*, 70–75.
92. Sims to Pratt, November 23, 1917, USNSF, TD file. A copy is also in the Sims Papers.

came a matter of constant debate and recrimination during the early months of 1918.

Meanwhile, Britain continued its pressure upon the United States to increase its production of merchant shipping. After the War Cabinet discussed indications that the United States was likely to fall far behind its initial commitments Lloyd George communicated his alarm in a letter to Colonel House. On the same day, however, the head of ship construction in Washington, Edward N. Hurley, told Wilson that the United States might possibly produce the amount of shipping promised—some 6 million tons.[93] Also in December, in order to assist the general inter-Allied effort to limit neutral trade with the Central Powers, the War Trade Board issued the first American "black list" of firms with whom Americans were not permitted to trade.[94]

At least some of the new energy and determination displayed in Washington was a response to growing domestic criticism of the American mobilization. The principal attack, emanating from Congress, was directed against the War Department and its head, Newton Baker.[95] The Navy Department also incurred some congressional ire. On December 22, Sims received a message from Benson asking for assistance. "Effort being made to credit impression you have been hampered by [failure] of Navy Department to meet your request for various things particularly personnel. I feel that a strong positive statement of [sic] this subject is highly desirable."[96] Sims responded in fairly helpful terms, but not without some slight intimation that the Navy Department might have acted more determinedly. "I strongly deprecate an impression that our Naval Forces in European Waters have been avoidably hampered by failure of the Navy Department to comply with my recommendations for various things particularly personnel." He conceded that some requests had not been fulfilled, but that the Navy Department had to

93. Minutes of the War Cabinet (WC 295), December 10, 1917, CAB 23, book 4; Ray Stannard Baker, *Woodrow Wilson: Life and Letters*, 8 vols., *War Leader* (New York, 1939), 7:41. For British alarms, see Maclay to Lloyd George, November 22, 1917, Lloyd George Papers, file F/35/2/33; Maclay to Lloyd George, December 5, 1917, Lloyd George Papers, file F/35/2/88.

94. Baker, *War Leader*, 7:391.

95. Daniel Beaver, *Newton D. Baker and the American War Effort, 1917–1919* (Lincoln, 1966), 79–109.

96. Benson to Sims, December 22, 1917, USNSF, TD file.

consider its support for his command in relation to other demands being made upon it.[97] To his wife Sims privately confided his real sentiments. He had not received any real assistance in respect to his staff until August, 1917, and had been "shamefully neglected" in this respect.[98] The Admiral was obviously much annoyed at the request that he pull the Department's chestnuts out of the congressional fire, given the accuracy of some of the charges he was expected to refute, but he followed the imperatives of loyalty rather than personal pique. If the domestic agitation soon subsided, the episode hardly boded well for the future.

✳   ✳   ✳   ✳

The trying year of 1917 now reached its end. The immediate future looked difficult indeed, as the Central Powers prepared for offensive operations in France to end the war. At sea the Germans continued their unrestricted submarine war. On the other hand, the debacles of 1917 had forced the western coalition into cooperative relations and arrangements that would permit a much more effective conduct of its over-all political, military, naval, and economic efforts during 1918. Sims continued to argue that an effective contribution to the submarine war in European waters would force victory and by itself create political conditions entirely favorable to the United States for a long period. He was convinced that Anglo-American combination during and after the war would guarantee national security. Officials in Washington were much less confident. Only the rapid development of the crisis forced the United States Government to those measures of cooperation advocated so powerfully by Sims and Page. Necessity rather than desire was the mother of American activity as 1917 came to its dreary and discouraging end. This obvious reality raised the question of whether the United States would revert to a prior order of things when victory hove in view. The superficial appearance of inter-Allied unity forced by the extreme political-military exigencies of November–December, 1917, concealed a broad range of conflicts, some of them irreconcilable.

97. Sims to Benson, December 23, 1917, USNSF, TD file. See also Baker, *War Leader*, 7:426.
98. Elting E. Morison, *Admiral Sims and the Modern American Navy* (Boston, 1942), 402–3.

CHAPTER 6

VICTORY IN THE ATLANTIC
January–September, 1918

Lloyd George believed that "the success of the steps taken to counter the submarine attack was the most important contribution made to victory during the year 1917." Of course Germany did not become immediately aware of the extent to which its undersea offensive had been checked. Its hope of victory depended on countering the novel antisubmarine tactics developed by the western coalition.[1] Ludendorff doggedly clung to the belief that Germany could force a decision on the Western Front if the U-boats sunk enough tonnage to prevent a rapid reinforcement of American troops.[2] He informed the Foreign Office on January 22, 1918, that "The effects of submarine warfare are undoubtedly very noticeable in England. Our immediate purpose is to bring England to her knees unswervingly and with all our energy."[3] Other observers were far less optimistic. General Groener caught the reality in a nervous passage in his diary: "Since we must count more and more on the arrival of American troops despite Tirpitz and the U-boats, the offensive [planned for the spring] becomes a last attempt to speed an end to the war."[4]

The German naval staff continued to believe that the U-boat could sink enough merchant ships to counteract new construction by the Allied and Associated Powers. It estimated that the U-boats could destroy about 650,000 tons per month. Since shipwrecks and other losses would account for another 45,000 tons per month and the enemy could build only about 345,000 tons per month, the net reduction would approximate 350,000 tons. By the middle of 1918 the Allied and Associated Powers would have only about 10.5 million tons of shipping to transport some

1. David Lloyd George, *War Memoirs of David Lloyd George*, 6 vols., *1917* (Boston, 1934), 4:580.
2. Erich Ludendorff, *Meine Kriegserinnerungen, 1914–1918* (Berlin, 1919), 332.
3. Ludendorff to Foreign Office, January 22, 1918, St. Antony's Papers, reel 13, Geheime Akten, vol. 59, frame 175.
4. Wilhelm Groener, *Lebenserinnerungen: Jugend; Generalstab; Weltkrieg* (Göttingen, 1957), 565.

60 million tons of supplies to Britain.[5] In order to increase the output of submarines, Ludendorff finally gave first priority to the construction of undersea craft.[6] Unfortunately for the Central Powers only seventy-four new U-boats were delivered during the first ten months of 1918, the consequence of failing to expand production at an earlier date.[7] Ludendorff also arranged procedures to deny neutral tonnage to the western coalition, but expedients of this nature did not work.[8] Instead of depriving the western coalition of about 700,000 tons of shipping per month, the actual average was less than 250,000 tons per month. The volume of sinkings in January was about 307,000 tons, the highest figure reached during 1918. In April 279,000 tons went down; by September the figure had declined to about 188,000 tons.

German hopes died slowly, perhaps sustained by indications of concern on the part of the enemy. Reports of domestic discontent in Britain continued to filter into Berlin. Admiral Sims himself noted the necessity of devoting every available ship to the supply of the British Isles in order to bolster civilian morale.[9] By early spring, however, Ludendorff finally realized that the submarine could not prevent the arrival of troop transports from the United States.[10] American vessels approached Europe on lanes far removed from the normal hunting grounds of the submarines. Ships used for this purpose were fast, and their routes were carefully concealed.[11] Antisubmarine methods developed in 1917 accomplished their purpose during 1918; not one transport approaching Europe fell victim to an undersea attack.

The German High Sea Fleet also lost offensive momentum. After an unsuccessful raid during late April in the North Sea,

5. Holtzendorff to Foreign Office, February 26, 1918, St. Antony's Papers, reel 14, Geheime Akten, vol. 62, frames 162–63.

6. Erich Ludendorff, *Urkunden der Obersten Heeresleitung Ueber Ihre Taetigkeit, 1916/18* (Berlin, 1922), 167–68.

7. Reinhard Scheer, *Germany's High Sea Fleet in the World War* (London, 1920), 335.

8. Ludendorff to Hertling, February 16, 1918, St. Antony's Papers, reel 14, Geheime Akten, vol. 62, frames 99–100.

9. Naval Attaché (Norway) to State Secretary of the Reichsmarineamt, March 3, 1918, St. Antony's Papers, reel 14, Geheime Akten, vol. 62, frames 212–13; Sims to Navy Department, February 2, 1918, USNSF, TT file.

10. Ludendorff, *Kriegserinnerungen*, 491; Erich Ludendorff, *Kriegsfuehrung und Politik* (Berlin, 1922), 207.

11. Otto Groos, *Seekriegslehren im Lichte des Weltkrieges* (Berlin, 1929), 227–28.

reaching as far as 60° N, it retired to its anchorages and never reappeared again.[12] This decline in activity emphasized the cumulative successes of the Allied and Associated Powers both on and below the surface of the sea. The frustration of the German submarine offensive and the High Sea Fleet contributed most importantly to the total triumph achieved by the western coalition in November, 1918.

I

Early in 1918 both American and British naval leaders evaluated the state of the naval war. Sims's planning section in London produced a broad-ranging estimate of the situation called "Problem No. 2," which began with a prediction of German intentions. Germany's naval mission was to mount the "maximum possible sustained attack on the sea communications of the Allies." The only means of attacking commerce was the submarine, and the High Sea Fleet was assigned the task of supporting submarine operations. What would the enemy fleet attempt to accomplish within the limits of its broad mission? It would continue the present unrestricted submarine war, enlarging its field of activity as antisubmarine measures in the danger area increased in effectiveness; it would utilize large cruiser submarines in distant waters to force dispersion of antisubmarine forces; it would maintain control of the Heligoland Bight, the Kattegat, and the Baltic Sea; it would use its air power only to protect naval bases; it would increase use of the submarine to support activities on land; and it would take extensive actions to frustrate Allied barrage operations. The High Sea Fleet would not come out in force for a fleet engagement, but would be deployed to immobilize as much Allied sea power as possible.

What courses of action were open to the Allies? Command of the subsurface was of *"paramount importance."* To achieve this end, concentration of effort and unity of command were essential. Disturbed by the lack of effective central direction, the planners held that "The success or failure of the present military and Naval councils depend on the extent to which they can

12. Ibid., 139; Karl Galster, *England, Deutsche Flotte und Weltkrieg* (Kiel, 1925), 122; Arthur J. Marder, *From the Dreadnought to Scapa Flow: The Royal Navy in the Fisher Era, 1904–1919,* 5 vols., *Victory and Aftermath (January 1918–June 1919)* (London, 1970), 5:143–56.

harmonize and co-ordinate the Allied efforts and bring about
unity of action for the purpose of winning the war." To achieve
command of the sea, it was necessary to launch offensives against
enemy ships and, if possible, their bases, as well as to undertake
effective defensive measures in order to protect commerce on the
high seas. Should the British Grand Fleet require reinforcement
—a possibility if Germany gained control of the Russian fleet—
the United States and Japan could send help. The destruction of
the Austrian fleet and more especially of the submarine bases in
the Adriatic would contribute importantly to the success of the
naval war in the Mediterranean. Attacks on enemy bases like
Wilhelmshaven and Kiel were impractical, but Zeebrugge might
be successfully neutralized. Another possible measure was to
construct effective barrages in places that could be patrolled,
such as the Adriatic and Aegean seas. Another means of strengthening the attack would be to concentrate available aircraft for
bombing attacks on accessible submarine bases. A North Sea
barrage would require control of a Norwegian base south of the
point where it approached Norwegian territorial waters.

The convoy system remained the best method of protecting
merchant shipping, and there were means of improving its efficiency. Convoys could be organized to achieve greater speed.
Merchant captains could be trained to higher efficiency. Merchant shipping and personnel might be placed under government control. The planners recognized that Germany might
undertake raids against commerce in American waters if the
convoy system foreclosed available targets in European waters.
In order to support the convoy system, it was necessary to seize
the offensive. "The ultimate solution to the submarine menace
is tactical and not strategic." The most effective method was all-
out use of depth charges by destroyers whenever a sighting was
made. Special note was made of the situation in the Mediterranean, where offensive endeavors had to be increased to stop
heavy losses to submarines in that area.[13]

These general principles were derived from the experience
of 1917, and they were generally followed during 1918. The
Planning Section considered a range of radical alternatives in
order to achieve a dramatic improvement in the general naval
situation, but most of these projects did not materialize. One

13. Planning Section Problem #2, January 12, 1918, USNSF, TX file.

recommendation, already in the process of implementation, was to expand mine barrages.[14] Another of the proposals, a major naval action in the Adriatic, was most seriously considered. This particular plan is discussed extensively in Chapter 7.

Admiral Sir David Beatty, commanding the Grand Fleet, precipitated some reconsideration of naval warfare in Great Britain. On December 29, 1917, he composed for the Admiralty a memorandum entitled "The Situation in the North Sea," which reflected his continuing anxiety. The Grand Fleet had the mission of engaging the High Sea Fleet at any cost. Beatty was concerned about this mission because of fleet weaknesses resulting from the detachment of destroyers and other supporting craft for antisubmarine duties. He proposed that the Grand Fleet engage the enemy only under favorable circumstances. "Our policy for the next few months should be to contain the enemy in his bases by extensive mining which would delay his exit and give us some prospect of collecting our Destroyers from other services; 2 or 3 days would enable this to be done." To strengthen his case, he wrote very seriously: "I reiterate that the situation is a dangerous one. . . . I feel that there may be a rude awakening for the Country if the Grand Fleet should have to meet the High Sea Fleet under the present conditions."[15] On January 9, Beatty revised his memorandum slightly to propose offensive actions against the Flemish coast and the closing of the Straits of Dover. This shift in basic naval strategy from forcing an engagement with the enemy fleet to containing it in its ports had numerous benefits, according to Beatty. It "would exert steady pressure, harass the enemy and weaken his morale, until the advent of additional destroyers and the replacement of our projectiles [certain shells considered inadequate] alter the situation in our favour."[16]

Sir Eric Geddes supported this proposal, recommending the containment policy as "a purely temporary measure." The reason was familiar. "The fact remains that a deficiency in destroyers exists, reflecting upon the fighting efficiency of the Grand Fleet, and necessitating the adoption of temporary measures . . . in

14. Planning Section Memorandum No. 18, Problem #10, n.d., USNSF, TX file.

15. Beatty memorandum, "The Situation in the North Sea," December 29, 1917, ADM 137, book 1937, 88–90.

16. Revised Beatty memorandum, "The Situation in the North Sea," January 9, 1918, ADM 137, book 1937, 91–94. Arthur Marder analyzes this document in detail in *Victory and Aftermath*, 131–38.

order to meet the situation created." He proposed various mine fields—the distant barrage in the North Sea, operations off the Heligoland Bight, and an extensive barrage in the Straits of Dover—in order to inhibit movements of the German fleet.[17] These recommendations were accepted in the War Cabinet, which also moved to increase production of destroyers. There was some concern that other types of vessels might not be completed until after the conclusion of hostilities. "The War Cabinet did not under-rate the importance of a *post bellum* naval supremacy, but before a final decision they felt it was imperative to ascertain the reaction of the naval proposals on other programmes of actual war construction."[18] Advocates of a "balanced" or "symmetrical" fleet were not lacking in Britain, but, as in the United States, their desires were largely set aside during the period of belligerency.

One reason for continuing concentration on the production of destroyers in Britain was doubt that the United States would fulfill its promises. Sir William Wiseman informed Sir Eric Drummond that it was always wise to "discount" estimates from the United States. "The country is so vast and disorganized, and so entirely unaccustomed to national organisation, that the very vastness of their resources prevent them from being brought speedily into play." He advocated insistence upon avoiding frills and concentration entirely upon "essentials." The United States, Wiseman believed, had learned its lesson and would take this road.[19] He warned against unduly direct pressures on the United States, telling Balfour that "President Wilson may be led but certainly not driven."[20] Evidently the young British officer had learned something from Colonel House.

Even at this juncture of the war the United States retained its suspicions of British motives. Austen Chamberlain told Sir Eric Geddes that Oscar Crosby, the American representative on the recently established Inter-Allied Council for War Purchases and

17. Geddes memorandum, "Naval Situation in the North Sea," January 17, 1918, ADM 137, book 1937, 104–9. The agreement of the War Cabinet on January 18, 1918, is recorded in ADM 137, book 1937, 111.

18. Minutes of the War Cabinet (WC 325), January 18, 1918, CAB 23, book 5.

19. Wiseman to Drummond, January 25, 1918, Lloyd George Papers, file F/60/2/42.

20. Wiseman to Balfour, January 25, 1918, Lloyd George Papers, file F/60/2/41.

Finance, was "evidently much disturbed by rumours that we are building a post-war fleet at American expense and has recurred to the question on more than one occasion."[21] There were no real grounds for this suspicion, although the Board of Admiralty, like the General Board of the United States Navy, on occasion made reference to the future. On February 14, probably reacting against opposition to a building program that would maintain the balance of the fleet, it solemnly recorded its view that "the question of maintaining the preeminence of the British Navy, not only in relation to the German Navy, was one of vital importance which must not be lost sight of."[22] The other navy of greatest concern, obviously, was that of the United States, but the building program of Great Britain was perforce concentrated to a remarkable degree on antisubmarine craft as against other types of fleet vessels during the remainder of 1918. The exigencies of the war allowed no other course.

If the Anglo-American evaluations of early 1918 brought forth some new proposals and resulted in some modifications of mission, they generally ratified the principles so painfully worked out in the atmosphere of intense crisis that endured throughout 1917. This circumstance strengthened the navies in the face of continuing challenges. In 1918 the principal inter-Allied crisis stemmed from the great German offensives launched along the Western Front during the period March–July. Those blows once again caused Admiral Sims to enunciate one of his favorite maxims. "It may be put down as a general rule that those military provisions which should be taken will not be taken until they are forced to take them." This, Sims thought, was true "particularly when there is distrust between . . . [allies]."[23] In any event, however, the western coalition met the test.

II

Official relations between the Navy Department and the London headquarters of Admiral Sims improved significantly

21. Chamberlain to Geddes, February 1, 1918, Geddes Papers, ADM 116, book 1806.
22. Minutes of the Board of Admiralty, February 14, 1918, ADM 167, book 53.
23. Sims to Benson, April 2, 1918, USNSF, TD file. A copy is in the Sims Papers.

after the visit of the House mission, but personal associations were by no means perfected. In addition some small annoyances caused a great deal of private recrimination, especially in Sims's organization. Among disturbing developments were the refusal of the Navy Department to allow Sims to accept an honorary appointment to the Board of Admiralty; the refusal of the United States Government to permit officers and men in Europe to accept foreign decorations; various efforts in Washington to interfere with Sims's powers; and a quarrel over the reluctance of the Navy Department to meet Sims's continuing demands for additional personnel. At times these difficulties obscured the general agreement between Washington and London that came about when Admiral Benson made his visit to Europe.

On November 22, 1917, Sir Eric Geddes explained to the Board of Admiralty that Admirals Sims and Benson had been proposed as "Honorary Lords of the Admiralty." In addition, Admiral Sims was to be invited to attend the meetings of the Board of Admiralty and the Admiralty Operations Committee. The King approved of these measures, and Benson was to ascertain the views of the United States Government.[24] All this was in line with Sims's sustained effort to maintain effective Anglo-American cooperation. Certainly the proposal was entirely unprecedented in the annals of British naval history.

Benson's inquiry went immediately to Washington, where the Secretary of the Navy discussed the matter with President Wilson. Daniels phrased the presidential decision in the briefest terms: "An emphatic *No.*"[25] The matter languished until early in January, 1918, when Sims mentioned the subject to Admiral Benson. "This honorary membership," he cabled, "would in no sense change my present position but would permit my attending all meetings at which important matters are discussed. I would of course have no voice and decisions would not interfere with our freedom of action." He was raising the question at the urging of Sir Eric Geddes, "who believes appointment would not only result in increased efficiency of cooperation but would

24. Minutes of the Board of Admiralty, November 22, 1917, ADM 167, book 53.

25. Daniels diary, November 26, 1917, E. David Cronon, ed., *The Cabinet Diaries of Josephus Daniels, 1913–1921* (Lincoln, 1963), 242.

have good effect."[26] Benson replied courteously but firmly. "Department fully appreciates feeling indicated by First Lord and realizes the good result to be obtained but fear knowledge of such action might create unfortunate feeling on part of other Allies and thereby weaken strong sense of cooperation now existing between all concerned."[27] Sims immediately responded that Geddes was disappointed. "He says it is difficult to keep me in thorough touch with everything if I have not had the privilege of listening to the discussions upon which decisions are based."[28] This message was an obvious effort to force a reconsideration.

When no further response came from Washington, Ambassador Page entered the lists in behalf of his naval friend. Late in January, urged on by Geddes, he cabled Wilson and Lansing to urge Sims's appointment. Page stressed the honorary nature of the position and also its uniqueness. "He regards it only as a mark of high esteem in which the British Admiralty hold the American navy and as an evidence of their cordial working relations." To obviate the possibility that the Sims appointment might injure Allied relations, the French Government would extend the same honor to Sims.[29] Benson had been hoist by his own petard! Two days later, Sims informed Benson that the King had shown an interest in the matter. "You can therefore readily imagine that the refusal of our Government to accept this invitation is a continuous embarrassment to me."[30]

Secretary Daniels, not impressed, continued to oppose the appointment. Benson agreed with him; it would do Sims harm because, "Officers were saying he looked too much to English approval." When Daniels discussed the question with the President, the latter took the view that acceptance of appointment would implicate Sims too deeply in British affairs.[31] On Febru-

26. Sims to Benson, January 4, 1918, Sims Papers.

27. Benson to Sims, January 9, 1918, Sims Papers.

28. Sims to Benson, January 10, 1918, USNSF, TD file.

29. Page to Wilson and Lansing, January 29, 1918, USDSM 367, 763.72/8698. A copy is in USNSF, TD file.

30. Sims to Benson, January 31, 1917, USNSF, TD file.

31. Daniels diary, January 31, 1918, Cronon, ed., *Cabinet Diaries*, 274. See also Daniels to Wilson, January 31, 1918, Wilson Papers, box 135. "I am glad you take the view of the matter you state in your letter with regard to Admiral Sims. There are other reasons why I was going to suggest that Sims do not accept the honorary membership and Admiral Benson holds the same opinion." See also Josephus Daniels, *The Wilson Era: Years of War and After, 1917–1923* (Chapel Hill, N.C., 1946), 494.

ary 2 Daniels informed the State Department, disposed to favor the appointment, that it was considered unwise.[32] The State Department waited until March 19 to inform Page that Sims could not accept appointment. To do so, wrote Lansing, who used language provided by Daniels, would be to violate "the general policy of declining to permit its officers to accept from foreign governments any decoration or distinctive honors in acknowledgment of their professional qualifications or as reward for meritorious service."[33]

The British project was now dead. On March 22, Geddes wrote to Sims what amounted to a letter of condolence. "I cannot help feeling that your Government has perhaps misinterpreted the intention underlying my proposal." It had not been proposed for "meritorious service," although Sims had indeed performed duty of that quality, but because it would have secured "an even closer relation, if possible, between the naval forces of the United States of America and our own." It was now time to give up the enterprise. "Perhaps in the circumstances you will not wish to press the matter with your Government, especially as the liaison between the two Navies is now so very complete; but I do wish you to know how much we should have welcomed you as a member of the Board."[34] Sims made no further effort to expedite his appointment, contenting himself with several mentions of the advantages it would have conferred.[35] Daniels later revealed that a naval officer, not identified, had told him at the time that his decision had earned him the "everlasting enmity" of Admiral Sims.[36] After the war ended, Sims was indeed unsparing in his criticism of Daniels during the well-publicized naval investigation of 1920.[37] The President probably thought that in refusing the honor for Sims he was pursuing his policy of retaining as

32. Daniels diary, February 2, 1918, Cronon, ed., *Cabinet Diaries*, 275. For the letter, see Daniels to Lansing, February 2, 1918, USDSM 763.72/8736.
33. Lansing to Page, March 19, 1917, USDSM 367, 763.72/8736.
34. Geddes to Sims, March 22, 1918, USNSF, TD file.
35. For examples, see Sims to Benson, April 2, 1918, USNSF, TD file; Sims to Pratt, April 29, 1918, USNSF, TD file.
36. Daniels, *Wilson Era: Years of War and After*, 495.
37. For a convenient summation of the hearings, favorable to Admiral Sims, see Tracy B. Kittredge, *Naval Lessons of the Great War: A Review of the Senate Naval Investigation of the Criticisms by Admiral Sims of the Policies and Methods of Josephus Daniels* (Garden City, N.Y., 1921).

much independence as possible from the Entente powers. Daniels's motives had perhaps been more personal.

In October, 1917, Sims had begun to recommend that some of the men in his command be allowed to accept the award of the Distinguished Service Order by Great Britain.[38] In this situation Daniels was also intransigent, although he wrote to Sims in quiet terms on the matter. He had publicized the British gesture, although the decorations could not be accepted.[39] In this instance Daniels also acted in accord with the President's wishes. A bit earlier, Wilson had told the Secretary that he would veto any legislation empowering American servicemen to accept foreign honors. "It would cause them to be trying to secure foreign favor & would be unAmerican."[40] Sims found this limitation impossible to endure in silence. As late as August, 1918, he was proposing acceptance of decorations like the British D.S.O. and the French *Croix de guerre*, but he could get no satisfaction from Daniels.[41] Like the exchange about the Admiralty appointment, this controversy did not improve the personal ties between the commander in London and his superiors in Washington.

Sims was sensitive to any activities that might interfere with the efficiency and the integrity of his command. Assiduous in seeking to impose his views on Washington, he was equally energetic in his desire to avoid undue regulation from the Navy Department. The adverse consequences of his strong stand were mitigated to some extent because he defined his principal task as one of providing a coordinating link between the Navy Department and the Admiralty. The Admiral's attitudes hardened as he improved his own organization in London while the Navy Department continued to flounder in Washington—or so he was informed by members of his staff who visited there.[42] His emis-

38. Sims to Pratt, October 15, 1917, USNSF, TD file; Sims to Benson, October 15, 1917, USNSF, TD file.

39. Daniels to Sims, December 15, 1917, USNSF, TD file.

40. Daniels diary, November 26, 1917, Cronon, ed., *Cabinet Diaries*, 242.

41. Sims to Benson, August 10, 1918, USNSF, TD file; Sims to Benson, August 30, 1918, USNSF, TD file.

42. For examples of reports on the situation in Washington by staff members, see McBride to Sims, January 9, 1918, USNSF, TD file; "Memorandum from Commander Babcock's Letters to Admiral Sims," n.d., ca. February, 1918, USNSF, TP file.

saries did all they could to counteract the assumption that Sims was unduly pro-British, but this effort proved fruitless.[43]

Sims became ever more insistent on sound relations between his organization and the naval staff at home. A year after the beginning of his mission he expressed clearly to Captain Pratt his conceptions of the relations between general headquarters and the theater commander:

I can understand perfectly well the disposition there must always be at the Navy Dept. to make decisions, even when they concern local affairs over here. Of course you know this is something which should be resisted as much as possible. The responsibility for local dispositions, and for their success must necessarily be on this side; we would of course be blamed for any failure. Moreover, we have the benefit here of discussion of all these matters with all of these able men belonging to our Allies. Do not misunderstand the extreme importance of this matter of discussion. It is really something to keep always in mind. It is wholly impossible to transmit by mail or by cable all of the details of a discussion which has arrived at a certain decision as to the disposition of forces, and so forth.[44]

In these terms Sims rehearsed the traditional outlook of the theater commander. Since, generally speaking, he was correct in his adherence to general policies established in Washington, he usually managed to maintain his prerogatives in sufficient repair as well as relations with the Navy Department in order to permit efficient conduct of his command.

Only a few incidents marred this record, although beneath the surface issues resided more than a little antagonism. In July, 1918, Benson cabled to Sims what amounted to a relatively severe reprimand after the theater comander had taken it upon himself to discuss certain arrangements for the repair of American destroyers in Great Britain that were deemed undesirable in Washington. Benson ordered him not to initiate general policies of an international character without prior permission from the Navy Department.[45] Sims replied politely but firmly; he had the impression that his arrangements with the British were acceptable in Washington, but nevertheless he had

43. For Daniels's record of the Babcock visit, see Daniels diary, February 12, 1918, Cronon, ed., *Cabinet Diaries*, 278.

44. Sims to Pratt, April 4, 1917, USNSF, TD file.

45. Benson to Sims, July 24, 1918, USNSF, TD file.

not made policy or committed the United States. He had said only that the British proposals would receive sympathetic consideration. He thought he had acted within the proper limits of his powers, arguing that an unduly restrictive attitude in Washington "would create a very difficult situation."[46] Benson responded in satisfactory terms, recognizing the prerogatives of the theater commander, but informing him that the policies he had discussed in London were not acceptable in Washington. Like other incidents of this nature, the tension did not lead to a confrontation. Sims took wicked pleasure in congratulating Pratt on some reorganization made in the Navy Department during the summer of 1918. "It is rather a curious reflection that the Navy Department should have watched a war for three years and been in a war for one-and-a half years without having organized a practical piece of machinery to carry on its work."[47]

In one respect—the preservation of his command—Sims received consistent support from Secretary Daniels. At times suggestions were made to send other ranking admirals to Europe. Admiral Mayo, the Commander of the Atlantic Fleet, was particularly interested in a European mission. Sims opposed this step, arguing that the United States Navy should act through one commander in Europe, and Daniels, with the backing of the President, supported this principle.[48] Sims was always receptive to staff visits from Washington, but he resisted all proposals to have him return there, arguing that it would have an adverse impact on public opinion.[49] In any event, he was able to avoid any such trip throughout the months of belligerency.

In one area of tension Sims never achieved a fully satisfactory arrangement with the Navy Department during 1918; as in 1917, he complained constantly of the Department's failure to honor

46. Sims to Navy Department, July 26, 1918, USNSF, TD file. The issue at hand—reimbursement for destroyer repairs—had been under discussion since the beginning of the year. See Minutes of the First Meetings, ANC, Fourth Session, January 23, 1918, USNSF, QC file.

47. Benson to Sims, August 1, 1918, USNSF, TD file; Sims to Pratt, August 13, 1918, USNSF, TD file.

48. Sims to Benson, February 15, 1918, USNSF, TD file; Daniels diary, April 15, 1918, Cronon, ed., Cabinet Diaries, 299. Sims later objected to completing reports asked for by Admiral Mayo, arguing that his command should be entirely separated from the Atlantic Fleet. Sims to Benson, June 4, 1918, USNSF, TP file.

49. Sims to Pratt, May 29, 1918, USNSF, TD file; Sims to Pratt, July 10, 1918, USNSF, TD file.

his requests for additional personnel. His activities finally elicited a comprehensive defense of the Department's personnel policies from Harris Laning, in charge of man power in the Navy Department. Laning pointed out that the Navy had only 2,394 experienced officers at the beginning of the American intervention. He defended the decision made early in the war not to detach officers from the battleship fleet for duty in European waters, a step that Sims had urged in order to obtain experienced commanders for antisubmarine vessels. Laning's response was that the Navy had to provide support for the second of its principal missions—the delivery of troops to France—as well as for antisubmarine activities. Sims considered only the antisubmarine mission. Moreover, seasoned professionals were desperately needed in Washington to fill staff positions. In short, Sims had ignored the full range of the demands being made upon the Bureau of Personnel.[50] The Force Commander responded in spirited terms, insisting that nothing should take precedence over the antisubmarine campaign; only trained and experienced commanders could hunt submarines effectively.[51] Disputes over personnel never culminated in a meeting of the minds; only the Armistice brought them to a halt.

As 1918 ran its course, the inter-Allied war against the submarines gradually achieved its objectives. The Germans sank fewer merchant ships, and the Allies destroyed more submarines. The First Lord of the Admiralty grew increasingly confident as spring merged into summer. In April he reported to the War Cabinet that more submarines were now being attacked successfully.[52] In May he attributed the decline in German success to the constant harassment of the submarines by antisubmarine forces, telling one correspondent that "life on a German submarine in these Northern waters must be getting pretty unbearable. In a recent week we made 65 separate attacks on submarines, and they are getting properly harried."[53] By June

50. Laning to Sims, August 26, 1918, USNSF, TD file. Laning had been disturbed by a strong defense of the Sims position included in a memorandum by W. R. Carter entitled "Set a Thief to Catch a Thief," forwarded by Sims to Pratt.
51. Sims to Laning, September 16, 1918, USNSF, TD file.
52. Minutes of the War Cabinet (WC 401), April 30, 1918, CAB 23, book 6.
53. Geddes to Sir Rennell Rodd, May 27, 1918, ADM 116, book 1649.

Geddes decided that the Allies were sinking far more submarines than the enemy was producing.[54]

In June the Prime Minister reviewed the inter-Allied political-
military situation for the Imperial War Cabinet. A great crisis
had resulted from the defeat of Russia, the slowness of the
American mobilization, the exhaustion of the Allied forces, and
the enemy's advantage in having a unified command, but against
these considerations he set "the comparative failure of the submarine campaign," success in Palestine and Mesopotamia, and
the breakdown of Germany's allies. These latter circumstances
"were elements of ultimate success which would increasingly
tell in our favour after the immediate crisis had been met."[55] The
Admiralty report to the Imperial War Cabinet was also per-
meated with quiet optimism. "Though the enemy's submarine
campaign is still the most important factor in the Naval situation
the position is steadily improving; the shipping losses are gradually decreasing, and it can be claimed that since January 1st
enemy submarines have been destroyed at least at the same rate
as the enemy has built them."[56] When Admiral Wester Wemyss,
Jellicoe's successor as First Sea Lord, made his report, Lloyd
George pointed out that "this was a pleasing contrast to the state
of affairs that used to be reported to the Imperial War Cabinet
at its meetings the year before."[57] The naval war, however, continued unabated, and it would still require extraordinary endeavors. The need for antisubmarine craft was still great. "Our
commitments in convoying and escorting, especially those enormous numbers of American troops, are putting the most tremen-
dous strain upon our destroyers," Wemyss told the War Cabinet.
On the other hand, the morale of the German submarine crews
was severely shaken. "It is a question of a hunter being hunted.
We hunt the enemy submarines; he is not merely hunting us."
Deep mine fields, depth charges, and hydrophones had vastly

54. Geddes to Calthorpe, June 13, 1918, Geddes Papers, ADM 116,
book 1809.
55. Minutes of the Imperial War Cabinet (IWC 15), June 11, 1918,
CAB 23, book 41.
56. "A General Review of the Naval Situation," June 15, 1918, ADM
137, book 1937, 115–24.
57. Minutes of the Imperial War Cabinet (IWC 19), June 20, 1918,
CAB 23, book 41.

increased the hunting capabilities of the antisubmarine forces.[58] The German submarines were indeed in deep travail. Severely challenged in the most heavily traveled sea lanes around the British Isles, submarine captains increasingly operated far out to sea or very close to shore, where antisubmarine forces were least effective. This change in tactics lessened the efficiency of the submarines, as opportunities to kill were reduced in exchange for enhanced safety.[59] The strain of the total war had taken its toll on German economic resources. By July, 1918, Ludendorff was prepared to acknowledge the failure of the submarine campaign, realizing that not enough U-boats could be produced to counter the antisubmarine tactics of the Allies because of other demands on German labor.[60] The German Navy now moved to establish a supreme command for itself comparable to that of the German Army. Admiral Scheer became the supreme commander of the Navy on August 11, and moved his headquarters to that of Hindenburg and Ludendorff at Spa in order to achieve more effective coordination with land operations.[61] This adjust-

1. Data on U-Boat Use, All Areas

	1916	1917	1918[1]
Average monthly total, U-boats in commission	103	163	172
Average monthly total, U-boats operational	71	129	123
Average number U-boats at sea daily	19	44	45
Number of U-boats constructed in year	108	93	80

Source: Adapted from a chart in Arthur J. Marder, *From the Dreadnought to Scapa Flow: The Royal Navy in the Fisher Era, 1904–1919*, vol. 5, *Victory and Aftermath (January 1918–June 1919)* (London, 1970), 118.
[1] January–October.

58. Minutes of the Imperial War Cabinet (Admiralty extract), June 27, 1918, ADM 116, book 1603.
59. R. H. Gibson and Maurice Prendergast, *The German Submarine War, 1914–1918* (London, 1931), 317.
60. Ludendorff, *Meine Kriegserinnerungen*, 348.
61. For information on the changes in the naval command and efforts to improve naval efficiency, see *The Kaiser and His Court: The Diaries, Note Books, and Letters of Admiral Georg Alexander von Mueller, Chief of the Naval Cabinet, 1914–1918*, Walter Goerlitz, ed. (London, 1961), 360, 378–79; Scheer, *Germany's High Sea Fleet*, 325, 327, 333; Gibson and Prendergast, *German Submarine War*, 301; Andreas Michelsen, *Der U-Bootskrieg, 1914–1918* (Leipzig, 1925), 70, 131–32, 138–39.

ment, however, came too late to reverse the unfavorable course of events on the Western Front.

Admiral Sims reflected the rapid reversal in the general military situation that began in July. During that month Gen. Ferdinand Foch's combined forces on the Western Front contained the final German thrusts and immediately assumed the offensive. Writing to President Wilson on July 13, Sims summarized the dominant inter-Allied view of the submarine situation—that it was well in hand. Germany would not give it up and losses would continue, but he thought it "perfectly apparent that the means of offense are gradually being improved and the number of antisubmarine vessels increased, while the submarines are decreasing in number and efficiency, so that they would appear no possibility of the enemy ever succeeding in destroying enough commerce to bring the Allies to terms." Sims predicted that Germany would attempt no more offensives, but would assume the defensive and attempt to arrange peace.[62]

The success of the antisubmarine war and the assumption of the offensive by the Allied and Associated Powers along the Western Front—to which the arrival of American troops contributed a good deal—drew Sims into a definite modification of priorities. Once the submarines were basically contained, the task of expediting the transport of American troops to Europe became paramount.

From General Pershing's arrival in Europe, Sims had been careful to maintain close working relations with the American Expeditionary Forces, despite his private belief that the Army was sometimes in serious error.[63] In April, 1918, Sims informed Pershing that "it is the sailor's function (1) to protect . . . lines [of communication] and (2) to attack the Hun pirates whenever we can find them." His difficulty was that escort duty required so many destroyers that not enough were available for hunting operations.[64] This order of priorities was quite acceptable to Pershing, who seems to have worked well with his naval counterpart in Europe. Sims lost no opportunity to ingratiate himself with Pershing, even to the extent of indulging in some naval self-abnegation, because he had seen so many examples of how detrimental interservice rivalries could be within European gov-

62. Sims to Wilson, July 13, 1918, USNSF, TD file.
63. Sims to Benson, April 2, 1918, Sims Papers.
64. Sims to Pershing, April 18, 1918, USNSF, TD file.

ernments.[65] In July he confirmed his earlier attitude in another message to Pershing:

I take every occasion to impress upon my forces that they are really a part of the American Army; that they are practically a part of the essential line of communications. I feel quite sure that they all understand this thoroughly and that their hearts are with your boys in the field who are bearing the brunt of the fighting. . . . In this war, in so far as actual fighting is concerned, the Navy is condemned to comparative inactivity. We so earnestly want to help that if you can suggest any way in which we could be of assistance, we would be very grateful.[66]

This general attitude was consistent with Sims's emphasis on winning the war by the very best available means without thought to special interests and aspirations, an attitude reflected also in his view of appropriate Anglo-American relations.

Sims brought these views to full expression in a letter to President Wilson on July 13, 1918. He was proud to report that the Navy had been able from the first to cooperate effectively with the Allies. "This is due to the fact that we recognized, and established as an inflexible policy from the first, that there should be in all of the various areas absolute unity of command similar to that which was established on the Western Front when the necessity became imperative." He recognized that "there is no real naval war going on on this side." The enemy was bottled up; he engaged only in submarine activity and some mining operations. Since the submarine avoided men of war, concentrating on commerce destruction, the Navy served principally as "defenders of the line of communication of the Army. This is completely understood between General Pershing and myself," he concluded, "and we are working together, not only in the most complete co-operation but in the most complete harmony and sympathy."[67] Apparently President Wilson was much more pleased with naval activity than a year earlier. In response he praised the Navy and invited Sims to "feel free" to write at any time.[68]

Sims did not vary from this policy during the remaining

65. Sims to Benson, June 19, 1918, USNSF, TD file.
66. Sims to Pershing, July 1, 1918, USNSF, TD file. A copy is in the Sims Papers. See also Sims to Roosevelt, July 7, 1918, USNSF, TD file.
67. Sims to Wilson, July 13, 1918, USNSF, TD file.
68. Wilson to Sims, August 2, 1918, USNSF, TD file. For mention of

months of the war.[69] Success had ratified it. Determined to pursue his conception of proper naval strategy and tactics, he was also assiduous in efforts to avoid misrepresenting the Navy's role in the conflict. When Daniels sought information on naval activities in Europe for publicity purposes in the United States, Sims responded in admonitory tones. "Although our record in proportion to numbers is one to be proud of, I consider it of extreme importance that public be not misled into an exaggerated view of our contribution as compared to that of our Allies who still bear the burden of the struggle." To prove his point he had recourse to some statistics.

The public should understand our relative size, for example:—our anti-submarine forces in Atlantic war zone are 5% of the total engaged; in the Mediterranean 6%: Britain's naval aviation effort alone was 4½ times larger than ours. In convoy system protecting allied trade we furnish 27% destroyer escorts and 35% cruiser escorts. British destroyers escort 62% of U.S. troops and about half of storeships for army.

These were sobering figures indeed. Sims concluded with a warning against building illusions about the naval effort that might cause a public reaction if a serious disaster overtook the country. In all probability he had in mind the possible sinking of a troop ship, a loss which would not in any case "compare at all with daily casualties on the Western Front."[70] It was broadly recognized that Sims was indeed an "original" man, and his attitude in this situation was striking proof of that reputation. Few commanders in the field have been so fulsome in praising the achievements of others. In this respect he stands in the most glaring possible contrast to that extraordinary specialist in public relations, Gen. John J. Pershing, whose reportage frequently left the powerful impression that he and his army were alone in France.

Despite continuing difficulties and crises, the United States Navy, both in Washington and London, carried out an intelli-

the Sims-Wilson exchange, see Ray Stannard Baker, *Woodrow Wilson: Life and Letters*, 8 vols., *Armistice* (New York, 1939), 8:313–14.

69. For a detailed exposition of these general ideas in terms of fleet orders, see the message from District Commander Lorient to All Ships and Stations, "Allied Naval Mission in the Present War," October 10, 1918, USNSF, TD file.

70. Sims memorandum for Daniels, August 17, 1918, USNSF, WV file.

gent naval policy with respect to the war in Atlantic waters during 1918. A great deal had been learned during 1917, and this education was put to good use during the decisive months of the war. If conflicts in doctrine and personality occurred on occasion, these unseemly events were remarkably few in number and were resolved in ways that did not interfere unduly with the prosecution of the war.

III

During 1917 the Navy had constantly interested itself in merchant shipping. After the Paris conference of 1917, however, this responsibility devolved principally upon various inter-Allied organizations, particularly the Supreme War Council, the Allied Maritime Transport Council, the military staffs of the various Allied and Associated Powers, and the principal political leaders. Secretary Daniels and others in the Navy Department provided what support and advice was called for, but the Navy played a distinctly subordinate role in policies related to merchant shipping. Its role in 1918 was confined principally to providing convoy.

Great plans had been laid in Europe by the member of the House mission concerned with shipping—Bainbridge Colby— who shared the general concern expressed by the mission about the problems of coordinating the vast inter-Allied effort required in 1918. One of two alternatives would solve the problem—"the advent of the Corsican figure, or the emergence of the solitary and ultimate strong nation"—that nation being, of course, the United States. As to shipping, Colby was firm in his view that the United States "must do more or leave the submarines in possession of the field."[71] In the wake of the conference the British recommended that the United States build 9 million rather than 6 million tons of shipping per annum; that it provide immediate emergency tonnage to Italy and France; that it allocate more tankers to Britain; and that it obtain additional tonnage from all other possible sources—neutral shipping, interned shipping, and Japanese shipping. Britain recommended that the United States eliminate every possible trade not connected with the war ef-

71. "Memorandum for Colonel House by Bainbridge Colby," December 14, 1917, USDSM 367, 763.72/13416.

fort.[72] The question of whether the United States should alter its plans for employing an independent army in Europe had also risen and was to become one of the most hotly contested inter-Allied issues during 1918. The argument for "amalgamation" was simple: more troops could be gotten to Europe and more tonnage released for other duty if the United States did not persist in following its policy of creating an independent army to fight in its own sector under its own commanders with its own services of the rear. General Pershing did not share Sims's attitude of all-out cooperation with the Entente powers. He refused to accept the "logical" solution as Sims had done in connection with the naval reinforcement. For Pershing considerations of national pride, military glory, and distrust of Entente efficiency were compelling reasons to oppose Allied arguments for amalgamation. Beyond these notions was the feeling that the United States would exercise more influence on the peace settlement if it organized and employed an independent army in Europe than if it allowed its man power to be utilized as replacements for the French and British formations on the Western Front.[73]

Sims privately favored amalgamation, and he also approved of the utmost efforts to construct merchant shipping.[74] The Navy Department did not share his views, but this conflict did not cause difficulties between the two headquarters, simply because neither Sims nor department officials took a leading role in the disputes over shipbuilding and amalgamation that marred inter-Allied harmony during 1918. In January Sims was temporarily hopeful that the United States would agree to amalgamation because it was looked upon favorably by the American military representative at the Supreme War Council—Gen. Tasker H. Bliss.[75] Pershing, however, remained intransigent and gained

72. Crawford to Polk, December 20, 1917, United States Department of State, Papers Relating to the Foreign Relations of the United States, 1917, 2 vols., supp. 2, 1:650–51.

73. For a detailed account of the amalgamation controversy, see David F. Trask, The United States in the Supreme War Council: American War Aims and Inter-Allied Strategy, 1917–1918 (Middletown, Conn., 1961), 70–100. General Foch was most critical of delays in the American reinforcement. Ferdinand Foch, Mémoires pour Servir à l'Histoire de la Guerre de 1914–1918, 2 vols. (Paris, 1931), 2:29–81.

74. Sims to Mrs. Sims [?], January 21, 1918, Sims Papers; Sims to Bayly, March 14, 1918, Sims Papers.

75. Sims to Bayly, January 24, 1918, Sims Papers. A copy of the letter to Bayly is in USNSF, TD file.

the support of President Wilson. In March Sims again recorded privately his feeling that it might be wiser to send supplies rather than troops to France, but he did not become actively involved in the continuing controversy over the utilization of American man power.[76]

Despite glowing promises, the United States never met its commitments to the Allies in respect to merchant-ship construction. During the period February-October, 1918, American shipyards turned out just less than a million tons, a miserably disappointing performance. The British War Cabinet regularly noted the gap between promise and fulfillment in the United States, but was at a loss to effect any great improvement in the situation. The British were increasingly convinced that the United States was developing its shipping program with an eye not simply to wartime needs but to the future, and in this opinion they were certainly correct.[77] The United States made various efforts to increase available tonnage. It undertook to charter and purchase Japanese tonnage, but expedients like this did not satisfy the British.[78] They were especially irritated at American insouciance about the shipment of troops to Europe, especially when this project required British tonnage. Lord Reading, Spring Rice's replacement as the British Ambassador in Washington, exploded privately to Lloyd George. "It is unfortunate indeed that our ships are to be taken to carry troops which our military people tell me cannot really be used for a very long time."[79] This frustration was to have its effects when the war approached its end, particularly in connection with a visit made to the United States by Sir Eric Geddes in early October and the pre-Armistice negotiations which took place in Paris during late October and early November after the collapse of the German Army. These events are discussed in Chapters 8 and 9.

The Allied Naval Council never became deeply concerned with shipping problems because they were assigned mostly to other agencies. About the only shipping issue of any substance

76. Notes for ANC meeting, March 11, 1918, USNSF, TX file.

77. Minutes of the War Cabinet (WC 355), February 27, 1918, CAB 23, book 5; Minutes of the War Cabinet (WC 394 and 395), April 18 and 25, 1918, CAB 23, book 6. Baker, *Wilson*, 7:285–86.

78. For documents relating to negotiations concerning shipping in relation to Japan, see Department of State, *1918*, supp. 1 (1933), 1:517–18, 521–23, 628–29.

79. Reading to Lloyd George, May 5, 1918, file F/60/2/59.

to interest that group was the question of whether to publish shipping losses. Some leaders wished to take this step in order to counteract exaggerated German claims of sinkings; others opposed the move out of fear that the extensive losses would have a depressing effect on civilian morale.[80] Sims favored publication. "It is only by [making] a plain, clear, and truthful statement of this kind that the civilian population of England and the other Allied countries can be brought to a realization that upon the shipbuilding industry depends the outcome of the war."[81] The French maintained their opposition to publication, thereby delaying the action favored by the other powers, but the issue gradually lost importance as the submarine war turned definitely in favor of the Allies.[82]

Despite the obvious interrelationship of naval policy and shipping policy, the western coalition for the most part chose to discuss questions of maritime transport outside formal naval channels. This tendency reflected the extreme importance of the question; it was too politically significant to be delegated to the admirals. If this practice might not have been the most rational of procedures, it spared Admiral Sims in London and his coadjutors in Washington the burdens of a most distressing and thankless problem.

IV

The dispute over amalgamation shook the western coalition in 1918, but the question of how to deal with the Bolshevik revolution was an even greater apple of discord. During 1917 the provisional government that overthrew the Czarist regime in March had constantly pressed for naval assistance to break a German blockade of Murmansk and Archangel on the White Sea.[83] When Sims was consulted he opposed any diversion of American forces from the submarine zone around the British

80. Sims to Benson, March 7, 1918, USNSF, TP file.
81. Sims memorandum, March 11, 1918, USNSF, TX file.
82. Minutes of the Second Meeting, ANC, First Session, March 12, 1918, USNSF, QC file. For Sims's report on this spirited discussion, see Sims to Navy Department, March 14, 1918, USNSF, QC file. See also Minutes of the Second Meeting, ANC, Appendix 3, March 12, 1918, USNSF, QC file.
83. For a request in April, 1917, see Department of State, *1917*, supp. 2, 1:32–33. See also Daniels diary, May 3, 1917, Cronon, ed., *Cabinet Diaries*, 145–46.

Isles, arguing that American assistance to Britain might allow that nation to send support to the White Sea.[84] The British did not share this opinion, and London asked Washington to provide aid to the hard-pressed Russians.[85] Daniels remained firm, reiterating Sims's view that American reinforcements for Britain would allow the Admiralty to direct assistance to the White Sea. "It is very necessary to the efficient employment of the United States forces," concluded Daniels, "that they be retained under one command and operated and administered as near as possible in one area."[86] The United States never really wavered from this general outlook.

The provisional government received some assistance from Great Britain, largely in the form of trawlers assigned as patrol craft in the White Sea. Russian efforts to augment this force at the London naval conference in September, 1917, met with little response except a promise not to withdraw the trawlers until the Germans ceased submarine operations for the season.[87] One reason for British reticence was a general feeling that the Russian fleet in the Baltic Sea had been entirely too inactive. At one point in October, 1917, the War Cabinet took the position that "if they want assistance from us the Russians must at least make a determined effort on their own behalf."[88]

After the Bolsheviks succeeded in overthrowing the provisional government in November, Lenin and Trotsky moved as rapidly as possible to take Russia out of the war. Almost immediately thereafter various schemes for Allied intervention at various places in Russia—particularly in North Russia at Murmansk and Archangel and in Siberia at Vladivostok—began to emanate from Britain and France. Such operations required naval participation, and the Navy Department began to consider the matter.

In January, 1918, Daniels met on several occasions with Acting Secretary of State Polk and other officials to consider what naval action the United States might take in connection with a possible Japanese intervention at the Siberian port of Vladi-

84. Daniels to Lansing, May 31, 1917, USDSM 367, 763.72/5004.
85. Crawford to Polk, June 1, 1917, USDSM 367, 763.72/5228.
86. Daniels to Lansing, June 22, 1917, USDSM 367, 762.73/5602.
87. Mayo to Daniels, September 8, 1917, USNSF, QI file.
88. Minutes of the War Cabinet (WC 253), October 19, 1917, CAB 23, book 4.

vostok.[89] At this early juncture Britain and France urged Japanese intervention upon Washington in the strongest terms. President Wilson, however, proved intensely reluctant to undertake such an adventure, and finally opposed it. He gave two reasons for this decision, which Daniels summarized in his diary. "We have not ships to send soldiers and besides if we invade Russia will not Germany say we are doing exactly what she is doing. We will lose our moral position."[90] Another motive, also of critical importance, was the fear that Japan would act in Siberia to further selfish expansionist interests rather than the general objectives of the Entente powers. Breckinridge Long summarized as well as anyone the distrust of Japanese motives that was general in Washington. "The real danger lies in the possible coalition of Japan and Germany—under an agreement for well defined spheres [in Siberia] & a sharp line of difference between the territories of each. The poor people of Siberia!"[91]

While these events took place, the Russian question began to enter into inter-Allied naval deliberations in London, particularly the situation in the Archangel-Murmansk region. Prior to the January meeting of the Allied Naval Council, France circulated a memorandum to the membership concerning the problems of assisting Allied citizens to escape from Russia and protecting some 210,000 tons of supplies intended for the Eastern Front, which were stored at Archangel. Would it be wise to prevent an enemy occupation of Murmansk and to protect the stores at Archangel?[92] The issue was discussed on January 22. Admiral Wemyss reported that the British had the *Glory* and some other vessels at Murmansk, although no ships were near Archangel. The Council decided to have Britain investigate the situation and if necessary seek assistance for operations from the

89. Daniels diary, January 2, 18, and 19, 1918, Cronon, ed., *Cabinet Diaries*, 261–62, 269, 270.
90. Daniels diary, March 1, 1918, ibid., 285. For an account of early efforts to arrange intervention in Russia, culminating in the President's refusal early in March, 1918, see Trask, *United States in the Supreme War Council*, 100–111. For another report of the Cabinet meeting of March 1, 1918, see Anne Wintermute Lane and Louise Herrick Wall, eds., *The Letters of Franklin K. Lane: Personal and Political* (Boston, 1922), 266–67.
91. Long diary, February 25, 1918, Long Papers.
92. French memorandum on North Russia, Minutes of the ANC, First Meeting, January, 1918, Appendix 6, USNSF, QC file.

French, who would dispatch a cruiser and personnel to make up an occupation force.[93] Sims then asked the Navy Department for any information it had on the situation.[94]

In March, prior to the second meeting of the Allied Naval Council, the British asked Sims whether the United States would send a cruiser to Murmansk. According to a British official, Sims replied that "the United States Government was not at present willing to order a cruiser to Murmansk, but that, if pressed by Lord Reading, they might reconsider their decision."[95] To Benson, Sims reported the absence of definite information on events in North Russia and took no positive position. "I do not think that it would require the services of one of our vessels for a long time, but of course that is more or less conjecture."[96] The Navy Department soon notified him that, after consultation with the State Department, a decision had been made not to send an American ship to North Russia.[97]

When the Allied Naval Council took up the question on March 12, it had before it reports from both Franch and Britain. The French informed the Council that about 200,000 tons of supplies were located at Archangel. Nothing was stored at Murmansk.[98] The British reported that they had decided to maintain their forces at Murmansk for the present, but that they had made arrangements for evacuation if it became necessary. Refugees at Murmansk would be evacuated and the stores would be moved to that port from Archangel. Britain—proceeding to reinforce its expedition—would take steps to prevent four Russian destroyers and nine trawlers from falling into the hands of the enemy.[99] The Council received the reports but elected to proceed cautiously. "It was agreed that all possible steps to meet the conditions at the moment had been taken, and that further

93. Minutes of the ANC, First Meeting, First Session, January 22, 1918, USNSF, QC file.

94. Sims to Navy Department, January 23, 1918, USNSF, QC file.

95. Minutes of the War Cabinet (WC 360), March 6, 1918, CAB 23, book 5.

96. Sims to Benson, March 7, 1918, USNSF, TD file. A copy is also in the TD file.

97. Sims notes for ANC meeting, March 11, 1918, USNSF, TX file.

98. French report on North Russia, Minutes of the Second Meeting, March 11, 1918, Appendix 6, USNSF, QC file.

99. British memorandum on Murmansk and Archangel, Minutes of the ANC, Second Meeting, March 3, 1918, Appendix 6, USNSF, QC file.

action must depend upon the course of events, which cannot be foreseen with any certainty."[100]

On March 15, 1918, a special political conference of the Allies took place in London at which the United States was not represented. This procedure was followed because of President Wilson's well-known objections to political decisions by inter-Allied agencies that might entangle the United States in activities that it could not condone. Among other things this conference asked the Allied Naval Council and the permanent military representatives to confer on the question of intervention in North Russia,[101] a request that precipitated decisions within the naval leadership. A special committee met at the Admiralty on March 19-20 and produced a recommendation. There should be no attempt to occupy Archangel without recognizing the strain it would place upon resources, something that aroused concern, since the small craft needed were required for the antisubmarine war elsewhere. The committee recognized, however, "that an occupation of Archangel would prevent valuable forces lying there from falling into German possession."[102] In this fashion, the Allied Naval Council decided that it would generally oppose extensive naval operations in North Russia unless extreme developments forced an alternative decision in the future.

In Washington Lord Reading and others were pressing the President to commit himself to another project for intervention, an expedition to Vladivostok. For a large number of reasons, among which was his belief that the operation was militarily unsound, the President resisted these clamors. He told Reading that "he did not trust their [military leaders'] wisdom. Thought it [intervention] most unwise."[103] Wilson remained convinced that meddling in the political affairs of Siberia would be productive only of political danger.[104]

100. Minutes of the ANC, Second Meeting, Second Session, March 12, 1918, USNSF, QC file.

101. Minutes of the political conference, March 15, 1918, Records of the Supreme War Council, War Department Records (Record Group 120), American Expeditionary Forces, National Archives, Washington, D.C. These records are cited hereafter as SWC-WDA.

102. Secret memorandum no. 93, "Archangel," printed for the ANC, April 3, 1918, MM, Es file, box 18. An undated copy is in USNSF, QC file.

103. Daniels diary, March 19, 1918, Cronon, ed., *Cabinet Diaries*, 292.

104. Daniels diary, March 20, 1918, ibid. For an account of the President's firm resistance to projects of intervention at this time, see Trask, *United States in the Supreme War Council*, 111-21.

On March 23, 1918, the Allied Naval Council discussed the Russian situation with the permanent military representatives of the Supreme War Council at Versailles. The gathering pronounced quite firmly against any expansion of effort in North Russia. As to Archangel, no military resources seemed available for an operation there. Shipping was a serious problem. "If this shipping was so devoted, its loss would be heavily felt both for anti-submarine purposes and those of transportation." To keep supplies at that place from falling into enemy hands, the group recommended that they be destroyed. As to Murmansk, the meeting decided that the same general considerations applied, but "the Naval steps actually being taken should be continued in order to retain this place in the possession of the Allies as long as possible."[105]

In Washington the old fear of a German-Japanese combination reappeared in this threatening climate. Captain Pratt thought that the antidote to any untoward Japanese activity was for the United States "to inaugurate or cause to be inaugurated an intensive counter offensive in the Far East, directed not against Russia, but in aid of Russia." The United States should accept the assistance of any power that could provide support on this front, an obvious reference to Japan. If that nation harbored dangerous motives, "there would seem no better way to expose it than by a frank, open, vigorous and straight forward policy, outlined immediately."[106] The President did not share this view, but on April 8 he informed Daniels that he could authorize the dispatch of a vessel to Murmansk if the Secretary thought it necessary, although he regretted its withdrawal from "the overseas convoy business."[107] This decision reflected a general tendency in Washington to concern itself less about intervention in North Russia than in eastern Siberia. The Japanese would not be involved in the North.[108]

As the British operation developed at Murmansk, Sims showed

---

105. Minutes of the Joint Meeting of Permanent Military Representatives and the Allied Naval Council (SWC Doc. 152), CAB 25, box 121. See also Secret memorandum no. 93. "Archangel."
106. Pratt memorandum for Benson, March 28, 1918, Sims Papers. A copy of this memorandum is enclosed with Pratt to Sims, April 2, 1918, USNSF, TD file.
107. Wilson to Daniels, April 8, 1918, Daniels Papers.
108. Trask, *United States in the Supreme War Council*, 118–19.

his usual proclivity to support Admiralty desires. Informing the
Navy Department of British efforts in the White Sea region to
protect the area generally, to evacuate refugees, and to guard
stores, he recommended that United States forces operate under
the command of the senior allied commander in that region, a
British rear admiral. He was careful to note that the British commander had been ordered "not to commit himself to land military
operations away from the port, but subject to this restriction he
may use the crews of the ships to stiffen local resistance against
Germans if found practicable."[109] The old *Olympia* was sent to
North Russia as part of the inter-Allied force under British
orders.

The North Russian expedition obtruded itself once again during the third meeting of the Allied Naval Council in late April.
Word of a potential threat to Murmansk from the Finnish White
Guard had been received. If that force could control the Kola
Inlet, it would close the White Sea.[110] Admiral Sims advanced a
political argument for retaining control of Murmansk and also
perhaps of Archangel. "It is necessary to do everything we can to
keep the sympathy of Russia," he told his colleagues, "so that if
the time comes when conditions change in that country, the Russians will again join with the Allies, and the fact that we have
done everything possible to maintain ourselves in the White Sea
ports against the Germans may perhaps have considerable influence in this respect." But Sims did not favor naval reinforcements; such assistance could not add to the security of the area
unless military forces were also sent, and none were available.
Admiral de Bon, the French representative, took the same view.
The Council as a whole reiterated its view that it would be desirable to maintain control of Murmansk, but it could not recommend the dispatch of naval reinforcements. The next day the
French representatives altered their position to support strictly
limited reinforcements. The Council then modified its position
slightly but continued to hold that the Allied navies "would not
be able to provide for the transport, escort, and maintenance of a
Military Expedition to Murmansk, even if this were limited to a
force of 6,000 men."[111] This discussion confirmed the strong ten-

109. Sims to Navy Department, April 13, 1918, USNSF, TT file.
110. British memorandum on Murmansk, Archangel, Finland, Minutes
of the Third Meeting, ANC, April 19, 1918, Appendix 5, USNSF, QC file.
111. Minutes of the Third Meeting, ANC, Second and Third Sessions,

dency of naval officials to oppose intervention in Russia because of their desire to concentrate available sea power against the German submarines in the Atlantic and Mediterranean. In this instance strategic considerations clearly overrode political objectives.

In June the Allied Naval Council once again discussed the North Russian situation, meeting after the permanent military representatives had approved a proposal for the occupation of Murmansk and Archangel.[112] Admiral de Bon observed that activities in the region were developing into extensive operations. He proposed that the Council refuse cooperation in any large operation, reflecting the views of General Foch, who was concerned about the diversion of troops and supplies intended for the Western Front to the North Russian area. Sir Eric Geddes argued for some change of attitude, recognizing new aspects to the situation, including conflicts between the Finns and Germans and the possibility that Murmansk in enemy hands might become a submarine base. Admiral Sims then supported De Bon. He thought that no one could oppose a small force, but the "Council ought to give some assurance that this Expedition would not extend beyond what the Allies were able to sustain from the Naval point of view." He recommended that the Council avoid "extensive operations in the White Sea regions which would very materially affect their Naval dispositions elsewhere." He maintained that if the Germans really wished to seize Murmansk, there was no way to prevent it. Geddes then proposed that a subcommittee meet to consider the question.[113]

The subcommittee report reaffirmed the general position taken by the Allied Naval Council throughout the period January–May, 1918. It recommended that the Supreme War Council reconsider the decision in favor of North Russian operations, arguing that the Allied Naval Council wished to retain naval forces

---

April 26–27, 1918, USNSF, QC file. See also Sims to Navy Department, April 30, 1918, USNSF, QC file.

112. Trask, *United States in the Supreme War Council*, 118–19. This recommendation was Joint Note no. 31. The Supreme War Council approved the project on June 3, 1918, and Britain immediately began to implement it.

113. Minutes of the Fourth Meeting, ANC, First Session, June 11, 1918, USNSF, QC file. The views of Geddes reflected memoranda prepared for the ANC on June 3 and 8, 1918, included in Minutes of the Fourth Meeting, ANC, Appendix 8, USNSF, QC file.

where they were presently concentrated. "The dispersion of forces necessary in order to safeguard the Northern routes to Murmansk and Archangel is undesirable from a strategic point of view, and can only be justified if the results to be obtained by the Military effort in the Murmansk and Archangel districts are adequate."[114] This relatively forceful pronouncement reflected some irritation at the failure of the Supreme War Council and its military representatives to consult fully with the Allied Naval Council prior to making a decision of considerable naval importance.

Events soon passed by the Allied Naval Council, as its resistance to North Russian operations proved unavailing. After extraordinary pressure was placed on President Wilson to condone interventions in North Russia and Siberia throughout June and early July by the Supreme War Council, the United States finally agreed to strictly limited expeditions.[115] This decision, made at the highest inter-Allied level, was not referred to the Allied Naval Council. It brought an unhappy end to that organization's effort to avoid a diversion of naval force to an enterprise that it considered injurious to the principal naval operations of the war—antisubmarine activities in the Atlantic and the Mediterranean. Once the Supreme War Council acted, the Allied Naval Council did what it could to provide the necessary naval support; but the navies, particularly that of the United States, played only a peripheral role in the extraordinarily important decisions and activities that marked the beginnings of the Allied reaction to the onset of the Bolshevik revolution.[116]

V

Throughout 1918 the United States Navy gave high priority to the one naval effort of its own devising that it succeeded in merchandising to the western coalition—the distant mine barrage designed to close off the North Sea. In 1917 the British Admiralty had been generally doubtful of success. Adequate

114. Minutes of the Fourth Meeting, ANC, Third Session, June 12, 1918, USNSF, QC file. See also Sims to Navy Department, June 15, 1918, USNSF, QC file.
115. Trask, *United States in the Supreme War Council*, 121–27.
116. Minutes of the Fifth Meeting, ANC, Second Session, September 14, 1918, MM, Es file, box 20. See also Sims to Navy Department, September 17, 1918, USNSF, QC file.

mines were not yet available, and the sheer length of the proposed barrage meant an enormous expenditure of time and effort. There was also the consideration that Admiral Sims had stressed; the barrage would not be particularly effective until practically complete. Despite these drawbacks the work went ahead.

Delays beset the project at all points in its development. Admiral Sims on occasion reported various reasons why it fell behind schedule. It proved difficult indeed, even with improved mines, to maintain them in position in stormy seas, and if they broke loose, they endangered friendly vessels.[117] It proved difficult to plan the location of "gates" or openings in the barrage through which Allied vessels could pass. There was also the tangled question of neutral rights; the barrage impinged on the Norwegian coast.[118] On occasion friction between British and American officers in charge of the mine-laying operations caused some loss of efficiency.[119] Nevertheless, dogged persistence forced the sea to yield to the extraordinary efforts of the British and American mine layers operating in the difficult northern waters, although the German submarines began to develop countermeasures in the last moments of the submarine war. Admiral Sims never became a truly enthusiastic supporter of the barrage.[120] The energies expended on it in the late summer and early fall indicate the general failure of the Allies to anticipate the remarkably rapid culmination of the war. The western coalition was truly caught by surprise when the Central Powers, at the end of September and in early October, suddenly began a serious attempt to end the war. The Armistice came before the northern barrage was quite complete.

Composed of some 70,000 mines, about 57,000 of which were laid by the United States, the barrage consisted of 15 strings of mines about 100 yards apart. It was about 30 miles wide and 230 miles in length. The cost approximated $40 million.[121] Even its most enthusiastic proponents were reticent in claiming great accomplishments for it, although it was, of course, difficult to

117. Sims to Benson, April 16, 1918, USNSF, TD file.
118. Sims to Benson, August 30, 1918, USNSF, TD file.
119. Sims to Admiral Joseph Strauss, September 7, 1918, USNSF, TD file.
120. Sims to Benson, September 17, 1918, USNSF, TD file; Sims to Benson, October 11, 1918, USNSF, TD file.
121. Elting E. Morison, *Admiral Sims and the Modern American Navy* (Boston, 1942), 415.

ascertain exactly its toll. Shortly after the war the United States
estimated that "at least six submarines were seriously damaged
while crossing the barrage and it is possible that several submarines have been sunk." More important, the barrage certainly
injured the morale of the U-boat crews, causing a notable decline
in efficiency.[122] The Navy Department had hoped that the barrage would rank as its most important and dramatic contribution
to victory over the submarines, but the conclusion of hostilities
precluded a definitive test of its efficiency.

2. Causes of U-Boat Losses, 1914–1918

	1914–1916	1917	1918	Total
Man of war ramming	2	0	1	3
Patrols and hunters	15	17	24	56
Decoy gunfire (Q-ships)	5	6	0	11
Merchant vessels and transports	0	3	4	7
Escorts	0	6	9	15
Mines	10	20	22	52
Accidents	7	9	2	18
Unknown	7	2	7	17
Totals	46	63	69	178

Source: Adapted from a chart in Arthur J. Marder, *From the Dreadnought
to Scapa Flow: The Royal Navy in the Fisher Era, 1904–1919*, vol. 5,
Victory and Aftermath (January 1918–June 1919) (London, 1970),
119–20.

One of the reasons for the extensive commitment to the northern barrage was the continuing fear that Germany would sooner
or later undertake submarine operations in distant waters, particularly in the mid-Atlantic and in waters adjacent to the American coast. Such an offensive could be undertaken by two types
of vessels: fast German cruisers might break out into the Atlantic
and undertake a massive raid on merchant shipping, or huge
submarine cruisers might come into play in areas where they
could not be counteracted by destroyer escorts. When it became
apparent that the convoy system was achieving satisfactory results, the Admiralty began to speculate on possible German
reactions. It was possible that "attack by battle-cruisers, co-
operating with large submarines, acting as scouts and screening

122. "Summary of Activities of U.S. Naval Forces Operating in European Waters," n.d. [but post-November, 1918], USNSF, WV file.

force, may be developed on the Atlantic trade routes."[123] At the inter-Allied naval conference in September, 1917, the Admiralty offered various proposals to counteract submarine cruisers of the *Deutschland* class.[124]

The Allied Naval Council frequently considered the possibility that Germany would launch battle cruiser and submarine cruiser raids. One remedy proposed was to provide escorts in the middle passage by larger vessels—old cruisers and battleships that had sufficient armament to counteract the large guns mounted on the battle cruisers. Another response was to create flying squadrons, groups of fast ships based on locations that would allow them to intercept German surface raiders upon their breakout into the Atlantic. Extension of the convoy system to all parts of the world was also planned.[125]

Admiral Sims did not become unduly alarmed about the possibility of German raids. He never felt that a battle cruiser raid was likely, but to provide for it he advocated cruiser and battleship escorts for convoys.[126] Because the large submarine cruisers were clumsy, he doubted that they constituted a truly serious threat. "All of our experience shows that these submarines are not dangerous to convoys," he told Benson in May, 1918; "otherwise they would have been attacking during the six months that they have been operating." Sims noted that "even the handier U boats and the still handier UB boats often let a convoy go by without attempting an attack." As always he was particularly anxious to avoid undue diversion of antisubmarine craft from the waters immediately adjacent to Britain:

There is no doubt in our minds over here, that what he [the enemy] seeks to do is to produce a moral and political effect, and that as the result of these effects, he can induce the Allies to disintegrate their submarine forces.

For example, if by sending one submarine to America to plant the

123. "Naval Weekly Appreciation, 10," August, 1917, ADM 137, book 511, 363.

124. Mayo to Daniels, September 8, 1917, USNSF, QI file.

125. Jackson notes on Paris meeting, November 30, 1917, USNSF, QC file; Minutes of the First Meeting, ANC, January 22, 1918, Second Session, USNSF, QC file; "Report of Sub-Committee on Ocean Convoys and Escorts," Minutes of the Second Meeting, ANC, March, 1918, Appendix 5, USNSF, QC file.

126. Sims to Benson, August 10, 1918, USNSF, TD file; Sims to Benson, August 30, 1918, USNSF, TD file.

few mines he can carry, or to sink the few ships that he can sink, he can through the influence of his presence upon public opinion, force our Government to keep a large number of destroyers on the other side or in any service not connected with the real anti-submarine campaign, he will have succeeded admirably in his objective.

The solution to the problem of submarine cruisers, he concluded, was not to divert antisubmarine craft needed elsewhere, but to instruct public opinion on the actual objectives of any submarine cruisers that might visit American waters. As he had argued in 1917, Sims held that any great effort in American waters would be highly injurious to the German cause. "To put the extreme case, if she should send all her submarines to the other side, the anti-submarine campaign would at once in consequence be successful."[127]

Sims was justified in his refusal to become unduly alarmed by the submarine raiders. Six of these vessels were converted merchant vessels of the *Deutschland* class, much too slow and clumsy to operate effectively against commerce. German designers had developed a new class of submarine cruisers specifically intended for commerce raiding, capable of a speed of fifteen knots. Only two of these vessels ever saw active service because of delays in production, and they did not prove efficient because they were beset by certain technical difficulties that could not be corrected in time. To add insult to injury the German naval staff never made effective arrangements for control of the submarine cruisers; each was maneuvered as an independent entity from Berlin.[128]

Sims and his British associates were correct in their belief that the convoy system had created great difficulties for the submarine; in the spring of 1918 the German naval staff began to consider ways of recovering the undersea initiative. On March 3, 1918, Holtzendorff informed Kuehlmann, the new foreign minister, that improved U-boats made possible an expansion of

127. Sims to Benson, May 17, 1918, TD file. For earlier mention of this problem, see the Sims-Benson correspondence for January-March, 1918, USNSF, TD file. See also Sims to Pratt, May 12, 1918, USNSF, TD file; Sims to Bayly, May 17, 1918, USNSF, TD file; Sims to Pratt, July 10, 1918, USNSF, TD file.

128. For information on the submarine cruisers, see Michelsen, *Der U-Bootskrieg*, 65–66, 178; Gibson and Prendergast, *German Submarine War*, 218–19; Arno Spindler, *Der Handelskrieg mit U-Booten*, 4 vols. (Berlin, 1941), 4:2; Goerlitz, ed., *The Kaiser and His Court*, 392.

operating areas. "The military necessity of scattering as much as possible the antisubmarine warfare of our enemies makes it necessary to increase the area of the blockaded zones." Naval estimates revealed that "the best chance of success lies in an increase of the unrestricted submarine warfare areas to the East Coast of the United States of America," because maritime traffic could be intercepted more easily at known assembly points than at unknown destinations. "Up to now political considerations and the lack of development in the effectiveness of the U-boats have prevented us from expanding the spheres of operation to the American coast. The technical obstacles . . . are no longer with us. In my opinion, political considerations no longer exist." He was planning to act in May, and the Kaiser had generally acceded to his plans.[129] Kuehlmann did not agree; then visiting in Bucharest, he quickly advised Holtzendorff that political considerations did indeed exist. Submarine activities on the American coast might arouse martial sentiment in the United States among those previously cool to the war. In addition, an extended war on commerce in American waters might interfere with Chancellor Hertling's hopes for peace, which he developed after President Wilson's announcement of the Fourteen Points.[130] General Ludendorff then entered the lists, strongly favoring the naval initiative, and reminded Kuehlmann of the importance of interdicting American reinforcements. "Political considerations must be dismissed due to the serious commitment of the United States to the war and due to the impotence of the antiwar elements before the dictates of military necessity."[131]

Delays ensued. The naval staff proposed specific dates for the opening of unrestricted submarine warfare on the American coast, but the Foreign Office sustained its opposition, continuing to cite political arguments against the military necessity argued by the Navy.[132] Hindenburg added his voice to those pressing for

129. Holtzendorff to Kuehlmann, March 3, 1918, St. Antony's Papers, reel 14, Geheime Akten, vol. 62, 172.
130. Kuehlmann to Foreign Office, March 5, 1918, St. Antony's Papers, reel 14, Geheime Akten, vol. 62, frames 182, 191.
131. Lersner to Foreign Office, March 7, 1918, St. Antony's Papers, reel 14, Geheime Akten, vol. 62, frame 194.
132. See for example, Holtzendorff to Kuehlmann, June 17, 1918, St. Antony's Papers, reel 14, Geheime Akten, vol. 64, frames 139–40; Kuehlmann to Holtzendorff, June 18, 1918, St. Antony's Papers, reel 14, Geheime Akten, vol. 64, frame 154.

the American campaign. The Kaiser seemed interested, but he continued to postpone the final decision.[133] Hindenburg became more and more insistent as he observed the decline of the German position on the Western Front, telling Wilhelm II that "The American army leaders are moving ever growing numbers of troops to the Western Front, so that every day takes on greater meaning."[134] Hindenburg had in mind attacks primarily on troop transports. On June 28, the Kaiser decided once again to refuse permission for the submarine offensive in American waters. Germany lacked sufficient resources to make a success of the effort; "One should not repeat the error of the Spring of 1915."[135] The Kaiser remained adamant, even after a face-to-face discussion with Hindenburg and Ludendorff on July 2. He insisted that Germany lacked sufficient strength to succeed in such an effort and also maintained that the policy would adversely affect the German position in South America. "So far opinion in Argentina and Chile is not at all unfavorable. We must prevent their giving out our ships under Wilson's pressure." This reference was to German shipping interned in Latin American harbors being sought by the United States. Chancellor Hertling stood firm against the soldiers and sailors. The Kaiser abruptly ended the discussion after a final naval plea, "I am of different opinion and it will remain with that."[136] Walther Rathenau reflected the disillusionment with the naval and military leaders that probably influenced the Kaiser and his Chancellor. The war leaders had promised earlier that no American army would ever land in Europe, but by July, 1918, over 1.2 million American soldiers were deployed in France, and additional detachments were arriving every day.[137] Further efforts to change the Kaiser's mind took place late in July, but when Admiral Scheer, about to as-

133. Berkheim to Foreign Office, June 23, 1918, St. Antony's Papers, reel 14, Geheime Akten, vol. 65, frame 27; Hindenburg to Hertling, June 24, 1918, St. Antony's Papers, reel 14, Geheime Akten, vol. 65, frame 35; Gruenau to Foreign Office, June 24, 1918, St. Antony's Papers, reel 14, Geheime Akten, vol. 65, frame 38.

134. Berkheim to Foreign Office, June 25, 1918, St. Antony's Papers, reel 14, Geheime Akten, vol. 65, frame 43.

135. Gruenau to Foreign Office, June 28, 1918, St. Antony's Papers, reel 14, Geheime Akten, vol. 65, frame 89.

136. Protocol of discussion, July 2, 1918, St. Antony's Papers, reel 14, Geheime Akten, vol. 65, frame 110. See also Goerlitz, ed., *The Kaiser and His Court*, 369–70.

137. Walther Rathenau, *Briefe*, 2 vols. (Dresden, 1926), 2:54.

sume the supreme naval command, came out in opposition to the plan, it receded from view.[138]

Some submarine cruisers did operate in American waters, observing the rules of cruiser warfare. Seven U-boat visits occurred in American waters during the summer of 1918, but as Sims had predicted, their accomplishments were minimal. The raiders sank only about 110,000 tons of merchant shipping.[139] In August Pratt told Sims of some difficulties on the American coast and reported preparations to put convoys into effect if major attacks were mounted against oil tankers in the Gulf of Mexico.[140] Sims responded acerbically, noting that any extensive response would play into the hands of the Germans.[141] Mercifully no loaded troopships were sunk. In early October Sims ventured the opinion that troop transports had been spared because the likelihood of successful attacks was small and the risk to U-boats great. There was more advantage in concentrating on merchant ships, and political considerations played a part. "I can hardly imagine the German High command deciding to make an effort to sink one of our troop convoys and at the same time deciding to make every effort to bring about a compromise peace, and there can be no doubt that they will make every effort to bring about such a peace."[142]

In a postwar retrospect, the Navy summarized the reasons why troopships avoided submarine attack. Troop transports moved at no less than twelve knots speed, and most reached fifteen to twenty-two knots, much faster than the submerged speed of seven or eight knots achieved by submarines. Destroyers provided unusually effective escort. Troop convoys moved through danger areas at night and were hard to locate. Finally, routes of convoys were constantly altered to confuse interceptors.[143] So ended the German submarine offensive, frustrated in the ex-

138. Gruenau to Foreign Office, July 18, 1918, St. Antony's Papers, reel 14, Geheime Akten, vol. 65, frame 129; Scheer, *Germany's High Sea Fleet*, 332; Discussion on the American Blockade, July 29, 1918, St. Antony's Papers, reel 14, Geheime Akten, vol. 65, frames 214–24; Goerlitz, ed., *The Kaiser and His Court*, 376; Hertling to Foreign Office, August 1, 1918, St. Antony's Papers, reel 14, Geheime Akten, vol. 66, frame 1.
139. Gibson and Prendergast, *German Submarine War*, 306–7, 310.
140. Pratt to Sims, August 15, 1918, USNSF, TD file.
141. Sims to Pratt, August 30, 1918, USNSF, TD file.
142. Sims to Benson, October 2, 1918, USNSF, TD file.
143. "Summary of Activities of U.S. Naval Forces Operating in European Waters," n.d. [but post-November, 1918], USNSF, WV file.

treme by effective countermeasures. No naval figure had been
more acute in his estimate of the situation and in his recommendations than Admiral Sims. Time after time he was proved correct in disputes with the Navy Department over the proper
American responses to the naval challenge. On October 10, the
German Admiralty recalled two ancient submarine cruisers
operating off the American coast in order to place relations with
the United States on a better footing as peace negotiations suddenly began.[144] The Allied Naval Council started to consider
armistice terms, an assignment that none of its members had
dreamed would be necessary until at least 1919.

✻ ✻ ✻ ✻

The western coalition survived the continuing submarine
challenge in 1918 by gradually perfecting the general antisubmarine policies that had been developed in 1917. The final German offensives in France had presumed effective interdiction of
American reinforcements. The failure of the U-boats to accomplish this mission was one of the most important reasons why the
Franco-British army on the Western Front was able to sustain its
defensive operations sufficiently to force the exhaustion of all
available German reserves. By October, 1918, when the German
Army was finally prepared to accept defeat, the German naval
offensive had been decisively contained. The victory at sea had
not been achieved without many difficulties within and between
the several navies of the Allied and Associated Powers, but the
western coalition had generated sufficient strength and coordination to ensure a splendid triumph.

To be sure, there had been some notable inter-Allied failures,
most of them mercifully obscured by the brilliant glow of victory
in 1918. One of these failures, never really explained by historians, transpired in the Mediterranean Sea and its tributary
bodies, the Adriatic and Aegean seas. Before turning to the culmination of the naval victory during the pre-Armistice discussions in Paris during late October and early November, 1918,
events in the Mediterranean Sea require analysis. The Allied
Naval Council gave more of its time to this endeavor than to any
other, and Admiral Sims became deeply involved in it. Frustration in the Mediterranean may help account for the general ob-
scurity of the Allied Naval Council in the pages of naval history.

144. Goerlitz, ed., *The Kaiser and His Court*, 404.

CHAPTER 7

FRUSTRATION IN THE MEDITERRANEAN

April, 1917–November, 1918

The western coalition coordinated its naval efforts in the Atlantic Ocean well enough to achieve a smashing victory in 1918, but the pattern differed in the other main theater of the naval war. Adolphe Laurens caught the reality in an expressive Gallic phrase: *"En Méditerranée tout se compliqué."*[1] The Mediterranean Sea, which constituted a vital link in the communications of Great Britain with its eastern empire, played a role of comparable importance for France and Italy and served also as the supply line to Allied armies operating in Palestine, Mesopotamia, and Macedonia. Among the major participants in the western coalition only the United States lacked significant Mediterranean commitments. The Entente powers had a common interest in preserving control of the Mediterranean, but divergent national objectives were everywhere in conflict. This situation naturally affected the naval effort of the western coalition in those waters.

In early 1917 the Central Powers had hoped to interdict Allied trade in the Mediterranean as well as in the Atlantic. When Germany decided to resume unrestricted submarine warfare it prevailed upon Austria-Hungary to undertake the same policy in the Mediterranean. Civilian leaders in Vienna, like their counterparts in Berlin, proved extremely hesitant to accept this decision, but naval officials waxed enthusiastic, and Austria-Hungary duly began unrestricted submarine warfare in the Mediterranean on February 1, 1917.[2] At that time it had only twelve submarines; its total undersea fleet grew during 1917–1918 to only twenty-seven boats. Germany agreed to reinforce the Austrian flotillas based on Pola and Cattaro, two ports on the eastern coast of the Adriatic Sea. Like Germany, Austria-

1. Adolphe Laurens, *Histoire de la Guerre Sous-marine Allemande (1914–1918)* (Paris, 1930), 369.
2. Edmund Glaise von Horstenau and Rudolf Kiszling, eds., *Oesterreich-Ungarns Letzter Krieg, 1914–1918*, 7 vols., *Das Kriegsjahr 1917* (Vienna, 1936), 6:7; Hans Hugo Sokol, *Oesterreich-Ungarns Seekrieg, 1914–18*, 4 vols. (Vienna, 1933), 3:338.

Hungary never developed a coordinated building program. Most of its vessels were relatively small and of ancient vintage, capable of operating for only two weeks at a time in coastal waters. The Austrian fleet undertook extensive operations against merchant shipping only after receiving German U-boats.[3] German submarines operating in the Mediterranean totaled only thirty-two, so that less than fifty submarines were available to the Central Powers there during 1917–1918, a remarkably small number.[4] The German U-boats remained under orders from Berlin, although the German naval staff consulted Vienna on their deployment.[5]

Austria's surface fleet, a relatively formidable force commanded by Adm. Nikolaus Horthy, consisted of three battleship divisions and a cruiser flotilla, along with supporting destroyers, mine sweepers, and the like.[6] Based on harbors in the northern Adriatic, this fleet occasionally mounted cruiser raids against the Italian Adriatic coast, thereby interfering with important coastal trade and terrorizing the civilian population. This policy immobilized most of the Italian Navy, which was kept in readiness for a general engagement should the main Austrian fleet venture into the Adriatic or attempt to break out into the Mediterranean Sea. The Austrians took full advantage of good anchorages on the Dalmatian coast, but the Italian coastline across the Adriatic was almost devoid of comparable locations, a considerable handicap to the Italian fleet.

Despite the urging of France and Britain, Italy stubbornly refused to adopt an offensive naval strategy, preferring simply to contain the Austrian fleet. A French observer summarized the situation aptly in July, 1916. His country's relations with the Italians were "courteous," but they did not inspire "the same confidence as those with the English." The Italians seemed to want mostly "to husband their ships and to avoid an encounter with the enemy; their tactics are purely defensive. . . . They wish to

3. For information on the Austrian submarines, see R. H. Gibson and Maurice Prendergast, *The German Submarine Warfare, 1914–1918* (London, 1931), 253; Charles Domville-Fife, *Submarines and Sea Power* (London, 1919), 55–56; Sokol, *Oesterreich-Ungarns Seekrieg*, 4:338–521.
4. Glaise von Horstenau and Kiszling, eds., *Oesterreich-Ungarns Letzter Krieg*, 6:8; Gibson and Prendergast, *German Submarine Warfare*, 239.
5. Andreas Michelsen, *Der U-Bootskrieg, 1914–1918* (Leipzig, 1925), 49; Walther Hubatsch, *Der Admiralstab und die Obersten Marinebehoerden in Deutschland, 1848–1945* (Frankfurt, 1958), 173.
6. Sokol, *Oesterreich-Ungarns Seekrieg*, 4:774.

MEDITERRANEAN SEA

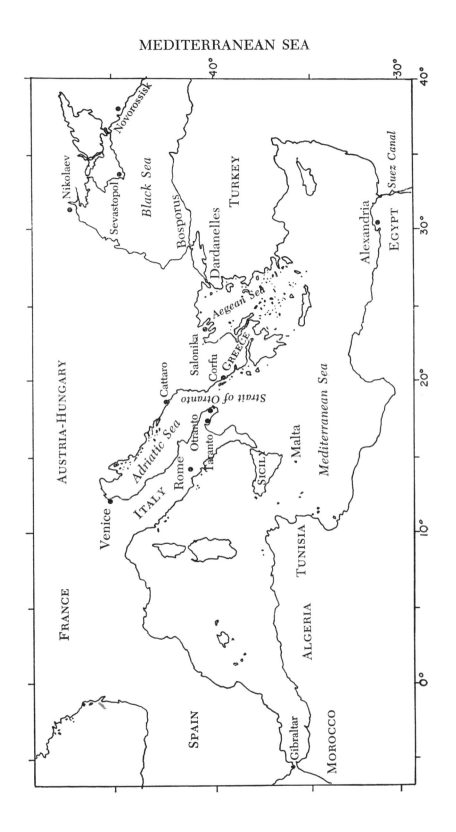

reserve the direction of operations in the Adriatic, and to maintain a barrier at Otranto."[7] The latter obstacle, intended to block the enemy submarines' exit to the Mediterranean, consisted of a surface patrol, augmented over time by an extensive mine and net barrage.

Throughout 1917–1918 France and Britain, ultimately supported by the United States, sought strenuously to energize Italian naval policy. The United States, of course, did not declare war against Austria-Hungary until December, 1917, a policy that severely restricted its role in Mediterranean affairs during the early months of its intervention, although U-boats operating in the area were under orders to attack American ships throughout the period February-November, 1917.[8]

Of course Italian naval policy reflected not only the requirements of belligerency with the Central Powers, but also long-run political considerations associated with historic imperial rivalries, particularly with France but to an important degree also with Great Britain. These political circumstances loomed as important in Italian calculations as the desire to contain the Austrian Navy; perhaps in the end they were more important. In particular Italy was determined to reap the benefits of the Treaty of London, concluded on April 26, 1915, which brought the country into the war on the side of the Entente powers. The Italians were promised the South Tyrol and Trentino, Gorizia, Gradisca, Trieste, Istria, certain Dalmatian islands, and the southern districts of Dalmatia itself along with Saseno and Valona. Rome weighed every wartime act in terms of whether it helped to guarantee the territorial annexations promised by the Treaty of London. Early in 1917 a French attaché in Rome drew attention to the naval consequences of Italian policy. Italy in the future would be "more attracted by the advantage that she ought to obtain from the war than the war itself." Without enlarging its naval or mercantile strength, Italy hoped "to profit from the situation and to assert herself in Mediterranean. This is why she systematically refuses all active cooperation in our enterprises and in our Mediterranean convoys."[9] At about the same time,

7. Report to French Etat-Major General (E.M.G.), July 9, 1916, MM, Es file, box 13.
8. Sokol, *Oesterreich-Ungarns Seekrieg*, 4:512.
9. French naval attaché (Rome) to E.M.G., February 15, 1917, MM, Es file, box 13.

Britain's ambassador in Rome, Sir Rennell Rodd, reported to Balfour on certain fixed attitudes of Sydney Sonnino, the Italian foreign minister. "One of these, on which he seems to have absolutely made up his mind, is that French policy is really anti-Italian, and that the French mean to dominate Italy in the Mediterranean and thwart her ambitions to expand." Rodd advised that Britain do all it could to smooth Franco-Italian relations; otherwise, "How shall we be able to retain the united face to the common danger after the war?"[10] Another British envoy, Lord Bertie in Paris, also drew attention to "an almost universal disgust and contempt" in France for Italy because of its policies in Greece and Asia Minor. "Her want of enterprise on land and at sea is partly attributed to an intention to reserve her military and naval forces as important assets when the time for peace negotiations approaches."[11]

The novelist Thomas Nelson Page, serving as the American Ambassador in Rome, informed President Wilson in February that Italy had responded unenthusiastically to the news of the German-American crisis. Italians were generally uninformed about the United States. More important, they feared that America might now divert to its own use shipments of war material previously intended for Italy. Even more significant was "the feeling, that in the event of our coming in you will have great influence in the peace congress, and may be opposed to the realization by Italy of Italian aspirations [with] regard to the extension of Italian territory."[12] Thereafter Page devoted himself to exerting pressures on Washington in behalf of Italian needs, stressing the importance of paying due attention to Rome. "Our friends in Italy," he told the President, "are very sensitive —especially sensitive to overtures of civility, and they have a feeling that what they have performed and suffered is by no means appreciated by the other powers."[13] He did not know that Sonnino harbored definite suspicions of American intentions. Italy's Foreign Minister told Sir Rennell Rodd in July, 1917, that "While Europe was struggling and exhausting herself, the United

10. Rodd to Balfour, February 19, 1917, Cabinet Papers, no. 82 (1917), FO 800, book 12.
11. Bertie to Balfour, February 21, 1917, Cabinet Papers, no. 93 (1917), FO 899, box 12. A copy is in the Bertie Papers, FO 800, book 169.
12. Page to Wilson, February 13, 1917, Wilson Papers, box 114.
13. Page to Wilson, July 16, 1917, Wilson Papers, box 123.

States were likely to become the dominant element in the world and this was a consummation he did not consider devoutly to be wished for."[14]

In October, 1917, combined Austro-German forces launched a powerful assault along the Italian front and achieved a great breakthrough at Caporetto, an event that placed Italian affairs at the forefront of Entente diplomacy for some time. Among other things the Italian disaster helped precipitate formation of improved institutions for coordinating inter-Allied endeavors. Most important among these organizations was the Supreme War Council, as well as the Allied Naval Council, the latter destined to devote much of its attention to Mediterranean questions. Because of this development Admiral Sims found himself deeply involved in Italian affairs during the last year of the war.[15]

I

Ambassador Page had urged an American declaration of war against Austria-Hungary for some time, obviously fearful that Italy might drop out of the war. Strong manifestations of confidence and support, he thought, would stiffen backbones in Rome. Russia's defalcation in early November particularly alarmed him. On December 1 he argued that a declaration of war "would have a strong moral effect here counteracting the Russian armistice and anti-war propaganda. Furthermore it would remove certain obstacles which make me feel sometimes that we are rather outside the circle here."[16] A few days later he spoke even more urgently. "Whatever can be done to fortify the Italian people should be done, and unless they are fortified I do not know what will happen."[17] Page's desires were finally

14. Rodd to Balfour, Cabinet Papers, no. 313 (1917), FO 899, book 13.

15. Italian questions first arose at the Allied Naval Council during its first session. See R. H. Jackson notes of the ANC meeting, November 30, 1917, USNSF, QC file; British memorandum of results at the first ANC meeting, November 29–30, 1917, ADM 137, book 1786, 45–54. See also Cusani memorandum for Benson, December 2, 1917, Benson Papers, box 42.

16. Page to Wilson, December 1, 1917, USDSM 367, 763.72/7929.

17. Page to Wilson, December 4, 1917, Wilson Papers, box 131. See also Page to Lansing, December 6, 1917, USDSM 367, 763.72/7997. This message is included in United States Department of State, *Papers Relating to the Foreign Relations of the United States, The Lansing Papers*, 2 vols. (Washington, D.C., 1940), 2:70. See also Robert Lansing, *War Memoirs of Robert Lansing, Secretary of State* (Indianapolis, 1935), 257–59.

met on December 7, 1917, when Congress responded to President Wilson's request for a declaration of war against Austria-Hungary.[18] Transported with joy, the Ambassador continued to call for direct American aid to Italy. "Every moment shows that Italy's needs of relief supplies are great, especially grain and coal. American troops sent here would have great moral effect even if number small."[19] He urged Colonel House, then in Europe attending the inter-Allied meeting in Paris, to visit Rome before returning to the United States, but the President's friend felt compelled to proceed immediately to Washington.[20] General Pershing strongly opposed diversion of American troops away from the Western Front, an attitude supported also by the French Commander in Chief, Gen. Philippe Pétain, so that nothing came of Page's recurrent suggestions that the United States "show the flag" on the Italian front.[21]

Just at the beginning of 1918, statements on war aims by both Prime Minister Lloyd George and President Wilson aroused new suspicion in Rome that the other belligerents did not intend to honor the territorial concessions envisioned in 1915. Wilson was less definite than his British counterpart, promising in the Fourteen Points only to adjust Italian boundaries according to the principle of self-determination. Secretary of State Lansing aptly summarized the naval aspects of the question, particularly in reference to the Adriatic Sea, where the Italian and Austro-Hungarian fleets confronted each other:

The Adriatic question of Italy is another of the problems which will have to be settled in the treaty of peace. Italy's retention of her right to occupy naval bases on the eastern shore of the Adriatic as a means of protection is not without merit. Of course it loses much of its force if the President's idea of an international guarantee of political and territorial integrity prevails and is effective. It seems to me that unless all doubt as to the efficacy of the proposed treaty is dispelled, the question will have to be solved.

If, as a result of the guaranty, all fortifications and naval bases on

18. For the message, see James Brown Scott, ed., *Official Statements of War Aims and Peace Proposals, December, 1916 to November, 1918* (Washington, 1921), 193–202.

19. Page to Lansing, December 12, 1917, USDSM 367, 763.72/8106.

20. Page to Wilson, December 15, 1917, Wilson Papers, box 132; Lansing to Page, December 15, 1917, USDSM 367, 763.72/8080.

21. *U. S. Army in the World War*, 17 vols., *Policy-Forming Documents* (Washington, D.C., 1948), 2:100.

the eastern shore are destroyed, ample protection to the low-lying indented coast of Italy might be furnished by an agreement of all the powers to prevent by force any attempt to fortify ports on the eastern shores. Unless that is done it would seem as if Italy might very properly claim the right to hold strategic harbors in Dalmatia and Albania. I think the whole question will have to be debated.[22]

Lansing proved correct in assuming that Italy would react negatively to Wilson's formulation concerning Italy's territorial claims. Page reported to the President: "It has become pretty generally accepted here that your expression eliminates a considerable part of what the Italians had been led to believe they might justly claim at the conclusion of the peace."[23]

Lansing now took what was for him an unusual step of urging a specific course of action upon the President. Writing on January 25, 1918, he rehearsed the views he had developed earlier and suggested that the Chief Executive seek without delay to head off a separate peace treaty between Italy and the Central Powers.[24] Recognizing the delicacy of the situation, President Wilson discussed the matter privately with the Italian Ambassador in Washington, Macchi di Cellere, telling him that he had

limited my statement about Italian rights as I did because I was taking my programme as a whole, including the league of nations through which mutually defensive pledges were to be given and taken which would render strategic conditions such as those affecting the Adriatic much less important. I told him that, failing a league of nations, my mind would be open upon all such matters to new judgments.

I am clear that I could not pledge our people to fight for the eastern shore of the Adriatic; but there is nothing in what I have omitted to say to alarm the Italian people, and it ought to be possible for Orlando to make that plain to his followers.[25]

The clarification probably amounted to cold comfort in Rome.

22. Lansing memorandum, diary, January 10, 1918, Papers of Robert Lansing, National Archives, Washington, D.C. Hereafter cited as Lansing Papers.
23. Page to Wilson, January 29, 1918, Wilson Papers, box 135. See also Page to Lansing, January 29, 1918, Department of State, *The Lansing Papers*, 2:96–98.
24. Lansing to Wilson, January 25, 1918, ibid., 89–90.
25. Wilson to Lansing, January 29, 1918, ibid., 94. See also Ray Stannard Baker, *Woodrow Wilson: Life and Letters*, 8 vols., *Armistice* (New York, 1939), 8:506–7.

Sonnino's prediction in 1917 that the United States might cause great difficulties had begun to materialize.

If Page reported a hardening of Italian opinion regarding war aims, attitudes within the American Government became more firmly opposed to unduly rapacious demands. The Ambassador informed the President that if Italy did not gain the Trentino, Trieste, and "certain strategic points on the eastern side of the Adriatic," the Italian people "would consider their failure to have them as tantamount to defeat." Once again he urged that the United States "show the flag" in Italy to counteract adverse public opinion.[26] Colonel House expressed to Wilson his firm opposition to Italian aggrandizement, but he urged caution in the light of the present military crisis. He did not think that Italy's desire for territorial aggrandizement was as strong as it was before Wilson made himself "the champion of the common people throughout the world." Waxing indignant, House denominated Sonnino "the worst reactionary that I know in Europe," but he was quick to point out that the Foreign Minister did not reflect Italian opinion well "on any subject excepting their desires of Austria." Recognizing the growing resentment of the United States in Europe, House pointed out that if peace negotiations were held at this juncture, "I think you would find some envy and resentment at your commanding position." Nevertheless, the prospects for the situation were favorable. "Unfortunately, the reactionaries are in control of almost all of the belligerent governments, but they represent the necessities of their people rather than their real sentiments." He proposed that the President "exercise great caution" in his next statement to the Congress because of the reactionary mood in Europe and also because a "false step" might head off growing sentiment for peace in Germany.[27] There was little encouragement in this private pronunciamento of the "new diplomacy" for the old-guard diplomatists of exhausted Europe. Pristine America was determined to clean out the Augean stables; events would continue to play into the hands of the western Hercules.

Lloyd George did not escape the wrath of the Italians for his restrained rendition of the terms contained in the Treaty of

26. Page to Wilson, February 5, 1918, Wilson Papers, box 135.
27. House to Wilson, February 1, 1918, Wilson Papers, box 135.

London. On January 10, Sonnino called in Sir Rennell Rodd and discussed the Adriatic question in great detail:

The all-important issue for Italy had been to release herself from the thralldom imposed upon her in 1866, and to secure freedom from constant menace in the Adriatic. What that implied the present war had revealed. With all the naval superiority of the Allies they had never been able to accomplish anything in that sea, which remained under the control and menace of the Power [Austria-Hungary] holding such immensely superior strategic positions, while the hopelessly exposed and harbourless coastline of Italy was at the enemy's mercy. It was admitted that Italy's claim to unite herself with the people of Italian language and race was included in the war aims of the Allies, but unless that aim included an improvement in geographical and strategic conditions, her sacrifices would have been in vain, because she was offered as much as that as the price of her neutrality. He did not mean to say that she had not had a duty to perform in associating herself with the greater issues for which the Allies were fighting, and indeed the Italian people had accepted the ordeal of war largely on ideal grounds. But they had concluded a definite pact regarding certain strategic advantages which they hoped to secure in order to make the future life and conditions of the country more tolerable.

The points which he was anxious should not be lost sight of were that this country was not actuated by imperialistic aims, but sought to improve her strategic position which had kept her under perpetual menace especially in the Adriatic; and secondly, that if there were any serious modification of the equilibrium in the eastern Mediterranean, it should not be modified to her disadvantage.[28]

Rodd insisted that every possible effort should be made at this juncture to bolster the "morally and materially weakest member of the alliance."[29] Premier Orlando soon went to London to secure a more explicit guarantee of Italian aims.[30] Sir William Wiseman notified London that the President wanted to be informed of the British response to Orlando's suit, not wishing to commit himself further to the Italians. "I gather," wrote Wise-

28. Rodd to Balfour, January 10, 1918, Cabinet Papers, no. 42 (1918), FO 899, book 14.
29. Rodd to Balfour, January 16, 1918, Cabinet Papers, no. 49 (1918), FO 899, book 14.
30. Page to Lansing, January 21, 1918, USDSM 367, 763.72/8592. See also Department of State, 1918, supp. 1, 1:35.

man, "that he is not very much in sympathy with Italy's war aims."[31]

These fundamental diplomatic considerations must be understood in order to appreciate both naval and military discussions among the Allies concerning the Italian theater. Italy was determined to gain security in the Adriatic against the Austrian enemy, but other members of the western coalition were less than enthusiastic about making new concessions that moved beyond the strict letter of the Treaty of London. Wilson had indicated that he was not willing to support even those claims if the League of Nations were brought into existence. These circumstances hardly predisposed Italy to forthright and cooperative relations with her wartime associates during the difficult months of 1918. In particular they interfered in numerous ways with naval cooperation in the Mediterranean Sea.

II

Figures of shipping losses in the Mediterranean compiled in January, 1918, indicated that the small enemy force of submarines was remarkably effective. Some 160 merchant vessels had gone down during the period August–December, 1917—45 in the British area, 68 in the French area, and 47 in the Italian area.[32] This information was before the members of the Allied Naval Council as it met for its first full session on January 22, 1918, in London. Italian questions appeared on the agenda for the second day. Admiral Wemyss presented a British plea for effective pooling of resources in the Mediterranean, to which Adm. Thaon di Revel, the Italian delegate, responded with an argument for destroyer reinforcements. Sir Eric Geddes then maintained that the navies must cease to assume that any one area of the sea was any given nation's domain, an obvious reference to the Adriatic; every sea should be considered "as belonging to all the Allies, who must do the best they can for the common good everywhere." He proposed that a naval mission

31. Wiseman to Drummond, Reading Papers, FO 899, book 23, US/2. See also Wiseman to Balfour, February 3, 1918, Reading Papers, FO 800, book 223, US/3.

32. Memorandum on losses in the Mediterranean Sea, January 14, 1918, ADM 137, book 1789, no. 6.

make a visit to the Mediterranean region to obtain information about its problems, to which di Revel responded affirmatively. Sims supported Geddes, arguing for a study of the whole question of the submarine war. "The Allies have only limited forces at their disposal, and the real question is, what is the best allocation of those forces." This view, of course, was more easily adopted by the United States than other nations, because it had only limited interests in the area. Sims recognized that the Adriatic question was particularly complex, since it was "partly political, partly military, and partly naval, and it is difficult to judge of the relative importance of the various questions."[33]

The Council finally decided to send a commission to Rome in order "to make a comprehensive study of the Mediterranean situation with particular reference to convoy system, allocation of additional vessels to Mediterranean and Otranto barrage." Sims himself planned to serve on the commission, telling Admiral Bayly that he would make the trip because he was the only American of suitable rank and also because there had been pressure for visits to Italy by high-ranking American officials. He thought the demands of Italy constituted the "most troublesome question" to come before the Allied Naval Council, and complained about the intrusion of political considerations.[34]

The commission met in Rome on February 8–9, 1918. Its deliberations proved relatively unimportant, but it at least helped to improve personal relations between the leaders of the navies operating in the Mediterranean. The British promised to make extensive contributions to the Otranto barrage, a project previously urged by the Italians and supported heavily by the French, in return for greater control over it, although Admiral de Bon preferred to keep the antisubmarine barrier under Franco-Italian auspices.[35] Otherwise, the Italians showed no inclination to accept significant changes in their naval policies.

33. Minutes of the First Meeting, ANC, Third Session, January 23, 1918, USNSF, QC file.

34. Sims to Navy Department, January 23, 1918, USNSF, QC file; Sims to Bayly, January 24, 1918, Sims Papers. A copy is in USNSF, TD file.

35. The Italian minutes of this meeting were printed in French. See "Commission Navale Interalliee de Rome, 8–9 Fevrier 1918," prepared by the Oficio del Capo di Stato Maggiore della Marina, MM, Es file, box 16. See also the official report to the Allied Naval Council, doc. no. 50, "Report of the Commission which Met in Rome on February 8th and 9th, 1918,"

As part of the information available to the conferees, Admiral di Revel presented some "Preliminary Notes to the Naval Inter-allied Conference at Rome—February 1918," in order to defend the naval viewpoints prevailing in Rome. This comprehensive statement provided a clear outline of the considerations underlying Italian naval policy. Di Revel dealt first with the Adriatic Sea. Should there be an offensive operation against Pola to destroy that base and perhaps force a fleet engagement with Austria? He thought not. The enemy fleet would not come out; defeat for Austria would mean "the loss of all military domain over the Adriatic." Its response to a naval probe would be to harass the assault force during its passage, exacting severe casualties. "An offensive by the Allied Fleet in the Adriatic would be an unpardonable error, and the only means of destroying the Austrian fleet is to attack it in its bases by special craft and by incessant bombardment from the air." Would Italy countenance changes in the distribution of naval craft in the Adriatic? Italy opposed the removal of any destroyers from the Adriatic; it sought a two-to-one ratio between its destroyer force and that of Austria, but at present it had only 30 such boats to Austria's 22. Would it be possible to take the offensive against submarines? Di Revel was convinced that only defensive tactics would yield desirable results.

There followed an extensive discussion of geographic considerations in the Adriatic Sea that affected naval operations. Austria had the use of "large sheltered harbours with deep water" on the eastern shore and could take advantage of islands, channels, and anchorages "which are always defensible and easily guarded." In contrast on the western shore Italy was left with "open beaches subject to the worst weather, no harbours and no islands. She is faced with the impossibility of defending her shore, whilst her deep waters are especially favourable to mines." Italian waters were "dark and turgid," while those of Austria were very clear. To add insult to injury, even the sea currents favored Austria; enemy mines that came loose were automatically carried to the Italian coast. All this established a forthright strategic generalization. "The power that possesses the eastern shore of the Adriatic has always been master of that

MM, Es file, box 16. Sims's summary report is in Sims to Navy Department, February 14, 1918, USNSF, TT file.

sea." As evidence the Admiral cited the case of Venice: "Whilst she paid little attention to the Italian Peninsula, her political sagacity, her arms and her money were dedicated exclusively to Dalmatia and hence she was mistress of the Adriatic."

Turning to the Mediterranean, di Revel noted the absence of a real fighting mission for capital ships. If enemy units came out, they faced almost certain destruction. The whole weight of operations therefore fell on light craft, whose most important task was the protection of seaborne traffic. "It is essential to emphasize that for Italy the security of her traffic is a mother of life and death, and that the limited means in her possession are far from assuring the arrival of the indispensable supplies which are the base-work of a further resistance." If there was a vast field of operations for enemy submarines, little opportunity presented itself to friendly submersibles.

All this background prepared the reader for the Italian argument concerning command arrangements and tactics in the area. In the Adriatic Sea, Italy faced Austria and its fleet. In the Mediterranean and Tyrrhenian seas it faced Germany and its submarines. The two theaters were completely distinct. *"For this reason it is not possible to relegate the necessary operations to pre-established and uniform lines, but instead the problems must be solved on grounds of most urgent necessity and with a view to the most rational employment of the scanty means available."* This statement implied that a fully unified command was a practical error; Italy must needs retain control of the Adriatic Sea. In those waters it would concentrate on containing the Austrian fleet by effective defensive measures and tactical attacks by small vessels and aircraft; in the Mediterranean and Tyrrhenian seas it would employ all available resources for the protection of seaborne traffic, particularly the Italian coastal trade. Its available escort and patrol craft were stretched quite thin because of long convoy routes from Suez to the east and Gibraltar to the west. This requirement established the need for reinforcements of light craft. Augmented convoy and escort operations would make possible the supply of Italy's most urgent domestic needs: coal, liquid fuel, steel plates, foodstuffs, and merchant tonnage.[36]

36. Admiral Thaon di Revel, "Preliminary Notes to the Naval Interallied Conference at Rome—February 1918," MM, Es file, box 16.

Di Revel's paper was in many ways a most distinguished elu-
cidation of the strategic and tactical questions associated with
naval operations in the Adriatic and Mediterranean seas, but it
aroused nothing but disgust in British and American minds, committed as they were to assumption of the offensive. Geddes
minced no words in commenting to Lloyd George on the memorandum. "A more plaintive wail was never, I think issued from
a Naval Commander-in-Chief and First Sea Lord." He thought
the document "unimportant in substance, but . . . useful as
showing the spirit in which they view the war."[37] Admiral
Wemyss agreed with Geddes, telling him that "You appear to
have been very successful with the Italians, but, Good Lord,
what a screed from di Revel. It is not pleasant reading when
one thinks that these are our allies."[38] Sims obviously shared
these opinions, but in his report to Admiral Benson he was
much more sensitive than his British colleagues to the political
considerations influencing the Italian outlook. Italy opposed
offensive operations in the Adriatic because such activities might
compromise its postwar position. "It is frankly acknowledged
that the Italians are not willing to trust either the French or
British to take possession of the Dalmatian Islands. They seem
to be in great dread lest some such measure should be taken and
that they should thereby be deprived of some of their future
influence in the Balkans." He observed that Italy was "not at
all pleased that the United States is actually in the war. That is,
it would seem that they would have preferred that we should
give all of the material assistance possible without actually being
a military ally." Sims concluded that the Italians "dread the
influence of America in European politics." President Wilson
would have a controlling position in determining the nature of
the peace settlement. "While this is admitted, it is perfectly
evident that the situation is not enjoyed by these people."[39]
Geddes and Sims were both convinced that their visit had been
beneficial as an exercise in friendly relations. They agreed that
their time had been well spent, and that Italy deserved some

37. Geddes to Lloyd George, February 9, 1918, Lloyd George Papers,
file F/18/1/6. A copy is in the Geddes Papers, ADM 116, book 1807.
38. Wemyss to Geddes, February 16, 1918, ADM 116, book 1806.
39. Sims to Benson, February 15, 1918, Sims Papers. A copy is in
USNSF, TD file. For a capsule rendition of the same analysis, see Sims to
Bayly, February 15, 1918, USNSF, TD file.

additional naval support.[40] Nevertheless, the burgeoning assumption that Italy, for reasons of state and because of faintheartedness, would continue its passive strategy, hardly boded well for the future development of the naval war in the Mediterranean.

If Admiral Sims grew in awareness of the political deeps in Mediterranean relations, he remained hopeful that the United States could make an important contribution to the campaign in the Adriatic by executing an audacious raid on an Austrian base along the Dalmatian coast. The history of this ill-fated endeavor provides an excellent lesson in the complexities of inter-Allied naval cooperation when fundamental diplomatic objectives are at cross purposes.

III

Admiral Sims had loyally adopted and conscientiously applied the general strategic principle that the United States Navy should operate as a reserve for the Allied naval forces in European waters. Nevertheless he could not completely fight down the idea of a dramatic American attack to demonstrate the prowess of the Navy. Was not President Wilson a convinced advocate of offensive action? He espied an opportunity to undertake such a project in the Adriatic Sea without compromising general naval requirements. Given the Italian distrust of British and French motives in the Mediterranean and also the seeming necessity of assuming the offensive in the Adriatic, was it possible that the Italians might look favorably upon an American initiative there, since the United States had no selfish interests in the area? Mediterranean possibilities received considerable attention in the Planning Section's Problem #2, prepared early in January, 1918, in which the planners drew attention to the completely unsatisfactory state of affairs in the Adriatic, calling for a "closer study of the Adriatic situation . . . with a view of greater concentration of offensive effort against enemy naval

40. The Italians lionized Geddes, who had taken an imposing delegation to Rome in order to impress the Italians with the extent of British interest and support. Admiral Saint-Pair took care to report to the French Minister of Marine that this activity did not imply any change in Franco-Italian naval relations, which he believed were in good repair. Rear Admiral F.G.P. de Saint-Pair to Georges Leygues, February 13, 1918, MM, Es file, box 16.

forces. We consider the entire problem of the Mediterranean and Adriatic a major problem in which the U.S. and the Allies are all greatly interested." In its conclusions the Planning Section proposed to develop plans for a surface attack against enemy bases in the Adriatic.[41]

The Planning Section accordingly produced a detailed proposal on January 30, 1918. Its foreword discussed certain general considerations, among them the value of adopting an offensive attitude whenever possible, the importance of unity of command, the soundness of concentrated effort, and the principle of attacking the enemy at its weakest point. Special circumstances in Italy should be taken into account. "The weakened morale of Italy due to recent reverses requires of the Allies that an extraordinary effort be made to build the morale up again to its former high standard." In addition, "success in the Adriatic would release large forces for other important operations and make possible a still greater concentration of effort in the areas which finally must be the areas of critical importance."

The basic strategic problem in the Adriatic derived from the enemy's position adjacent to maritime lines of supply and communication. The Austrians, especially because of their position at Cattaro, "lie close on the flank of all communications between Gibraltar and Salonika and between Gibraltar and Egypt. They also threaten with almost equal facility all lines of communication leading from Gibraltar to Italian and French Mediterranean ports." The high ground and the island chain from Cattaro to Trieste on the eastern Adriatic coast greatly benefited the enemy. Austria's objective in the Adriatic was to maintain freedom of passage for submarines to and from their bases. If the Allies took no action, the enemy would continue to hold its capital ships in reserve in northern Adriatic ports, use Cattaro as a base for operations against the Otranto barrage, supply submarines at Cattaro for operations on Allied lines of supply, and continue to raid the Italian coast for "moral effect."

The planners concluded that only an offensive in the Adriatic could counteract these activities. Even if an attack on the Austrian enemy only partially succeeded, it would have "a very depressing effect on his morale, as present reports indicate decided unrest and hardship in Austria," and it would have real

41. Planning Section Problem #2, January 12, 1918, USNSF, TX file.

benefits in Italy. "The political situation in the Adriatic is such as to demand that extraordinary effort be made to revive a confidence in both the military and civil forces that victory will eventually rest with the Italian forces in that region." The moment of offensive opportunity was now at hand.

The rest of the memorandum discussed a possible attack on the enemy base at Cattaro. The initial step would be to cut off communications between Cattaro and Pola to the north by occupying a west-east line across the Adriatic from Gargano Head on the Italian coast to Curzola, one of the Dalmatian Islands. Mine barrages would be placed in waters from Gargano Head to Curzola Island or from Nuova Point to Grossa Island. The first line seemed preferable because of the excellent anchorage between Curzola and the Sabbioncello Peninsula. A land raid would intercept communications along the coast from Cattaro to the north. Cattaro could then come under attack from the air and by land. Patrolling and hunting operations would continue in the Adriatic to intercept submarines until the base at Cattaro fell to Allied hands.

Italy and the United States would divide assignments for the attack. Responsibility for air raids and mining operations would fall to the Italians. The Americans, "not being affected by any Balance of Power in the Mediterranean," were to provide battleships to launch raids on enemy bases, as well as mines, listening devices, and patrol boats for antisubmarine operations.[42] In this fashion the United States might contribute importantly to the acquisition of command of the sea in the Adriatic and the Mediterranean, departing from the immensely useful but undramatic pattern of its naval activity in the Atlantic waters surrounding Britain and the French coast. Here was an arresting proposal indeed, stirring historic memories of Farragut and Dewey.

In a message to the Navy Department urging approval of the plan Sims summarized its principal components. An anchorage would be seized between Curzola and Sabbioncello Peninsula at the same time that land raids interdicted railroad traffic to Cattaro. A mine barrage would halt travel on the surface of the

42. Planning Section Memorandum No. 9, January 30, 1918, USNSF, TX file. The memorandum was printed in Minutes of the First Meeting, ANC, Appendix 6, memorandum no. 49, USNSF, QC file. A copy is in MM, Es file, box 16.

sea between Cattaro and more northerly ports. Various islands in the area of operations would be seized when forces became available, and certain of these (Lagosta, Gazza, and Pelagosa) would be fortified to support light craft patrolling the mine barrage across the Adriatic. An American battleship raid would be launched against Cattaro, and the Allied vessels would actually enter the harbor if possible. The Otranto patrol would be reorganized and equipped with listening devices and multiple depth charges. General command in the Adriatic would be assigned to an American admiral. Air raids would harass Cattaro after the base had been isolated. Mine fields would be laid in the vicinity of Cattaro. All aircraft not required for the attacks on Cattaro would take part in the surface patrol. If the plan were adopted, the United States would be required to contribute 25,000 mines, 5 battleships, and supporting destroyers as well as 36 submarine chasers. Sims concluded earnestly: "I deem it very important that radical steps be taken in the Adriatic. I request earliest possible information of Department's view of above proposals."[43] On February 10, when Sims was in Rome, Admiral Benson responded favorably to the general plan, approving further study and consideration. According to Benson, the operation promised two notable benefits. It would have a political effect of great consequence—an apparent reference to the shaky Italian situation—and it would be a logical accompaniment to the distant barrage being prepared in the North Sea. Details could be considered later.[44]

The plan was discussed at the Rome meetings, but no decision was reached; the Allied Naval Council was authorized to consider the project at its next session after it had been developed further in conjunction with the British Admiralty. Sims reported that it was "considered necessary to success of plan that troops for landing operations be American or British. Our marines would be especially desirable."[45] Marine forces, of course, were closely affiliated with the Navy and trained for amphibious operations.

Despite these preparations Sims was not very confident of ultimate success. He had read di Revel's estimate of the naval

43. Sims to Navy Department, February 2, 1918, USNSF, TT file. A copy is also in the QC file.
44. Benson to Sims, February 10, 1918, USNSF, TT file.
45. Sims to Navy Department, February 14, 1918, USNSF, TT file.

situation, including its definitive opposition to offensive operations in the Adriatic, and the French Admirals de Bon and Ratyé had told him that the Italians "are now, and always have been, opposed to any energetic naval action in the Adriatic." Perhaps their attitude would soften if the Americans undertook the enterprise, but Sims was "not hopeful that they will decide upon the kind of offensive that we would like to see carried out." The Italians opposed operations by any other power, refusing to take action themselves "until they are practically sure they can do so with success, and particularly without much material loss."[46] He told Admiral Bayly of Italian fears that "if a landing was ever effected in that neighborhood, . . . it would be difficult, if not impossible, to get us out."[47]

Sims's principal representative in Rome, Comdr. C. R. Train, shared these impressions. He also believed that an "ulterior motive" would prevent the acceptance of the American scheme. "Personally, I believe that they are afraid of it, that in case of failure, the very strong anti-war spirit might sweep aside the government, with possible revolutionary results." He was convinced that the operation would never take place unless the United States accepted full responsibility for it.[48] These considerations hardly augured well for the future.

In London the Planning Section matured its project. Discussion with Admiralty planners led to a few emendations. It was necessary to heed "the supreme importance of planning the operation on an adequate scale," even if it meant a radical reduction of naval forces elsewhere. If successful, it could become "the deciding factor of the war." Anglo-American collaboration would eliminate language difficulties and related problems. Adriatic patrol would have to be sufficient to preclude any reaction by enemy surface craft. An admonitory comment came from the planners, who were "constrained to believe that, unless the Allies are able to inaugurate offensive operations in contradistinction to purely defensive operations, the outlook as to our success in this war is extremely dubious."[49]

46. Sims to Benson, February 15, 1918, USNSF, TD file. A copy is also in the Sims Papers.
47. Sims to Bayly, February 15, 1918, USNSF, TD file.
48. Train to Sims, February 15, 1918, Sims Papers. A copy is in USNSF, TD file.
49. Planning Section Memorandum No. 16, "Memorandum on Adriatic Project," March 7, 1918, USNSF, TX file. See also Sims to Navy Depart-

In Paris, however, the reaction was distinctly cool; the Fourth Section of the E.M.G. raised some serious objections. Would not the operation seriously detract from the numbers of light craft needed for convoy and patrol elsewhere? In addition the reach from Gargano Head to Curzola Island was long and deep, a highly unfavorable location for a mine field. Why not concentrate instead upon the Franco-British barrage at Otranto considered at the Rome conference?[50] In another document, memories of an earlier disaster came back to haunt the E.M.G. "The lesson of the DARDANELLES ought not to be forgotten; a second reverse of the same nature would be equivalent to a disaster."[51]

On March 12, Sims received a message from the Chief of Naval Operations asking whether the plan had yet been submitted to the Supreme War Council and the British War Cabinet and raising some problems. How would the plan affect other commitments? "The logistic demands now to supply the needs on the Western Front are so great that no eccentric move regardless how attractive its local aspect may be can be contemplated without full consideration by all parties concerned." The Navy Department "must not be committed to any plan until full details are submitted and our decision rendered."[52] Clearly Washington shared with Paris a considerable concern about the broader ramifications of the Adriatic scheme for other Allied operations, deeply impressed as were all the Western Powers with the likelihood of a great land battle in the near future on the Western Front. In London Sims prepared for the second meeting of the Allied Naval Council. In his notes for use during those sessions, he summed up the situation. The Rome meeting did not accept the American plan; it had turned instead to aug-

---

ment, March 8, 1918, USNSF, QC file. A copy is in the TT file. In this dispatch Sims reported progress in consultations with the Admiralty and urged that American preparations begin immediately—even before the plan was adopted—to be prepared to execute it rapidly.

50. "Etudes du Memorandum Americain sur la Situation dans l'Adriatique," March 10, 1918, MM, Es file, box 17.

51. "Au Sujet du Memorandum de la Marine des Etats-Unis sur: 'La Situation dans L'Adriatique; sa Repercussion en Mediterranee et les Decisions qu'il Faudrait Prendre pour Asurer le Succes de la Guerre," March 10, 1918, MM, Es file, box 17. Titles and punctuation given for French naval documents are as found in the French naval archives. Diacritical marks are often missing in the originals.

52. Benson to Sims, March 12, 1918, USNSF, TT file.

mentation of the Otranto barrage. If the British supported the proposal, it would be urged upon the Council; if no agreement seemed possible, it would be wise to drop the matter for the moment. "In any case," he concluded, "a re-examination of the plan may be desirable in view of the possibility of a German offensive towards Greece or through Northern Italy, as either one of these situations might result in an entirely different situation in the Eastern Mediterranean from that existing today."[53]

On March 12, the Allied Naval Council took up the American plan. Di Revel immediately expressed reservations, arguing that Italian estimates indicated a need for 25,000 troops rather than the 10,000 envisioned by the Americans. He saw as advantages of the operation the desirable effect on Italian morale and the seizure of Cattaro as a means of cutting Austria's north-south communications on the Adriatic. Sims interjected to state that the concept was not to seize and hold Cattaro but to raid it and cut its railroad communications. Di Revel expressed further doubts. The issue was "essentially an Italian question, since if any reverse were incurred Italy primarily would be affected. He considered therefore that any such action in the Adriatic should be controlled by an Italian officer, since Italy joined the war purely on the question of the Adriatic." (Apparently di Revel was not as careful as Sonnino to argue the disinterested idealism of Italy.) Georges Leygues, the French Minister of Marine, then made the familiar argument that the coalition must avoid its earlier tendency to take an unduly narrow view of the war, noting that "the power of our enemies lies in the cohesion resulting from the concentration of all their forces under one single command." He was most sensitive to the importance of the issues at hand. "The day on which we lost the Mediterranean would be a day of disaster for the Allies." De Bon then urged further study, but the Japanese representative Admiral Funakoshi supported the proposal.

Sims then made his case for the American plan. He dissented from di Revel's view that the question was essentially one for Italy; the United States would provide the necessary ships. "His desire was that this Council should at these Meetings decide definitely that some form of offensive action ought to be taken in the Adriatic as soon as possible, so that the necessary prepa-

53. Sims notes, March 11, 1918, USNSF, TX file.

rations could be proceeded with." Details could be decided later. "It was a matter of indifference to him who undertook the command so long as he was a fighter." The outcome was a decision to form a special committee to consider the matter further.[54]

The special committee reported to the Allied Naval Council on March 13 and unanimously recommended the operation. Since military support was needed, it referred two questions to the permanent military representatives of the Supreme War Council: Were troops, artillery, and material available, and if so, when? How much force was required to seize and hold the island objectives? An early meeting was scheduled to discuss these matters with the permanent military representatives, and di Revel once again insisted on Italian command.[55]

On March 14, the Allied Naval Council met in joint session with the permanent military representatives to explain the proposal. Sims argued that the operation would make important contributions to the antisubmarine campaign. Since it responded to growing demands for an aggressive naval policy, it would have desirable effects on the morale of the western coalition. Probability of success was very high, and the interruption of communications by land and sea would seriously discommode the enemy. General Rawlinson, the British military representative, wanted to consider the plan in terms of its effect on the over-all operations of the Allies, particularly on the Austrian front. General Giardino, the Italian military representative, then maintained that the assault would require more troops than contemplated by the United States and that Italy had none to offer. Sims demurred, but Giardino extended his critique to argue that the operation involved too much dispersion of forces and was probably impractical. The permanent military representatives agreed only to consider the project carefully and to report back their ultimate conclusions, a highly unsatisfactory result from the naval point of view.[56]

54. ANC doc. no. 81, "Adriatic," March 28, 1918, MM, Es file, box 17. Apparently this colloquy was not included in the official minutes because of its extremely secret nature. See also the Minutes of the Second Meeting, ANC, First Session, March 12, 1918, USNSF, QC file.

55. Report of the special committee (de Bon, Wemyss, di Revel, Funakoshi, and Sims), March 28, 1918, MM, Es file, box 17. See also Sims to Navy Department, March 14, 1918, USNSF, TT file.

56. ANC doc. 81, "Adriatic," March 28, 1918, MM, Es file, box 17. The notes on this meeting are dated March 16, 1918.

The matter now languished for a month. Germany's massive offensive in France had finally begun on March 21, and for some time it absorbed most of the energies of the western coalition. Early in April Sims informed the Navy Department that no movement had taken place since the meeting of March 14. "In view of the present situation on Western Front, it is improbable that this project will receive much consideration for the present, and may prove to be unnecessary or impractical, depending on outcome of present German offensive."[57] When, on April 15, the permanent military representatives returned their opinions on the questions addressed to them, their report proved unfavorable. For the present no military forces could be diverted to the Adriatic operations, but the military representatives would keep the project under consideration.[58]

Despite this discouraging communication the project dragged on. At the third meeting of the Allied Naval Council in late April, Sims urged that the planning continue "with a view to the project being completely ready for execution later if a favourable opportunity arose." Since the position on land and at sea might change unexpectedly, it would be "wiser to develop the plans completely now, as it is impossible to say with certainty that the operation will not be carried out this summer." His colleagues concurred, and the Council decided to convene a special planning subcommittee in Rome on May 15.[59] Sims assigned a member of his planning section, Capt. H. E. Yarnell, to represent the United States and provided him with detailed instructions, stressing particularly the preparation of information requested by the permanent military representatives. The subcommittee was not to prepare detailed operations plans; these should be left to the commander designated for the operation.[60] Sims also sought permission from Washington for Yarnell to promise

57. Sims to Navy Department, April 5, 1918, USNSF, TT file. Copies are in the TP and QC files.

58. Reply of the Permanent Military Representatives, April 15, 1918, SWC doc. no. 159/1, CAB 25, box 121 (SWC). See also the Minutes of the Meeting of the Permanent Military Representatives, April 8, 1918, SWC doc. no. 163, CAB 25, box 121 (SWC). For Sims's report of this outcome, see Sims to Navy Department, April 19, 1918, USNSF, QC file. A copy is in the TP file.

59. Minutes of the Third Meeting, ANC, Second Session, April 26, 1918, USNSF, QC file. See also Sims to Navy Department, April 30, 1918, USNSF, QC file.

60. Sims instructions to Yarnell, May 8, 1918, USNSF, QC file.

that the United States would subsidize mining, urging the Navy Department to proceed without concern about financial loss. Immediate preparations were necessary to ensure effective execution of the project, if it were finally approved by the Supreme War Council.[61]

Little took place during the Rome Conference except a rehearsal of the various positions and arguments adduced earlier. The Americans and the British supported the enterprise, but the Italians sustained their objections to various aspects. French delegates were less than enthusiastic, continuing to emphasize development of the barrage at Otranto as an alternative. America's willingness to provide extensive support—particularly mines and marines—did not have any measurable effect on the Italian delegation.[62]

The proposed assault now entered the last stages of its consideration. On June 10, Sims reported despairingly to the Navy Department that opposition forced him to drop the project for the moment, since Italy and France would support only the Otranto barrage. He did not know whether his plan would ever rise again.[63] The Allied Naval Council gave the American plan a decent burial during its fourth meeting on June 11.[64] Admiral Sims was not to have an opportunity to damn the torpedoes or to give the order to fire when ready, and the Navy would not

61. Sims to Navy Department, May 6, 1918, USNSF, QC file.

62. For information on the meetings in Rome, May 15–21, 1918, see the following: American memorandum on capital ships required at Sabbioncello, ca. May 15, 1918, ADM 137, book 1792, also available in USNSF, QC file; Memorandum by Colonel H. Cavallero, Italian Army, May 15, 1918, MM, Es file, box 19; "Memorandum on the Strategic Situation in the Adriatic, and the Consequent Demands upon the Italian Navy, by the Italian Representatives," May 16, 1918, USNSF, QC file; "Memorandum on Adriatic Operations by British Delegates," May 19, 1918, ADM 137, book 1792, also available in MM, Es file, box 19; "Report of the Sub-Committee on Plans which Met in Rome on May 15th to May 21st, 1918," with various attachments, MM, Es file, box 18; "Memorandum by Italy on the Occupation of the Sabbioncello Peninsula at Least as Far as the Isthmus of Gradina, of Curzola, and Successively of the Other Islands in the Middle Adriatic," prepared by Admiral Thaon di Revel, May 29, 1918, MM, Es file, box 19.

63. Sims to Navy Department, June 10, 1918, USNSF, QC file.

64. Minutes of the Fourth Meeting, ANC, Second Session, June 11, 1918, USNSF, QC file; Crease to Heaton-Ellis, June 15, 1918, CAB 25, box 121 (SWC). See also Minutes of the Fourth Meeting, ANC, June 15, 1918, Appendix 4, USNSF, QC file; Sims to Navy Department, June 15, 1918, USNSF, QC file.

achieve an exploit during World War I to compare with earlier triumphs at Mobile and Manila.

Naval warfare in the Mediterranean varied considerably from that in the Atlantic. The problem was similar—how to contain the enemy's surface fleet while counteracting the operations of submarines against merchant commerce—but everything else was different. Italy's national interest forced naval decisions much at variance with those desired by the other partners in the western coalition. Rome was bound and determined to maintain a defensive policy against the Austrian surface fleet and the submarines operating from Adriatic bases. Fearful of the effect of a naval disaster upon domestic public opinion, mindful of arduous tactical difficulties in the way of offensive operations, and intensely desirous of maintaining every possible political advantage vis-à-vis not only its enemies, but also its friends in anticipation of the postwar distribution of the spoils, the Italian Navy tenaciously clung to its policy of avoiding battle.

The United States hoped that it might make signal contributions to the naval war in the Mediterranean because it was the most disinterested of the powers. Admiral Sims saw in the Adriatic impasse an opportunity for the dramatic exploits that he had unselfishly foresworn in the Atlantic, where the logic of the situation suggested a naval policy entirely subordinated to that of the British Navy. Aware almost from the beginning of long-standing Franco-Italian and Anglo-Italian rivalries—aside from historic Austro-Italian hatreds that reached back to the unification of the Italian peninsula—Sims manfully but unsuccessfully sought ways of transcending their wartime consequences. He was not helped by a general Italian mistrust of the United States and of President Wilson, nor by the great German offensive in France from March to July, 1918.

The failure of the plan for an offensive in the Adriatic only inaugurated Sims's difficulties in the Mediterranean. He found himself deeply involved in a whole range of additional inter-Allied negotiations concerning the Mediterranean from January to October, 1918. Various alarms, of which none was more influential than the possibility that the Russian Black Sea Fleet might fall into German hands, forced the British, French, and Americans to exert strong pressures on their Italian associate to accept altered naval organization in the Mediterranean. To establish command of the sea, they advanced proposals for redistribution of surface craft in the Adriatic and Aegean seas; to contain the submarine they gave first priority to the construction of a great barrage across the Straits of Otranto like that being developed in the North Sea, and they moved to perfect their arrangements for convoy of merchant shipping from Suez to Gibraltar. Ultimately they attempted to establish a supreme naval command for the Mediterranean somewhat analogous to General Foch's position on the Western Front.

IV

Russia's departure from the war exerted unexpected influence on naval planning for the Mediterranean during 1918. In one respect, it greatly enhanced Allied trepidation concerning the much-discussed end-the-war offensive Germany planned to launch early in the year. It also created the possibility that Germany might acquire the Russian Black Sea Fleet, then at anchor in various Black Sea ports. If these vessels augmented German and Turkish ships located at Constantinople, and if this combined force managed to link up with the Austrian battle fleet, all manner of difficulty might result. The Suez Canal could be blocked, or lines of communication to the eastern empires of Britain and France might be interdicted. The Central Powers could conceivably cut off communications to Allied expeditions operating in Palestine, Mesopotamia, and Macedonia, or they might launch a massive attack on merchant commerce. Above all Italy might be forced out of the war if any of these eventualities came to pass.[65] As early as January the Allied Naval Council took note of the danger in the Black Sea and its members discussed the question in a relatively desultory fashion for several weeks.[66] It first took up the matter in detail during the March meetings of the Council.

65. For early concern about this problem, see Memorandum by Sydney R. Fremantle for the British Admiralty, December 31, 1917, ADM 137, book 2180; "Examen de la Possibilite d'Achat par L'Allemagne de la Flottee Russe de la Mer Noire qui Serait Armee par Elle pour des Operations en Mediterranee," January 20, 1918, MM, Es file, box 14. This document appears in the Minutes of the First Meeting, ANC, January 20, 1918, Appendix 6, USNSF, QC file.
66. Minutes of the First Meeting, ANC, January 22, 1918, First Session, USNSF, QC file; Sims to Navy Department, January 23, 1918, USNSF, QC file; Planning Section Memorandum No. 9, January 30, 1918, MM, Es file, box 16; Gauchet to Leygues, February 9, 1918, MM, Es file, box 14;

Britain and France presented complementary memoranda on the general situation in the Mediterranean at the March meetings of the Allied Naval Council. The Admiralty document noted the overwhelming numbers of Allied capital ships in the Mediterranean, but it also conceded that the combined forces had failed miserably in efforts to control the submarine offensive. Drawing attention to the Russian Black Sea Fleet, reported to consist of 2 dreadnoughts, 13 destroyers, and 6 submarines, the British judged that nothing could be done to prevent the Germans from seizing it, a step that might be taken since it would force the Allies to strengthen their forces in the Aegean. To guard more effectively against surface dangers, Franco-British vessels might be concentrated at Corfu, from which they could maneuver effectively to cover both the Adriatic and Aegean seas.[67] The French memorandum emphasized particularly the possibility that the Allies might have to respond to surface raids in the Mediterranean, particularly if Austria's fleet came out of the Adriatic to link up with the combined Turco-German force at Constantinople reinforced by the Russian Black Sea Fleet. The enemy might threaten either the base at Salonika, which supplied the Macedonian expedition, or the Suez Canal. France proposed to counteract this possibility by concentrating its forces at Corfu, strengthening various points in the Aegean, and laying a material barrage off the Dardanelles to hinder the exit of enemy forces from that passage.[68]

An American memorandum on the Mediterranean prepared by the Planning Section took a different direction and concentrated on a political solution, raising the possibility of negotiating a separate peace with Turkey. "The Turk came into the war primarily to protect himself against Russian aggression; and, now that danger is eliminated, he does not relish the inevitable German domination which will follow a German victory." Many advantages might flow from a separate peace,

---

Minutes of the War Cabinet (WC 349), February 19, 1918, CAB 23, book 5; Gough-Calthorpe memorandum, February 20, 1918, ADM 116, book 1798.

67. British memorandum on the Mediterranean, Adriatic, and Black Seas, Minutes of the Second Meeting, ANC, n.d., Appendix 6, USNSF, QC file.

68. French memorandum on the general situation in the Mediterranean, Black Sea, and Adriatic, Minutes of the Second Meeting, ANC, n.d., Appendix 6, USNSF, QC file.

although some concessions would have to be made to Turkey. Aside from the political gain, forces committed in the East could be redeployed elsewhere, and the Allies might be able to obtain command of the Black Sea. As to the Russian Black Sea Fleet, if it should become a factor, a redistribution of forces as the situation required would be essential by the commander in chief in the Mediterranean.[69] This intriguing document harmonized generally with the French and British proposals to neutralize the Russian fleet, but it introduced a political dimension that went unmentioned in the other appreciations.

Sims was not unduly concerned about the Black Sea question, relying upon the Admiralty to deal effectively with it.[70] Other Mediterranean questions seemed to him much more important at the time, particularly the plan for the Adriatic raid. He was preoccupied generally with the need to coordinate the several naval forces in the Mediterranean and to make certain that their operations were integrated with those of the land forces.[71]

During its March meetings the Allied Naval Council decided that if Germany acquired the Russian vessels there would be sufficient warning to respond efficiently, and forces in the eastern Mediterranean could be redistributed to deal with them.[72] The Admiralty re-examined the question later in March and concluded that the danger could be counteracted by combining the French and Italian surface forces in the Adriatic and by reinforcing the Aegean fleet with French battleships. France had agreed to these measures, and they were being taken up with Italy.[73]

69. Planning Memorandum No. 15, March 4, 1918, USNSF, TX file. Printed in Minutes of the Second Meeting, ANC, n.d., Appendix 6, USNSF, QC file.

70. Sims to Benson, March 7, 1918, USNSF, TP file. A copy is in the TD file.

71. Sims notes for ANC meeting, March 11, 1918, TX file.

72. Minutes of the Second Meeting, ANC, March 12, 1918, Second Session, USNSF, QC file.

73. For the Admiralty consideration, see Geddes to Admiralty Operations Committee, March 14, 1918, ADM 116, book 1798; Minutes of the War Cabinet (WC 369), March 21, 1918, CAB 23, book 5; Minutes of the War Cabinet (WC 373), March 23, 1918, CAB 23, book 5; "Admiralty Memorandum for the War Cabinet on the Russian Black Sea Fleet and the Effect of Possible Capture by the Germans," prepared by Admiral Wemyss, March 29, 1918, ADM 116, book 1769; Memorandum by R. A. Nugent, April 1, 1918, ADM 116, book 1798.

Suddenly, however, concern grew to considerable proportions. Anglo-American and French frustration with Italian intransigence had been mounting rapidly for some three months. The crisis in France raised the specter of early disaster on land. And finally, intelligence information indicated that Germany had decided to employ the Russian Black Sea Fleet. French sources reported early in April that a detachment of German sailors had passed through Kiev on its way to the Black Sea.[74] Wemyss immediately reported this information to the War Cabinet, although he cast some doubt on its authenticity and reminded the group that "sufficient forces were available to counteract any such movement." He advocated an early meeting of the Allied Naval Council with the proper instrumentalities of the Supreme War Council, "in order that any necessary concerted action by the Allied fleets could be taken," and Sir Eric Geddes immediately began to arrange this consultation.[75.]

The First Lord of the Admiralty apparently saw in the situation an opportunity to force the issue of Italian cooperation and settle it once and for all. On April 6, he explained to Lloyd George that he hoped to achieve three desirable ends: consolidation of French and Italian forces in the Adriatic at Corfu; reinforcement of the Aegean squadron with three French battleships and two cruisers; and provision for the transfer of destroyers and submarines from the patrol on the Straits of Otranto to the fleets in the Adriatic and the Aegean, in the event that fleet actions appeared imminent. The news from the Black Sea required that he "begin at once to persuade the Italians to assent to it [his project], which will, I think, be a matter of time." Geddes, certainly an optimist, was yet aware of the difficulties. "The matter must be carefully handled from the commencement, and I believe that the best way to proceed would be to deal with it primarily through the Supreme War Council."[76] That group could engender sufficient pressure to force the hand of Italy. Geddes then acquainted the Allies with his in

74. Fourth Section, E.M.G., to Leygues, April 3, 1918, MM, Es file, box 14.
75. Minutes of the War Cabinet (WC 380), April 2, 1918, CAB 23, book 6; Memorandum for Crease, Secretary of the ANC, on proposed meeting with the SWC, April 5, 1918, ADM 116, book 1604.
76. Geddes to Lloyd George, ADM 137, book 1786, 600–602. A copy is in ADM 116, book 1604. The contents of this letter were reported to Paris in Rothiacob to de Bon, April 6, 1918, MM, Es file, box 21.

tentions by means of a communication from Lloyd George to Clemenceau and Orlando on April 12, describing the potential threat posed by the Russian Black Sea Fleet and calling for the desired redistribution of forces.[77]

The next step was to bring the proposal for redistribution of the navies before the Allied Naval Council during its third meeting in late April, which took place in Paris. As might have been expected, the Italian representative Admiral di Revel proved entirely unready to accept the British proposal, despite the support lent to it by all the other nations. He would condone in principle the transfer of Italian dreadnoughts to Corfu, but not surrender of control to a French admiral. The Italian vessels "must keep intact their character of distinct grouping and be always ready to transfer themselves and intervene anywhere that it would appear desirable with regard to the Adriatic situation." Di Revel was unalterably opposed to the Aegean proposal. "The advisability of such a movement is exclusively dependent upon events in the Adriatic, which cannot be foreseen and may not be related to those in the Aegean."[78]

Sims accurately summarized the Italian tactics in his report to the Navy Department:

It was apparent that Italian Admiral was instructed to agree in principle to transfer of battleships, but to obstruct the plan by raising all possible objections to its practical execution. . . . As Vice Admiral di Revel is both Chief of Staff and Commander-in-Chief of the Fleet he loses the most important part of his command by this transfer of battleships and his opposition may be due in part to personal motives, but it is thought that the policy now controlling the Italian Navy is one of saving their ships so as to be superior to Austria after the war. It is the impression in the British Admiralty that Admiral di Revel must be removed from both of his present positions before any real work can be expected from the Italian Navy.[79]

77. Lloyd George to Orlando and Clemenceau, April 12, 1918, ADM 137, book 1786, 604–5. The plan was explained to the War Cabinet in great confidence on the same day. See the Minutes of the War Cabinet (WC 390a), April 12, 1918, CAB 23, book 14 (secret minutes). Appendix 1 of the minutes contains a copy of the message to Orlando and Lloyd George.
78. Minutes of the Third Meeting, ANC, April 26–27, 1918, USNSF, QC file. The quotation is from Minutes of the Third Session, April 27, 1918. For the memorandum on which the British proposals were based, see Minutes of the Third Meeting, ANC, n.d., Appendix 4, USNSF, QC file.
79. Sims to Navy Department, April 30, 1918, USNSF, QC file.

Sims obviously shared the British distaste for di Revel, but he realized that reasons of state conditioned the Italian position. Summarizing the discussion at the Allied Naval Council for Admiral Benson, he once again noted the Italian distrust of France and Britain. "I think it very difficult for anyone who has not seen the clash of national interests continuously over here to realize how much the things that are done in this war are influenced by what the various nations expect will be done after the war. This [is] not only in reference to military power and prestige, but also in reference to commercial interests." Sims was also sensitive to growing dislike of the United States in Europe. "Of course we are not free from the suspicion of acting in the same way. . . . There is not only envy of our usual prosperity, but just now there is particular envy over the position that it is likely that we will occupy after this war is over."[80]

When the Italians blocked the British proposals at the Allied Naval Council the scheme of achieving a decision at the Supreme War Council went into operation. At Abbeville early in May the Supreme War Council approved a resolution calling upon the Italian Government to accept the principle of concentrating surface craft at Corfu so that the French could reinforce the Aegean squadron. This step set the stage for a month of extensive inter-Allied negotiations.[81]

Premier Orlando had been placed in a difficult position; he wished to meet the desires of his fellow premiers, but he faced powerful resistance from his naval advisers.[82] On May 10, di Revel produced another extensive memorandum restating his previous views. He remained convinced that capital ships should put to sea only to meet a similar enemy force and then "*only*

80. Sims to Benson, April 30, 1918, Sims Papers.
81. See the minutes of the Supreme War Council, May 2, 1918, in Minutes of the Third Meeting, ANC, n.d., Appendix 4, USNSF, QC file. The Minutes of the Supreme War Council, Fifth Session, May 1–2, 1918, are in SWC-WDA. The French showed great interest in supporting the British proposal. Leygues to Gauchet, May 8, 1918, MM, Es file, box 14; Clemenceau to Lloyd George, May 10, 1918, MM, Es file, box 14; de Bon to Gauchet, May 12, 1918, MM, Es file, box 14.
82. Orlando to Marquis Imperiali (Italian Ambassador in London), May 6, 1918, MM, Es file, box 14. This cable emphasized a technical problem (fear of loss of ships) and a political problem (loss of control of Italian fleet). The MM records contain a number of cables between Rome and London sent by the Italians. It is possible that these were obtained by espionage.

*when there is a fair probability of forcing them to fight without
our own forces being compelled to remain too long at sea.*" (This
argument bore marked similarity to that of Admiral Beatty in
January, 1918, which had resulted in some alterations in the
mission of the British Grand Fleet.) Di Revel maintained that
the best response to the Austrian challenge was "to intensify
the use of Submarines and of extensive mine-fields, that is, to
resort to the same devices that the Central Powers are so effectively employing against our own traffic." The enemy had the
power to decide the time and place of a fleet engagement; there
was no way to alter this circumstance at the moment.[83] Di Revel's
logic was hard to refute, but he had not taken into consideration
the possible challenge of the Russian Black Sea Fleet.

The British now advanced a new solution to the problem of
Italian opposition. In a special *aide-mémoire* entitled "Note
upon Naval Situation in the Mediterranean, Adriatic, and Aegean," approved by the War Cabinet on May 11, 1918, the
British summarized the position. Germany's acquisition of the
Russian Black Sea Fleet posed "a new and dangerous situation.
. . . It is essential not to allow questions of National amour propre
to bring about a naval disaster." The proper response to the new
threat was to send six French battleships from Corfu to the
Aegean and to replace the loss at Corfu with four Italian ships;
also a unified naval command seemed necessary. Unfortunately,
the French were no more willing to surrender the supreme command in the Mediterranean than the Italians were to transfer the
Adriatic command. A possible way out was to appoint a British
admiralissimo "to serve under the Allied Naval Council and to be
bound as regards the general disposition of the Naval Forces under him by the decisions of the Allied Naval Council approved by
the Supreme War Council." This arrangement would leave un-
disturbed local commands like that of the Italians in the Adriatic
and the French in the Aegean. It might not be necessary to
transfer the Italian vessels from Taranto to Corfu, "as they

83. Memorandum by di Revel, "Some Notes on the Conduct of the
Naval War," ANC doc. no. 133, May 10, 1918, MM, Es file, box 19. This
document—printed in the Minutes of the Fourth Meeting, ANC, May 10,
1918, Appendix 8, USNSF, QC file—aroused the usual British contempt.
See Geddes to Rodd, May 27, 1918, ADM 116, book 1649. "I doubt,"
wrote Geddes, "that the Italian Battleships, since the beginning of the
war, have steamed as many miles as the Grand Fleet Battleships do each
month."

would all be under one Admiralissimo, and their co-ordination with the Corfu forces would thus be assured."[84] Lloyd George notified Clemenceau of the proposal on May 13, indicating that he had Lord Jellicoe in mind for the supreme command.[85] If the attempt to redistribute the naval forces did not succeed, the United States might be asked to send a division of battleships to the eastern Mediterranean. Sims alerted Benson to this possibility on May 13 and also reported that the Allied Naval Council would hold an emergency meeting on May 15 to consider the Mediterranean question.[86]

The principal political stratagem behind these maneuverings was to obtain the support of Premier Orlando against di Revel. Commander Train, the American naval representative in Rome, reported that di Revel was "suspicious of everything that is French" and maintained that "the Italian Navy will never get a proper show with Revel at its head."[87] This view, quite general in France and Britain, was part of the motivation for the proposal to create an admiralissimo, an arrangement that would weaken di Revel's baneful influence. In Rome Sir Rennell Rodd had approached Orlando with the Franco-British proposals for redistribution. The Premier had overruled di Revel's opposition to the dispatch of Italian ships to Corfu, but "he could not accept suggestion of incorporating them in a French fleet." The proposal of an admiralissimo removed his objections, and he would welcome it. Rodd argued that "There is more than amour propre on the part of Ministers on this issue. It is public opinion of the country which they cannot help considering."[88]

On May 15, the Allied Naval Council held an emergency meeting in London to consider the Mediterranean. It confined its discussion to a recommendation from the permanent military

84. "Note upon Naval Situation in the Mediterranean, Adriatic, and Aegean," May 11, 1918, ADM 116, book 1649. This memorandum was sent to the British ambassadors in France (Derby) and Italy (Rodd) on May 11. See also Minutes of the War Cabinet (WC 409a), May 11, 1918, CAB 23, book 14 (secret minutes); Balfour to Derby, May 11, 1918, MM, Es file, box 14.

85. Lloyd George to Clemenceau, May 11, 1918, ADM 116, book 1649. The message, along with the aide-mémoire, was not sent for two days.

86. Sims to Benson, May 13, 1918, USNSF, QC file. A copy is in the TT file.

87. Train to Sims, May 9, 1918, USNSF, TD file.

88. Rodd to Foreign Office, May 13, 1918, ADM 116, book 1649.

advisers that the United States declare war against Turkey and
Bulgaria, with the proviso that this action would not lead to a
diversion of American troops from the Western Front, a possibility earlier advanced by Sims's Planning Section. This step was
recommended because of its moral effect on the peoples of the
Ottoman Empire and Bulgaria; because it would allow the
United States, if necessary, to take an active role in the eastern
theater; and because it would stimulate additional support for
the Allies in the Middle East. Sims was somewhat reluctant to
act, despite the previous interest within his staff in this initiative.
To begin with, he was miffed at the intervention of the permanent military representatives, since the matter seemed to him
much more a naval than a military concern. He also had in mind
Washington's desire that its representatives in inter-Allied bodies avoid involvement in political questions that were of no
interest to the United States. Therefore he preferred merely a
statement of the naval consequences that would follow such declarations of war. Wemyss argued for a more general pronouncement, placing heavy stress on the importance of the United States
being able to act against the Russian Black Sea Fleet. In addition an American entry would present a picture of complete
inter-Allied unity in the Middle East. Sims remained adamant,
so the Council confined itself to a simple statement: "The Allied
Naval Council wish to record their opinion that from the Naval
point of view also it is desirable that the action recommended by
the Military Representatives should be taken."[89] Nothing came
of this proposal, a reflection of the general tendency of the
United States to avoid adventures not essential to its principal
military-naval objective—the defeat of Germany by the most
expeditious procedure that would not prejudice its political objectives. Sims appears personally to have favored declarations
of war against Turkey and Bulgaria, but he did not press the
matter.[90]

Meanwhile, a more important negotiation was about to occur
elsewhere. As soon as Clemenceau officially indicated his acceptance of the proposal for an admiralissimo, Geddes traveled

89. Minutes of the Emergency Meeting, ANC, May 15, 1918, USNSF,
QC file.
90. Sims to Benson, May 17, 1918, USNSF, TD file. This message contains a report on the meeting of May 15.

to Paris in order to complete the arrangement.[91] Sims and his friends in the Admiralty now hoped for a desirable settlement, because the Italians had agreed in principle to a supreme commander. This expedient obviated the usual difficulty of Franco-Italian rivalry. Franco-British rivalry, however, posed a second problem. Sims told Benson that the French "will doubtless be rather tenacious of the position that they have held in the Mediterranean and will not want to give it up, but I am in hopes that the present crisis is such that they will give way."[92]

Sims was correct about French naval concern. On May 16, the Ministry of Marine produced a paper that objected strongly to the appointment of an admiralissimo, interpreting it as part of the British effort to achieve dominance in the Mediterranean. It proposed that Jellicoe be allowed to coordinate rather than to command naval forces in the Mediterranean. On May 21, Admiral de Bon summarized for Georges Leygues the principal French naval interests in the Mediterranean—maintenance of communications to Algeria and Morocco and also to the Allied expedition at Salonika, largely composed of French forces. The admiralissimo arrangement might affect these interests. De Bon favored a revision of the naval accords of 1914 with Great Britain and of 1915 with Italy to re-ensure French interests.[93]

Clemenceau began the meeting on May 17 by announcing that he would consider the proposal for a British admiralissimo if the Italians refused to transfer their ships to Corfu. He then raised the consideration that had excited the Ministry of Marine, pointing out that "by naval custom the French were entitled on account of the preponderance of their force in the Mediterranean to claim command and that the British had very small forces out there." Geddes retorted that the British predominated in the number of craft most needed in the Mediterranean, namely destroyers. Clemenceau then said that he needed three or four days before he could act. It was necessary "to lead public opinion to the right point of view," and he proposed his

91. Clemenceau to Lloyd George, May 15, 1918, ADM 116, book 1649; Sims to Navy Department, May 15, 1918, USNSF, TT file.

92. Sims to Benson, May 17, 1918, USNSF, TD file. See also Sims to Train, May 16, 1918, Sims Papers.

93. Ministry of Marine memorandum, "Note sur la Repartition des Forces Navales Alliees en Mediteranee," May 16, 1918, MM, Es file, box 14. De Bon memorandum for Leygues, May 21, 1918, MM, Es file, box 14.

formula for the arrangement: "Admiral Jellicoe is charged by the British and French Governments with coordinating the action of the Allied Fleets in the Mediterranean for the preparation and conduct of naval operations." This definition, in accord with the recommendation made by the Ministry of Marine, stopped well short of conferring supreme command upon Jellicoe. The British were expected to obtain the consent of the Italians, Japanese, and Americans. Clemenceau informed Geddes that he would telegraph permission to proceed in three or four days and would be prepared later to accede to an extension of Jellicoe's powers as he had in the case of General Foch. In a special note it was agreed to place the admiralissimo directly under the Allied Naval Council rather than the Supreme War Council—a reflection of naval dislike of the military-political organ at Versailles as well as the British desire to retain every possible influence over naval policy. The British, of course, had a much greater voice in the Allied Naval Council than in the Supreme War Council, where French opinions were generally most influential.[94]

Geddes and Lord Derby, the British Ambassador to France in succession to Lord Bertie, welcomed the outcome. The First Lord of the Admiralty explained to Lloyd George that the delay was "merely to put . . . [Clemenceau] in the right strategic position politically." France's Premier wanted to be "able to say publicly if necessary and at any rate to his colleagues, that the Italians had forced him into accepting a British admiralissimo because they refused to put their ships under a French Commander in the Mediterranean."[95] When the Italians definitely refused to place their ships under French command, Jellicoe would receive his appointment, and his powers would be increased gradually to ensure efficiency.[96] Sims defined Jellicoe's powers as "the idea that he will control simply the strategy of the Mediterranean, that is, the disposition of the forces that may be rendered necessary by any future action taken by the enemy."

94. "Memorandum of meeting on the subject of Naval Command in the Mediterranean held at the Ministry of War today Friday, May 17th, [1918]," ADM 116, book 1649. See also Geddes to Wemyss, May 17, 1918, ADM 116, book 1649.
95. Geddes to Lloyd George, May 17, 1918, ADM 116, book 1649. See also Derby to Balfour, May 18, 1918, Lloyd George Papers, file F/52/1/33.
96. Geddes to Wemyss, May 17, 1918, ADM 116, book 1649.

The naming of Jellicoe was an important aspect of the scheme, because he was "a man whose name is thoroughly well known to everybody in Europe."[97]

On May 21, Orlando notified the French Ambassador in Rome —Barrere—that Italy could not accept the proposed redistribution of forces in the Mediterranean; it would place Italian vessels under French command. Besides, the Black Sea Fleet could be contained by other methods.[98] Two days later Clemenceau sent his promised message to London, angrily reporting that Orlando had reneged on his promise to accept the transfer of Italian vessels to Corfu. He did not, however, propose to move on with the proposal for an admiralissimo until the British accepted an addendum to the formula agreed to on May 17. "Each commander-in-chief has the right to appeal to his Government, if in his opinion his command [armée] is placed in danger by any instructions received from Admiral Jellicoe." A comparable proviso, he noted, had been attached to Foch's authority.[99]

On the same day—May 23—Geddes reported developments to the War Cabinet, reviewing the arguments for the appointment of Jellicoe and indicating his confidence that the arrangement would mature.[100] He proposed to Lloyd George a reply to Clemenceau's proposal in these terms: "I think you will appreciate that the rapidity with which a Naval battle situation develops makes the clause of different import to what obtains in land warfare." He also urged preparations to bring the whole matter before the Supreme War Council.[101] All attention now centered on the meeting of that body, to which Orlando was bringing Admiral di Revel.[102]

97. Sims to Benson, May 19, 1918, (addendum to the letter of May 7, 1918), USNSF, TD file.

98. Orlando to Barrere, May 21, 1918, MM, Es file, box 14. Official notification to Paris is in Orlando to Clemenceau, May 23, 1918, MM, Es file, box 14. For a British account of the Franco-Italian conversations on redistribution, see British naval attaché (Rome) to Admiralty, May 23, 1918, ADM 116, book 1649.

99. Clemenceau to Lloyd George, May 23, 1918, Lloyd George Papers, file F/50/2/41. Copies are in MM, Es file, box 14, and ADM 116, book 1649.

100. Minutes of the War Cabinet (WC 415), May 23, 1918, CAB 23, book 6.

101. Geddes to Lloyd George, May 24, 1918, Lloyd George Papers, file F/18/1/21. A copy is in ADM 116, book 1649.

102. Minutes of the War Cabinet (WC 420), May 29, 1918, CAB 23, book 6; Barrere to Foreign Office, May 29, 1918, MM, Es file, box 14.

On June 1, a special private meeting of the British, French, and Italian premiers took place to arrange the appointment of an admiralissimo. Lloyd George summarized the necessity for arrangements to counteract the threat that the Russian Black Sea Fleet might combine with the German battle cruiser *Goeben* based at Constantinople in order to make a dangerous sortie in the Mediterranean. He thought it in the Italian interest to appoint a British admiralissimo, since it would guarantee the domination of the Mediterranean so essential to the supply of Italy. Unable to resist a gibe at di Revel, he said that the Admiral, "he had no doubt, was a very good sailor, but in his statement he really seemed to suggest that ships ought not to run any risks." This rendition was a misrepresentation of di Revel's actual position, as Sonnino pointed out later in the discussion. Orlando rose to di Revel's defense, citing the familiar technical and political objections advanced previously by Italy. "He was all in favour of unity, but we must leave the Italian Fleet alone." It might be argued that this was not a time to raise arguments of national *amour propre*, but his argument was more than sentimental in nature. The proposed redistributions "might affect the feelings of the Fleet so strongly as to be injurious, and the effect on the Italian people also could not be disregarded." Despite this exchange, the meeting decided to appoint Jellicoe with the understanding that he would be "in effective strategic [not tactical] command in the Mediterranean, Adriatic, and Aegean."[103] The matter seemed settled.

Much to the annoyance of the French and the British, Premier Orlando suddenly withdrew his acceptance the next day and forced another discussion. He proposed that the Supreme War Council accept two modifications: "The conduct of all special operations of war regarding the Adriatic is assigned to the Italian Commander-in-Chief." This was too much for the testy Clemenceau, who shouted that "the Italians appeared to want a single command but did not propose themselves to be bound by it." Orlando replied that he was simply drawing a distinction

103. Notes of the private consultation, June 1, 1918, ADM 116, book 1649. The official minutes are in SWC-WDA. See also the American report of the meeting, in Frazier to Lansing, June 2, 1918, USDSM 367, 763.72/Su 48. See also Department of State, 1918, supp. 1, 1:245–46. Maurice Hankey describes the situation in *The Supreme Command, 1914–1918*, 2 vols. (London, 1961), 2:811.

between strategic and tactical command. Leygues, Geddes, and de Bon all criticized various aspects of the Italian proposal, but to no avail. Sonnino, apparently unwilling to leave matters to Orlando, proposed alternative wording that made no real substantive improvements. Orlando then voiced the familiar Italian plaint concerning the vulnerability of the western Adriatic coast to enemy attack. Geddes objected to this argument, citing changes in the situation since the early years of the war. Italy's attitude was tantamount to declaring the Adriatic a closed sea. "This would create an impossible situation, since the principal enemy submarine bases were situated in the Adriatic and in the Dardanelles." Di Revel did not help matters when he reiterated the argument most offensive to British ears: the transfer from Taranto to Corfu meant that his ships "would have to run the very risks which he was anxious to avoid." After de Bon attempted unsuccessfully to obtain acceptance of an alternative proposal, Lloyd George abruptly withdrew his proposal for an admiralissimo. "If necessary," he said, "special arrangements could be entered into between France and Great Britain."[104]

The official minutes did not do justice to the intensity of the discussion. Sir Maurice Hankey, who was present, commented somewhat critically on the British position. "I am bound to say that Geddes was just as difficult and uncompromising as the Italians. On one hand he would concede nothing to Italian *amour-propre*, and on the other he would insist on Jellicoe's dispositions being subject to the Allied Naval Council which the Italians would not accept."[105] The American liaison officer at the Supreme War Council, Arthur Hugh Frazier, caught the real anger displayed at the meeting in his report of the denouement:

Lloyd George said in view of the attitude of the Italian representatives that any agreement which they might reach would only be a sham, and he would not subject such a fine man as Sir John Jellicoe to the indignity of occupying a position which would not be a reality. He therefore withdrew his resolution. Baron Sonnino with much heat protested that Italy had conceded a great deal already and that he would yield nothing further. He remarked that Italy had not been

104. Notes of the Supreme War Council discussion, June 2, 1918, ADM 116, book 1649. The official minutes are in SWC-WDA. See also Frazier to Lansing, June 2, 1918, USDSM 367, 763.72/13361.
105. Hankey, *Supreme Command*, 2:812.

forced to go into the war, in fact, she had been promised a good deal to remain neutral. Much surprise was caused by Admiral [di Revel's] statement that none of his battleships had been sunk for sixteen months because he had not allowed them to go to sea.[106]

Geddes refused to accept defeat, even trying to revive the project during the late moments of the meeting, but his efforts were doomed to failure.[107] The indefatigable First Lord of the Admiralty then prepared for another attempt at the imminent fourth meeting of the Allied Naval Council.[108]

The Council met in London on June 11–12, but it failed to break the deadlock over policy in the Mediterranean. Admiral Sims angrily reported to Washington Italy's refusal during the gathering to send battleships to Corfu to participate in joint training in anticipation of combined operations, to pool facilities for repair, and to permit detachment of light craft and cruisers based on the Otranto barrage for emergency fleet operations. Admiral Triangi, sitting for Italy, would consider redistribution only if the Black Sea danger actually materialized. Sims strongly supported the Franco-British position, but to no avail.[109] Geddes now informed Sir Rennell Rodd in Rome of his present views:

The French and the Americans and ourselves all feel that the Italians do not intend in Naval matters to co-operate at all. They do not intend to run any risks with their main forces; they do not intend to throw their Naval Forces into the general pool and use them on lines which are agreed, even by them, to be the best in the circumstances; and they are only prepared to share as long as they have something to gain in the sharing. . . . The Italians are prepared to set up any Allied organisation we like provided that they are represented on it, provided it facilitates their obtaining materials from us, but provided we exclude from its purview every Italian warship facility. . . . I see a widening rift between ourselves with the French and Americans on one hand, and the Italian Naval Authorities on the other.

106. Frazier to Lansing, June 3, 1918, USDSM 367, 763.72/Su 46. For another view, see Bliss to Baker, June 8, 1918, Wilson Papers, box 142. Geddes summarized these events in an angry letter to Sir Rennell Rodd, June 13, 1918, ADM 116, book 1649.
107. Memorandum by Geddes, "Memorandum on Command in the Mediterranean," June 3, 1918, ADM 116, book 1649; Minutes of the War Cabinet (WC 426), June 5, 1918, CAB 23, book 6.
108. Admiralty memorandum by Geddes, "Command in the Mediterranean," June 9, 1918, ADM 137, book 1937, 128–30; Geddes to Rodd, June 13, 1918, ADM 116, book 1649.
109. Minutes of the Fourth Meeting, ANC, June 11–12, 1918, USNSF, QC file; Sims to Navy Department, June 14, 1918, USNSF, QC file.

Geddes hoped that a threat to stop certain assistance to Italy might force some concessions, but he concluded that "as long as di Revel is in power we shall have difficulties in trying to get him to move at all."[110]

Geddes was a nonpolitical man of action, convinced of his own rectitude, and it was most difficult for him to consider the Italian case objectively. In his mind any resistance to general inter-Allied proposals was sheer perversity. Di Revel exemplified such interference par excellence, and Geddes came to dislike him intensely. He all too easily attributed Italian intransigence merely to the personality of the naval chief. "Admiral di Revel, and he alone, is responsible for the present state of affairs," trumpeted Geddes, and he claimed that Wemyss, de Bon, and Sims all shared this view.[111]

Geddes now attempted to force some change in Italian attitudes by mobilizing inter-Allied diplomatic pressure on Rome. After the First Lord held a meeting with his French and American colleagues, Sims informed the Navy Department: "It was agreed that each member would urge on his Government the desirability of bringing such pressure to bear on Italy as would induce her to cooperate heartily with the other Allies." Italy, he continued, had made inter-Allied naval consultations "more or less of a farce." Britain and France could bring great pressure to bear on Italy, but hesitated to go beyond a certain point because "anything in the nature of an ultimatum might have the effect of taking Italy out of the war altogether." Some diplomatic activity was called for: "It would seem at least that our Government could express their displeasure over the attitude of Italy in this respect."[112]

The project did not immediately come to fruition. Clemenceau demurred, not because he opposed the idea, but because the

110. Geddes to Rodd, June 13, 1918, Drummond Papers, FO 800, book 329. A copy is in ADM 116, book 1649.

111. Geddes memorandum for the War Cabinet, "Command in the Adriatic," June 13, 1918, continuing his memorandum of June 9, 1918, ADM 116, book 1649.

112. Sims to Navy Department, June 14, 1918, USNSF, QC file. For Geddes's project, see "Command in the Adriatic," June 13, 1918, ADM 116, book 1649; Geddes report to the Imperial War Cabinet in "A General Review of the Naval Situation," June 15, 1918, ADM 137, book 1937, 119; Minutes of the War Cabinet (WC 431), June 17, 1918, CAB 23, book 6.

timing seemed inappropriate to him.[113] In the United States Benson reported the Italian difficulty to the State Department, and shortly thereafter the President, according to Secretary Daniels, instructed Lansing "to talk to the Italian Ambassador and tell him how embarrassing it was."[114] In Rome Sonnino held his ground with Ambassador Page, who reported that Italy had "a feeling . . . that France is playing her own hand against Italy and that Greece is fomenting this. So far as Balkans are concerned I question whether Italy would agree to a single Naval Commander, if he were French, but think she would if British."[115] This outcome hardly served Geddes's purposes, and his enterprise was further undermined when France ended her efforts to rearrange the command in the Mediterranean.[116]

For a few weeks British and American leaders consoled themselves with private recriminations about di Revel. Sir Rennell Rodd reported to a friend in the Foreign Office that the Admiral was a trial at home as well as abroad. "[Thaon di Revel] is a heavy cross to bear and somehow or other he manages to impose his will. Orlando told me he was most difficult and hinted that our people had had their difficulties with wooden-headed soldiers, and might sympathize with him and have patience."[117] Sims told Commander Train that the Italian Navy was a fine force, but he could hardly recommend either Triangi or di Revel for the American Military Cross. He did concede that they were "undoubtedly bound down by political instructions."[118] Even Thomas Nelson Page expressed displeasure with di Revel.[119] Lloyd George agreed with Geddes that Sonnino and di Revel represented "strong Military and Jingo interest in the Italian

113. See the covering letter by Geddes, June 17, 1918, for his memorandum on "Command in the Mediterranean," ADM 116, book 1649.

114. Benson to Lansing, June 20, 1918, USDSM 367, 763.72/10605; Daniels diary, June 18, 1918, E. David Cronon, ed., *The Cabinet Diaries of Josephus Daniels, 1913–1921* (Lincoln, 1963), 312; Sims to Train, July 1, 1918, USNSF, TD file.

115. Page to Lansing, June 24, 1918, USDSM 367, 763.72/10507. See also Train to Sims, June 25, 1918, USNSF, TD file, which reports some details of the Page-Sonnino conversation.

116. Saint-Pair to Leygues, June 15, 1918, MM, Es file, box 19; de Bon to Saint-Pair, June 18, 1918, MM, Es file, box 19.

117. Rodd to Lord Hardinge, June 23, 1918, Lloyd George Papers, file F/3/3/15.

118. Sims to Train, July 1, 1918, USNSF, TD file.

119. Page to Wilson, July 2, 1918, Wilson Papers, box 143.

Government." He proposed to bypass them by taking up naval questions with the much more reasonable Minister of the Treasury, Nitti.[120]

These developments set the stage for an exercise in personal diplomacy by the ebullient Assistant Secretary of the Navy, Franklin D. Roosevelt, who had finally been granted his wish to make a visit to Europe.[121] Geddes succeeded in convincing Roosevelt that the British had a sound view of the situation in Italy, and he enlisted the active intervention of the American. Roosevelt informed Daniels that he planned to rectify the difficulty during a forthcoming sojourn in Rome. "I hope by my visit to lay the foundations for more unified action between the many Allied naval units in the Mediterranean, and also for more actual offensive work against the Austrians on the Dalmatian Coast."[122] Geddes recognized in the impending visit of F.D.R. to Rome another opportunity to press for the unified command. Nothing if not a persistent man, he obtained permission from Balfour and Lloyd George to accompany Roosevelt to Italy for private talks with the Italians. The French, who had been increasingly difficult to deal with on this question, would not participate in the expedition.[123] Roosevelt, however, was not interested in a joint mission. He simply went off to Rome by himself, quite properly, and Geddes was not able to take part in his conversations with the Italian naval leaders. "I think that Geddes rather wanted to go to Italy with me," he wrote Daniels, "but it would be a great mistake for us to go together, and I think I have succeeded in heading him off." He believed that he could achieve more on his

120. Geddes minutes on conversation with Lloyd George, July 16, 1918, ADM 116, book 1649.

121. For scattered comments on the Italian question, see Roosevelt's brief journal in Assistant Secretary file, Roosevelt Papers, box 7.

122. Roosevelt to Daniels, August 2, 1918, Daniels Papers. See also Frank Freidel, *Franklin D. Roosevelt: The Apprenticeship* (Boston, 1952), 351.

123. Geddes to Balfour, August 3, 1918, Balfour Papers, FO 800, book 207; Geddes to Roosevelt, August 3, 1918, Balfour Papers, FO 800, book 207; Balfour to Geddes, Balfour Papers, August 5, 1918, FO 800, book 207. Copies of the last two letters are in ADM 116, book 1649. British assumptions that the French were growing suspicious of the admiralissimo project were accurate. The French Ambassador in Rome asked the Foreign Office for permission to counteract Rodd's efforts to gain the command of the Mediterranean for the British. Barrere to Foreign Office, July 17, 1918, MM, Es file, box 14.

own. "The Italians may not love us, but at least they know that we have no ulterior designs in the Mediterranean."[124]

Roosevelt did not persuade the Italians to alter their naval policy, although he did succeed in irritating some of the officials with whom he discussed the situation. In order to meet the Italians halfway, he apparently sympathized with their desire to retain control of the Adriatic. This breezy concession of course placed him at cross-purposes with the British Admiralty, although he came to share that agency's criticism of Italian inactivity. At one point he inquired why the Italian fleet did not put to sea for training exercises. The response was that it was unnecessary because the Austrians had also confined themselves to their harbors. "This is a naval classic which is hard to beat," Roosevelt recorded, "but which perhaps should not be publicly repeated for a generation or two."[125] The French Ambassador took umbrage at Roosevelt's activity, reporting angrily to the Foreign Office that the Americans and the British had approached Italy behind the back of France in search of postwar advantage.[126] When Roosevelt quit Italy he wrote in discouraging terms to Geddes. "My visit to Italy not only made me feel that it will be impossible to get the Italian battleship force placed under Allied command, but the whole political situation down there is such that we should not attempt to force this issue."[127]

Roosevelt's activities apparently led to an inquiry into the status of his mission in Washington by French Ambassador Jules Jusserand. He reported to Clemenceau, quite accurately, that Roosevelt's enterprise was not to be taken seriously. When Secretary Daniels heard of this matter from Lansing, he explained

124. Roosevelt to Daniels, August 2, 1918, Daniels Papers. See also Roosevelt to Daniels, August 13, 1918, Daniels Papers.

125. Roosevelt diary, August 10, 1918, quoted in Freidel, *Roosevelt: The Apprenticeship*, 363; Roosevelt to Daniels, August 13, 1918, Daniels Papers; Naval attaché (Rome) to Geddes, August 27, 1918, ADM 116, book 1649; Roosevelt journal, August 2, 1918, Assistant Secretary file, Roosevelt Papers, box 7.

126. Barrere to Pichon, August 17, 1918, MM, Es file, box 14. For British activity, see Rodd to Geddes, August 15, 1918, ADM 116, book 1649; Geddes to Rodd, August 17, 1918, ADM 116, book 1649; Geddes to Rodd, August 17, 1918, ADM 116, book 1649. This exchange arranged an approach to Rome through the Italian envoy in London—the Marquis Imperiali.

127. Roosevelt to Geddes, August 28, 1918, ADM 116, book 1649.

that Roosevelt had no authority to discuss the appointment of Admiral Jellicoe. Roosevelt had been informed only that the United States favored a unified command; it had not supported any given candidate.[128] Thus came to a rather dubious end the Italian adventures of the Assistant Secretary.

That most dogged of sea dogs, Sir Eric Geddes, still continued his effort to secure Italian agreement to an admiralissimo for the Mediterranean. Rome apparently was prepared to accept the proposal only with the understanding that the command did not extend to the Adriatic, that national commanders could appeal to their respective governments, and that Jellicoe would function under the authority of the Supreme War Council. The last proviso bypassed the Allied Naval Council, to which Geddes raised great objection. He deemed the Supreme War Council unwieldy and slow to act; only the naval organization could control the situation properly. "Naval warfare is so much more fluid and less fixed than is land warfare; it is much more technical and much more detailed in the disposition of the forces and a consideration of their various qualities."[129] He was nevertheless convinced that a unified naval command became more urgent with every passing day, and he received the permission of the War Cabinet to continue negotiations.[130]

In late September Geddes left Britain for a visit to the United States; after his departure Sir Rennell Rodd attempted to carry on in Rome, but nothing came of his efforts. Writing to Rodd, Wemyss ruefully admitted a salient weakness in the British position: "The truth is that we really have very little knowledge as to the state of affairs obtaining in the Black Sea." The First Sea Lord saw clearly the adverse consequences of Franco-Italian

128. Daniels diary, September 3 and September 5, 1918, Cronon, ed., *Cabinet Diaries*, 333, 334.

129. Geddes to Lloyd George (with enclosed memorandum), September 17, 1918, Lloyd George Papers, file F/18/1/18. A copy is in ADM 116, book 1649. See also "Memorandum by the Admiralty on the Proposal of the Italian Government for the Appointment of an Admiralissimo in the Mediterranean," September 17, 1918, ADM 116, book 1649; Geddes memorandum, "Some Important Aspects of the Naval Situation and Submarine Campaign," September 25, 1918, Cabinet Memorandum no. 791, FO 899, book 4.

130. Minutes of the War Cabinet (WC 479), September 27, 1918, CAB 23, book 7. See also Geddes memorandum, "Naval Situation in the Black Sea and Command in the Mediterranean," September 25, 1918, ADM 116, book 1771.

rivalry that greatly complicated the situation.[131] He did not realize the extent to which the French had become alarmed at the British initiative. Ambassador Barrere sought permission to block the enterprise, referring to it as an *"entente clandestine."*[132] The breakdown of Anglo-French cooperation ensured the failure of the eleventh-hour effort to alter the attitude of Italy.

Anglo-French tensions erupted into a serious quarrel over policy in the Mediterranean when it became apparent early in October that a Turkish surrender was imminent. Both nations wished to command the occupation force to be sent into the Dardanelles. Britain made a most extensive effort to obtain the command for one of its admirals, but Clemenceau refused to concede this privilege. London, he argued, had agreed to French command in the Mediterranean in August, 1914, and that arrangement was the controlling consideration.[133] Disarray among the Entente powers concerning Mediterranean policy was not the least of the problems confronting those who gathered to draft the naval terms of armistice in Paris in late October, 1918.

What was the actual situation in the Black Sea? The evidence is relatively sparse, but although Germany did seek control of the Russian fleet, there is every indication that Germany never intended a major sortie into the Mediterranean.[134] In April, 1918, the Russian fleet was located in three different ports. The largest part of the fleet was in Russian hands at Sevastopol; another small contingent under Bolshevik command was based on Novorossisk; and the newly independent Ukrainian government at Nikolaev had control of another flotilla. When the Bolsheviks began to utilize the ships under their control in operations against the Ukraine, Germany considered the occupation of

131. Wemyss to Rodd, October 3, 1918, ADM 116, book 1649.
132. Barrere to Army GHQ, September 23, 1918, MM, Es file, box 14.
133. For information on the Anglo-French dispute over command of the expedition to the Dardanelles, see Minutes of the War Cabinet (WC 484), October 1, 1918, CAB 23, book 42; Lloyd George to Clemenceau, October 15, 1918, Lloyd George Papers, file F/50/3/37; Derby to Lloyd George, October 18, 1918, Lloyd George Papers, file F/52/2/40; Derby to Balfour, October 18, 1918, Lloyd George Papers, file F/52/2/41; Clemenceau to Lloyd George, October 21, 1918, Lloyd George Papers, file F/52/2/43; Lloyd George to Clemenceau, October 25, 1918, file F/50/3/39.
134. For an account by the German naval commander in the Black Sea, consult Admiral Albert Hopmann, *Das Kriegstagebuch eines deutschen Seeoffiziers* (Berlin, 1925).

Sevastopol.[135] The German Foreign Office notified Holtzendorff that Germany could not employ the Russian fleet unless it was purchased from the Bolsheviks after signature of peace. This policy forced the Navy to postpone a projected seizure of the ships lying at Nikolaev.[136] When Russia failed to deliver the ships at Novorossisk into German hands at Sevastopol, Ludendorff wanted to sink them, but he was overruled by the Foreign Office and the naval staff. Ultimately German military movements forced the Russians in July to destroy the vessels at Novorossisk —a battleship and some destroyers. Germany now had control of 9 battleships, 6 cruisers, 10 destroyers, 10 U-boats, and some lesser craft at Sevastopol and Nikolaev.[137] Ludendorff and Holtzendorff then agreed that Germany should obtain direct control of all the battleships, 5 destroyers, and all the submarines, placing them in the hands of German crews. Austria could have some destroyers if it could provide crews. Turkey could have only enough ships to secure the Dardanelles. Bulgaria would receive none.[138] On August 8, 1918, Germany concluded an agreement with the Bolsheviks that recognized Russian ownership of the Black Sea Fleet, but provided for German retention of its vessels until the conclusion of a general peace.[139] In September the German naval staff arranged for the seizure of certain ships at Sevastopol still in Russian hands.[140] Throughout this period arguments over the command of operations in the Black Sea area between the army and the navy interfered with rapid and efficient operations.

135. Bussche to Mirbach, April 23, 1918, TA-191-D 75683, German Naval Record Collection of the U.S. Naval History Division, Washington, D.C. Hereafter this collection is cited as Tambach records. The collection is now in the National Archives, Washington, D.C.

136. Foreign Office to Holtzendorff, April 25, 1918, Tambach records, TA-191-D 75683; Admiralty statement on the Black Sea Fleet, May 10, 1918, Tambach records, TA-191-D 75683.

137. Report of Ludendorff-Holtzendorff conference, May 15, 1918, Tambach records, TA-136-D 67476; Hindenburg to Kaiser Wilhelm II, June 10, 1918, Tambach records TA-191-D 75683; German naval attaché (Sevastopol) to Holtzendorff, July 19, 1918, Tambach records, TA-190-D 75679, frame 22199B.

138. Naval Representative at G.H.Q. to Naval Staff, July 10, 1918, Tambach records, TA-190-D 75679, frame 20476; Holtzendorff to Hindenburg, July[?], 1918, Tambach records, TA-190-D 75679, frame 20916.

139. Supplementary Russo-German agreement, August 8, 1918, Tambach records, TA-190-D 75679, frame 24739B.

140. For information about this enterprise, see Tambach records, TA-191-D 75681, especially frames 29649, 27700.

The Russian vessels were never placed in operating condition. On October 27, the naval staff reported that three or four weeks must elapse before the ships could be repaired and crews transferred to the Black Sea from Flanders.[141] With the onset of the Armistice Germany undertook to insure that the Allies respected the arrangements it had made with Russia for the return of the Black Sea Fleet at the end of hostilities. The Armistice terms had provided that the ships be turned over to the victors.[142] Given the great emergency developing on the Western Front, Germany could hardly give first priority to naval operations in a peripheral region, especially given the strength of the various Allied navies located in the Mediterranean. If German efforts to utilize the Russian Black Sea Fleet never amounted to very much and ultimately came to naught, they certainly aroused a great amount of consternation and conflict within the western coalition.

Thus culminated ingloriously what had never approached any likelihood of historical approbation. The unsatisfactory naval situation in the Mediterranean by early 1918 had prompted the British to seek redistribution of Allied naval forces and the appointment of an admiralissimo to direct them. Italy from the first opposed all such endeavors, fearful that its naval interests, particularly in the Adriatic, would be sacrificed by its associates. France initially supported the British effort, but its enthusiasm declined as Italian resistance hardened and as Anglo-French tensions matured during the summer and fall of 1918. The chief naval argument for the changes—a possible enemy attack in the Mediterranean from the Black Sea—never became credible. This fact deprived the British of a truly cogent rationale. American support for the British was at best halfhearted; Admiral Sims sympathized with the Admiralty campaign, but he could not act effectively without active support from Washington. The fiasco over fleet redistribution and command in the Mediterranean during 1918 must go down as a classic example of the ways in which inter-Allied political differences precluded desir-

141. Naval staff report, October 27, 1918, Tambach records, TA-191-D 75681.
142. See various documents in Tambach records, TA-190-D 75679; Minutes of the German Cabinet meeting, November 16, 1918. See also Records of the German Foreign Ministry, Alte Reichskanzlerei 2744, Beihefte zur Kabinetts-protokollen, 1917–1919, filmed at Whaddon Hall, England, 1954, serial #9246H, frames E653467. Hereafter this collection is cited as Whaddon Hall microfilms.

able naval cooperation. Efforts to combat the submarine menace were more successful, but inter-Allied conflicts also beset improvement of the Otranto barrage and convoy operations in the Mediterranean.

IV

The Allied Naval Council made its most important contribution to Mediterranean operations by supporting construction of the Otranto barrage and improvement of convoy operations in the Mediterranean. For the most part the United States and France concurred in barrage and convoy policies advocated by the British Admiralty, but as in other contexts Italy proved contentious. That country was most anxious to expedite the Otranto barrage and also to improve convoy operations, but it withheld contributions to these endeavors deemed essential to success by the other powers. Inter-Allied controversy and delay account in part for the effectiveness of Austro-German submarine warfare in the Mediterranean long after its efficiency had been vastly reduced in the Atlantic.

Britain raised the problem of Mediterranean convoy at the first meeting of the Allied Naval Council in January, 1918. Seeking to introduce "freedom of movement and general elasticity," it proposed that Italy "consent to the proposal that Italian vessels now employed in protecting Allied shipping . . . be pooled with those of France and Great Britain under the general control of the British Commander-in-Chief [Gough-Calthorpe] leaving sufficient forces with which to protect their purely local coastal traffic." France supported this general concept, although it recognized that Italy was in desperate need of light craft to secure its position in the Adriatic.[143] The Italian memorandum on convoy was hardly encouraging. Admiral di Revel concentrated on the necessity of supplying destroyers for the Adriatic and also opposed any interference with coastal convoys on the west coast of Italy and in Sicilian and Sardinian waters. These early discussions resulted in appointment of a special commission to shape definite plans for the Mediterranean.

The special commission met in Rome on February 8–9 and

143. British and French memoranda on Mediterranean convoy, Minutes of the First Meeting, ANC, n.d., Appendix 6, USNSF, QC file.

made some useful decisions, its principal achievement being to arrange for development of the Otranto barrage. In return for contributions of materials Britain obtained command of the surface patrol on the barrage. The United States was asked to contribute some of its new submarine chasers for the patrol. Admiral di Revel once again reminded the conference of the need to guarantee the security of convoys bringing much-needed coal and food to Italy.[144] The outcome of these negotiations encouraged Sir Eric Geddes, although he told Admiral Wemyss that "if we are going to down the submarines in the Adriatic there is no doubt we have got to do it ourselves."[145] Admiral Sims was prepared to allocate submarine chasers to the Adriatic, but he urged that such decisions be made by the Allied Naval Council in order to avoid unnecessary confusion and conflict.[146] The chasers became particularly important when Japan refused to send additional antisubmarine craft to the Mediterranean.[147]

In March the Allied Naval Council approved the proposals of the Rome conference and took further steps to develop the Otranto barrage;[148] it also discussed allocation of American submarine chasers. Sims insisted that the small vessels be deployed "on broad strategical grounds and not after considerations of only a part of the theater of war." The Council ultimately agreed to send the first two squadrons to the Adriatic—some thirty-six

144. "Report of the Commission which met in Rome on February 8th and 9th, 1918," Minutes of the Second Meeting, ANC, n.d., Appendix 1, USNSF, QC file; Sims to Navy Department, February 14, 1918, USNSF, TP file.

145. Geddes to Wemyss, February 14, 1918, Geddes Papers, ADM 116, book 1807.

146. Sims to Benson, March 7, 1918, USNSF, TD file. The submarine chasers were 110 feet long, displaced sixty-five tons and were driven by three engines. They mounted a three-inch gun and depth charge launchers. Their complement was two officers and about twenty-two men. "The American Effort in the Mediterranean," ca. November, 1918, USNSF, WV file.

147. French memorandum on Japanese and American assistance, Minutes of the First Meeting, ANC, n.d., Appendix 6, USNSF, QC file; Japanese memorandum on aid in Mediterranean, Minutes of the Second Meeting, ANC, March 7, 1918, Appendix 6, USNSF, QC file.

148. Minutes of the Second Meeting, ANC, Second Session, March 12, 1918, USNSF, QC file; British memorandum on the Otranto barrage, Minutes of the Second Meeting, ANC, n.d., Appendix 1, USNSF, QC file; di Revel memorandum on the Otranto barrage, Minutes of the Second Meeting, ANC, March 12, 1918, Appendix 2, USNSF, QC file.

boats—for use as patrol rather than escort craft. The rest of the chasers building—over a hundred—would be utilized around the British Isles.[149]

The Allied Naval Council met again in late April, but it took little action on the Mediterranean convoy and barrage activities. Efforts to centralize control of convoy operations had to be delayed because of confusing recommendations from the various concerned nations, despite the insistence of Sims on an early settlement.[150] The Council did set up a special subcommittee to plan the pooling of Allied repair facilities.[151] It met in Rome during the period May 9–14, but accomplished very little. France's participant reported to the E.M.G. that the British and the Italians were at loggerheads on the question because the latter strictly opposed centralization of authority.[152] Great controversies then raging over redistribution of surface units and appointment of an admiralissimo obviously interfered with progress in the campaign to restrict enemy undersea operations in the Mediterranean. Sir Eric Geddes told the War Cabinet that arrangements for that area were still "totally inadequate." Admiral Wemyss attributed some of the difficulty to the fact that so many destroyers were needed to escort American troopships approaching France.[153]

After the demise of the American plan for an amphibious offensive in the Adriatic, Admiral Sims and the Navy Department turned their attention to the Otranto barrage and other mining

149. Minutes of the Second Meeting, ANC, Second Session, March 12, 1918, USNSF, QC file; United States note on submarine chasers, Minutes of the Second Meeting, ANC, n.d., Appendix 6, USNSF, QC file; Sims notes for ANC meeting, March 11, 1918, QC file; Sims to Navy Department, March 16, 1918, QC file; French memorandum on distribution of American submarine chasers, Minutes of the Second Meeting, ANC, n.d., Appendix 6, USNSF, QC file.

150. Minutes of the Third Meeting, ANC, April 27, 1918, Third Session, USNSF, QC file.

151. Minutes of the Third Meeting, ANC, April 26, 1918, First Session, USNSF, QC file.

152. Engineer Labeuf, "Rapport de Mission a Rome (9–14 Mai 1918)," May 16, 1918, MM, Es file, box 18; "Report of Sub-Committee appointed to consider the Arrangements for Repair of Allied Warships in the Mediterranean," Minutes of the Fourth Meeting, ANC, May 14, 1918, Appendix 6, USNSF, QC file.

153. Minutes of the War Cabinet (WC 417), May 24, 1918, CAB 23, book 6.

projects in the Mediterranean. The Department interested itself particularly in a proposed barrage stretching from Sicily to North Africa at Cape Bon, a project that would close the western Mediterranean to submarines operating from the Adriatic and the Dardanelles. Sims recognized the merits of the proposal but explained that it was not likely to be adopted because it would not protect lines of communication eastward to the Suez Canal. For this reason the Entente powers would concentrate primarily on developing barrages in the Straits of Otranto and off the Dardanelles.[154]

The fourth meeting of the Allied Naval Council produced few decisions relating to convoy and barrage operations in the Mediterranean, preoccupied as it was with the dispute between the British and the Italians over redistribution and command of the surface fleets. A report from the subcommittee on pooling repair facilities came before the group, but differences between the Anglo-American and the Franco-Italian combinations prevented action.[155] Italy complained about the slow development of the Otranto barrage. When Geddes requested American assistance in order to speed its completion, Sims promised to make inquiries in Washington.[156] The question of American submarine chasers rose once again. Sims insisted that the next seventy-two available be assigned to the Irish Sea and the English Channel; if utilized in those waters, they would help protect American troopships going to France. He effectively opposed British efforts to allocate some of the vessels to the Gibraltar area and French efforts to place others off their own coast. None of this group of submarine chasers was sent to the Mediterranean.[157] If one considers the needs of the Mediterranean theater, these were meager accomplishments indeed. Admiral Wemyss reported to the Imperial

154. Benson to Sims, May 27, 1918, USNSF, QC file; Sims to Benson, June 10, 1918, USNSF, QC file.

155. Minutes of the Fourth Meeting, ANC, June 11, 1918, First and Second Sessions, USNSF, QC file.

156. Minutes of the Fourth Meeting, ANC, Second Session, June 11, 1918, USNSF, QC file.

157. For various memoranda by the United States, Britain, and France on the allocation of chasers, see Minutes of the Fourth Meeting, ANC, June 11–12, 1918, Appendix 8, USNSF, QC file. For the Council's discussion, see the Minutes of the Fourth Meeting, ANC, June 11, 1918, First Session, USNSF, QC file. See also Sims to Bayly, May 17, 1918, TP file; Sims to Navy Department, June 15, 1918, USNSF, QC file.

War Cabinet in June only that "on the whole the situation is getting better, and certainly is not getting worse."[158] A report compiled by the Admiralty in July bore out this conclusion. Tonnage loss in the Mediterranean from the first quarter to the second quarter of 1918 had declined by 16 per cent, compared with a decrease in home waters of 21 per cent. The risk percentage in the Mediterranean was 1.5 per cent; in home waters it was 0.6 per cent. Some 258 ships had gone to the bottom in the Mediterranean from November, 1917, through June, 1918—an average of thirty-four per month—amounting to some 800,000 tons.[159]

The Mediterranean was now more critical than the Atlantic, and a more vigorous policy was required. Admiral Sims seized the initiative, chairing a subcommittee of the Allied Naval Council to expedite mining policies in the Mediterranean. On July 23, the Council held an emergency meeting to consider his recommendations. First of all Sims obtained acceptance of certain general principles deemed essential to effective mining operations. Then the Council agreed to develop an over-all barrage plan. The United States would supply necessary mines and mine layers in association with the Allies. It was agreed that the completion of the Otranto barrage (Otranto to Corfu via Fano Island) should receive first priority. The next effort would be in the Aegean (Euboea to Cape Kanapitza via Andros, Tinos, Mykoni, Nikaria, Furnia, and Samos islands), followed by the Sicily-Cape Bon project. A committee meeting at Malta was to produce detailed recommendations.[160] After the action of the Allied Naval Council, Sims cabled earnestly to the Navy Department: "I request the Department's specific approval in order to strengthen my hands in this matter, as I think there may be

158. Wemyss statement to the Imperial War Cabinet, June 27, 1918, ADM 116, book 1603. See also Admiralty Memorandum for the Imperial War Cabinet, "A General Review of the Naval Situation," June 15, 1918, ADM 137, book 1937, 119.

159. Report on Mediterranean sinkings by Lt. Col. J. G. Beharrell, July 25, 1918, ADM 116, book 1604.

160. Minutes of the Emergency Meeting, July 23, 1918, printed as Appendix 1, dated July 24, 1918, in the Minutes of the Fifth Meeting, ANC, September 13–14, 1918, MM, Es file, box 20. See also Rothiacob to de Bon, July 25, 1918, MM, Es file, box 21; ANC Memorandum No. 163 by the United States, "The Desirability of Undertaking New Mine Barrage Operations in the Mediterranean," July 11, 1918, MM, Es file, box 19; Sims to Train, July 24, 1918, USNSF, TD file.

some disposition to favor the use of our minelayers for other purposes less important strategically. The exact location of barrages must depend somewhat on tactical considerations presented by the Allied Commanders in the Mediterranean."[161] Soon thereafter he proposed to the Navy Department that it assign an admiral to the Allied headquarters at Malta because of growing American interest in the Mediterranean.[162] Sims's initiative resulted in a major conference on mining operations in the Mediterranean on Malta in early August, which produced detailed plans for the general operations that had been approved on July 23.[163]

The Navy Department was remarkably slow in responding to the many messages of Sims regarding barrage operations in the Mediterranean. When it did so it must have seemed entirely irresponsible to the Commander in London. After a strong appeal from Sims, Secretary Daniels finally reacted on September 4, 1918. He recognized the importance of barrage operations, but drew attention to the lack of coordination that had so far characterized inter-Allied activities. As a general principle, the Department would approve plans that coordinated military and political interests in the eastern Mediterranean and the Adriatic with naval operations, so long as the arrangement in turn was integrated with "the more important military campaigns conducted elsewhere"—a reference to the Western Front. Daniels authorized Sims to proceed with the barrages in the Straits of Otranto and in the Aegean Sea. Then, however, the Secretary took a surprising tack: He revived the plan for a mid-Adriatic barrage from Gargano Head to Curzola Island!

There had been evidence of "grave unrest" across the Adriatic. A military operation might provide opportunities for "a disruptive [propaganda] effort in the rear." Sims was instructed to take up the matter with the Supreme War Council through the Allied Naval Council.[164]

161. Sims to Navy Department, July 25, 1918, USNSF, QC file. See also Sims to Strauss, memorandum entitled "Mine Barrages in the Mediterranean," July 27, 1918, USNSF, TT file.

162. Sims to Benson, July 28, 1918, USNSF, TD file.

163. The Report of the Malta Conference, August 6–9, 1918, is printed as Appendix 1 of the Minutes of the Fifth Meeting, ANC, September 13–14, 1918, MM, Es file, box 20.

164. Daniels to Sims, September 4, 1918, USNSF, QC file. The message promoting this cablegram is Sims to Navy Department, September 3, 1918, USNSF, QC file.

Sims dutifully proceeded with what he must have known was a fool's errand. On September 13, at the Allied Naval Council he reintroduced the Gargano Head-Curzola Island project. Di Revel immediately responded that the first effort should be to complete the Otranto project and, for a change, received the support of both Wemyss and de Bon. Sims argued further, but ultimately accepted a decision to proceed first with the barrage at Otranto. The Council then made arrangements for logistical support.[165] Sims's cable reporting the outcome was suitably terse. "Council considered Military situation would not justify revival of consideration Mid-Adriatic Mine Barrier at this time, and did not consider expedient refer question to supreme war council."[166]

Another outcome of the fifth meeting of the Allied Naval Council was an agreement to dispatch additional submarine chasers to Italian waters. As usual the Italians were pressing for further protection of shipping in the Mediterranean, provided they were utilized for hunting operations rather than escort.[167] Di Revel accepted this proposal.[168] Sims justified this arrangement to the Navy Department on psychological as well as naval grounds. "Not only can they be advantageously employed in the indicated locality [Straits of Otranto and Sicilian coasts], but their assignment will be particularly pleasing to Italian authorities, who feel that their requests for assistance usually receive scant consideration."[169]

The Department responded favorably to Sims's recommendations, and he busied himself with various mining projects in the Mediterranean throughout September and October until the onset of the pre-Armistice discussions.[170] Ironically the end of

165. Minutes of the Fifth Meeting, ANC, First Session, September 13, 1918, MM, Es file, box 20. See also Minutes of the Fifth Meeting, ANC, Second Session, September 14, 1918, MM, Es file, box 20; Conclusion of the Fifth Meeting, ANC, September 13–14, 1913, USNSF, QC file.

166. Sims to Navy Department, September 15, 1918, USNSF, QC file.

167. Italian memorandum, "Inferiority of Anti-Submarine Protection Measures in the Mediterranean," Minutes of the Fifth Meeting, ANC, August 27, 1918, Appendix 7, MM, Es file, box 20.

168. Minutes of the Fifth Meeting, ANC, First Session, September 13, 1918, MM, Es file, box 20.

169. Sims to Opnav, September 14, 1918, USNSF, QC file.

170. For correspondence dealing with this effort, see Sims to Benson, September 17, 1918, USNSF, TD file; Sims to Aminfor, Inverness, September 19, 1918, USNSF, QC file; Sims to Benson, October 2, 1918,

the war precluded completion of these endeavors—the only ones
for the Mediterranean that ever gained general inter-Allied support. As Sims had argued, mine barrages did not become efficient until actually completed, and none of the Mediterranean
projects achieved that status. Losses in the Mediterranean would
have been more serious than they were, had the Central Powers
been able to send more submarines to the region. Their undersea
flotilla suffered grievously from lack of adequate repair facilities.[171] As it was, maritime traffic declined greatly; at one point
in 1917 the Suez Canal was carrying only 40 per cent of its normal peacetime volume. Only ten U-boats were sunk in the Mediterranean.[172] It is not clear that the Otranto material barrage destroyed a single U-boat, although, like its counterpart in the
North Sea, it certainly constituted an increasingly demoralizing
harassment, which took its toll on the morale of the submarine
crews. As in the Atlantic the volume of sinkings declined precipitously in the last months of warfare. Lack of effective naval
coordination in the Mediterranean Sea greatly inhibited antisubmarine operations there, and it created an important quan-
tum of the dissension that inhibited inter-Allied cooperation
during and after the war.

After the pre-Armistice negotiations in Paris, Sir Rennell Rodd
told Balfour that "The naval obligations in co-operation with
the land forces [of Italy] have, to a great extent, justified the
plea of the chief of the naval staff [di Revel] for the necessity of
keeping the Italian fleet in the Adriatic, and for liberty of action
in local operations."[173] Anglo-American naval leaders would

USNSF, TD file; Sims to Navy Department, October 9, 1918, USNSF, QC
file; Sims to Navy Department, October 16, 1918, QC file; Chief of Staff,
London, to Secretary, ANC, October 16, 1918, USNSF, QC file; United
States Memorandum on mining operations in the Mediterranean, in Minutes of the Sixth Meeting, ANC, Seventh Session, November 9, 1918, Appendix 50, USNSF, QC file. The last document summarizes the planning
for barrage operations. See also "Policy in the Mediterranean, and the
Manner in Which Our Vessels are Employed to Carry Out That Policy,"
September 17, 1918, ADM 137, book 1437, 185–88.

171. For information on this situation, see Michelsen, *U-Bootskrieg*,
130–53; Gibson and Prendergast, *German Submarine Warfare*, 263–64;
Arno Spindler, *Der Handelskrieg mit U-Booten*, 4 vols. (Berlin, 1941),
4:466.

172. Robert M. Grant, *U-Boats Destroyed: The Effect of Anti-
Submarine Warfare, 1914–1918* (London, 1964), 130.

173. Rodd to Balfour, November 5, 1918, Cabinet Papers, no. 264
(1918), FO 899, book 14.

hardly have accepted this estimate. Admiral Sims recognized
that Italy had fought well, but he realized also that "she has
also made a great deal of friction." No one knew this better than
he! He drew a comparison between Italy and the United States.
"It is inevitable she should have a rather bad reputation because
she hesitated so long about coming into the war. We suffered
from the same cause."[174] Others were not so charitable. The
course of policy and strategy during the Great War deepened
not only Italy's distrust of Britain and France, but also the almost
universal international aversion to Italian statecraft. The consequences for the United States, that relatively innocent bystander,
were ultimately serious indeed.

American naval leaders as well as their political associates
grew rapidly in their comprehension of the Italian situation during 1918, but they succeeded neither in concerting policies designed to ensure the future of Italo-American relations nor in
making an effective contribution to victory in Italy during the
year of decision. Admiral Sims's efforts reflected his central preoccupation with the means of defeating the submarine campaign of the Central Powers rather than with specific political
interests of a territorial and economic nature in the Mediterranean. He tirelessly sought to assist Italy in various ways, proposing an American naval attack in the Adriatic, supplying
submarine chasers, and working out arrangements for American
contributions to mine barrages and convoy operations. Some
seventy-five ships and 5,542 officers and men served in the Mediterranean.[175] If these activities were appreciated in Rome, Italian
leaders took a different view of American support for Anglo-
French attempts to achieve a redistribution of fleets in the
Mediterranean and the appointment of Jellicoe as admiralissimo. Rome of course reacted strongly against clear indications
that President Wilson opposed Italian territorial aspirations in
Dalmatia and elsewhere violative of the principles of self-
determination. In the end, all of Sims's endeavors to conciliate
the Italians were futile, lost in the clash of interests and aspirations during the hectic negotiations that took place in Paris in
1919.

174. Sims to Train, November 4, 1918, USNSF, TD file.
175. "The American Effort in the Mediterranean," ca. November, 1918,
USNSF, WV file.

CHAPTER 8

THE GEDDES MISSION
August–October, 1918

Early in October, 1918, Sir Eric Geddes made a rapid visit to the United States, delivering a few public addresses and attending some conferences in Washington. The visit aroused relatively limited curiosity because President Wilson's dramatic negotiations with Germany, which led to the pre-Armistice negotiations in late October, overshadowed it. In recent years, however, certain scholars have shown some interest in the Geddes mission. Mary Klachko, for example, explains that the First Lord hoped to coordinate the shipbuilding efforts of the United States and Great Britain, but she also speculates that he was instructed to oppose Wilsonian deals with Germany that were repugnant to the War Cabinet.[1] It is now possible to make a relatively detailed analysis of the Geddes mission because of the opening of the British naval archives. The activities of Geddes in the United States constituted an interesting prelude to the negotiation of the naval armistices in Paris only a few short weeks later.

I

As the United States became more and more deeply involved in the Great War, the tradition of Anglo-American mistrust was largely suppressed, so were mutual suspicions entertained in London and Washington concerning postwar trading policies and naval building programs. Nevertheless, these questions on occasion concerned statesmen in both countries during 1917–1918. In communications with British officials President Wilson was careful to stress his intention to act in the general interest of the western coalition, but privately he expressed strong distrust of British intent.[2] To Secretary Daniels he once burst out: "Fear

1. Mary Klachko, "Anglo-American Naval Competition, 1918–1922," Ph. D. diss., Columbia University, 1962, pp. 41–45, 51–52. See also Warner R. Schilling, "Admirals and Foreign Policy, 1913–1919," Ph. D. diss., Yale University, 1953, pp. 136–37.
2. Wiseman memorandum on conversation with President Wilson, April 1, 1918, Balfour Papers, BM, book 49741.

I will come out of the war hating English."[3] The tradition of
Anglophobia, latent, remained an important element condi-
tioning Anglo-American relations. Charles Lyell, observing the
American scene in April, 1918, described the situation accurately for Sir Eric Drummond. There was still "a very curious
amount of anti-British feeling which every now and again crops
up in unexpected ways in the Press; tendencies to belittle British
performance in the field and to glorify French, Canadian, and
Austrian efforts." He noted, however, that "this subterranean
feeling does not dare show itself openly and is entirely overlaid
by an intense desire to understand and be the best possible
friends with Great Britain."[4] Captain Pratt, a dedicated Anglophile, occasionally reported to Sims on anti-British sentiment in
the United States and argued the importance of frank Anglo-
American exchanges to prevent a future rupture of friendly
relations.[5]

In Britain various irritations also interfered with the development of full confidence in the United States. Fear that the
United States would appropriate British markets in Latin America was one of the reasons why Sir Maurice de Bunsen led an
extensive mission to that area in 1918.[6] Concern about the effect
of President Wilson's League of Nations on the future of the
Grand Fleet also created some difficulties. Walter Hines Page
summarized this situation well. Noting that the Grand Fleet had
over and over again preserved Britain from its enemies, the
Ambassador stated that one of the reasons why "the British
general mind has not got firmly hold on a league is the instinctive
fear that the formation of any league may in some conceivable
way affect the Grand Fleet." Another reason was "the general
inability of a somewhat slow public opinion to take hold on
more than one subject at a time or more than one urgent part of
one subject."[7] Perhaps the most important source of irritation in
Britain, however, was the feeling that the United States had not
made its maximum effort in the naval war. This feeling grew as

3. Daniels diary, April 14, 1918, E. David Cronon, ed., *The Cabinet
Diaries of Josephus Daniels, 1913–1921* (Lincoln, 1963), 299.
4. Lyell to Drummond, April 25, 1918, Drummond Papers, FO 800,
box 329.
5. See, for example, Pratt to Sims, August 15, 1918, USNSF, TD file.
6. Klachko, "Anglo-American Naval Competition," 26–32.
7. Page to Wilson, March 7, 1918, quoted in Burton J. Hendrick, *The
Life and Letters of Walter Hines Page*, 3 vols. (New York, 1922), 2:356.

the United States fell far, far behind its promised rate of military and merchant ship production. This development especially annoyed Sir Eric Geddes, the principal exponent of British naval interests.

In 1917 the United States had slowly but surely accepted the British argument that it should postpone the building of capital ships in favor of antisubmarine craft. On November 30, Secretary Daniels made his recommendations concerning naval appropriations for the coming year. He informed President Wilson of "the paramount necessity of building a large fleet of destroyers and merchant ships," but he also sought appropriations for capital ships that had been authorized before the war. "I think the money should be provided to carry out the full three-year building program," he argued, "and with the money provided, as soon as possible we can begin their construction." Daniels here made reference to the Naval Act of 1916, which had authorized a three-year building program aimed at developing a navy second to none—that is, one that at least equalled that of Great Britain. Congress lent support to the construction of 10 battleships, 6 battle cruisers, 60 destroyers of various types, 67 submarines, and 14 other vessels of miscellaneous types to achieve its objective. William Braisted accurately notes that the plan of 1916 had "little or no relation" to the war. "It was primarily designed," he asserts, "to prepare for a later contest in which the United States might face a coalition attacking in both oceans."[8] The exigencies of 1917 had played havoc with the rational program of construction that had been started before the United States entered the war. Those in the Navy Department committed to the concept of a navy second to none detected in the improving naval situation an argument for early resumption of the interrupted building schedule.

On April 2, 1918, Admiral Sims received an important message from Captain Pratt. "I would like an estimate from your point of view of the time when we should begin to change our present building policy (which you know is a drive on the destroyer, chaser, submarine, and merchant ship programme) and return to the big ship programme." He asked for detailed specifications

8. Daniels to Wilson, November 30, 1917, Wilson Papers, box 130. Braisted's views are in William Reynolds Braisted, *The United States Navy in the Pacific, 1909–1922* (Austin, 1971), 201. For a careful discussion of the legislation passed in 1916, see ibid., 171–208.

of desirable types and also "the political or other conception on which we should base our standards as to the proper numbers to be incorporated in a building programme."[9] Sims assigned this task to his Planning Section and in early May that group produced Memorandum No. 21, entitled "U.S. Naval Building Policy." It began with an intriguing statement on national policy, summarizing the Monroe Doctrine, the Open Door Policy, and freedom of the seas. Special note was taken of the need, for reasons of geography, "to control the Panama Canal and its approaches, including the Caribbean Sea. For racial and economic reasons it is essential that we adhere to the policy of exclusion of . . . Asiatics from our country." The planners concluded that in the final event, force was the only sure support of diplomacy. In this respect, "our primary weapon, either for offense or defense, must be the Navy; . . . our Navy must be more powerful than any Navy that may oppose it."

There followed a discussion of relations with various other naval powers. Britain was an aggressive naval power, but if that country might not come to the aid of the United States in some circumstances (a reference to the Anglo-Japanese alliance) it was unlikely to precipitate hostilities. If Germany should win the war, that country would certainly pose a challenge in the Western Hemisphere. The Germans would also seek help from Japan in an attempt to dominate the Pacific. Japan was a particularly important concern because the American policy of racial exclusion would try its temper; pressure at home would force overseas expansion; and the Japanese would ultimately fight to expand southward, motivated not only by population pressures but also by the need for various raw materials. To protect the Philippines the United States would require a naval force superior to that of Japan. Even if the Islands were granted independence, the United States would continue to have a moral obligation to them. This survey prompted a general conclusion that the most powerful naval combination that might challenge the United States was that of Germany, Austria, and Japan. "Considering national temperaments, interests and tendencies we cannot assume we have a due degree of security unless we are prepared to fight at sea the German, Austrian and Japanese Navies simultaneously."

9. Pratt to Sims, April 2, 1918, USNSF, TD file.

The Planning Section by no means assumed that the Great War would end all wars. "Past history has demonstrated the instability of human society after great wars. New wars are apt to break out, new groupings of Powers to be made, new boundaries and new spheres of influence defined." The United States must prepare for "the possibility of sudden war, which may involve us in effort as far afield as the present one." The most likely theater of war was the Pacific. "The growing need of Japan for opportunity to expand, the [helpless] situation of China, the vulnerable conditions of the Philippines, and our great interest in Chinese markets, make the Western Pacific an area of intense interest to us; one requiring not only firm and tactful diplomacy, but the readiness of our naval forces to act in those distant waters." All this suggested a basic naval doctrine:

The Navy of the United States shall be a self-contained organisation designed to exercise, in the Pacific, a commanding superiority of naval power, and, in the Atlantic, a defensive superiority of naval power against all potential enemies who may seek to expand their spheres of interest over, or to impose their sovereignty on, any portion of the American Continent or Islands contiguous thereto, not now in their [possession], or who may unjustly interfere with our international rights or our trade expansion.

Here was an ambitious objective indeed, one that automatically required an extraordinary building program.

Given the immediate requirements of the European war, what adjustments should be made in the building program? The Planning Section was unequivocal in its belief that "our basic naval policy should not ultimately be modified, but . . . we should for the present bend all our energies towards winning the present war by completing our Destroyer and Chaser programmes as soon as possible, and by increasing in every possible way the output of our present tonnage." When should the United States revert to its regular naval building program? The Planning Section believed that this change should occur when the war ended, or when shipping was no longer a controlling factor in the conflict.

There followed a discussion of German naval intentions in the western Atlantic in the event that the Central Powers achieved victory. Germany would seek bases in the Azores, Cape Verde Islands, Dakar, Venezuela, and Samana Bay. If Germany acquired these positions, it could proceed as it pleased. The proper response was to secure such places in the Caribbean Sea and to block German acquisitions in the Atlantic region. It would be difficult to prevent German operations in the eastern Atlantic, but appropriate dispositions in the Caribbean would provide security in the western latitudes. Samana Bay should be acquired. The harbor at St. Thomas in the newly acquired Virgin Islands was too small for a large fleet, but would serve well as an advance base for submarines, destroyers, and other light craft. "Without these bases secured for our fleet, an active enemy may seize them before we can mobilize." A comparison of the American fleet with the combined Austro-German fleet, excluding obsolete types, showed that the United States was superior only in destroyers, 318 to 248. The balance against the United States included 11 dreadnoughts, 4 battle cruisers, 33 light cruisers, 8 mine-laying cruisers, and 102 submarines. As to types, the Planning Section recommended superiority of fighting power and radius of action.

What would be required in the event of a Pacific war? Regardless of whether there was a simultaneous war in the Atlantic, the United States would have to control the defensive line Kiska-Honolulu-Panama. If a two-ocean war broke out, the United States would have to assume the defensive in the Pacific until a decision was reached in the Atlantic. "We can never hope to invade Japan, so we must base our plans for success on economic pressure through naval action." Hawaii must be developed as the principal base, with Guam as a forward base. The United States then could carry on a minor offensive in the Pacific, if it were also engaged in the Atlantic. It could launch a major offensive if engaged only against Japan.

Given all these considerations, the Planning Section made its estimate of over-all building needs. These included 21 dreadnoughts, 10 battle cruisers, 24 fighting scouts, 54 superdestroyers, and 54 scout submarines. In establishing building priorities it assumed as conditions an adverse battle cruiser position in the Pacific, adverse battleship position in the Atlantic, war weariness in Europe, extensive Japanese ambition, necessity for construction of all types to maintain them in up-to-date conditions, and the great importance of homogeneous tactical units. The proper building policy, then, should be to construct vessels in intact units; build eight battle cruisers as soon as immediate shipping requirements were met; aim thereafter to achieve superiority in battle cruisers over Japan and in battleships over the combined force of Austria and Germany; lay down six fighting scouts as soon as possible, sustaining the effort until the program was completed; and adjust the super-destroyer and scouting submarine programs to the availability of shipyard facilities.[10] In a special message to the Navy Department Sims summarized the proposal:

> The United States should prepare now for the most vigorous possible resumption of the big-ship building programme and should undertake that programme when merchant tonnage demands of the present war permit. Fundamental policy governing numbers and types of battleships and battle cruisers should be: Numbers equal to Japan, Germany, and Austria combined; type to be superior in speeds, radius and gun power, to beat foreign types.[11]

Clearly Admiral Sims and his staff did not anticipate a great era of peace in the aftermath of World War I!

On September 10, 1918, the General Board recommended a program that superseded all its previous proposals. It called for the construction of 28 capital ships beyond those authorized in 1915, some of which had not been built as yet. The program included 12 battleships and 16 battle cruisers, three less *in toto* than recommended by the Planning Section, ensuring the Navy a total of 61 ships—39 battleships and 22 battle cruisers.[12] Captain Pratt, realizing that this decision would arouse considerable concern in Great Britain, went out of his way to justify the decision to a British naval representative in Washington.[13] Warner Schilling has aptly summarized the significance of this program. The United States Navy did not believe that victory in Europe would guarantee American security. "In fact, the end of the war was to be the occasion for a very large increase in the size of the American Navy." The Navy entertained a given conception of international political realities:

> The war was considered the natural consequence of economic competition among the Great Powers. This competition was rooted in human nature and would continue after the war, leading, in time, to new wars. Naval planners did not even anticipate significant short-

10. Planning Section Memorandum No. 21, "U.S. Naval Building Policy," May, 1918, USNSF, TX file.

11. Sims to Navy Department, May 4, 1918, USNSF, TX file.

12. Schilling, "Admirals and Foreign Policy," 121–22.

13. Draft for Pratt to Benson, October 25, 1918, Benson Papers.

run changes in the policies and relative strength of the Great Powers as a result of the war.[14]

There was one important reaction to the victory of 1918 only ten days after the Armistice. In London the Planning Section produced a memorandum entitled "United States Building Programme," which assessed the implications of the German defeat. Its basic premise was that "additions to the British Fleet must be made with reference to the United States as a possible enemy," and, conversely, "Any additions made to the United States Fleet must be made with reference to Great Britain as a possible enemy." The planners thought such a conflict unlikely, but they listed several sources of tension: trade rivalry, disputes over freedom of the seas, repressive reactions against the expansion of American trade, the present international instability, and other conditions mentioned in Memorandum No. 21. There were additional reasons, quite aside from the possibility of war with Great Britain, "why the U.S. Navy should be as powerful as any other Navy." The United States had new interests and duties to fulfill:

We have taken the lead in certain world policies. We have been able to do this through the known unselfishness of our motives and chiefly through the sudden rise in importance of our naval and military power. We are interested in seeing the growth everywhere of American ideals of international justice and fair dealing. There is no surer way of furthering this growth than in providing diplomacy with the sanction of a naval power that by reason of its greatness will be fearless.

The outcome of the war had vastly enlarged the horizons of naval expansionist thought among those in the London Planning Section. This memorandum reflected the necessity of rationalizing naval expansion in terms of general Wilsonian outlooks, even though the planners probably did not endorse them. In terms of building calculations the planners recognized that the new standard must be calculated relative to Great Britain and Japan. "In interpreting the basic naval policy [as stated in Planning Memorandum No. 21] we should consider for the present the British Navy as the maximum probable force which we must be prepared to meet. We should always have in mind the possibility of the co-operation of the British and Japanese Navies."

14. Schilling, "Admirals and Foreign Policy," 124.

The United States should immediately cease construction of antisubmarine vessels, a response to the complete defeat of Germany.[15]

In all these planning proposals the prospect of an Anglo-American war was never entertained seriously, but the likelihood of peaceful economic competition and political disputation on various questions was always recognized. The planners kept in mind the special exigencies of the war, but they did not fail to consider the future. The Navy obviously had no intention of abandoning its quest for a navy second to none after the victory of 1918. These very broad and general considerations undergirded American naval thought as Sir Eric Geddes began to prepare for his mission to Washington.

II

On July 27, Franklin D. Roosevelt, then visiting in Europe, wrote to Secretary Daniels about a conversation with Admiral Wemyss and Sir Eric Geddes. The British wanted to discuss "dovetailing the British programme for new construction in with our programme, in order that between us we may not build too many of one type of vessel, and in order that we may have an understanding in regard to the need for new types for next year's operations." Geddes thought that there was no need for additional chasers and other types of small craft, preferring to proceed with destroyers and "a new type of escort vessel for the convoys, a ship with less speed and better sea-going qualities than a destroyer."[16] There was more to this conversation than Roosevelt realized at the time. The First Lord of the Admiralty had begun a major effort to force a significant alteration and increase in American ship construction.

On August 1, Geddes informed the Board of Admiralty that he was preparing a memorandum for the War Cabinet on the naval effort of the United States and Great Britain. The memorandum would point out "the prejudicial position in which this country will be placed if they [the British] continue to bear the very

15. Planning Section Memorandum No. 67, "(United States) Building Programme," November 21, 1918, ca. October, 1918, Benson Papers.

16. Roosevelt to Daniels, July 27, 1918, Daniels Papers. A copy is in USNSF, TD file. See also Frank Freidel, *Franklin D. Roosevelt: The Apprenticeship* (Boston, 1952), 350.

heavy burden cast upon them of supplying without compensation the needs of the Allies both as regards warships and mercantile tonnage." He had in mind to negotiate with the United States a joint construction program for 1920 designed to improve the British position.[17]

The memorandum itself began with the observation that warship construction in the United States for the period January–May, 1918, had been "extremely disappointing," but that the production of mercantile tonnage in American shipyards had been "somewhat higher than we thought they could possibly achieve, although of course considerably below the optimistic forecasts made in the States during 1917." Geddes wished, therefore, to submit certain important considerations to the War Cabinet, although he wished "to state at the outset that I am making no complaint against our American Allies as regards their War effort." The United States had built some 838,000 gross tons of merchant shipping in the period January–June, 1918, whereas Great Britain had produced 763,000 tons:

This abnormal development, especially having regard to the relative sizes of the two Mercantile Fleets, raises not only a War, but a post-War problem. The British Mercantile Marine is not being rebuilt at the same speed as would be possible if the Naval effort which the country is called upon to make were not so great or if America took a larger Naval share, and the time seems opportune for considering the question of the total Maritime effort of America and ourselves. For the successful waging of war we are equally dependent on the maintenance of the mastery of the Sea, as is indeed the whole Alliance.

The British merchant marine was being sacrificed because of the great naval shipbuilding effort, the burden of repairing Allied and neutral shipping in British yards, and the use of shipping to transport American troops to France.

What were the possible consequences? If the war continued for another few years, Britain would have built a large battle fleet and repaired many vessels for its associates, but "the Americans will have built up a Mercantile Fleet approaching that of Great Britain, whereas before the War they only owned one-fourth of our tonnage." The situation was not uncomplicated:

It is exceedingly difficult to determine the relative Naval effort which should be put forward by the United States and this Country. Our

17. Minutes of the Board of Admiralty, August 1, 1918, ADM 167, book 53.

position as an Island Empire demands a large Naval force, whilst the
fact that the United States are engaged in a land war across thousands
of miles of water necessitates a Naval protecting force which they do
not at present possess, and which their programme of Naval construction even if realized, will not afford.

The matter required negotiation with the United States.

In addition to naval considerations there were obvious economic aspects. Geddes asked whether Britain should continue
"its policy of accepting responsibility for the whole burden of
Naval warfare, less such contributions as our Allies feel disposed
to make, to the sacrifice of other vital demands on our resources."
Further, he asked whether Britain should "go on losing ships in
our Allies' immediate interest, and repairing ships for them
while they overtake us in our Mercantile Marine." Geddes sought
the guidance of the War Cabinet because he was then preparing
the building program for 1920, which he "must discuss with Mr.
Roosevelt before he goes back to America."[18] This memorandum,
detailed and explicit, was the basis of all subsequent developments leading to the dispatch of the Geddes mission to the
United States.

On August 2, Geddes had occasion to address a group of
visiting American congressmen—members of the Committee on
Naval Affairs—and he took the opportunity to begin educating
his American cousins to the necessity of changes in building
policy. After describing in great detail the imposing naval contribution of the British, he emphasized the need for "quick, fast
craft and the patrol craft, light cruisers and destroyers, and a
good, simple, comparatively slow seagoing escort ship." He included a plea for the suspension of the American battleship program until the immediate needs of the war were met. Although
the First Lord did not state his main point explicitly, he was in
fact arguing that since Britain had made its great effort in the
past it was time for the United States to recognize this sacrifice
by making reciprocal sacrifices of its own.[19]

18. Geddes memorandum for the War Cabinet, "Naval Effort—Great
Britain and the United States of America," August 2, 1918, ADM 116,
book 1771. A copy is in the Geddes Papers, ADM, book 1809.
19. Geddes speech to American Congressmen, August 2, 1918, Geddes
Papers, ADM 116, book 1809. Others were also aware of the American
tendency to emphasize merchant shipbuilding. At a meeting of the Imperial War Cabinet, Premier W. F. Massey of New Zealand said that "a
prominent shipping man had informed him that the United States of

The War Cabinet took up the Geddes memorandum on August 9. The First Lord reported on conversations with Roosevelt, the American congressmen, and the Prime Minister. He was now hopeful that the United States would agree to an expanded naval building program of the kind desired by the British. He received support from a representative of the Ministry of Shipping, Sir Leo Chiozza Money, who thought that if anything Geddes might have underestimated the pace of the American program. "It was not improbable that—by 1920 or 1921—if the present conditions continued the United States would actually have a bigger mercantile marine that we should have." The War Cabinet established a committee including the First Lord, the Minister of Shipping, the Ambassador to the United States, and the Foreign Secretary to consider the matter further.[20] A few days later Lloyd George supported the Geddes position in another meeting of the War Cabinet. The shipping question remained critical because so much tonnage was allocated to the United States for transport of its troops to Europe. "The Americans were under the impression that we were not disclosing all our available tonnage, and it was quite certain that we had the same suspicions of the United States Government, and with more reason." He was in favor of establishing clearly the extent of the British shipping effort and he proposed to discuss the matter with Herbert Hoover, then visiting in Europe, before the American food administrator returned to the United States.[21]

The special committee met at the Foreign Office on August 16 to concert its strategy. The members first decided that "it was not advisable to make any requests to the United States Government for the material replacement of British merchant tonnage lost." It was, however, not unreasonable to ask the United States to adjust its production so that the ratio between naval construction and mercantile construction would be the same in both nations. The plan was not to be executed until Geddes discussed

America were, in certain directions, continuing and developing lines of trade with a view to their post-war position." Minutes of the Imperial War Cabinet (IWC 27C), August 6, 1918, CAB 23, book 44.

20. Minutes of the War Cabinet (WC 456), August 9, 1918, CAB 23, book 7.

21. Minutes of the War Cabinet (WC 458), August 14, 1918, CAB 23, book 7.

the question with Roosevelt.[22] Five days afterward the Ministry of Shipping proposed that the United States actually produce warships at a pace beyond the British ratio, but Balfour vetoed the suggestion. Lord Reading had advised that there was no chance of its acceptance in the United States and that it might prejudice the ratio plan in entirety.[23]

Meanwhile, American activities irritated Sir Eric Geddes more and more. In a memorandum for the War Cabinet he explained his unsuccessful efforts to obtain compensation from the United States for the cost of repairs made on American ships in British yards. Sims had approved, but the Navy Department had refused payment. Implying that this response was an aspect of the United States policy of developing the greatest postwar merchant marine, he thought that the War Cabinet should give the matter further attention.[24] Sims received what amounted to a severe reprimand from Secretary Daniels for his part in the exchange, an indication that feelings were decidedly high in the United States as well as in Britain:

Department feels that in initiating policy [decidedly] contrary to the wishes and intentions of this government you have committed an error in judgment. In future do not initiate general policies of international character without first communicating with the Department, giving your views and obtaining views of this government through the Department, before taking up with foreign official matters, affecting international policy.[25]

This message angered Sims. He believed it completely unjust, but in the future he was careful to specify that he always avoided commitments until he had received clearance from Washington. He eschewed involvement when Roosevelt held his conversations with Sir Eric Geddes regarding the proposed dovetailing of the British and American building programs.[26]

22. Balfour minutes on meeting, August 16, 1918, Balfour Papers, book 49748.
23. Balfour to Maclay, August 21, 1918, Balfour Papers, book 49748.
24. Geddes memorandum for the War Cabinet, "Naval Effort of Great Britain and the United States of America," August 24, 1918, Geddes Papers, ADM 116, book 1809.
25. Daniels to Sims, July 25, 1918, USNSF, TT file.
26. Sims to Benson, August 10, 1918, USNSF, TD file; Sims to Pratt, August 30, 1918, Sims Papers. A copy is in USNSF, TD file.

Evidence of American interest in postwar trade considerations mounted in Britain. On August 20, Sir William Wiseman reported to Lord Reading a serious protest from President Wilson about a bellicose speech Lloyd George had made on July 31 before the National Union of Manufacturers, in which the Prime Minister had adverted to the destruction of German trade after the war. He wanted the Ambassador to urge upon the Prime Minister the need for "common policy" on trade. "Colonel House says he fears that, if the Allies persist in making similar statements regarding their economic policy, the President will feel obliged, as he did once before, to make some statement dissociating this country with that policy."[27] Clearly Lloyd George was most accurate in his belief that suspicions were mutual.

Geddes became increasingly anxious to undertake his negotiation with the United States. On August 26, he pressed Lloyd George for action on his proposals to obtain American construction agreements that would allow reduction of man power commitments in shipyards by 20,000 men, compensation by the United States for refitting its vessels, and compensation for British tonnage lost in the American service. He initially thought that he could undertake the negotiation through Assistant Secretary Roosevelt, but he discovered that Roosevelt lacked sufficient power to act for his government. "I also find that Mr. Roosevelt, like all capable men, while his energy is much admired, is not without his own difficulties, and I am told that any agreement come to with him, or any agreement which he recommended as a result of a conference here, would start prejudiced." Geddes had apparently been informed, perhaps by Roosevelt himself, of his difficulties with the Benson-Daniels faction in the Navy Department. Geddes recommended as an alternative a flying visit to the United States, because no American with sufficient powers was available in Europe for negotiations and because the matter was too complex to be settled by exchanges of messages.[28] The next day Secretary Balfour approved of Ged-

27. Wiseman to Reading, August 20, 1918, Reading Papers, FO 800, book 225. The previous incident took place in early 1918 in reference to a rather bellicose statement of the Supreme War Council. See David F. Trask, *United States in the Supreme War Council: American War Aims and Inter-Allied Strategy, 1917–1918* (Middletown, Conn., 1961), 48–50.

28. Geddes to Lloyd George, August 26, 1918, Lloyd George Papers, file F/18/2/11. A copy is also in the Geddes Papers, ADM 116, book 1809.

des's first two subjects, but he opposed an effort to obtain compensation for lost ships because "it was quite certain that the request would be refused." He gently suggested to Geddes that Anglo-American relations were not in the best repair at the moment and that he would be well-advised to have Lord Reading test the situation in the United States in order to be able to render helpful advice.[29]

On August 28, Lord Reading asked Wiseman to send information on recent American refusals of British requests for assistance. "I should like to know whether there are any grounds for believing that this is part of a deliberate policy due either (a) to some action of ours which has antagonized U.S.G. or (b) to some change of policy for other reasons."[30] Wiseman replied early in September, reporting that the situation was not a deliberate policy but a product of wartime tensions. He thought that "the real danger point . . . is in trade relations." He believed that Lloyd George should "explain our policy and programme without reserve and in our dealings avoid any suggestion of bargaining for our own trade advantage after the war." He hoped that Great Britain would adopt a "sympathetic and helpful" attitude towards the United States. "We should always have in view the real tie which binds us together—that of our common traditional ideals and our sense of what is fair."[31]

Admiral Sims was especially concerned about the problem of economic rivalry, fearful that it would interfere with Anglo-American cooperation in the postwar years. He reminded Captain Pratt that he had "recommended measures which would show our good faith in this respect before the war is ended. I was reprimanded in a very severe cable for making a suggestion which would have shown that we were willing to cooperate in this way." Unrepentant, he was convinced that the United States

See also Roosevelt to Geddes, August 28, 1918, Geddes Papers, ADM 116, book 1809.

29. Balfour to Geddes, August 27, 1918, Geddes Papers, ADM 116, book 1809.

30. Reading to Wiseman, August 28, 1918, Reading Papers, FO 800, book 225.

31. Wiseman to Reading, September 5, 1918, Reading Papers, FO 800, book 225. For a message reporting the President's great irritation at a report that Prime Minister Hughes of Australia would visit the United States and make a bellicose speech on trade retaliation, see Wiseman to Reading, August 30, 1918, Reading Papers, FO 800, book 225. Wiseman wanted some action taken to head off Hughes.

could demonstrate its good intentions effectively by announcing to Allied and neutral powers that it would return vessels commandeered during the war. These remarks preceded mention of the projected Geddes mission. Sims believed that a satisfactory arrangement of the Anglo-American building program on the basis of reciprocity would be "the best possible opportunity for the United States to show that they are willing to cooperate in a way which will promote good relations." He was, however, quick to deny any complicity in the Geddes project. "I did not even suggest the policy which will be put up to our Government, I had absolutely nothing whatever to do with it."[32]

On August 30, Geddes sought the permission of the War Cabinet to visit the United States, having "ascertained that Mr. Roosevelt had no powers as regards the allocation of naval ships." The War Cabinet, however, proposed an alternative procedure. Perhaps E. N. Hurley, head of the American Shipping Board, might come to Europe—a more desirable negotiating situation from the British point of view. To strengthen his case for the American negotiations Geddes mentioned that he had in motion a scheme to transfer some 20,000 men from warship construction to merchant shipbuilding in connection with the American arrangement.[33] On the same day Secretary Daniels dispatched a cablegram welcoming a Geddes visit to the United States.[34] The Hurley visit did not materialize.

The transfer of man power to merchant-ship construction was an important aspect of the Geddes project. After clearing the general idea with Lloyd George he proceeded through the mechanisms of the Admiralty to obtain the necessary decision. On August 27, he convened a meeting of the Operations Committee with Admiral Sims present. Geddes was careful to specify that "it was not intended that any views that he [Sims] expressed should be recorded as binding him or his Navy Department." The committee considered possible reductions in the British building program, arriving at a series of agreements concerning

32. Sims to Pratt, August 30, 1918, USNSF, TD file. A copy is in the Sims Papers.

33. Minutes of the War Cabinet (WC 466), August 30, 1918, CAB 23, book 7.

34. Daniels to Geddes, August 30, 1918, Geddes Papers, ADM 116, book 1809.

several classes of vessels. Sims was helpful in respect to destroyers, stating that "no possible doubt existed as to the ability of the United States to allocate this number by the date indicated."[35] Two days later the Board of Admiralty accepted the recommendations for building reduction, subject to the proviso that the 22,000 men released from the naval program would not be subject to military service and could be recalled to naval construction in case of an emergency.[36] On August 31, Geddes prepared an Admiralty memorandum for submission to the War Cabinet explaining the proposed reductions. The program depended on American cooperation, but the Board of Admiralty believed that the United States could meet the British suggestions. In its final form the Admiralty suggested that Britain cut back its naval building program as follows: light cruisers: 6 projected, 5 postponed; flotilla leaders: 7 projected, 3 postponed; destroyers: 90 projected, 42 postponed; mine sweepers: 72 projected, 36 postponed; trawlers: 168 projected, 72 postponed; submarines: 48 projected, 24 postponed. The United States would be asked to supply 128 destroyers, 45 mine sweepers, and trawlers at the rate of 9 every two months until the end of 1919.[37] All this activity of course met with the strong approbation of those responsible for merchant shipbuilding.[38] While these arrangements were made Geddes once again communicated the British viewpoint to Roosevelt. In a detailed letter, Geddes placed special stress on the importance of the United States concentrating on lighter craft. "I appreciate that I am treading upon somewhat delicate ground in referring to this matter," he told the Assistant Secretary, but "I venture to suggest to the United States Navy Department that as long as there is a deficiency in essential craft, it is a matter for the most serious consideration whether they are justified in continuing to build capital ships, which I

35. Minutes of the Admiralty Operations Committee, August 27, 1918, ADM 116, book 1798.

36. Minutes of the Board of Admiralty, August 29, 1918, ADM 167, box 53.

37. Admiralty memorandum for the War Cabinet, "Battle Cruiser Position and Ship-Building Program," August 31, 1918, Geddes Papers, ADM 116, book 1809. A copy is in ADM 116, book 1771.

38. Memorandum by Lord Pirrie, Controller-General of Merchant Shipbuilding, "Merchant Shipbuilding Position," September 3, 1918, ADM 116, book 1771.

understand they are still doing in accordance with the instructions of the Congress."[39]

Geddes now proceeded to obtain final permission from the War Cabinet to undertake his mission to the United States. Lloyd George once again noted that Britain "had to bear in mind, from a *post*-war point of view, the extensions that were being made to the American mercantile marine, and the effect on our welfare of the loss of nearly half a million tons of shipping on our part." Geddes then received authority to undertake negotiations in Washington with the understanding that he cooperate with Lord Reading. He specified that he desired no reduction in British naval construction until the agreement was reached with the United States.[40] The War Cabinet agreed to this proviso two days later, after the Board of Admiralty exerted pressure.[41] On September 9, Geddes informed Secretary Daniels of his coming, indicating that he hoped "to discuss with you and your Naval Advisors the general Naval situation, the co-ordination of Naval effort from our two countries, and the Naval building programme of the two countries."[42] Daniels replied in suitable terms: "We anticipate with pleasure a discussion of general naval situation. This exchange of views will aid promotion of existing desire for co-ordination on the part of both our countries joined in a common cause."[43]

A delay ensued, occasioned in part by Lord Reading's business in Britain, but Geddes took advantage of these weeks to systematize his objectives in the United States. In a memorandum for the Operations Committee of the Admiralty he specified five distinct endeavors. First, he would discuss the general naval

39. Geddes to Roosevelt, August 31, 1918, Wilson Papers, box 137. A copy is in the Geddes Papers, ADM 116, book 1809. Some copies are dated September 2, 1918, including those in USNSF, TD file, and the Sims Papers.

40. Minutes of the War Cabinet (WC 469a), September 6, 1918, CAB 23, book 14 (secret minutes).

41. Minutes of the War Cabinet (WC 470a), September 6, 1918, CAB 23, book 14 (secret minutes). See also Geddes to Lloyd George, memoranda of the Board of Admiralty, September 5, 1918, ADM 167, book 55; Minutes of the Board of Admiralty, September 5, 1918, Geddes Papers, ADM 116, book 1809; Minutes of the Board of Admiralty, September 12, 1918, ADM 167, book 53.

42. Geddes to Daniels, September 9, 1918, Geddes Papers, ADM 116, book 1809.

43. Daniels to Geddes, September 13, 1918, Geddes Papers, ADM 116, book 1809.

situation in order to communicate "the magnitude of our effort compared wtih the effort which the Americans have so far been able to put into the Naval war." Second, he would seek a desirable allocation of American vessels about to proceed to European waters. Third, he would urge the program of American naval construction developed by the Admiralty. Fourth, he would discuss compensation for repair of ships in British yards, suggesting in this regard the transfer of five American oilers to the British. Finally, he would discuss the submarine situation and the measures required to continue an effective campaign against the German U-boats.[44] At the same time he received reports from various sources providing exact details on the requests to be made of the United States and a careful comparison of the American and British naval efforts.[45]

In August, 1918, Geddes had been relatively optimistic about the future of the submarine war, but by late September he had altered his views. On August 5, he informed General Sir Edmund Allenby that the submarine menace was well in hand. "We may have a recrudescence of activity and an increased effort, sinkings may go up for a time, but I think, without being unduly optimistic, one may see that the submarines as a feature cannot make us lose the war."[46] On August 27, however, the Operations Committee noted that the decline in sinkings had stopped and also that attacks were taking place farther out at sea, a circumstance that prompted a decision to seek additional assistance for mid-ocean escort from the United States.[47] On September 17, Geddes informed the Cabinet that the tonnage situation was likely to get worse, "owing to the fact that we were not sinking so many submarines as formerly, mainly in consequence of the requirements for convoy of American troops, and that the enemy were making

44. Geddes memorandum for the Operations Committee, Minutes of the Operations Committee, September 19, 1918, ADM 116, book 1799. The memorandum was approved on September 25, 1918, Minutes of the Operations Committee, ADM 116, book 1799. A copy of the memorandum is in the Geddes Papers, ADM 116, book 1809.

45. Memorandum by Admiralty Director of Plans on American assistance, September 22, 1918, Geddes Papers, ADM 116, book 1809; Memorandum by J. G. Beharrell, Admiralty Director of Statistics, on comparison of naval efforts, September 22, Geddes Papers, ADM 116, book 1809.

46. Geddes to Allenby, August 5, 1918, Geddes Papers, ADM 116, book 1808.

47. Meeting of the Operations Committee, August 27, 1918, ADM 116, book 1789.

a greater effort in output and in increased activity."[48] By September 25, he was writing that the enemy now had 160 submarines and would have 180 by the end of the year. The War Cabinet "should realize that a great enemy submarine offensive is not only threatened but is materializing."[49] Two days later he told Admiral Beatty of his growing concern about the decline in the efficacy of antisubmarine weapons. "Although we know, to a great extent, the reason, there is no doubt that the submarine fleet is growing on us."[50] The "reason," of course, was the use of antisubmarine vessels as escorts for American troopships rather than as hunters.

There was some substance to Geddes's alarms. About 255,000 tons of shipping had been lost in June. In July the figure increased to 261,000 tons and in August to 284,000 tons. These were the statistics that concerned Geddes. Actually the figures declined precipitously in September (188,000 tons) and October (119,-000 tons). The upsurge of the summer stemmed not only from dispositions of antisubmarine craft, but also from a final great effort in Germany. German naval officials remained committed to the last to unrestricted submarine war. During the late summer and early fall of 1918 Germany abandoned all construction of surface vessels in order to concentrate its production entirely on U-boats. General Ludendorff finally agreed to supply man power for the naval yards. The Germans hoped to increase submarine output from sixteen per month during the last quarter of 1918 to thirty per month during the third quarter of 1919 and after.[51] Of course this effort never materialized, but it might have altered the course of the submarine war to some extent if the great conflict had extended into 1919. Admiral Sims took note of increased submarine activity at the beginning of October and of the declining "kill ratio," but he doubted that the German effort could be sustained for any length of time.[52]

48. Minutes of the War Cabinet (WC 473), September 17, 1918, CAB 23, book 7.

49. Geddes memorandum for the War Cabinet, "Some Important Aspects of the Naval Situation and Submarine Campaign," September 25, 1918, Cabinet Memorandum no. 791, FO 899, book 4.

50. Geddes to Beatty, September 27, 1918, Geddes Papers, ADM 116, book 1809.

51. For information on this effort, see Reinhard Scheer, *Germany's High Sea Fleet in the World War* (London, 1920), 337, 344; Andreas Michelsen, *Der U-Bootskrieg, 1914–1918* (Leipzig, 1925), 132.

52. Sims to Benson, October 2, 1918, USNSF, TD file.

Nevertheless, the worsened submarine situation lent additional cogency to the arguments Geddes proposed to offer in the
United States. On September 27, just before his departure, Geddes told the War Cabinet of the new submarine danger. "He
wished therefore to bring before the Cabinet the fact that we
are going to have an anxious time and might have to face enormous monetary losses in ships and cargoes. The latest German
submarines were of an improved type and our sinkings of the
enemy were not keeping pace with his new construction." Adverting once again to the fact that the diversion of escort to
American troopships had disorganized the antisubmarine effort,
he criticized the American building effort in blunt language.
"United States promises were apparently as untrustworthy in
Naval as they had been in Military matters." The Americans had
produced only seven new destroyers in the first seven months of
1918 and no more were to become available until January, 1919.
"Moreover it was always possible that the Americans would retain their output for the protection of their own waters." He
might therefore have to argue for the re-establishment of domestic naval construction as a first priority.[53]

Geddes justified his departure in advance of Lord Reading on
the ground that the submarine war was likely to intensify once
again. "There is no doubt that the Submarine effort in March,
April and May of last year was far weaker than the Submarine
effort which we have got to meet in the first quarter of next year
and possibly later." He recognized that the recent statistics on
sinkings were at their lowest level since March, 1917, but these
figures might be misleading. "We must recognize that protecting ships from attack, however successful it may be, is unsatisfactory with an increasing submarine fleet unless we also kill
submarines, and undoubtedly at the present time we are devoting ourselves far too much to defensive and safeguarding convoy
work, and far too little to offensive work."[54]

In all these discussions no one raised the possibility that the
war might come to an early end. While Geddes was in transit
the Central Powers sent their initial peace notes to Washington
—first Austria-Hungary and then Germany. President Wilson

53. Minutes of the War Cabinet (WC 479a), September 27, 1918,
CAB 23, book 14 (secret minutes).
54. Geddes to Lloyd George, September 27, 1918, Lloyd George Papers, file F/18/2/22.

quickly inaugurated a correspondence with both Vienna and Berlin concerning a basis for an armistice and an eventual peace settlement. The rapidity of these developments caught everyone by surprise, including the British Admiralty and its First Lord. Wilson's negotiations with the Central Powers proved to be extraordinarily clever, but throughout these exchanges, which continued through the first three weeks of October, he failed to consult the Entente powers. This policy was a logical culmination of the consistent Wilsonian tendency to preserve full freedom of action in advance of the postwar peace negotiations. The President obviously planned to further his own war aims and peace proposals, and this intention naturally aroused serious misgivings in Europe, particularly in France and Italy, but also to a considerable degree in Great Britain.[55] Among those most disturbed was the aggressive First Lord of the Admiralty, and by chance he was the most important British official in the United States when the President conducted his skillful correspondence with the Central Powers. This unexpected development had measurable consequences for the Geddes mission. Obviously Geddes had developed his plans for the mission in terms of a critical postwar consideration—the relation between the British and American merchant marines. But he was also directly interested in the conduct of the naval war itself and concerned about the inadequacy of American assistance. He had acted on the assumption that the war would not come to an end until 1919 and probably not until later. When this assumption proved invalid it naturally created unexpected circumstances which, from the British point of view, were also unpalatable.

III

Despite its outward appearance of cordiality the United States Government entertained vague suspicions of Geddes's motives —a logical consequence of heightening Anglo-American tensions as the war approached its climax. Franklin D. Roosevelt did his best to prepare the way for the British visitor, informing Secretary Daniels that he had discussed the dovetailing of naval construction with Geddes when he was in Europe "in a purely tentative way." He argued that "common sense requires that we

55. These developments are traced in Trask, *United States in the Supreme War Council,* 147–58.

should, as far as possible, seek to avoid duplication of effort in the United States and Great Britain, and in so doing should be perfectly frank in our discussions and meet Great Britain half-way."[56] The President was not so reasonably inclined. In preparation for the Geddes visit Daniels had sent various documents to the White House, including a copy of the speech Geddes had made to the visiting American congressmen on August 2. Wilson's comment on this information was frigid indeed. "As I said to you the other day, I don't like it even a little bit."[57] Generally, however, Washington seems to have been remarkably unexcited at the advent of the First Lord. Of course the presidential correspondence with Austria-Hungary and Germany tended to obscure the coming of Geddes.

During the voyage to the United States Geddes and his associates completed preparations for the forthcoming negotiations. They wrote various memoranda summarizing the arguments they intended to present in Washington and the evidence supporting their contentions. These materials merely summarized and organized the points of view that had emerged during the prehistory of the mission in Britain during August and September.[58] Meeting on October 5, just before the landfall of the *Alsatian*, the mission considered its tactics for the last time. The greatest difficulty was that the United States might not wish to come to a "conclusive arrangement." The Navy Department "would be likely to argue that the matters were proper subjects for consideration in the first instance by the Inter-Allied Council, and it was felt that if the U.S. Navy Department took up this attitude it would be difficult to beat." To minimize this difficulty the mission decided to eliminate the Mediterranean zone from its discussion, assuming that if it concentrated on the Anglo-American zone the United States would find it more difficult to utilize delaying tactics.[59] All was now in readiness for the confrontation in Washington.

56. Roosevelt to Daniels, October 1, 1918, Daniels Papers.
57. Wilson to Daniels, October 2, 1918, Daniels Papers. See also Schilling, "Admirals and Foreign Policy," 136–37.
58. "Notes for Guidance as to the Line to Be Adopted in Conferences with United States Navy Department and in Informal Conversations," n.d. (but about October 1, 1918), Geddes Papers, ADM 116, book 1809.
59. Notes of meeting of the Geddes mission on board the *Alsatian*, October 5, 1918, Geddes Papers, ADM 116, book 1809.

The signs and portents for success were hardly as favorable as Geddes might have liked; the Americans continued to manifest suspicion of Britain's postwar intentions. During a meeting of the War Cabinet on October 9, Lord Reading drew attention to the refusal of the United States to pay for the transport of American troops on British vessels and to a disturbance over the price paid for wool purchased in Australia. Balfour thought it best to give way on these issues, but he could take this line only "on the understanding that they [the difficulties] could not be dealt with on any logical basis."[60] Mutual suspicions, although kept firmly below the surface during the negotiations in Washington, greatly conditioned the atmosphere of the talks.

The consultations in the American capital city began on October 8 and continued for several days. Geddes dominated the first meeting, explaining British views in detail. He anticipated no difficulties with the German surface fleet until perhaps 1920, when the enemy's preponderance in battle cruisers might constitute a serious problem. If necessary the British would build two more battle cruisers in addition to one already on the ways. He explained the manifold frustrations encountered in attempting to coordinate the inter-Allied effort in the Mediterranean, including the controversy about the appointment of an admiralissimo. (Daniels interjected to state that the State Department was exerting pressure to expedite this arrangement.) Geddes also believed that difficulties in the eastern Mediterranean were under control. The great problem was in the Atlantic, where submarine kills had declined as a result of the shift of antisubmarine forces from hunting to escort duties. Then Geddes made the case for increased American production of antisubmarine craft.[61] Separate technical discussions during the period October 8–10 dealt with this problem in detail.[62] On October 10, Geddes introduced the delicate question of compensation for ship repairs.[63]

On October 11, the United States responded to the British

60. Minutes of the War Cabinet (WC 483), October 9, 1918, CAB 23, book 8.
61. Memorandum of conference, October 8, 1918, Geddes Papers, ADM 116, book 1809.
62. Memorandum of meetings of the technical staffs at the Navy Department, October 8–10, 1918, Geddes Papers, ADM 116, book 1809.
63. Geddes to Daniels, October 10, 1918, Geddes Papers, ADM 116, book 1809.

requests. The United States hoped to place 128 destroyers in European waters by August 31, 1919. It could be certain of sending 94. As a temporary expedient it would dispatch 34 of its new "Eagle" boats. An additional 200 of this type would ultimately be supplied. Any deficiency in the destroyer reinforcement would be made up as quickly as possible after August 31, 1919. The United States could not provide large mine layers as it had planned and therefore would convert 8 destroyers for this purpose as soon as the destroyer program was completed. It could not develop a new type of patrol boat and would therefore substitute 54 Eagle boats as soon as possible in 1919. Finally, the first of 45 mine sweepers of American trawler design would arrive in Europe in July, 1919.[64]

Geddes was by no means satisfied with this outcome. He reported to Lloyd George that his visit had been "only partially successful owing to the really serious failure of their Destroyer building programme upon which they have been very unduly optimistic." Admiral Sir Alexander Duff, however, thought that the Americans had agreed to everything "their limited production capacity at present permits." Geddes was pleased with the tone of the discussions. "The negotiations and intercourse have been of a most satisfactory and cordial nature."[65] In his official report of the outcome—not presented to the War Cabinet until November 8—he repeated this view and summarized the naval situation somewhat somberly. He anticipated a renewal of submarine warfare much more extensive than any previous effort. The United States would continue to be a naval liability through 1919: "That is to say, her demands for transport protection will exceed the contribution she makes in light craft for escort purposes." Finally, the British submarine effort since April last had been "sacrificed in favour of the war on land, the British provision of light craft having been diverted from offensive to defensive purposes." He envisioned three alternatives for 1919. Britain could continue, in part or in whole, its destroyer program to the detriment of merchant shipbuilding; it could reduce the

64. Memorandum of meeting at the Navy Department, October 11, 1918, signed by Admirals Benson for the United States and Duff for Great Britain, October 11, 1918, USNSF, TT file. A copy is also in the Geddes Papers, ADM 116, book 1809.

65. Geddes to Lloyd George, October 13, 1918, Geddes Papers, ADM 116, book 1809.

volume of escort it provided American troopships in order to reinforce its antisubmarine offensive; or it could assume the conclusion of the war in 1919, accepting "a growing and formidable submarine menace which may, and probably will, have serious results in the latter half of that year."[66] The report reflected no awareness of the impending Armistice, probably because it was actually prepared as Geddes returned to Europe for the pre-Armistice discussions. It was hardly an optimistic document. Geddes revealed in this report something of the feelings of frustration that he had experienced when his Italian project had come to naught.

When in the United States, Geddes had occasion to speak publicly—notably in an interview with *The New York Times* on October 10 and in an address to the Pilgrim's Club. The interview bristled with distrust of the Germans; by implication it was critical of the President's bilateral exchanges with the Central Powers. "Let the Kaiser talk while Foch shoots." Wilson apparently was much annoyed by it.[67] Before speaking to the Pilgrim's Club Geddes consulted Lloyd George on the content of his remarks.[68] The Prime Minister replied in cautionary language, reflecting the antagonism Wilson had engendered among the Entente powers by undertaking negotiations with the Central Powers without consulting the European associates:

You should be careful to express no approval or disapproval of Wilson's attitude toward Prince Max's Note about which we were not even consulted. As you are aware we cannot accept his views about the Freedom of the Seas and our own military advisers including Foch consider that the conditions he seems to contemplate for an Armistice are inadequate. You can of course say that the British Empire is resolute that there shall be no sham or humbugging peace. We do not mean to let them off by an armistice the terms of which will be more helpful to them than to us or to sign any peace which will give militarism a fresh lease on life.[69]

66. Admiralty memorandum for the War Cabinet, "Warship Building Programme," November 8, 1918, ADM 116, book 1771.
67. See for this incident, Klachko, "Anglo-American Naval Competition," 42–43.
68. Geddes to Lloyd George, October 11, 1918, FO 371, book 3493 (file 169051).
69. Lloyd George to Geddes, October 12, 1918, FO 371, book 3493 (file 169051). A copy is in the Geddes Papers, ADM 116, book 1809.

The British war leader obviously was deeply suspicious of the German peace feelers and doubtful of the President's capacity to deal with them effectively.

On October 13, Geddes had a detailed interview with President Wilson that turned on a discussion of possible peace terms. Reporting later to Lloyd George, Geddes stressed Wilson's belief that the western coalition must sustain an unremitting effort while the German peace notes were being considered. Recognizing the necessity of consultation with the Allies, Wilson was dispatching Colonel House to Europe. The President revealed his attitudes toward the military and naval terms of an armistice with the Central Powers, stating that they "must be viewed in spirit that undue humiliation would be inexcusable except insofar as such terms are necessary to prevent enemy taking advantage of armistice to reform their forces and better their position." Wilson was "cordial" in his disposition, recognizing the necessity of consultations with the Allies, but he was "outstandingly fearful that the Naval and Military Authorities may urge an armistice so humiliating that the German people could not accept it."

The critical question of freedom of the seas also came up during the talk. Geddes thought the President's views "obviously unformed," but he seemed to plan "acceptance of principle that no one Power in League of Nations should exercise its naval strength to crush a belligerent Power without consent of League leaving until occasion arises any decision as to nationality of Naval police force." Geddes attempted to explain to Wilson that "of all belligerent nations our views would naturally be strongest on this point on account of our geographical position and overwhelming Naval superiority."[70] Discussing the question later with House, Geddes said that the President wanted all outlaw nations, "as Germany was today, . . . to feel the weight of the united naval power of the world. He was distinctly opposed to any one nation exercising this power." House understandably tried to soothe the feelings of his visitor, telling Geddes that he "thought if they were fair-minded we could get together on some plan which would be of benefit to all."[71] Wilson also

70. Geddes to Lloyd George, October 13, 1918, Wiseman Papers. Copies are in the Geddes Papers, ADM 116, book 1809, and the Lloyd George Papers, file F/18/2/23.
71. House diary, October 13, 1918, House Papers.

thought that an international conference might be needed to curb the submarine. He also sensed a possible need to enlarge territorial waters because of modern naval artillery and to undertake a redefinition of blockade.[72]

The President revealed to a certain extent his jealous desire to keep a close rein on the terms of the final peace settlement. He told Geddes of his opposition to the publication of a British proposal concerning the postwar security organization—the Phillimore report—giving as his reason the necessity of avoiding "controversy" and "feeling" at a critical moment. It might divert statesmen and peoples in the Allied countries from vigorous prosecution of the war. It would "give opportunity for every crank to urge views to the distraction of Statesmen's minds from vital war issues, and his desire is to postpone the discussion . . . until Peace Conference."[73]

House expressed to Balfour the opinion that "No mission has produced a more favourable impression both among the members of the Administration and the People generally," but many important people in Washington seemed unwilling to alter their views of future naval policy.[74] The General Board of the Navy at that very moment was calling for a building program that would give the United States "the biggest Navy in the world by 1925."[75] Wilson demurred somewhat to this advice, believing it "not wise while discussing reduction of armament in case of peace to increase our program." But he was willing to endorse another three-year program like that of 1916.[76] When Daniels discussed what he called "GB's selfish policy" with the President, Wilson told him: "I want to go into the Peace conference armed with as many weapons as my pockets will hold so as to compel justice." He recognized some progress in respect to Britain. "England has agreed to trade conditions as I proposed. We must pool raw material & not permit it to be used for speculative purposes."[77]

Upon his return to Great Britain Geddes received effusive

72. Geddes to Lloyd George, October 16, 1918, Geddes Papers, ADM 116, book 1809.

73. Geddes to Lloyd George, October 15, 1918, Geddes Papers, ADM 116, book 1809.

74. House to Balfour, October 13, 1918, Geddes Papers, ADM 116, book 1809.

75. Daniels diary, October 14, 1918, Cronon, ed., *Cabinet Diaries*, 341.

76. Daniels diary, October 15, 1918, ibid.

77. Daniels diary, October 17, 1918, ibid., 342.

congratulations, but the maritime situation still seemed dangerous.[78] Sir Robert Cecil and the Minister of Shipping agreed
that the shipping situation had become even more threatening.
A public declaration calling for the "strictest economy" was
deemed necessary because "transport of American troops more
than off-set the advantage from increased shipbuilding."[79] Admiral Sims summarized the outcome of the Geddes mission as
well as anyone:

It will probably not make much difference whether the British Mission was a complete success or not. I have never been told what they
accomplished or what we agreed to so I can express no opinion. It is
of course good that our people and the British got together and discussed conditions which are undoubtedly going to help after the war
is over. When peace is signed there will be many very serious problems to solve and I would be glad if our people showed a little more
willingness to cooperate than they apparently do.[80]

Just a week before the conclusion of World War I the American
Naval Commander in Europe was still annoyed at the tendency
of the Navy Department to ignore his counsel and irritated by
the more general tendency of the United States to avoid that
close association with Great Britain which he thought vitally
important not only during the war but afterward as well.

     ✿   ✿   ✿   ✿

In her valuable work on "Anglo-American Naval Competition,
1918–1922," Mary Klachko deduces from a fugitive statement
by Geddes that he wanted in Washington to discuss a matter of
"pressing and supreme importance"—the conclusion that he
was sent principally to warn Wilson against any premature set-
tlements with the Central Powers.[81] Actually Geddes's statement
referred to his belief that Germany would launch an unparal-
leled submarine effort in 1919; his principal concern was to obtain American consent to an expanded naval building program
and to coordination of ship construction with that of Great

78. Wemyss to Geddes, October 22, 1918, Geddes Papers, ADM 116,
book 1609; Barclay to Balfour, October 18, 1918, FO 371, book 3493 (file
169051).
79. Minutes of the War Cabinet (WC 487), October 16, 1918, CAB
23, book 8.
80. Sims to Pratt, November 4, 1918, USNSF, TD file.
81. Klachko, "Anglo-American Naval Competition," 41–45, 51–52.

Britain. Like practically every important Allied statesman he was taken completely by surprise when the prospect of a sudden peace materialized in late October. Lloyd George explicitly instructed the First Lord to avoid extensive comments on the peace settlement. Yet Dr. Klachko's deduction that Geddes was not uninterested in postwar concerns is clearly borne out by the full record. One of Geddes's principal reasons for coming to the United States was to make arrangements that would allow the British to meet the postwar challenge of the American merchant marine. While in the United States he did discuss the peace settlement to some extent with President Wilson and others. The negotiations revealed that the surface appearance of complete Anglo-American cooperation concealed a number of important points of difference, particularly in relation to freedom of the seas and international trade. The Geddes mission anticipated a new form of dispute that would arise very shortly thereafter as the Allied and Associated Powers gathered for meetings of the Supreme War Council to consider the political, military, and naval terms of armistices for the several Central Powers. The anxious deliberations in Paris culminated the long effort of the western coalition during 1917–1918 to concert its naval-political activities as one important way of obtaining a decisive victory over the central coalition and guaranteeing a just and lasting peace.

CHAPTER 9

THE NAVAL ARMISTICE
November, 1918

The sudden onset of armistice negotiations in October, 1918, took the western coalition by surprise. Marshal Foch's victories on the Western Front and achievements in other theaters—particularly in Macedonia—convinced the German High Command that defeat had become unavoidable, but this prospect was difficult to grasp elsewhere. In September Lord Reading reported accurately the general feeling in Allied military circles: "With great effort the War might be ended in 1919 . . . and all energies should be concentrated in this direction. A definite policy to this effect had not been recorded or even agreed between all the ALLIES, but tendencies are in this direction."[1] The German naval leaders continued to argue that a massive reinforcement of the submarine campaign would yet yield victory, but the army and the civilian leadership thought differently.[2] Early in October German U-boats began to evacuate their bases in Flanders, and the pace of the submarine war slackened rapidly. After Germany finally accepted Wilson's conditions for an armistice, all submarines were recalled to German ports.[3] These entirely unanticipated events forced the naval leadership of the western coalition to consider not only the terms of armistice but also the ultimate naval settlement to be arranged during the postwar peace congress.

1. Reading to Wiseman, September 12, 1918, Reading Papers, FO 800, book 225.
2. *The Kaiser and His Court: The Diaries, Note Books, and Letters of Admiral Georg Alexander von Mueller, Chief of the Naval Cabinet, 1914–1918*, Walter Goerlitz, ed. (London, 1961), 366; Protocol of German Cabinet meeting, October 17, 1918, *Ursachen und Folgen vom Deutschen Zusammenbruch 1918 und 1945 bis zur staatlichen Neuordnung Deutschlands in der Gegenwart*, Herbert Michaelis, et al., eds., 8 vols. (Berlin, n.d.), 2:416–17; Report of Konteradmiral von Levetzow about the events of October 20–22, 1918, ibid., 423.
3. Robert M. Grant, *U-Boats Destroyed: The Effect of Anti-Submarine Warfare, 1914–1918* (London, 1964), 137; Goerlitz, ed., *The Kaiser and His Court*, 408, 410; *Ursachen und Folgen*, 2:432; Walther Hubatsch, *Der Admiralstab und die Obersten Marinebehoerden in Deutschland, 1848–1945* (Frankfurt, 1958), 179; R. H. Gibson and Maurice Prendergast, *The German Submarine War, 1914–1918* (London, 1931), 324.

Two naval questions loomed above all others. What disposition would be made of the enemy's sea power? What response
would be made to President Wilson's call for freedom of the
seas? These questions would be decided primarily by Great
Britain and the United States—the principal naval powers in
the western coalition. From the viewpoint of London, the war
had certainly stimulated a desirable change in American attitudes toward Great Britain, but Sir William Wiseman anticipated some difficulties:

Against this improvement in attitudes we must put the growing
consciousness that after the war there will be only two great powers
left—Great Britain and the United States. Which is going to be the
greater, politically and commercially? In that constantly recurring
thought may be found much of the Anglo-American friction that
arises.[4]

The war aims and peace plans of the United States and Great
Britain were much more congruent than those of any other
combination of the victorious powers, but there was by no means
a close identity of interest. The sudden onset of the pre-Armistice
negotiations, before careful preliminary preparations could be
made, ensured a measurable degree of conflict when the leaders
of the western coalition gathered at Paris in late October to discuss the military and naval terms of the armistice and their
political basis.

I

When news of President Wilson's exchanges with the Central
Powers came to Europe, the Entente nations hurriedly arranged
a special consultation in Paris for October 7. At that meeting,
which was not considered an official session of the Supreme
War Council because the United States did not participate,
delegates from Britain, France, and Italy drew up a list of eight
basic principles to govern the negotiation of armistices. The
military terms rested on the concept of evacuating all conquered

4. Memorandum by Wiseman, "The Attitude of the United States and
President Wilson towards the Peace Conference," n.d., Balfour Papers, FO
800, book 212. See also a quotation from Wiseman to Arthur Murray, October 4, 1918, cited in Wilton Fowler, "Sir William Wiseman and the
Anglo-American War Partnership, 1917–1918," Ph. D. diss., Yale University, 1966, p. 240.

territory. The naval terms stressed the immediate cessation of the submarine war. A special joint meeting of the permanent military representatives and the members of the Allied Naval Council to be held on the following day was to discuss the eight principles.[5] Before the joint session the Allied Naval Council met separately to concert its views. The British representative— Adm. G. P. W. Hope—outlined the basic Admiralty position. Submarine warfare must cease immediately; all enemy craft must remain in or return to harbor; there must be no restraints on Allied naval operations. These ideas governed a long list of specific provisions. Enemy surface fleets would assemble at ports designated by the Allies and remain there. Sixty German submarines would proceed immediately to an Allied port. The Central Powers would reveal the location of their mine fields and allow the Allies to sweep them. Various coast lines of the English Channel, the Adriatic, and the Black Sea would be evacuated, leaving facilities and equipment intact. Naval blockade would continue in force, and enemy merchant ships found at sea would be liable to capture. The permanent military representatives added another clause with a naval aspect—the surrender of certain enemy forts, including Heligoland, because of the consideration that Germany's "word cannot be believed, and that it denies any obligation of honour." Nothing was said about the final disposition of the German and Austrian surface fleets, an omission that soon aroused concern in the Admiralty.[6] General Bliss, the American military representative to the Supreme War Council, did not participate in the joint meeting and did not sign the document that reported the general conclusions, pleading lack of instructions as his excuse.[7]

During the meeting in Paris the Entente leaders did not attempt to conceal their anger at Wilson's unilateral initiative. Cecil informed Balfour that "Lloyd George and Clemenceau vie

5. Joint opinion of the Prime Ministers, October 7, 1918, Wilson Papers, box 150. Copies are in SWC-WDA, entitled "Principles Submitted by a Conference of Prime Ministers to a Joint Meeting of the Military and Naval Representatives."

6. "Joint Resolution regarding Conditions of an Armistice with Germany and Austria-Hungary," October 8, 1918, SWC-WDA. A copy is in CAB 25, box 123 (SWC). For Admiralty consensus, see Minutes of the War Cabinet (WC 484), October 11, 1918, CAB 23, book 42.

7. W. B. Wallace to Secretary, British Section, SWC, October 16, 1918, CAB 25, box 123 (SWC).

with each other in scoffing at the President, and Sonnino is almost openly apprehensive of allowing him to interfere in European politics." Cecil recommended that President Wilson come to Europe, or at least that Colonel House be dispatched immediately.[8] Balfour replied somewhat discouragingly that the President could not come until after the fall elections in the United States and that House was needed where he was until Lord Reading returned to the United States. "The only course open seems to allow matters to develop trusting that events will compel Prime Ministers to co-operate with President and to persuade House to come here immediately after Reading returns."[9] The British mission at the Supreme War Council was quite positive in its views of a proper armistice. It must give "Full and acceptable guarantees that the terms arranged with be complied with. There must be a clear understanding that Germany accepts certain principles as indisputable, and reserves for negotiation only such details as, in the opinion of the Associated Powers, are negotiable." Among the subjects not considered negotiable were claims for damage, removal of barriers to trade, disposition of German colonies, the League of Nations, and certain Wilsonian principles such as avoidance of war, reduction of armaments, freedom of the sea and of the air, and regulation of international maritime traffic. The concept of the free development of all peoples must underlie the projected international organization.[10] While not unfriendly to much of the Wilsonian program the British mission clearly reflected European fears that the President would botch the negotiations with the Central Powers.

Admiral Sims asked permission to sign the joint proposal, reporting that the naval terms seemed satisfactory in general. He believed that enemy forces at sea should not be allowed to return to their home bases, but should be held as hostages in Allied ports. They would then be forced to surrender if an armistice were violated. He also wished to arrange for Germany to turn over during each month of the Armistice a number of sub-

8. Cecil to Balfour, October 7, 1918, Balfour Papers, book 49692. See also C. E. Callwell, *Field-Marshal Sir Henry Wilson: His Life and Diaries*, 2 vols. (London, 1927), 2:134–36, 139–41.

9. Balfour to Cecil, October 8, 1928, Balfour Papers, book 49692.

10. Memorandum by the Policy Committee of the British War Mission, October 9, 1918, Balfour Papers, FO 800, book 212.

marines equal to its building capacity.[11] General Bliss recognized the extent to which the rapid development of events had taken the Allies by surprise:

None of them believed that resistance would collapse in certain quarters so completely and suddenly as it has, or that there would be such evidence of a general collapse of it everywhere, before at least next year. They have dreaded to get together and try to settle the "after-the-war" difficulties. They have foreseen the possibilities of the discord that would result from throwing the golden apple into the ring. They have feared (and perhaps wisely) that it might bring about a lack of cohesion in their alliance or entente which would weaken them and encourage the enemy. At any rate, they have done nothing and now find themselves confronted with the fact that the settlement of some of these difficult questions is pressing them.

Bliss believed that the joint proposal was a relatively pointed method of informing the United States that the Entente would not treat with the Central Powers "on the terms of Wilson's fourteen propositions or on any terms." He ended his observations by stating a view that he sustained throughout the pre-Armistice negotiations, one that was remarkable for a military man. "The realization of the President's declaration as to the reduction of armaments is absolutely vital to any proposition for the destruction of militarism and the effective creation of a League of Nations."[12] Bliss was sick to death of damage and destruction.

The Entente initiative aroused a strong negative reaction in Washington. Daniels immediately cabled to Sims: "The whole matter was done without consultation with the President and he feels that no instructions can be given you until he is informed by the Civil authorities of the Governments concerned of the purpose and significance of what they have done."[13] Sims tried to pour oil on troubled waters by pointing out that the document was of an entirely preliminary nature, designed merely to indicate "what the terms of an armistice would be pending the cessation of hostilities." His own view was bluntly stated. "Per-

11. Sims to Navy Department, October 9, 1918, USNSF, VA file, "Armistice." A copy is in the Wilson Papers. Sims was not in Paris for the meeting. See R. H. Jackson to Sims, October 14, 1918, USNSF, VA file, which records events of that day.
12. Bliss to Newton D. Baker, October 9, 1918, Wilson Papers, box 150.
13. Daniels to Sims, October 9, 1918, USNSF, VA file.

sonally I would be in favor of terms much severer than those laid down."[14] Once again Sims was in accord with Admiralty opinion.

The United States and Great Britain now engaged in two weeks of preparation for an inter-Allied conclave in Paris to settle the final terms of an armistice. Nothing could be done officially until Colonel House arrived in Europe, a visitation that the British finally decided was necessary.[15] In the United States the President prepared to execute the next phase of his grand design. Throughout 1917–1918 he had held aloof from political commitments to the Allies, believing that his bargaining power would increase markedly as the United States completed its mobilization and Europe exhausted itself. In Europe the Entente statesmen slowly grasped the Wilsonian intent. The President was now about to accept the role pressed upon him by Pope Benedict XV, who urged strongly that he arrange peace negotiations. "Divine Providence has reserved for you and the great Republic over which you preside the immortal glory of restoring bleeding humanity to peace, which will mark a new epoch in the history of the world."[16]

If the President was ready for the negotiations in Paris, the United States Navy was not. It too had not anticipated the rapidity of the German collapse. Warner Schilling aptly states another reason for confusion. "There was little in their [the naval leaders'] intellectual tradition which had prepared them for this experience, much less for the more complicated task of anticipating their own interests and the probable interests of other Powers at a post-war conference."[17]

II

On October 13, the British chargé d'affaires in Washington— Colville Barclay—delivered a message to the President from Balfour that stated the latter's position regarding the ongoing

14. Sims to Benson, October 11, 1918, USNSF, TD file.

15. Minutes of the War Cabinet (WC 484), October 1, 1918, CAB 23, book 42.

16. Pope Benedictus to Wilson, October 11, 1918, Wilson Papers, box 150. Wilson replied in conciliatory but noncommittal terms. Wilson to Pope Benedictus, October 17, 1918, Wilson Papers.

17. Warner R. Schilling, "Admirals and Foreign Policy, 1913–1919," Ph. D. diss., Yale University, 1953, p. 125.

exchanges with the Central Powers. Germany was apparently prepared to concur in the American plans for peace. Great Britain agreed with the general tenor of the Fourteen Points, but it had some observations on them. They had not yet been discussed by the Allied and Associated Powers as a whole; they were subject to diverse interpretations, some of which Great Britain would resist most strongly; other terms were probably in existence, for example on the topic of shipping, to which the President had not referred and upon which Great Britain would have to insist. Great Britain believed that in shaping the terms of armistice "care must be taken to prevent the Allies from being deprived of the necessary freedom of action in the settlement of the final terms in the Peace Conference and that steps should be taken immediately by the chief belligerent powers to discuss the doubtful points and to come to some agreement amongst themselves with regard to them."[18]

In London the Admiralty was hard at work shaping its mature position on the naval terms. On October 13, an unidentified author prepared a memorandum entitled "The Case for the Surrender of the German Fleet as an Article of the Armistice," in which two central positions were taken: that the terms of the armistice must guarantee that Germany would not improve its position if the conflict were resumed and that the enemy must be placed in a position that would preclude refusal of the final peace settlement. The proper criteria for both military and naval terms were evacuation and surrender of war material. In respect to the peace treaty the great issue was security of communications, to which the German fleet posed the only possible threat. Therefore, "surrender of the German Fleet is the only compensation we can accept as the consequence of our great and successful naval efforts in the war. It is our only guarantee of security in the future if we are not to recommence an era of bloated navy estimates and of a navy continually on a war footing."[19] On the next day the War Cabinet discussed the second crucial question—freedom of the seas. Lloyd George thought the concept "capable of wide variation in interpretation." Austen Chamberlain was convinced that no time should be lost in

18. Balfour to Barclay, paraphrase for Wilson, October 13, 1918, Wilson Papers, box 151.
19. "The Case for the Surrender of the German Fleet as an Article of the Armistice," October 13, 1918, USNSF, TX file.

informing the United States that Great Britain could not accept the German interpretation of freedom of the seas.[20] The War Cabinet decided not to contact President Wilson immediately, but Andrew Bonar Law, one of Lloyd George's advisers, expressed a general feeling when he complained bitterly that the President "ought not to make these pronouncements without first consulting the other Allies." Lord Reading defended Wilson. "He had so manoeuvered that the Germans were unlikely again to try to make peace through him."[21] No one seemed aware that the President had been proceeding for a year and more in ways to ensure that he would have the greatest possible freedom of action in respect to the determination of the peace—sufficient flexibility to act independently if it became necessary.

By October 17, Admiral Wemyss had prepared an Admiralty memorandum on the freedom of the seas. The application of this principle was intended to safeguard neutral and belligerent trade in time of war; it would preclude blockades against commerce and hamper purely naval operations of battle fleets:

> It would prevent us from using our strongest weapon and place in the hands of our enemy a power which he does not possess. The value of military power, both for attack and defence, would be enhanced, and its radius of action increased, while the value of naval power for attack and defence and its radius of action would be correspondingly diminished.

These considerations explained why Germany favored freedom of the seas. "Germany, whose whole industry is war, saw a military advantage in the proposal." Wemyss took note of Wilson's plan to use sea power to police the peace. "The conditions of the British Empire, however, are so unique and its dependence on sea communications so vital, that it is impossible even to contemplate committing its whole destinies at sea to any League or combination of nations." The British had an alternative interpretation of freedom of the seas:

> The British idea of the freedom of the seas is free and unfettered access in time of *peace*, to all the seas by all who wish to cross them "upon their lawful occasions"; in time of *war* this privilege must be fought

20. Minutes of the War Cabinet (WC 438), October 14, 1918, CAB 23, book 8.

21. Minutes of the War Cabinet (WC 486), October 15, 1918, CAB 23, book 8.

for by belligerent navies, causing as little inconvenience as possible
to neutrals, but maintaining the rights of capture of belligerent merchant ships and of searching neutral merchant ships in order to veri-
fy their nationality and prevent their aiding a belligerent.

Wemyss pressed on to inevitable conclusions:

Acceptance of this proposal [Wilson's] would result in making
sea-power of little value to a nation *dependent upon it* for existence
whilst providing a military Power with free lines of oversea communication.
The right to decide for ourselves questions which concern such
vital interests, could not be surrendered to any League or combination of nations for by assenting to the proposal we should give up by
a stroke of the pen the sea-power we have for centuries maintained
and have never yet misused. On this basis the British Empire had
been founded, and on no other can it be upheld.[22]

Here was a forceful restatement of traditional British naval policy; the Admiralty by no means intended to sacrifice its interests to the whims of a quixotic American President. Wilson, of
course, reiterated the historic American view of neutral rights
on the high seas that had been advanced since the time of
Independence.

The Admiralty had also considered the question of specific
armistice terms extensively.[23] Its final demands considerably
stiffened the terms discussed in Paris. All submarines were to
surrender in Allied ports at the time of the armistice. All surface
ships were to withdraw to certain specified locations, and certain ships were to surrender at Allied bases. All Allied prisoners
of war were to be returned immediately, along with Allied subjects interned in neutral countries. Heligoland was to be surrendered within forty-eight hours of the armistice. Merchant
vessels in enemy or neutral hands were to be returned to bases
specified by the Allies. The German surface vessels to be surrendered numbered 10 battleships, 6 battle cruisers, 8 light
cruisers including 2 mine layers, and 50 of the most modern

22. Admiralty Memorandum by Wemyss for the War Cabinet, "An
Inquiry into the Meaning and Effect of the Demand for 'Freedom of the
Seas,' " ADM 116, book 1771.
23. See memoranda from various Admiralty officials on surrender of
German surface and undersea vessels, October 14, 1918, in memoranda for
the Board of Admiralty, ADM 167, book 55. See also Minutes of the Board
of Admiralty, October 14, 1918, ADM 167, book 53.

destroyers.[24] All submarines were to be surrendered because they had been used by Germany "in contempt of the rules of International Law and of the dictates of humanity." The step would be "recognised and approved by the whole of the civilised world." The surrender of surface vessels was necessary to make certain that the Allies did not lose "the advantage of the Naval initiative, which, as a result of our continuous activity, we have gained and the enemy has lost."[25] Clearly, considerations of prestige were involved as well as strictly naval desiderata.

The severity of the Admiralty proposals somewhat disturbed the War Cabinet. At the meeting on October 19, Lloyd George, Milner, and Law all thought that some relaxation might be appropriate, but General Sir Henry Wilson, the Chief of the Imperial General Staff, supported the Admiralty. At this meeting the extreme British annoyance with the performance of the American Army in France was particularly manifest. The Americans had earlier refused to brigade their troops by smaller units. Then, their independent Army had performed badly:

The only way to press the Americans was to threaten to withhold shipping. . . . When Colonel House arrived in this country he ought to be told straight that the Americans were making a mess of it. At present the American Press were sending out the most absurd accounts of the prowess of their Army, and President Wilson was undoubtedly being misled. In his late Note [to Germany], President Wilson had spoken of the supremacy of the troops of the United States and their Allies, or some such phrase. It was very important that Marshal Foch should talk very straight to Colonel House.[26]

These irritations had some effect on the naval terms; Britain thought that its naval contributions entitled it to a pre-eminent voice in the naval settlement.

Admiral Wemyss, a prime exponent of the theory that the terms of the armistice were of great importance because they

24. "Draft of British Admiralty Proposals for Conditions for an Armistice," October 16, 1918, USNSF, VA file; Elncase to Sims, October 17, 1918, USNSF, QC file; Elncase to Sims, October 19, 1918, USNSF, VA file; Memorandum by Admiral Beatty on proposed armistice terms, October 18, 1918, memoranda for the Board of Admiralty, ADM 167, book 55.

25. Admiralty Memorandum for the War Cabinet, "Naval Conditions of Armistice," October 19, 1918, ADM 116, book 1771.

26. Minutes of the War Cabinet (K-29), October 19, 1918, CAB 23, book 17 (very secret minutes).

would probably approximate the terms of peace, presented this view to the War Cabinet on October 20. He feared that the Grand Fleet might not receive its proper share of the spoils. To relax the naval terms "might mean that while we had been victorious on shore, we would not reap the fruits of our victory at sea. This naval victory was no less real because it was not spectacular, for the Admiralty claimed their strategy to have imposed their will upon the enemy." Wemyss brought Admiral Beatty to the meeting to support his contentions. "Like the First Sea Lord, he also based his views on the assumption that hostilities were not likely to recommence after an armistice, and consequently that the terms of armistice must be as near as possible to the terms of peace." Those terms must ensure that the enemy had no future capability to reduce the strength of the British fleet by methods such as submarine warfare. It was also of great importance to reduce those enemy fortifications that precluded effective assault on the submarine nests.[27] The Admiralty gained additional support from France, when the E.M.G. urged almost identical conditions.[28]

One source of British fear dissipated in the next few days. On October 21, Balfour had cabled to the President the British concern that the President might agree to arrangements with the Germans that did not guarantee an effective armistice—an armistice that would preclude the resumption of hostilities. Absence of concrete military and naval terms of armistice would cause great difficulties. "Our experts assure us that the effect of any such policy would be to give the Germans what they most want—time to reorganize and a short and defensible front. Peace negotiations carried on under such conditions could never secure the terms desired by the associated governments."[29] On October 24, when Wilson had concluded his negotiations with Germany, Lloyd George conceded to the War Cabinet that Wilson had respected the British concern. "The diplomatic wrangle was now over, and the President had made it clear that

27. Minutes of the War Cabinet (WC 489b), October 21, 1918, CAB 23, book 14. These minutes also contain a long memorandum by Beatty.

28. De Bon to Mercier de Lostende, October 22, 1918, MM, Es file, box 21; "Note by France on the Essential Naval Conditions of an Armistice with the Enemy," October 22, 1918, USNSF, VA file.

29. Balfour to Barclay, paraphrase for Wilson, October 21, 1918, Wilson Papers, box 151. For a letter urging this message, see Cecil to Balfour, n.d. (but about October 20, 1918), Balfour Papers, FO 800, book 207.

the terms of the armistice would be such as to prevent the resumption of hostilities by the Germans." [30]

There remained a final War Cabinet decision on armistice terms. Lloyd George was by no means convinced that an armistice was desirable at the present time. On October 25, the War Cabinet heard the Prime Minister claim "an open mind" on the matter. "The issue really was whether we should grant what might be termed a good peace now, or whether we should impose such drastic terms for an armistice that the enemy could not accept, our intention being utterly to crush him next year, with the idea of obtaining better security for peace for the future." At the same meeting the group agreed to send a message to the United States stating the inability of Great Britain to accept the Wilsonian doctrine of freedom of the seas. [31]

The next day Lloyd George returned to both questions. In regard to an armistice, Balfour, Chamberlain, and Curzon supported peace if the victors could negotiate reasonable armistice terms. Geddes wanted to "insist on the surrender of so much of Germany's naval and military power as to reduce her to a second-class Power." General Smuts particularly opposed continuance of the war, giving as his reason the impending predominance of the United States. "As Europe went down, so America would rise. In time the United States of America would dictate to the world in naval, military, diplomatic, and financial matters. In that he saw no good." Lord Reading lent strong support to Smuts. At the moment Britain and America dominated the situation as partners, but further warfare would strengthen the American position. Concerning freedom of the seas, Lloyd George wanted to withhold the message to America, believing that "If all the Allies would agree on a joint declaration it would be much better than a separate declaration by the British Government." Austen Henderson thought that the other Allies might not agree. He favored dispatch of the message to leave no doubt of the British position. Balfour then proposed that a message be sent specifying that Britain could not accede to freedom of the seas until the proposed league had proved effective. Lloyd George pointed out that Wilson favored limits on sea power but

30. Minutes of the War Cabinet (WC 490), October 24, 1918, CAB 23, book 8.

31. Minutes of the War Cabinet (WC 491a), October 25, 1918, CAB 23, book 14 (secret minutes).

not on land power. "We ought to state quite definitely that we could not associate ourselves with this doctrine. Public opinion in this country would never stand for it." Geddes claimed that the President would not press the matter very strongly. Wilson was "rather bitten with the effectiveness of sea power. . . . He probably wished, under the League of Nations, to take a large share in the policing of the seas." Balfour then raised a truly critical point. "At Versailles the problem would be for us, in discussing the question of an armistice, not to commit ourselves too deeply on the question of the Fourteen Points." Reading then argued that Colonel House was strongly in favor of freedom of the seas. Lloyd George held that the best procedure would be to "challenge the doctrine of the Freedom of the Seas altogether." Austen Chamberlain wanted to take the position that sea power should be limited exactly as was land power, but Balfour detected the flaw in that position. The seas were international, whereas the land areas were not. Geddes made another appeal for the dispatch of the message, but Smuts held out for withholding it.

Lloyd George took a more conciliatory position on the question of the surrender of German vessels, particularly the submarine fleet. Geddes argued that the larger issue was whether the Allies would discuss or dictate the peace terms. The Admiralty believed that the armistice terms would approximate the terms of peace and wished to settle the matter immediately. Smuts and Reading dissented, arguing that the long-term control of the German Navy should be determined by the peace conference rather than the armistice. Lloyd George maintained that surrender at the peacemaking was more humiliating than surrender at the armistice. Geddes then cited President Wilson's belief that if the Germans were beaten they would accept any terms, but Lloyd George thought this view crude because there were various degrees of defeat.

After these debates the War Cabinet made its decisions. Lloyd George and Balfour were instructed to inform the conference that Britain did not accept the doctrine of freedom of the seas and that Germany must receive notice of this fact before the beginning of peace negotiations. It is of interest that the freedom of the seas was the only one of the Fourteen Points subjected to extensive discussion by the Cabinet prior to the climactic negotiations in Paris. As to the German fleet and the naval armistice the War Cabinet decided that "The naval conditions of the armistice should represent the admission of German defeat by sea in the same degree as the military conditions recognise the corresponding admission of German defeat by land." Sir Eric Geddes was to accompany Lloyd George and Balfour to the Paris meetings and be present during discussions of the naval conditions of the armistice and the freedom of the seas.[32]

Before departing for Paris Geddes consulted the Board of Admiralty as to the formula for discussion of naval terms. In treating the surrender of submarines, the Board decided that enough should be surrendered to preclude the resumption of submarine warfare if the armistice broke down. This proviso required the surrender of substantial numbers, in any event something more than half of the total. As to the surface fleet, the Board decided that enough ships must be surrendered to "reduce Germany to a second-class Naval Power so as to enable the Allies to enforce the Terms of the Armistice."[33] The preliminaries were now over in Britain; the main bout was soon to take place across the English Channel.

For its part, the United States also made preparations for Paris. While Colonel House journeyed across the sea to Europe, President Wilson pressed his negotiations with the Central Powers to a successful conclusion. He obviously shared the suspicions of European intent that some of his correspondents expressed to him. Henry Hollis wrote of jingo tendencies in the Entente countries and made a shrewd point in this connection: "If we are to get a fair and permanent peace, we do not want Germany beaten any worse than she is. If she should be reduced to a point where England and France should think they did not need our help any more, they would rub it in beyond reason." Fortunately America's Army and wealth conferred great bargaining power upon the President. Hollis hoped that Wilson would not have to exert pressure, but if he did he would "know how best to use it."[34]

32. Minutes of the War Cabinet (WC 491b), October 26, 1918, CAB 23, book 14 (secret minutes). Balfour's proposed message, dated October 26, 1918, is printed as Cabinet Memorandum no. 792, FO 899, box 14.

33. Minutes of the Board of Admiralty, October 26, 1918, ADM 167, book 53.

34. Hollis to Wilson, October 15, 1918, USNSF, VA file.

Wilson had already expressed to Sir Eric Geddes his belief that the time was ripe for peace. "The spirit of the Bolsheviki is lurking everywhere, and there is no more fertile soil than war-weariness." He also had in mind conditions in Germany. "If we humiliate the German people and drive them too far, we shall destroy all form of government, and Bolshevism will take its place. We ought not to ground them to powder or there will be nothing to build up from." His general views on the armistice were clear. He thought it possible to obtain one that would "safeguard us against any possible treachery." The heads of governments would probably have to modify the terms proposed by the military and naval people, "because the soldiers and sailors will make them too severe. We must not make them impossible, or even humiliating."[35] Prince Maximilian of Baden, the new Chancellor of Germany, accurately gauged Wilson's desires in proposing a given response to the one of the President's notes. He was anxious to place the President, "who according to his previous statements should shrink back from a war of total victory, in the position of *arbiter mundi* and further give him the opportunity of trying to moderate the fanatical aspirations of his 'Associates.' "[36] Wilson's skillful procedure was well described by Sen. John Sharp Williams, who recommended that the Central Powers be allowed to "wobble on the gudgeon."[37]

The President would extract a commitment from the Central Powers to end the war whilst he could still exercise a dominating influence on armistice negotiations and the peace settlement. His supporters cheered him on, many of whom were violently distrustful of Entente motives. Edward N. Hurley, the shipping expert, wanted him to keep tight hold on the "throttle of war and peace." He feared the consequences if the Entente leaders, "whose chief thought is their prestige and power," succeeded in seizing the diplomatic initiative. Hurley believed that only editorial writers and politicos opposed the President. The people everywhere were for his policies. "The spirit of America, I am

35. Geddes memorandum on interview with President Wilson (October 13, 1918), October 16, 1918, Balfour Papers, FO 800, book 212.
36. Memorandum by Chancellor Max von Baden, October 16, 1918, Whaddon Hall microfilms, serial #9246H, frames E65331–65333.
37. Wilson to Williams, October 17, 1918, Wilson Papers.

convinced, will give a million lives for justice, but not a single life for vengeance."[38] Wilson knew that the Allies were restive. He told his Cabinet on October 22 that the European associates "needed to be coerced, that they were getting to the point where they were reaching out for more than they should have in justice."[39] His strategy during the armistice discussions was designed to preserve equity while ensuring that Germany did not get off without severe penalties. Secretary Baker summed up the American position in instructions for General Pershing: "In general, the President feels the terms of the armistice should be rigid enough to secure us against renewal of hostilities by Germany but not humiliating beyond that necessity, as such terms would throw the advantage to the military party in Germany."[40] He did not say that unduly harsh terms might ultimately play into the hands of Entente statesmen.

Meanwhile the naval headquarters in London made its analysis of the proper terms of the naval armistice.[41] Earlier, Sims had generally concurred in the terms arranged in Paris, suggesting only minor modifications.[42] He feared that a political settlement might undercut the objectives of the military and naval leadership, telling Admiral Bayly in Queenstown that "You may be sure that we military men will do all we can to keep the politicians from letting us down. The great danger is that there will be disagreement among the Allies as to what the terms of Peace should be." He was irritated that the President had not consulted the Entente leaders before making his arrangements with Germany.[43] Just as Sims expressed these sentiments Wilson notified Prince Max that he was now satisfied with the German position and would refer the correspondence to an inter-Allied meeting for the final decision.

38. Hurley to Wilson, October 23, 1918, Wilson Papers, box 151.

39. Anne Wintermute Lane and Louise Herrick Wall, eds., *The Letters of Franklin K. Lane: Personal and Political* (Boston, 1922), 295.

40. Baker to Pershing, October 27, 1918, Wilson Papers. For additional evidence relating to this attitude, see David F. Trask, *The United States in the Supreme War Council: American War Aims and Inter-Allied Strategy, 1917–1918* (Middletown, Conn., 1961), 155–64.

41. The Navy Department had requested the view of the London headquarters. Department to Sims, October 15, 1918, USNSF, VA file.

42. Sims to Navy Department, October 15, 1918, USNSF, VA file.

43. Sims to Bayly, October 23, 1918, USNSF, TD file.

The Planning Section at length produced a memorandum on "Armistice Terms." Its analysis and proposals generally paralleled those of the Admiralty, with some important distinctions. It proposed internment rather than surrender of all surface vessels and submarines. The surrender principle might cause "possible serious disagreement amongst the Allies." The only exception was the Russian fleet, which should be surrendered and returned to Russia "when a stable government has been established there." Another significant variation concerned Heligoland. "We consider that the disadvantages of the question raised by the surrender of Heligoland will outweigh the advantages it might give temporarily."[44] There was no discussion of the political basis of the armistice or of freedom of the seas.

In Washington at about this time the planning committee established within the Navy Department also produced a series of recommendations dealing briefly with armistice terms but mostly with the final conditions of peace. As terms preliminary to an armistice the Washington committee called unequivocally for unconditional surrender. The Central Powers must evacuate occupied territory; Germany must withdraw into its own territory as far as the Rhine; the armies must be disarmed and disbanded; the fleets must be surrendered and located in ports designated by the Allies; and the Hohenzollerns and Hapsburgs must abdicate their thrones. As an aspect of the peace settlement the document called for "Absolute freedom of navigation upon the seas, outside territorial waters, alike in peace and war, except as the sea may be closed in whole or in part by international action for the enforcement of international covenants." Here was a forceful document indeed, calling for a victor's armistice but opting in general for the broad principles of President Wilson. The Washington planners voiced some concern about entanglement. "It will be unwise for the United States to enter into any agreements or pledges that will jeopardize our future welfare or safety. World history in the past has shown swift and startling changes in national relations and the intense commercial competition that will inevitably take place after the

44. Planning Section Memorandum No. 59, "Armistice Terms," October 24, 1918, USNSF, TX file. The specific recommendations are summarized in Sims to Navy Department, October 25, 1918, USNSF, VA file.

war is to be considered as causes [*sic*] of future friction among the great nations."[45] There is no indication that this document of itself played any role in the negotiations in Paris, but it represented the views of many within the Navy Department, including Admiral Benson who had accompanied House to the inter-Allied conference. The Chief of Naval Operations joined Sims in the Allied Naval Council.

One other recommendation of naval terms was in being as the inter-Allied conference began its deliberations on October 28. General Pershing had met with Marshal Foch, General Pétain, and Field Marshal Haig at Senlis on October 25 to consider the terms of the armistice. He concurred in a recommendation for the "surrender of all U-Boats and U-Boat bases to the control of a neutral power until their disposition is otherwise determined";[46] there was no mention of surface vessels. The Senlis proposals reflected Foch's primary interest in the land armistice; they gave only minimal consideration to the naval terms.[47] Wilson reacted strongly to the naval proposal. Secretary of War Baker cabled significantly to Pershing on October 28:

The President believes it would be enough to require internment of U-Boats in neutral waters, as a further pledge and also to further unrestricted transportation of American material . . ., but does not think terms of armistice should suggest ultimate disposition of such U-Boats, nor that U-Boat bases should be occupied under armistice, as that would mean Allied or American occupation of German soil not now in their possession.[48]

On October 28, the President transmitted to House and Benson his detailed suggestions of naval terms. The enemy was to cease submarine operations upon the signature of the armistice. No mine laying was to take place outside of territorial waters during the armistice. The enemy was to disclose the location of his mine fields near Allied and neutral shores and to forbear from mine sweeping outside his territorial waters. Blockade and restrictions on oceanic traffic would continue during the armi-

45. Planning Committee, Washington, to Benson, n.d. (but ca. October, 1918), USNSF, VP file. Benson probably received this document before departing for Paris, but there is no direct evidence on this point.

46. Pershing to War Department, October 25, 1918, Wilson Papers. See also John J. Pershing, *My Experiences in the World War*, 2 vols. (New York, 1931), 2:359–63.

47. Ibid.; Trask, *United States in the Supreme War Council*, 159–60.

48. Baker to Pershing, October 28, 1918, Wilson Papers.

stice. The enemy would evacuate all coasts and ports of occupied countries, as well as all coasts and ports of disputed territories evacuated by military forces, including those formerly a part of Russia. No damage or removal of supplies would be permitted in evacuated regions. Enemy vessels would withdraw to their own waters, except for Russian vessels, which would be surrendered. The peace conference would decide the final disposition of the enemy fleets. Submarines would be interned in neutral ports under conditions that prevented their departure. The naval aircraft of the enemy would be concentrated at an enemy base specified by the Allies. Finally, all these terms would be executed in the shortest possible time.[49]

The President had made his position clear. He favored relatively moderate naval terms that precluded resumption of naval warfare but avoided undue humiliation of Germany. His views must have angered those in Washington—like Franklin D. Roosevelt—who desired strict terms.[50] He remained firm in his conviction that the freedom of the seas should be established by international covenants. If there was broad correspondence of view concerning the naval armistice within the western coalition, there were at least two divisive issues—freedom of the seas and disposition of the German fleet. These questions dominated the discussion of naval terms at the pre-Armistice negotiations in Paris.

III

The naval leaders met in Paris on October 28. Georges Leygues first stated three general principles to govern their discussions of armistice terms: a large number of submarines should be surrendered; a certain number of surface ships should be surrendered; and the blockade should be maintained. Sir Eric Geddes then made a statement that no needed arrangement should be excluded because it conflicted with the Fourteen Points, a clear indication that the American negotiators might encounter difficulties later on. He suggested a fourth general principle, that

49. Navy Department to Sims for Benson and House, October 28, 1918, Wilson Papers. Sims transmitted the message on October 29. A copy is in the House Papers.

50. Frank Freidel, *Franklin D. Roosevelt: The Apprenticeship* (Boston, 1952), 370–71.

the Allied navies be given free access to the Baltic, Black, and the Adriatic seas, as well as other locations. He wanted to consider first the terms for Germany, proceeding afterwards to those for Austria-Hungary.

The four principles were then applied to the enemy navies. Rather than requiring surrender of the entire underseas fleet the negotiators agreed to demand 160 German submarines. Approximately half of the German surface fleet must be surrendered. "The end of the war must leave the German Fleet reduced to impotence and unable at will to disturb the peace of the world." Terms contained in the naval armistice would be substantially those of the final peace treaty. A special committee was set up to decide upon the exact vessels to be surrendered, basing its deliberations on the Admiralty calculations of the required reduction (10 battleships, 6 battle cruisers, 8 light cruisers including 2 mine layers, and 50 of the most modern destroyers). Enemy crews would be repatriated to Germany, and the final disposition of the vessels surrendered would be left to the peace conference. Blockade would be maintained, and the enemy would allow access to various bodies of water under their control. The same general decisions were reached with respect to the Austrian fleet, with di Revel to designate those Austrian vessels to be surrendered.[51]

President Wilson's message of October 28 on naval terms did not reach Admiral Benson until the next day. When he received it he immediately informed his fellow negotiators that he had to reserve his views on the question of disposition. Since Benson favored the terms of the Allied Naval Council, he asked Washington for instructions to permit acceptance of them, noting that Colonel House had approved his referring the matter to Washington.[52] He thus placed himself in opposition to the moderate terms desired by the President.

Meanwhile Colonel House had begun his campaign for moderate terms in a characteristic manner. He communicated his views privately to certain British officials who he knew would pass them on to Lloyd George:

51. Minutes of the Conference of Naval Representatives, October 28, 1918, USNSF, QC file.
52. Benson to Daniels, October 29, 1918, Wilson Papers. Benson's reservation is recorded in Minutes of the Sixth Meeting, ANC, October 29, 1918, First Session, USNSF, QC file.

I told Wiseman and later today told Reading, that if the British were not careful they would bring upon themselves the dislike of the world. The British Navy seemed to me to be analogous to the German Army, except the German Army is under the direction of an autocracy while the English Navy is under the direction of a democracy. I did not believe the United States and other countries would willingly submit to Great Britain's complete domination of the seas any more than to Germany's domination of the land, and the sooner the British recognized this fact, the better it would be for them. I told them, furthermore, that our people, if challenged, would build a navy and maintain an army greater than theirs. We had more money, we had more men, and our natural resources were greater. I believed such a program would be popular in America and should England give the incentive, the people would demand the rest.[53]

This was tough talk indeed, designed to achieve some modification of the British naval terms by private methods rather than public disputation.

House received some unexpected support from no less a figure than Marshal Foch. The Generalissimo wrote to Clemenceau on October 29 warning against undue demands on the German Navy. He did not think that strict terms could be adopted "because, if they were too rigorous, they would result in making the land armies continue a most costly struggle for advantages of questionable effect."[54] After Clemenceau pointed out the difficulties raised by Foch, House wanted to know what the Allies intended to do with the ships taken from Germany. After this discussion House reported a moderating trend. "We all agreed that the articles drawn up by the Navy are entirely too severe and we propose to soften them. We plan to eliminate the German battle cruisers and submarine fleet which will be all that is necessary." He dispatched this news to President Wilson on October 30,[55] but House reckoned without Sir Eric Geddes. As the Allied Naval Council discussed naval terms on October 29, Geddes burst into the meeting to bring the news of Foch's state-

53. House diary, October 28, 1918, House Papers.
54. Ferdinand Foch, *Mémoires pour servir à l'Histoire de la Guerre de 1914–1918*, 2 vols. (Paris, 1931), 2:284.
55. House diary, October 29, 1918, quoted in Charles Seymour, ed., *The Intimate Papers of Colonel House*, 4 vols., *The Ending of the War* (Boston, 1928), 4:117–18. House to Wilson, October 30, 1918, United States Department of State, *Papers Relating to the Foreign Relations of the United States, 1918*, supp. 1, 3 vols., *The World War* (Washington, D.C., 1933), 1:425–27.

ment and to propose angrily that the various representatives
express themselves on this matter to their respective prime
ministers.

Geddes was intent upon adding to the statement of naval
terms a pronouncement that it had been negotiated on the assumption that the enemy had been decisively defeated. He had
argued this view earlier in sessions of the British War Cabinet as
a means of maintaining British naval prestige vis-à-vis that of
Haig's land forces, but also as a basis for strict terms. In the debate Geddes argued the view that Germany was preparing a vast
new submarine offensive, the line he had taken so vigorously
during his mission to America. Admiral de Bon saw no reason to
adopt the statement urged by the First Lord, but it was finally
accepted.[56] The first basic draft of naval terms for Germany and
Austria-Hungary was now complete, and it followed the general
lines of the Admiralty proposal. The United States had reserved
its views on the disposition of the German surface fleet. Benson
reported the outcome of the discussions to Colonel House, noting
that the word "surrender" had been used to avoid any German
misinterpretation of the harshness of the terms. He thought it
"possible that the military terms of the armistice will be sufficiently drastic to warrant the amelioration of the Naval terms
while still retaining complete security against the possibility of
the resumption of hostilities."[57]

There was now a distinct gulf between the terms approved by
the Allied Naval Council and those desired by President Wilson.
The principal distinction, of course, was that the President
favored internment of submarines and the return of the enemy
surface fleet to its home bases, whereas the Allied Naval Council
called for the surrender of 160 submarines and a large number
of enemy surface vessels. The President and the Council both
provided for final disposition of the enemy fleets by the peace
conference, but the terms of the Council left much less to be
decided later than did the President's terms.[58] House persisted
in the view that the civilian leaders did not agree with the Allied

56. Minutes of the Sixth Meeting, October 29, 1918, ANC, First Session, USNSF, QC file.
57. Benson to House, October 30, 1918, USNSF, VA file.
58. For a detailed analysis of the distinctions, see "Memorandum for
Admiral Benson," n.d. (but ca. October 30, 1918), USNSF, VA file. A
copy is in the TX file.

Naval Council and informed the President: "It is my view that privately [Lloyd] George and Balfour believe that the proposed terms of the naval armistice and those of the military armistice are too severe. They wish to get just as much as they can but they wish to be able to continue negotiations in the event that Germany refused to accept the terms proposed."[59] In Washington Captain Pratt drew Secretary Daniels's attention to the discrepancies between the President's terms and those of the Allied Naval Council. He favored the moderate arrangements. If a new government came to power in Germany it would need assistance in order to ensure that it was "neither autocratic and military or bolshevik. Such a government being assured, it ought to be supported and the armistice terms not made too humiliating, in order to guard most carefully the future." He was fearful that if the Germans could not accept an armistice they would launch extensive naval operations against Britain's lines of communications and American convoys, utilizing surface units as well as submarines.[60] Admiral Benson shared this concern. On November 1, he asked House to send a special message to Washington. "In view of possibility of desperate action being attempted by German naval forces or a part of it upon receipt of armistice terms, strongly recommend sailing of troops be delayed until definite information is received."[61]

As the plight of Germany became apparent in September, Admiral Sims took note of British interest in the possibility of a final desperate sortie by the German High Sea Fleet. If the German vessels ventured into the North Sea, Sims thought that they would avoid an all-out engagement, because a defeat would completely destroy the morale of the German people. In an addendum to his initial expression of views Sims reported positively: "I have found nobody in the Admiralty or outside of it that believes in the probability of the High Sea Fleet giving battle."[62] He retained this view well into October.[63] As it happened Germany did consider a major naval engagement in October to raise

59. House to Wilson, October 30, 1918, Department of State, 1918, supp. 1, 1:422–23.

60. Pratt to Daniels, October 31, 1918, USNSF, VA file.

61. House to Wilson, November 1, 1918, USDSM 367, 763.72/13377.

62. Sims to Benson, September 17, 1918 (with addendum, September 18, 1918), USNSF, TD file.

63. Sims to Benson, October 11, 1918, USNSF, TD file.

civilian morale and possibly to turn the tide at the last moment. At worst even a defeat for the German Navy might so cripple the British fleet that it would become a doubtful political tool for the future.[64] Changes in the naval command left the High Sea Fleet free to contemplate action without fear of undue interference or restraint from military or political leaders.[65] On October 22, Admiral Scheer ordered the commander of the German High Sea Fleet—Admiral Hipper—to raid the English coast in order to draw the Grand Fleet into battle on terms advantageous to Germany.[66] Admiral Hipper seriously considered asking the Kaiser to participate personally in the naval strike against England.[67] On October 28, the fleet began to move into position, but a mutiny on several vessels brought an abrupt halt to the dramatic operation. Hipper dispersed various units to isolate the mutinous crews and re-establish order.[68] Thus ended ingloriously the last German endeavor to alter the course of the war by use of its sea power. The collapse of naval discipline in the High Sea Fleet was another link in the chain of circumstances that strengthened the likelihood of a relatively severe set of naval terms.

While the Allied Naval Council hammered out its first version of the naval terms, the civilian leaders began to discuss the political basis of the armistice. When the President's Fourteen Points were first discussed on October 29, Clemenceau, Lloyd George, and Sonnino all raised objections— the British leader adverting particularly to freedom of the seas. House, immedi-

64. See the report of Konteradmiral von Levetzow, October, 1918, *Ursachen und Folgen*, 2:500.

65. Germany, Nationalversammlung, 1919–1920, Untersuchungsausschuss ueber die Kriegsverantlichkeit, *Das Werk des Untersuchungsausschusses der Verfassungsgebenden Deutschen Nationalversammlung und des Deutschen Reichstages 1919–1928: Die Ursachen des Deutschen Zusammenbruchs im Jahre 1918*, Albrecht Philipp, ed., 12 vols. (Berlin, 1928), vol. 9, pt. 1, 188–89, 193, 198.

66. Reinhard Scheer, *Germany's High Sea Fleet in the World War* (London, 1920), 353–54; *Ursachen und Folgen*, 2:200–202; Grant, *U-Boats Destroyed*, 137–38; Hans Kutscher, *Der letzte Einsatz der deutschen Hochseeflotte und der Ausbruch der Matrosen Revolte* (Stuttgart, 1933), 48.

67. Hubatsch, *Der Admiralstab*, 181.

68. Scheer, *Germany's High Sea Fleet*, 354–57; *Ursachen und Folgen*, 2:502–4; Wilhelm Groener, *Lebenserinnerungen: Jugend; Generalstab; Weltkrieg* (Göttingen, 1957), 442.

ately convinced that the Entente leaders would attempt to seize control of the peace negotiations and frustrate the plans of President Wilson, quickly argued that any such departure would mean repudiation of the President's prior arrangements with the Central Powers. The American negotiator now prepared to employ his trump card. When Clemenceau broached the possibility that if frustrated in respect to the Fourteen Points the United States might withdraw from the war and make a separate peace with the Central Powers, House replied significantly: "It might."[69] Although Germany and Austria-Hungary were close to complete collapse, the defalcation of the United States might well revive their spirits and correspondingly depress those of the Entente nations, who were in desperate need not only of American wartime assistance but also of aid during the immediate postwar period.

One of the principal Entente complaints about Wilsonian diplomacy was that the Fourteen Points were frequently vague and therefore susceptible to diverse interpretations. This was true of the principle of freedom of the seas as advocated in Point II: "Absolute freedom of navigation upon the seas, outside territorial waters, alike in peace and in war, except as the seas may be closed in whole or in part by international action or the enforcement of international covenants."[70] To clarify this principle as well as others Colonel House asked Frank Cobb, the editor of the New York World, and Walter Lippmann, a liberal journalist then in Army Intelligence, to prepare a "gloss" on the Fourteen Points, eliminating some of their ambiguities. The Cobb-Lippmann gloss explained that Point II had to be read in connection with Point XIV, which called for the establishment of a league of nations. It referred to navigation on the high seas under three conditions: general peace, general war, and limited war. There was no serious dispute about navigation in conditions of general peace. During a general war fought by the league under international covenants, an outlaw nation would justly experience complete nonintercourse. The difficulty arose in connection with limited wars, which did not violate the obligations of the international covenant. What was the meaning of freedom

69. Trask, *United States in the Supreme War Council*, 165–66.
70. For an account of the drafting of Point II, see Seymour, ed., *Intimate Papers*, 3:327.

of the seas when the league remained neutral? "Clearly, it is the intention of the proposal that in such a war the rights of neutrals shall be maintained against the belligerents, the rights of both to be clearly and precisely defined in the law of nations."[71] The prime British objection to freedom of the seas was that it might outlaw the right of blockade. Charles Seymour insists that Colonel House had no such intention. He sought "a codification of maritime usage that would sanctify the doctrine of the immunity of private property at sea in time of war." This distinction carried little weight with Britain, dependent as it was upon its sea power.[72] In Paris the prime difficulty for Great Britain was that it had made no great protest against Point II before the pre-Armistice negotiations. Silence presumed tacit consent. Those who now opposed the principle would subject themselves to the charge that they had broken faith.[73]

In Washington the President prepared to weather the Entente attack on the Fourteen Points. On October 29, he sent House a blunt message insisting that the settlement must be made on the basis of his principles. "If it is the purpose of the statesmen to nullify my influence let me speak of it boldly to all the world as I shall." Wilson was convinced that he possessed the necessary position of strength. "England cannot dispense with our friendship in the future and the other Allies cannot without our assistance get their rights as against England."[74] The President's tactic was quite transparent. House should force the issue because the Entente powers were in no position to withstand the American demand.

On the next day—October 30—President Wilson commented directly to House on the freedom of the seas and repeated his threat to make a public statement on the question:

I feel it my solemn duty to authorize you to say that I cannot consent to take part in the negotiation of a peace which does not include freedom of the seas because we are pledged to fight not only to do away with Prussian militarism but with militarism everywhere. Neither

71. Ibid., 4:193. The complete text of the gloss is ibid., 192–200.

72. Ibid., 4:164; Seth P. Tillman, *Anglo-American Relations at the Paris Peace Conference* (Princeton, 1961), 45, 48.

73. Mary Klachko, "Anglo-American Naval Competition, 1918–1922," Ph. D. diss., Columbia University, 1962, 70.

74. Wilson to House, October 29, 1918, Wilson Papers.

could I participate in a settlement which did not include league of nations because peace would be without any guarantee except universal armament which would be intolerable. I hope I shall not be obliged to make this decision public.[75]

Clearly the war leader was in a belligerent mood and had no intention of moderating his program in the hour of victory.

House prepared to execute the President's wishes. He informed Wilson of his intention "to tell the Prime Ministers today [October 30] that if their conditions of peace are essentially different from the conditions you have laid down and for which the American people have been fighting, that you will probably feel obliged to go before Congress and state the new conditions and ask for their advice as to whether the United States will continue to fight for the aims of Great Britain, France, and Italy." He agreed that firmness was both right and expedient. "The last thing they want is publicity and they do not wish it to appear that there is any difference between the Allies. Unless we deal with these people with a firm hand everything we have been fighting for will be lost." House had in mind also to threaten a withdrawal of economic assistance.[76]

When House made his dramatic announcement to the assembled prime ministers it brought about a measurable change in their positions. Each government had prepared commentaries on the Fourteen Points, but when House issued his threat only the document prepared by Great Britain remained before the group. It dealt with only two matters. First, Britain insisted on reserving complete freedom of action on the freedom of the seas. Second, to satisfy the French, the Italians, and the Belgians, the British also required that the enemy make "compensation" for damages to civilians and property during the war. Wilson had not discussed this question in his various statements on war aims.[77] House now began to prepare the President for what he deemed necessary but acceptable concessions to the Entente powers. He was careful to assure Wilson that "You will have as free a hand after the armistice as you now have. It is exceedingly important that nothing be said or done at this time which may in

75. Wilson to House, October 30, 1918, Department of State, *1918*, supp. 1, 1:423.
76. House to Wilson, October 30, 1918, House Papers.
77. Trask, *United States in the Supreme War Council*, 168–69.

any way halt the armistice which will save so many thousands of lives."[78]

The President was not as yet fully prepared to accept the Colonel's plan and quickly responded to House's proposition:

I fully and sympathetically recognize the exceptional position and necessities of Great Britain with regard to the use of the seas for defence both at home and throughout the Empire and also realize that freedom of the seas needs careful definition and is full of questions upon which there is need of the freest discussion and the most liberal interchange of views, but I am not clear that the reply of the Allies . . . definitely accepts the principle of freedom of the seas and means to reserve only the free discussion of definitions and principles. . . . I cannot change what our troops are fighting for or consent to end with only European arrangements of peace. Freedom of the seas will not have to be discussed with Germany if we agree among ourselves beforehand but will be if we do not.

Wilson made one conciliatory statement in order to relieve the principal British concern. "Blockade is one of the many things which will require immediate redefinition in view of the many new circumstances of warfare developed by this war. *There is no danger of its being abolished.*"[79]

If the President remained firmly convinced that the United States must continue to insist on freedom of the seas, the navalist faction in the British War Cabinet was also determined to prevent any serious concessions. Balfour made this point clearly to Lloyd George, evidently concerned that the flexible Prime Minister might waver under specific American pressure for freedom of the seas and general French pressure for the relaxation of the naval terms of armistice. "We are after all a much greater *proportionate* factor in the Naval Situation than Foch & Co. are in the military Situation and (quite apart from merits) we have to consider the views of our own people and of the Dominions."[80]

House persevered in private discussions with important British officials, but could make no real progress:

I cannot bring them to the point of even admitting that the matter is one for discussion at the Peace Conference. It is the most extraordi-

78. House to Wilson, October 31, 1918, House Papers.
79. Wilson to House, October 31, 1918, Department of State, *1918*, supp. 1, 1:427–28. Italics added.
80. Balfour to Lloyd George, November 1, 1918, Drummond Papers, FO 800, book 329.

nary attitude I have ever known and is sure to lead to trouble if not modified. Reading said if they admitted that "freedom of the seas" was a matter for discussion, it was like a man admitting that another man could discuss with him whether or not his house was for sale. I immediately seized this illustration he uses to prove the British attitude, that is, they considered the seas as much their private property as a man does his own house. I asked if they did not consider the rules of warfare on land were a fit subject for discussion at a peace conference. Reading admitted this without question. Then, I asked, why not the rules of the sea also open to discussion[?][81]

Despite tireless efforts, the Colonel failed to break the opposition of Lloyd George. Even dire threats did not prevail. If Britain persisted in forcing a naval building contest, House argued, it would suffer the same eclipse as had Germany. "The United States had more resources, more men and more money than Great Britain and in a contest, Great Britain would lose." Lloyd George replied forcefully: "Great Britain would spend her last guinea to keep a navy superior to that of the United States or any other power. . . . No Cabinet official could continue in the Government in England who took a different position." House replied that the United States did not desire a naval building contest, but "it was our purpose to have our rights at sea adequately safe-guarded. . . . We did not intend to have our commerce regulated by Great Britain whenever she was at war."[82]

Finally the impasse was resolved; the result was in effect a British victory. On November 3, Lloyd George sent Colonel House a letter in which he agreed to discuss the question of freedom of the seas and its application at the peace conference, although he could not admit the principle.[83] House accepted this promise, despite an explicit threat from the President to outbuild the British Navy if Lloyd George did not bend. It was the only concession that he could wheedle from the determined British.[84] On November 4, the Supreme War Council approved the so-called pre-Armistice agreement, which became the political basis of the armistice. The agreement pointed out that "Clause 2, relating to what is usually described as freedom of the seas, is

81. House diary, November 2, 1918, House Papers.
82. House diary, November 4, 1918, House Papers.
83. Lloyd George to House, November 3, 1918, in Seymour, ed., *Intimate Papers*, 4:184–85.
84. House to Wilson, November 3, 1918, Department of State, *1918*, supp. 1, 1:448; Wilson to House, November 3, 1918, Wilson Papers.

open to various interpretations, some of which [the Allies] could not accept. They must therefore reserve to themselves complete freedom on this subject when they enter the peace conference."[85] House urged acceptance of the agreement; "Any other decision would cause serious friction and delay."[86]

President Wilson now faced a crucial decision. He had insisted in the strongest terms on the acceptance of freedom of the seas. His representative in Paris had fought doggedly for the principle. How would he respond to the reservation? After receiving news of the British exception, the President called Secretaries Daniels, Lansing, and Baker to the White House. Daniels described the outcome. "Great Britain raised question of freedom of the seas—did not understand exactly what is meant by it—and wished that left open to discussion." Wilson had threatened that if Britain proved intransigent, "we would use our facilities to build the greatest navy." France supported the principle of freedom of the seas. The group finally decided to accept the reservation, "inasmuch as G.B. agreed to all other 13 points & did not actually dissent from that in order to have unity." The President consoled himself with the resolve "in later conference to win over the other countries to our point of view, and secure it from League of Nations." Daniels was much disappointed, but Lansing and Baker believed that the situation would work itself out satisfactorily.[87]

Despite his strong views President Wilson proved capable of sustaining a significant setback in order to gain acceptance of most of his program. It was another signal concession in the distinguished history of Anglo-American negotiations, one that was ultimately in the best interest of both countries and in the interests of others as well, in that it was a major contribution to the achievement of the political agreement required as a basis of the military and naval terms of the armistice to be offered to Germany.

While the statesmen discussed the basic political question, the sailors concentrated on the disposition of the German fleet.[88] The

85. Transmitted to Washington in House to Wilson, November 4, Department of State 1918, supp. 1, 1:461.

86. House to Wilson, November 3, 1918, ibid., 457.

87. Daniels diary, November 4, 1918, E. David Cronon, ed., *The Cabinet Diaries of Josephus Daniels, 1913–1921* (Lincoln, 1963), 346.

88. The naval terms for Austria-Hungary posed less difficulty than the German terms. They were quite severe—even more so in relative terms than

American delegation had received firm instructions to support the policy that enemy vessels interned or surrendered should be disposed of not by terms of armistice but by the peace conference. The British delegation wished to negotiate terms of armistice as close as possible to the ultimate peace terms. This difference of view caused another extensive controversy in Paris. On November 1, House reported progress in his effort to bring about a relatively moderate settlement, informing Wilson that Clemenceau and Lloyd George both realized that the terms as proposed by the Allied Naval Council were "somewhat harsher than is necessary to fulfill your conditions regarding the making of it impossible for Germany to renew hostilities. We are modifying the naval program in the interest of commerce."[89] Lloyd George proposed a compromise: surrender the battle cruisers, light cruisers, and destroyers, but intern ten dreadnoughts.[90] Here was a logical approach, but House reckoned without the stubborn Sir Eric Geddes, who manifested his usual tendency to block compromise.

On the afternoon of November 1, the Allied Naval Council gathered to discuss proposed revisions in the naval terms. When the question of whether the German battleships to be detached from the High Sea Fleet were to be interned or surrendered came up for discussion Geddes admitted that the prime ministers had internment in mind but that he favored surrender. He would consider a reduction in the number of vessels to be surrendered only for the period of the armistice. He took this position because "Germany would inevitably look upon these ships as pawns

those ultimately imposed on Germany—although they were modified to some extent at the instigation of the civilian leaders. Austria-Hungary was forced to surrender 3 battleships, 3 light cruisers, 9 destroyers, 15 submarines, and a number of lesser craft. Austria-Hungary actually turned its fleet over to the Yugoslavs on November 1, but the Supreme War Council arranged for its surrender to the Allies at Corfu. The complete collapse of Austria-Hungary strengthened the Italian hand in the negotiations in Paris. Lord (Maurice) Hankey, *The Supreme Command: 1914–1918*, 2 vols. (London, 1961), 2:846–48; Minutes of the Eighth Session, SWC, Appendix B, November 4, 1918, SWC-WDA; Minutes of the Sixth Meeting, ANC, October 28–November 4, 1918, USNSF, QC file. American suspicions of Italian intentions are apparent in Planning Section Memorandum No. 63, "Proposed Decisions in the Event of a Revolution in Austriahungary [*sic*]—from a Naval View Point," November 3, 1918, USNSF, VA file.

89. House to Wilson, November 1, 1918, Department of State, *1918*, supp. 1, 1:438.

90. Seymour, *Intimate Papers*, 4:128–29.

at the Peace Negotiations when these arrived, which they might perhaps get back at the Peace since they had not been definitely taken away at the Armistice." Admiral Benson proposed that, if the battle cruisers and destroyers were surrendered, the dreadnoughts and perhaps the light cruisers might be interned. De Bon saw no reason to change the previous decision; he wanted to guarantee that Germany could not remain a first-class naval power. Citing Foch's view that the victory on land was decisive, he insisted that "eventual victory on our own terms was absolutely assured, and there was no reason whatever for timidity in fixing the terms of the Armistice." Geddes reported the view of the civilian leaders that it would be dangerous to risk refusal of the armistice over the seemingly minor distinction between surrender or internment of ten battleships, but he reiterated his opinion that the Allied Naval Council "must also consider the situation that would exist after the War if the ships now proposed to be interned were by any chance of negotiation to be returned to Germany." He saw the fundamental issue in simple terms. "The real question to decide, therefore, was whether the war was to be permitted to end with Germany at the same relative strength at sea as when she provoked it." When Benson claimed that there was no thought of returning the interned vessels, Geddes and Leygues both argued that the possibility of return might arise later. Benson remained firm during further debate, although he agreed that the German fleet should in no circumstances be permitted to retain the strength it possessed at present. De Bon complained bitterly that if the ships were interned and then returned to Germany, "It would appear that the Associated Navies had been half defeated, instead of being entirely victorious on the sea as was the fact."

The discussion turned to the question of ultimate disposal. Geddes reported his impression that ships surrendered would not be returned to the Germans but that ships interned would be the subject of future negotiations. Leygues of France and Grassi of Italy both spoke against internment, as did Iida, the Japanese representative. Geddes then raised an interesting question. How could the Allied Naval Council justify its demand that Germany turn over about half of its battleships to the victors if Foch insisted upon relatively less stringent military terms? Wemyss and Leygues argued that the German Navy would have been liquidated if it had come out and fought. They also drew distinctions between military and naval forces. Ships were much less easily replaced than troops. Geddes then raised another problem. How long must the war continue in order to obtain half of the German fleet? Sims exploded at this inquiry. "It would be almost as pertinent a question to ask how long it would take the Grand Fleet to capture Berlin." He felt that the Allied Naval Council should discuss terms with the permanent military representatives in order to be able to rely on proper understanding and coordination. Underlying this statement was naval irritation at what were considered the cavalier attitudes of the Supreme War Council and its military representatives. The conference concluded much as it began. The Allied Naval Council decided to reiterate its previous recommendation for the surrender of vessels, but Benson reserved the right to attach to the decision a letter expressing his view that "the 10 Battleships could, without danger, be required under the Armistice to be interned in Neutral Ports during the Armistice, their final disposition to be settled at the Peace Conference."[91]

On November 2, Rear Adm. G. P. W. Hope presented the naval views to the Supreme War Council. Germany had increased its strength in dreadnoughts from 13 to 25 during the war. It now had 9 battle cruisers as against the 4 in hand at the outset of hostilities. "It was clear then that unless the German Navy was reduced at the conclusion of peace by the numbers proposed by the Allied Naval Council, Germany would end the war in a far stronger position than at its commencement and she would remain a permanent menace to the peace of the world." Surrender was a better course than internment. Lloyd George wanted to delay a decision. If Austria left the war it would be possible to increase the severity of the terms for Germany. House demurred at delay, but when Clemenceau supported Lloyd George the decision was postponed until November 4.[92]

Foch remained convinced that the naval terms should be sufficiently moderate to ensure German acceptance of the armistice, since the military terms would guarantee victory on the land.[93] Sims informed his confidant at Queenstown, Admiral

91. Minutes of the Sixth Meeting, ANC, November 1, 1918, Fifth Session, USNSF, QC file.
92. Minutes of the Eighth Session of the Supreme War Council, Third Session, November 2, 1918, SWC-WDA. See also Seymour, ed., *Intimate Papers*, 4:132–33.
93. Foch, *Mémoires*, 284.

Bayly, that the Allies had two goals in drafting the naval terms. "One is that these terms shall be a demonstration to the German people that they have been definitely defeated, and the other is that they shall be such as to render it impossible for Germany to enter into a race of armaments with Allies in the immediate future."[94] The Board of Admiralty remained firm in its earlier opinions. On November 3, it recorded the view that "no question of internment of German men-of-war is admissible, and that the only condition to which the German men-of-war mentioned in the draft Terms of Armistice should be subjected, is surrender to the Allied and United States Navies."[95]

In Washington President Wilson faced a moment of decision. When Benson first reported the controversy over the disposition of the German fleet the President had indicated that the ships should be held in trust for disposition by the peace conference, but he had given no further guidance. After a White House conference reconsidered the issue Secretary Daniels was instructed to have Admiral Benson take a relatively firm line. Daniels's message to Paris lent additional support to the position that the American Admiral had already taken in the Allied Naval Council. "In advising Col. House with regard to the terms of armistice, you are authorized to use your judgment, but the President's judgment is clear that it ought to be distinctly understood that all armed vessels taken should be held in trust and that it is quite possible to [go] too far in demanding security."[96]

In London the War Cabinet discerned difficulties with the Lloyd George formula. "It was felt that such a distinction would be liable to misinterpretation by the public, both here and in Germany, and either all should be surrendered or all interned." One comforting bit of information was that the United States delegates "had made it quite clear that they did not contemplate the return of any warships to Germany as part of the Peace Terms."[97] In Paris, however, Lloyd George continued to advance the internment principle, receiving the willing support of Colonel House. Admiral Benson proposed that the ships to be taken

94. Sims to Bayly, November 3, 1918, USNSF, TD file.
95. Minutes of the Board of Admiralty, November 3, 1918, ADM 167, book 53.
96. Daniels to Sims, November 3, 1918, Cronon, ed., *Cabinet Diaries*, 345. Another copy, undated, is in USNSF, VA file.
97. Minutes of the War Cabinet (WC 496), November 4, 1918, CAB 23, book 8.

from Germany be sunk after their acquisition—a means of destroying German naval power without strengthening that of the Entente powers—but this suggestion was not accepted. He did obtain from Geddes a clear statement that the ships taken from Germany would not be added to the Entente navies after the war. Geddes also favored their destruction.[98]

The issue finally came to decision on November 4. At a hastily convened meeting of the Allied Naval Council, Admiral Hope reported on a conference of the prime ministers and Colonel House. He had been asked to convey to the Council a request from that group to reconsider and to report again on the alternatives of internment or surrender. A note from Admiral Benson, he reported, had "largely influenced the Conference in the course that they had subsequently taken." Benson's message had stressed the importance of making terms that would not preclude acceptance of the armistice by the enemy. "In order to save life, every possible effort should be made to submit such Terms as will satisfy the required conditions and at the same time bring an end to hostilities." Admiral Hope said that the Supreme War Council was not asking for advice—having decided in favor of interning all of the seventy-four ships in question—but rather whether the Allied Naval Council would support its view. Hope was not prepared to recommend acquiescence unless it was clearly understood that the ships would never be returned to Germany. Benson concurred in this course. De Bon held out for surrender, but the Japanese and Italian delegates supported internment. De Bon finally gave way, subject to the understanding that he reserved the right to express his opposition before the Supreme War Council. The decision of the Allied Naval Council accepted internment and disarmament of specified German vessels in neutral ports on the understanding that "this is an Armistice term only and that these Ships will not, under any circumstances, be returned to Germany on the conclusion of the Armistice, or at any time."[99]

When the Supreme War Council met later that day, Sir Eric Geddes reported the decision of the Allied Naval Council. After House reaffirmed that the heads of government desired intern-

98. Seymour, *Intimate Papers*, 4:131; copy of Benson to Daniels, undated but early November, 1918, House Papers.

99. Minutes of the Sixth Meeting, ANC, November 4, 1918, USNSF, QC file.

ment the First Lord said that the Allied Naval Council did not approve this course. De Bon then made his statement, placing on the record his opposition to internment in neutral ports. Clemenceau and Orlando supported him, but Benson thought internment quite manageable if the endeavor received the support of both belligerent coalitions. Finally Sir Eric Geddes spoke: "He wished once more to make it clear that the Allied Naval Council did not agree but accepted the decision of the ministers."[100] The argument was over. When the Allied Naval Council met briefly that day it provided that, if the victors had difficulty finding neutral ports for the internment procedure, they would utilize Allied ports.[101]

After the decision was reached Colonel House made a curious remark to Sir Eric Geddes when he said that he preferred the resolution for internment supported by Lloyd George, but "I would have followed England in the naval terms as I had followed Marshal Foch in the military terms."[102] If the Colonel really meant what he said, he would certainly have placed himself in opposition to the evident desires of the President. Wilson wanted terms sufficient to prevent a resumption of hostilities, but he also wanted them as restrained as that requirement would allow.

When Lloyd George reported the final outcome to the War Cabinet he sweetened the pill a bit by noting that all nations, including the United States, had agreed that Germany would not recover any of the ships interned in neutral ports. "In regard to this, America was absolutely committed, and their assent was duly recorded." He had not weakened with respect to freedom of the seas. The only peace terms discussed at Paris were freedom of the seas and indemnities, "the former because it was included in President Wilson's Fourteen Points, and the latter because it was omitted." He "had made it perfectly clear that we were unable to accept the proposals regarding the freedom of the seas, and that, if necessary, we should continue to fight alone rather than give way upon this point."[103] The Board of Admiralty,

100. Minutes of the Eighth Session, SWC, November 4, 1918, SWC-WDA.

101. Minutes of the Sixth Meeting, ANC, November 4, 1918, USNSF, QC file.

102. Seymour, *Intimate Papers*, 4:135–36.

103. Minutes of the War Cabinet (WC 497), November 5, 1918, CAB 23, book 8.

strongly opposed to the internment principle, contented itself with a sour statement that Lloyd George had known of its objections and that the Allied Naval Council in general and the First Lord in particular had expressed their dissent "in unmistakable terms."[104]

Sir Maurice Hankey believed that Lloyd George won a great victory for the British Navy at Paris.[105] The British Prime Minister assuredly gained the decision on the political question of the freedom of the seas. On the other hand the American preference for internment rather than surrender of the German ships to be detached from the High Sea Fleet at the time of the Armistice—along with the understanding that the final disposition of the enemy navies would be decided at the peace conference—was a considerable victory for Colonel House. Marshal Foch had lent important support. There is no direct evidence that an Anglo-American *quid pro quo* was worked out during the pre-Armistice negotiations, but the denouement had that effect. The controversy had an unfortunate outcome. It fed the generalized suspicions in both Britain and the United States vaguely entertained throughout the period of American intervention that the wartime partners planned competitive naval and commercial policies after the victory.

Sir Eric Geddes defended the naval terms against the angry criticisms of Admiral Beatty who reflected the feeling of the Grand Fleet, but he left Paris with deep suspicions of American intent.[106] In a memorandum entitled "United States Naval Policy," he recalled that when he had visited Washington he learned that President Wilson wished to utilize naval power to enforce the decisions of the League of Nations. He also discovered that the United States had continued its program of capital-ship construction "when the whole of her energies ought to have been thrown into building destroyers for convoying and escorting her own Army across the Atlantic." In Paris "the one outstanding feature" of the American naval attitude was that "nothing that we did there should in any way pre-judge or have any influence upon the disposal of any war ships of which Ger-

104. Minutes of the Board of Admiralty, November 7, 1918, ADM 167, book 55.
105. Hankey, *Supreme Command*, II, 858–63.
106. Geddes to Beatty, November 9, 12, 13, 1918, Geddes Papers, ADM 116, book 1809.

many may ultimately be deprived after Peace." His conclusion was that "President Wilson wished to create a sea power other than ours." The American had in mind three means of achieving this end: American building, use of former German ships, and combinations with other naval powers to achieve a force that was the "equivalent of, or greater than, the sea power of the British Empire." In a word, the President was "pursuing the 'Balance of Power' theory, which has hitherto so much influenced European policies, and applying it in sea power only to world politics."

Geddes reported an intriguing conversation with Colonel House in which he "got an interesting but rather unaccountable confirmation" of his interpretation. "Colonel House told me that the President had realised how sea-power had built up and maintained the British Empire, and how the absolutely essential importance of it had been demonstrated by the present War, and that the League of Nations would control recalcitrant members in the future by the exercise of sea-power." Geddes thought that this statement confirmed his dark suspicions of American intent; House was "the last man to suspect of thoughtlessly indiscreet utterances, but I am convinced that by the methods I have set out above, it is the aim and purpose of the President to reduce comparatively the preponderance in sea-power of the British Empire."[107]

If Geddes was highly suspicious of American plans for the future, the naval leaders of the United States harbored considerable reservations of their own regarding the intentions of the Entente powers. On November 4, the London Planning Section produced a memorandum entitled "United States Naval Interests in the Armistice Terms," which summarized its analysis of Allied motivation during the discussion of internment versus surrender. The memorandum began with the observation that the Great Powers, quite legitimately, sought "by the terms of armistice and by the terms of peace to strengthen to the maximum their position in the world. That they are following this policy astutely and consistently admits of no doubt." The planners believed that the Entente powers had struck a bargain between them. Britain and France would dictate the naval terms for

107. Geddes memorandum for the War Cabinet, "United States Naval Policy," November 7, 1918, ADM 116, book 1771.

Germany, and Britain and Italy would determine the Austrian terms, "Italy being accorded practically everything she asked for." The basis of this understanding was an agreement on the distribution of the German fleet. "In other words there have been councils on this subject of vital importance to us from which we have been excluded." In this connection the reader was reminded that "we have strong evidence of an agreement between Great Britain and Japan by which not less than five British dreadnoughts are to be transferred to Japan after the Peace."

A comparison of the various fleets followed, in which the planners argued that the German and Austrian fleets would be divided among the victorious powers as indicated:

	Dread- noughts	Battle Cruisers	Destroyers	Submarines
Great Britain	2	6	24	70
France	4	0	12	35
Italy	4	0	12	35
Japan	3	0	11	35
United States	0	0	0	0

A comparison of the five principal navies in terms of capital ships on the basis of this distribution revealed the following outcome:

	Capital Ships Before	Capital Ships After
Great Britain	43	51
United States	17	17
France	7	11
Japan	13	16
Germany	27	11

Japan and Britain together would have 67 capital ships to 17 for the United States. Britain alone would have three times as many as the United States. The conclusion was indisputable. "This in itself is an intolerable situation, but if we join to the mere recital of figures political considerations which we know have governed in the past, we shall see more clearly that our national interest demands that this distribution of vessels shall not take place."

The prospects for Anglo-American rivalry were now most considerable. Britain had already met in turn the challenges of Spain, Holland, France, and Germany. "A fifth commercial power, the greatest one yet, is now arising to compete for at least commercial equality with Great Britain. Already the signs of jealousy are visible. Historical precedent warns us to watch closely the moves we make or permit to be made." If the German and Austrian fleets were reduced by the armistice figures and those vessels were later destroyed, Great Britain would face no naval challenge in Europe. If that nation favored distribution, then "she has solely in view her future relations with the United States." The planners then quoted an unidentified Briton who had expressed the view that if the United States wanted freedom of the seas it would have to fight for it. It was necessary to provide for some "restraining influence" on the British fleet, because it would

be able to exert throughout the world an influence unknown to her in time of peace in the recent past. It may be right and proper that she shall have a greater Navy than any other European Power since she must by the very nature of her insular position assure to herself the opportunity to live by the importation of food. It is not, however, in the interest of humanity that she shall occupy so commanding a naval position that she may regulate the high seas through the world in accordance with her will.

On this basis the proper policy was (1) to arrange the destruction of the German and Austrian ships; (2) to prevent any augmentation of any fleet from the defeated navies; (3) to ensure that the German Navy remain strong enough "to exercise a distinctly conservative influence on the application of British Sea Power" by taking no more than ten German battleships; and (4) to prevent any transfer of British vessels to Japan, "as the move would be distinctly hostile to American interests."[108] This document expressed overtly that generalized American suspicion, muted throughout 1917–1918, that peace would breed Anglo-American rivalry. It also revealed once again the inveterate naval assumption that trade competition was at the root of international conflict.

Admiral Sims was relatively inactive during the pre-Armistice negotiations because of the presence of Colonel House and Admiral Benson. Desirous of rigorous exactions, he was generally pleased with the terms of armistice, assuring one of his correspondents that "as a matter of fact an armistice of this kind is only another name for practically unconditional surrender."[109]

108. Planning Section memorandum, "United States Interests in the Armistice Terms," November 4, 1918, USNSF, TX file.
109. Sims to Captain Hutch I. Cone, November 5, 1918, USNSF, TD file.

On the other hand he was suspicious of the proposed League of Nations, telling Admiral Bayly: "I am glad to say that I have not yet run across anybody who believes a League of Nations is possible, that is, in the accepted interpretation of the phrase of Simon Pure pacifists." He thought that some such organization would be created and would meet at least occasionally, concluding somewhat mordantly: "These are certainly interesting times in which we live."[110] Deeply acquainted with the stresses and strains of the wartime association, Sims looked forward to the future with some trepidation, but ultimately he could not repress his usual optimism, expressing his sentiments in a letter to Captain Train in Italy:

When you consider the spirit that is now being shown between the Allies and the practically complete distrust between all of the others, you can see that it does not offer very much encouragement for the type of "League of Nations" which must be based on the brotherhood of men. Since the Armistice was signed a new war began: it is going on here as furiously as it is down your way. You do not see much about it in the papers but it is going on all the same. It is the clash of national and economical interests that is going to give the trouble complicated to a certain extent by the people who have always lived up in the clouds. However, I have no doubt that they will reach a common conclusion in time. They must reach a common conclusion or else settle down to the same state of affairs that we had before the war.[111]

Sims remained true both to Admiral Mahan and to his Anglophile past.

Admiral Benson's report to Daniels stressed the difficulties he had entertained during the naval negotiations. In Paris he had taken the view that the original naval terms should "neither be humiliating in expression nor impossible of acceptance because of their severity"—a policy that had "practically isolated me from the rest of the group at once." He therefore "could not escape the impression that an agreement had been entered into by some of the other representatives as to the final disposition of the various vessels to be taken over, and I felt strongly, if such a thing were true, that every effort should be made to thwart it." Even as it was, he doubted that the Central Powers would have accepted the Armistice if domestic catastrophes had not loomed

110. Sims to Bayly, November 9, 1918, USNSF, TD file. A copy is in the Sims Papers.
111. Sims to Train, November 19, 1918, USNSF, TD file.

on the horizon. Like Sims he was concerned about the future of Anglo-American relations. "There is a marked feeling of anxiety, if not one of uneasiness, on the part particularly of our English friends in regard to our building program, both naval and commercial." He was taking steps to clarify the American position.[112]

       ❀   ❀   ❀   ❀

The necessity of close cooperation on land and on the sea among the Allied and Associated Powers in the face of a great German challenge of 1917–1918 certainly minimized various inter-Allied conflicts of interest, but with the approach of peace, political aspiration replaced military necessity as the prime determinant of national policies. When the prospect of an armistice materialized quite unexpectedly at the end of October, the western coalition gathered in Paris to define the demands it would make upon the Central Powers. The United States was intent upon an armistice severe enough to protect against the resumption of hostilities but moderate enough to maintain President Wilson's strong bargaining position into the postwar conference, at which gathering he hoped to make a settlement consonant with the Fourteen Points. Great Britain was intent upon a settlement that preserved the British Empire and the primacy of British sea power. Italy and France wished utterly to crush the land power of Austria and Germany and to establish strategic boundaries sufficient to ensure their security vis-à-vis central Europe into the distant future. The interests of the Entente powers brought them into various disagreements with certain of the Fourteen Points. Of all the European states Great Britain was least opposed to the President's program. Ironically, she was the principal beneficiary of the few concessions the United States was forced to make during the pre-Armistice negotiations.

By October, 1918, Wilson held the whip hand. The power of the United States was just materializing fully, while the Entente powers were close to exhaustion. The prospect of continued warfare filled European leaders with foreboding, because civil disturbance was conceivable in all the Allied countries as well as in the homelands of the Central Powers. The result was that Colonel House could generally force agreements in Paris that met

112. Benson to Sims, November 10, 1918, Daniels Papers. See also "Statement of Admiral Benson in Connection with His Mission of American Representative on the Interallied Naval Council," USNSF, UB file.

the basic desires of the President. The Allies accepted thirteen of the Fourteen Points as the basis of negotiations with the Central Powers and agreed at least to discuss freedom of the seas. If the military and naval terms were more severe than necessary to meet the President's minimum requirements, they were kept within tolerable limits.

The pre-Armistice conference was not without its drawbacks. It brought fully into the consciousness of American naval leaders suspicions that Great Britain entertained the prospect of injurious naval and commercial policies at the conclusion of the war. These forebodings found their mirror image in Great Britain, alarmed both by the American naval building program and the great expansion of the American merchant marine. The horrible memory of the death and destruction wrought by more than four years of the greatest war in the history of the race guaranteed that the peace negotiations would be long and difficult. Conflicts arising from differences in the war aims of the various victorious nations became evident in Paris even before Germany accepted the armistice terms. Already the fundamental dislocations wrought by the war years had begun to cast long shadows over the men who would make peace during 1919.

CHAPTER 10

CONCLUSION

Two days after the Armistice the Allied Naval Council gathered in emergency session and officially confirmed a decision actually made the previous day in Paris to anchor the German vessels soon to be surrendered in Scapa Flow rather than in a neutral port. "All the Members would appreciate that it was most undesirable that the German ships should be sent to Neutral Ports, and the proposal was full of difficulties."[1] Germany was in no position to resist this significant alteration in the naval armistice, plunged as it was into widespread revolutionary discontent. The government of Max von Baden desperately sought relaxation of the Allied blockade, but Marshal Foch responded only with the statement that the Allied and Associated Powers "contemplate the provisioning of Germany during the Armistice as shall be found necessary."[2] The lot of the vanquished is hard.

Very soon after the Armistice German submarines began to appear in Allied ports. At war's end Germany did not have as many as 160 U-boats in seaworthy condition. Apparently the Germans desisted from destroying the submarines because Foch had arranged for the occupation of Heligoland if the naval terms of the Armistice were not honored.[3] Ultimately 176 submarines were surrendered to the Allied and Associated Powers.[4]

1. Minutes of the Emergency Meeting, ANC, November 13, 1918, USNSF, QC file. A memorandum of the meetings in Paris on November 12, 1918, is attached to the minutes. For some minor changes in the naval terms of the armistice arranged by Marshal Foch, see Minutes of the Sixth Meeting, ANC, November 11, 1918, Seventh Session, Appendix K, USNSF, QC file.

2. German Minister of Foreign Affairs to Lansing, November 10, 1918, USNSF, VA file; Minutes of the Sixth Meeting, ANC, November 11, 1918, Appendix K, USNSF, QC file.

3. R. H. Gibson and Maurice Prendergast, *The German Submarine War, 1914–1918* (London, 1931), 330–31; Records of the German Foreign Ministry, Whaddon Hall microfilms, serial #9246H, frames E653456–653458.

4. For information on the surrender of the U-boats, see E. Freiherr von Spiegel, *U-Boot im Fegefeuer: Ein Buch ueber den U-bootkrieg 1914–1918* (Preetz/Holstein, n.d.), 289; Gibson and Prendergast, *German Sub-*

After various delays the German surface ships designated for internment arrived at Scapa Flow. The flotilla included 11 battleships, 5 battle cruisers, 8 light cruisers, and 50 destroyers. It lay in Scottish anchorage while the peace negotiations took place in Paris during the first six months of 1919. When the full extent of the exactions to be imposed upon Germany by the Treaty of Versailles became known, including surrender of the ships at Scapa Flow and dismantling of those in German hands, the commander of the German flotilla took decisive action. On June 17, 1919, he secretly ordered the ships prepared for scuttling. Vice Adm. Ludwig von Reuter based his decision on orders issued by the Kaiser in 1914 stating that German ships were not to be surrendered to the enemy under any circumstances. At 1:00 P.M. on June 21, his officers executed the order. Germany later claimed that some of the German seamen who had abandoned ship were rammed and machine-gunned while in lifeboats, resulting in casualties of nine killed and twenty-one wounded. Of the German vessels Britain preserved only 21 destroyers, 1 battleship, and 3 light cruisers. For its deed, Germany was forced to deliver 5 more light cruisers and some 400,000 tons of dredges, cranes, tugs, dry docks, and the like.[5] Thus ended in utter degradation the proudest era in German naval history.

Immediately after the Armistice both Britain and the United States began preparations for the naval aspect of the peace conference. Some observers saw no real problem ahead. A respected British journalist, Lionel Curtis, told General Bliss shortly after the Armistice that "It made no great difference to English feeling whether we [the United States] build a great navy or not; that we could lay five keels to their one if we wanted to, and that they

marine War, 275–80, 330–32; Hans Hugo Sokol, Oesterreich-Ungarns Seekrieg 1914–1918, 4 vols. (Vienna, 1933), 4:737, 743; Robert M. Grant, U-Boats Destroyed: The Effect of Anti-Submarine Warfare, 1914–1918 (London, 1964).

5. For information on the events at Scapa Flow, see "Denkschrift ueber Britische Voelkerrechtsverletzungen begangen an der Besetzung der in Scapa Flow versenkten deutsche Flotte," (Berlin, 1921) Tambach collection, TA-112-D 64936; Seth P. Tillman, Anglo-American Relations at the Paris Peace Conference (Princeton, 1961), 172; Karl Galster, England, Deutsche Flotte und Weltkrieg (Kiel, 1925), 166; Arthur J. Marder, From the Dreadnought to Scapa Flow: The Royal Navy in the Fisher Era, 1904–1919, 5 vols., Victory and Aftermath (January 1918–June 1919) (London, 1970) 5:275–93.

would still regard them all as being in a common pool to attain a common end."[6] Captain Pratt and some of his associates in the Navy Department sought escape from difficulty during the peace negotiations by proposing to establish a League of Nations navy based on Anglo-American parity.[7] Most of the responsible naval officials, however, girded their loins for a serious conflict of wills.

The United States began its planning even before the Armistice; on November 7, the Planning Section produced a memorandum on "Freedom of the Seas," generally reiterating those classic aspects of international law on which American statesmen had taken their stand since the famous "Plan of 1776." Absolute freedom of the seas was deemed impractical, but the rules of visit, search, blockade, contraband, and other traditional principles enunciated by the United States as recently as the period of American neutrality from 1914 to 1917 were all solemnly endorsed by the planners. The Navy Department continued to press its extensive building program. Daniels complained when someone opposed this effort; it was required "because we need to strengthen our Navy and as a good instrument to use at the Peace Conference."[8] A Planning Section memorandum on the "Building Programme," issued late in November, 1918, agreed thoroughly with the estimate of the Secretary.[9] The General Board and the Washington planning committee reiterated some old and some new arguments for naval expansion. Naval leaders had to bear in mind the likelihood that world conditions would remain unsettled for some time to come; the millennium was hardly at hand: "World history in the past has shown swift and startling changes in international relations, and the intense commercial competition that will inevitably take place after the war is to be considered as cause of future friction among the great nations."[10] Moreover, "Navies must be the

6. Bliss diary, December 22, 1918, Bliss Papers.
7. Pratt to Sims, November 12, 1918, USNSF, TD file. A copy of the plan for the proposed League of Nations navy, dated November 11, 1918, is in the Daniels Papers.
8. Planning Memorandum No. 70, "Freedom of the Seas," November 7, 1918, USNSF, TX file; Daniels diary, November 20, 1918, in E. David Cronon, ed., *The Cabinet Diaries of Josephus Daniels, 1913–1921* (Lincoln, 1963), 350.
9. This document is analyzed in Chapter 9. Planning Memorandum No. 67, "Building Programme," November 21, 1918, USNSF, TX file.
10. Planning Committee to Chief of Naval Operations, November 27, 1918, Records of the General Board.

principal supports of a League of Nations, and the United States, from its influence and power, will be called upon to contribute a very large share of the international police force which will have to be created."[11]

In Britain the Admiralty continued to prepare its case against the freedom of the seas, but it manifested a desire to avoid head-on conflict with the United States.[12] A memorandum for the Operations Committee of the Admiralty, undoubtedly prepared by Sir Eric Geddes, took up the British building program. The general situation was too fluid to permit hard decisions, but possibly the building program could be kept within reasonable limits. The American naval program would be cancelled; it was difficult to believe that within three to six months Britain would not "come to some agreement with America, either for a Naval holiday or for a limitation of armaments." In addition, "We have more than a moiety of the second most powerful Navy in the world interned in our Ports."[13] Some confirmation of this analysis came during a conversation between Lord Grey and an American official. Paul Cravath thought that if Britain were to transfer some "first-class fighting ships" to the United States, "the effect might be enormous and might lead to the present American programme being very greatly diminished." Also Cravath argued that "if Great Britain and the United States came to an agreement to have equality of naval forces the question of the freedom of the seas would no longer be pressed. He quite understood that it was necessary for us [Great Britain] to maintain a standard ensuring us completely against European aggression."[14] In these fragmentary considerations one discerns the genesis of the arrangements forthcoming not only in Paris during 1919, but also in Washington during the naval conference of 1921–1922.[15]

11. Badger to Benson, December 2, 1918, Records of the General Board.

12. Admiralty memorandum for the War Cabinet, "The Freedom of the Seas," December 21, 1918, ADM 116, book 1772.

13. Memorandum for the Operations Committee, November 22, 1918, ADM 116, book 1604.

14. Drummond to Balfour, November 27, 1918, Drummond Papers, FO 800, book 329.

15. For valuable information of relatively recent vintage, see Warner R. Schilling, "Admirals and Foreign Policy, 1913–1919," Ph. D. diss., Yale University, 1953; Mary Klachko, "Anglo-American Naval Cooperation, 1918–1922," Ph. D. diss., Columbia University, 1962; Tillman, *Anglo-American Relations at the Paris Peace Conference*. Of course, these ques-

❁   ❁   ❁   ❁

During 1917–1918 the United States accepted the basic strategic decisions of the European Allies—both on land and sea. General Pershing, with the full support of the government in Washington, did not vary from the Entente view that the land war should be waged primarily on the Western Front against the principal enemy—Germany. Similarly, Admiral Sims never wavered in his support of the British belief that the central naval effort should be the maintenance of a blockade of the Central Powers, supplemented by strenuous antisubmarine policies to frustrate the enemy counterblockade. Pershing's opposition to the amalgamation of American forces into European formations was no contradiction of grand strategy, any more than was Sims's early interest in convoy operations.

Two fundamental realities led American leaders to accept European leadership in respect to grand strategy:

1. No opposition to European ideas emerged within the leadership elite of the American military and naval establishment. The absence of civil-military conflict within the American Government during World War I stemmed from the simple fact that few really important differences of view ever materialized; civilians agreed with warriors that Entente directions were sound. The principal desideratum of the United States was the defeat of Germany, an outcome that would prepare the way for the President's achievement of his political objectives. Germany could best be defeated by concentrating land power in France and by concentrating naval power against the enemy submarines in the Atlantic and the Mediterranean. Naval leaders almost universally persisted in the assumption that success against the submarine would guarantee victory.

2. The fundamental strategic decisions of the Allies did not endanger American political objectives. President Wilson, of course, was unwilling to condone military and naval activities that might prejudice his peace plans. He wanted to encompass the defeat of the Central Powers without surrendering his freedom of diplomatic action to the Allies. Concentration in France and antisubmarine activities on the surrounding seas seemed unlikely to prejudice the American bargaining position at the

tions are also dealt with in the older standard accounts of the Paris Peace Conference and the Washington Naval Conference.

end of the war. Wilson was capable of frustrating, delaying, or minimizing military and naval plans—like those for massive inter-Allied intervention in Russia—when he deemed them militarily or politically unwise. As it happened few such difficulties came to the fore during 1917–1918. Wilson generally sought to avoid undue interference with military and naval decisions, as long as those decisions comported with his political designs— the reason why he plays a modest role in the events that have been chronicled in this book.

Americans were preoccupied with military and naval means rather than ends during 1917–1918. With respect particularly to naval activity this concern dictated emphasis on methods of achieving effective Anglo-American cooperation at sea. Given this circumstance the choice of Admiral Sims as Force Commander in European waters turned out quite well. A notorious Anglophile, he also possessed the qualities of leadership— courage and firmness—required in the situation. On the other hand, the presence of Admiral Benson as Chief of Naval Operations was somewhat unfortunate, precisely because he was deeply suspicious of the British and an uninspiring leader. To some extent historic Anglo-American rivalry interfered with effective cooperation at sea, but this constraint became relatively unimportant during the height of the naval war. The two great English-speaking nations kept disputation at a minimum not only because of common danger but also because of their basic agreement on grand strategy.

In making decisions concerning naval activity in the Atlantic Ocean the British and the Americans acted largely on their own, and their monopoly of the decision-making process was an important reason why they were able to conduct effective operations in that area. London and Washington occasionally disagreed about antisubmarine methods, building programs, and the like, but each government recognized its dependence upon the other. Great Britain understood that wholehearted American support was essential to victory. The United States recognized that it could not bring its power to bear in Europe unless the submarine menace was controlled—a feat that could be accomplished only by extraordinary exertion on the part of the British Navy. Antisubmarine operations in Atlantic waters were brought to a successful conclusion because the combined Anglo-American Navy had the necessary power and the two nations were able to achieve a degree of coordination sufficient to gain their objectives.

The situation in the Mediterranean Sea was in stark contrast. Those Allied Powers engaged there—Italy, France, and Great Britain—were in deep disagreement over both policy and strategy. The most irrepressible obstacle to cooperation against the common enemy was Franco-Italian rivalry, but Anglo-Italian and Anglo-French differences also played a considerable role in precluding a truly well-organized naval effort. Imperial obligations bound Great Britain to the advocacy of policies designed to protect its communications to Asia. Italy and France both hoped to improve their power positions in the Mediterranean at the expense not only of the enemy, but also Great Britain and each other. A common interest and a common danger were not sufficient to overwhelm significant conflicts of interest. The United States, a relatively disinterested party, attempted to serve as an honest broker in the Allied Naval Council, but no amount of energy and good will succeeded in breaking down the welter of inter-Allied rivalry that frustrated or debilitated practically every plan of cooperation in the Mediterranean. Historians have paid little attention to the Allied Naval Council because it concentrated much of its activity on Mediterranean questions and had little to show for its efforts when the war came to its end.

The special circumstances of 1917–1918 imposed a peculiar relationship between Sims in London and his superiors in Washington. The American fleet was not deployed as an independent entity and instead became engaged in various operations supportive of the British fleet and ultimately of the Allied armies engaged on the land. It undertook no independent fleet operations. The naval staff in Washington had to concentrate primarily on organizing forces for disposition by Admiral Sims in accord with basic strategic and tactical decisions made by the British Admiralty.[16] Sims's own list of American naval accomplishments during the war reflects the unusual character of the

16. See the statement of Captain William V. Pratt quoted in Josephus Daniels, *The Wilson Era: Years of War and After, 1917–1923* (Chapel Hill, N.C., 1946), 502–3. See also Frothingham, *Naval History of the Great War*, 3:28–29, 122, 129; William Sowden Sims, in collaboration with Burton J. Hendrick, *The Victory at Sea* (Garden City, N.Y., 1920), 245–46; Daniels to Geddes, August 20, 1918, Geddes Papers, ADM 116, book 1809.

national effort. The Navy transported about 45 per cent of the American troops sent to Europe—about 900,000 men. It provided 27 per cent of the convoy escort; supplied 12 per cent of the battleship strength of the British Grand Fleet; laid 80 per cent of the great barrage in the North Sea; and maintained twenty-three naval stations distributed along the French, Irish, English, and Italian coasts. To conduct its operations the Navy placed 368 ships in European waters, including 128 submarine chasers and 85 auxiliary vessels. The force aggregated 70,000 men and 5,000 officers.[17]

The strong-willed Sims naturally manifested the outlook of a theater commander in his dealings with Washington. During the war he managed for the most part to keep his temper, but after the Armistice he finally exploded upon reading a statement by the Navy Department that seemed to him to misrepresent the realities:

The whole trouble seemed to have been the inability of you people at home to adopt and play up to the very mission that you now state . . . , that is, to treat our Service and our facilities and material as "reserves" and to throw them in wherever we could bolster up in any way a weak spot in the forces of our allies over here. It meant nothing else but disintegration of our Fleet, and those bald words seemed to be the stumbling block. We did not seem to be able to get away from our habits of peace, the Fleet must have its Train, although there were excellent Navy Yards there which could easily have taken the place of the Train—Navy Yards which were unmolested by the enemy in any way. Even to this day, with one or two outstanding exceptions, our forces have not been thrown into the game as they might have been.[18]

In the stress of the emergency Sims had abandoned the hallowed doctrine of Adm. Alfred Thayer Mahan—to develop and deploy the battle fleet as a complete and independent entity. He was convinced that the dead hand of the past had precluded a comparable reaction at home. Like so many theater commanders before and since, Sims sometimes failed to recognize that the general headquarters in Washington had to consider all manner of contingencies.

Ironically, the very qualities that sometimes caused difficulties with the Navy Department and even with President Wilson

17. Sims to Navy Department, November 13, 1918, USNSF, WV file.
18. Sims to Pratt, January 28, 1919, USNSF, TD file.

made Admiral Sims uniquely acceptable to the British Government. He was not the least of America's contributions to inter-Allied unity during 1917–1918. Sims realized that allies must sometimes put aside particular concerns in the interest of common victory. He was able to "ignore such secondary considerations as national pride, naval prestige, and personal ambitions."[19] Sometimes he could not accept the fact that national objectives might on occasion force less than wholehearted commitment to coalition objectives. Such contradictions are inherent in the system of nation-states. Wrangling between the United States and Great Britain was relatively restrained because the British could simply not afford to antagonize the Americans beyond a certain point and because there was certainly at least a broad correspondence of political viewpoints between the two nations.

At the outset of this study the principal question posed for examination was the nature of relations between American policy and naval strategy, given the inter-Allied context of 1917–1918. The general relation is clear: American sea power was organized to help encompass the defeat of the German submarine offensive—in close cooperation with the naval forces of Great Britain—because victory would presumably place President Wilson in the position of being able to dictate a peace settlement of his own devising. The principal American associate—Great Britain—had already defined the prime naval objective, although of course with different political aims in mind. Basic naval disagreements between Great Britain and the United States did not materialize precisely because both countries saw the requirements of sea warfare in broadly the same light. In short the United States did not have to define grand naval strategy when it entered the war; Britain had already accomplished that task.

In 1917 the United States Navy provided what emergency assistance it could to frustrate the extraordinary submarine offensive of Germany in the Atlantic Ocean and the Mediterranean Sea while it prepared to play a vastly increased role in the naval war during the decisive stages of the conflict.

In 1918 the planning of 1917 had a measurable impact, although the sudden and unexpected termination of the struggle

19. Sims, *Victory at Sea*, 246.

in November came before the American naval effort could materialize to its fullest extent.

The war interfered with the development of a "balanced" American Navy because the United States bowed to the insistent argument of British leaders—strongly supported by Admiral Sims—that construction of capital ships must be deferred in favor of antisubmarine craft. On the other hand, the British clearly recognized that the United States might well improve its commercial potential in world markets as a consequence of events during 1917–1918. Wartime tensions indicate why naval building programs and international trade questions were so important in the calculations of the great naval powers during negotiations in Paris during 1919 and in Washington during 1921–1922.

Anglo-American differences began to emerge as the war came to its end, when the necessity of unity had begun to pass. Admiral Sims played a limited role in the postwar naval negotiations. His last public activity was an acrimonious controversy with Secretary Daniels in 1920. He was equipped to further Anglo-American cooperation, not conflict.

The dislocations created by World War I ultimately brought to light international problems of far greater complexity and danger than it was supposed to resolve. The naval-political history of 1917–1918 was part of the making of those postwar tensions. Of course once international violence breaks out, some methods of conducting naval-political negotiations are more efficacious than others. An understanding of successes and failures during World War I might be instructive to those who wish to concert constructive actions at some point in the future.

BIBLIOGRAPHICAL ESSAY

This study rests on certain extensive archival collections of un-published diplomatic and naval records. Since the work stresses Anglo-American relations, the chief reliance is upon governmental and private repositories in the United States and Great Britain. I have generally refrained from listing below certain materials that are of great importance for an understanding of international politics and strategy during World War I but not of particular use for investigations of naval-political questions during 1917–1918. A number of items of this nature are mentioned in the reference notes, but for particularly extensive listings, see the bibliographies in Seth P. Tillman, *Anglo-American Relations at the Paris Peace Conference of 1919* (Princeton, 1961); Lawrence E. Gelfand, *The Inquiry* (New Haven, 1963); Paul Guinn, *British Strategy and Politics: 1914 to 1918* (London, 1965); and N. Gordon Levin, Jr., *Woodrow Wilson and World Politics* (New York, 1968).

UNITED STATES

The principal United States material is in the Naval Records Collection of the Office of Naval Records and Library, particularly the subject file for the years 1911–1927, included in Record Group 45, housed in the National Archives, Washington, D.C. Subject headings such as Adm. William S. Benson's personal correspondence (UB file); Adm. William S. Sims's personal correspondence (TD file); the Records of the Allied Naval Council (QC file); "General Plans and Naval Policies, U.S. Naval Forces in Europe. . . ," (TP file); and "Joint Arrangements, U.S. and other Navies, including cooperation and lack of cooperation," (TT file); are to be found in the collection. These and other materials have become available only in recent years, and historians have only begun to utilize them. For highly important supplementary material, one may consult the Records of the General Board of the Navy and the war portfolios of that agency in the Archives of the Naval History Division, held by the Naval Historical Foundation, Washington, D.C.

More familiar to historians are the diplomatic records of the United States for this period. Two volumes in the supplement to the *Foreign*

Relations series entitled *The World War* proved particularly useful: United States Department of State, *Papers Relating to the Foreign Relations of the United States, 1917, The World War*, supplement 2, vol. 1 (Washington, 1932), and *Papers Relating to the Foreign Relations of the United States, 1918, The World War*, supplement 1, vol. 1 (Washington, 1933). For the most part these documents appear in the much more extensive collection of material on microfilm prepared by the National Archives, Washington, D.C., *Records of the Department of State Relating to World War I and Its Termination, 1914–29* (Microcopy No. 367, 1962). Other published and microfilmed records of the Department of State—such as the annual volumes in the *Foreign Relations* series and microfilm collections of materials relating to specific states in the decimal files for the period 1910–1929— do not contain much information on naval-political questions.

Among sources available for President Woodrow Wilson are his voluminous private papers deposited at the Library of Congress, Washington, D.C., and his published state papers edited by Ray Stannard Baker and William E. Dodd, *The Public Papers of Woodrow Wilson: War and Peace*, vol. 1 (New York, 1927), 6 vols. The appropriate volume of Baker's standard biography also reprints a great deal of source material: *War Leader*, vol. 8 (New York, 1939), *Woodrow Wilson: Life and Letters*, 8 vols. The standard biographies of Wilson give little or no attention to naval-political questions.

Materials for members of President Wilson's Cabinet are plentiful. The private papers of Secretary of State Robert Lansing are in the Library of Congress, and some of his memoranda are reprinted in *War Memoirs of Robert Lansing, Secretary of State* (Indianapolis, 1935). A selection of his papers is in United States Department of State, *Papers Relating to the Foreign Relations of the United States: The Lansing Papers, 1914–1920*, 2 vols. (Washington, 1939–1940). The Papers of Assistant Secretary of State Breckinridge Long are also of some use and are in the Library of Congress. Of far greater importance than either the Lansing or Long collections are the Papers of Edward M. House in the Yale University Library. The important biography edited by Charles Seymour must be used with caution: *Into the War*, vol. 3 (Boston, 1928), *The Intimate Papers of Colonel House*, 4 vols. The Papers of the Counselor of the Department of State, Frank L. Polk, are also in the Yale University Library. The Private Papers of Secretary of the Navy Josephus Daniels are in the Library of Congress; his manuscript diary has now been beautifully edited by E. David Cronon, *The Cabinet Diaries of Josephus Daniels, 1913–1921* (Lincoln, 1963). For additional information, see the Secretary's own memoir history of the First World War entitled *The Wilson Era: Years of War and After, 1917–1923* (Chapel Hill, N.C.,

1946), and also Carroll Kilpatrick, ed., *Roosevelt and Daniels: A Friendship in Politics* (Chapel Hill, 1952). The Private Papers of Secretary of War Newton D. Baker are in the Library of Congress. A detailed study of the Secretary during World War I, which revises earlier efforts by Frederick Palmer and C. H. Cramer, is Daniel Beaver, *Newton D. Baker and the American War Effort, 1917–1919* (Lincoln, 1966). Materials for Daniels's chief assistant are the Papers of Franklin D. Roosevelt at the Franklin D. Roosevelt Library, Hyde Park, New York. The most useful biographical account is Frank Freidel's *Franklin D. Roosevelt: The Apprenticeship* (Boston, 1952), which makes good use of the Hyde Park information.

The Private Papers of Ambassador to Great Britain Walter Hines Page are in the Houghton Library of Harvard University, Cambridge, Massachusetts. Some of these are reprinted in Burton J. Hendrick, *The Life and Letters of Walter Hines Page*, vol. 2 (Garden City, N.Y., 1922), 3 vols. A careful modern biography that corrects the Hendrick volumes in important respects is Ross Gregory's *Walter Hines Page: Ambassador to the Court of Saint James's* (Lexington, 1970). A less useful published source is *The War Memoirs of William Graves Sharp: American Ambassador to France 1914–1918*, edited by Warrington Dawson (London, 1931).

Scattered information of marginal use for this study is found in the private papers of two prominent Republicans—Chandler P. Anderson and Elihu Root—located in the Library of Congress, and in a collection of letters of the Secretary of the Interior edited by Anne Wintermute Lane and Louise Herrick Wall, *The Letters of Franklin K. Lane: Personal and Political* (Boston, 1922). The memoir of the Secretary of Agriculture is David F. Houston, *Eight Years with Wilson's Cabinet: 1913 to 1920: With a Personal Estimate of the President*, 2 vols. (Garden City, N.Y., 1926).

Secondary works on the general question of American naval participation in World War I, particularly ones that deal with strategic and political questions, are few and far between. The standard general account is Thomas G. Frothingham, *The Naval History of the World War*, 3 vols., *The United States in the War, 1917–1918* (Cambridge, 1926). Two useful dissertations are Warner Roller Schilling, "Admirals and Foreign Policy, 1913–1919," Ph. D. diss., Yale University, 1953, published in microfilm by University Microfilms, No. 54–11, 383; and Mary Klachko, "Anglo-American Naval Competition, 1918–1922," Ph. D. diss., Columbia University, 1962, published in microfilm by University Microfilms, No. 63–3685. The Papers of Chief of Naval Operations, Adm. William S. Benson, have become available at the Library of Congress, but there is no memoir or biography. The private papers of the American naval commander in

Europe, Adm. William S. Sims, are deposited in the Archives of the Naval Historical Division, held by the Naval Historical Foundation in Washington, D.C. Sims published a striking memoir in collaboration with Burton J. Hendrick, *The Victory at Sea* (Garden City, N.Y., 1920). Elting E. Morison's biography, *Admiral Sims and the Modern American Navy* (Boston, 1942), is remarkably astute despite the fact that government archives were closed when he completed his research. Tracy B. Kittredge produced a highly polemical defense of Admiral Sims in the wake of the naval investigation of 1920 entitled *Naval Lessons of the Great War: A Review of the Senate Naval Investigation of the Criticisms of Admiral Sims of the Policies and Methods of Josephus Daniels* (Garden City, N.Y., 1921). The record of the investigation itself, by the Naval Affairs Committee of the United States Congress, is *Naval Investigation, Hearings before subcommittee*, 2 vols. (Washington, 1921). The Papers of Capt. (later Adm.) William V. Pratt, Sims's closest associate in the Navy Department, are in the Archives, Naval Historical Foundation, Washington, D.C.

Certain military records supplement the naval materials. The archives of the American section of the Supreme War Council are found in the Records of the American Expeditionary Forces, Record Group 120, in the National Archives. Some records of the Supreme War Council are reproduced in the microfilm (M 367) cited above. For important military policy papers, see *Policy-Forming Documents*, vol. 2 (Washington, 1948), *United States Army in the World War*, 17 vols. The Private Papers of the American commander in Europe, Gen. John J. Pershing, are in the Library of Congress. Of interest also is the General's memoir, *My Experiences in the World War*, 2 vols. (New York, 1931). The Papers of the American Military Representative at the Supreme War Council, Gen. Tasker H. Bliss, are also in the Library of Congress. For a work on political-military history that gives much attention to Bliss, see David F. Trask, *The United States in the Supreme War Council: American War Aims and Inter-Allied Strategy, 1917–1918* (Middletown, Conn., 1961). The Papers of Chief of Staff Gen. Peyton C. March in the Library of Congress are disappointing. For a biography, see Edward M. Coffman, *The Hilt of the Sword: The Career of Peyton C. March* (Madison, 1966), and for a memoir, see Peyton C. March, *The Nation at War* (Garden City, N.Y., 1932).

GREAT BRITAIN

The principal British information is drawn from the recently opened records of the War Cabinet, the Foreign Office, and the Admiralty, available at the Public Record Office, London, England. The principal Cabinet materials include the Minutes of the War Cabinet and the Imperial War Cabinet, cited in the reference notes as CAB 23. These detailed accounts of discussions are supplemented by various papers and reports. An important category of Foreign Office papers is FO 800, which includes collections of individual statesmen's manuscripts. These collections are mentioned individually below. Some important information was located in the political correspondence of the Foreign Office, cited in the reference notes as FO 371. The most useful Admiralty collection was ADM 137, which consists of collections of documents on multifarious subjects collected for use by the authors of official naval histories. ADM 116 includes the minutes of the Board of Admiralty.

The Private Papers of Prime Minister David Lloyd George are deposited in the Beaverbrook Library, London, England. The war leader's memoirs are of great importance, although they must be utilized with caution, particularly *War Memoirs of David Lloyd George: 1917* (New York, 1934). Two collections of papers of Foreign Secretary Arthur James Balfour are available: one in FO 800, in the Public Record Office, and the other in the British Museum, London, England. The several biographies of Balfour proved relatively unrewarding for the study of naval-political questions, although Balfour was a former First Lord of the Admiralty. Some papers of Balfour's assistant, Sir Eric Drummond, are in FO 800. Two collections of the papers of Sir Robert Cecil, an important official in the Foreign Office, are also available, one in the Foreign Office Records, FO 198, and the other in the British Museum, but the latter collection proved unimportant for this study.

Among the papers of British overseas representatives are those of the Ambassador to the United States during 1917—Sir Cecil Spring Rice—in FO 800. For additional information, one may consult *The Letters and Friendships of Sir Cecil Spring Rice*, vol. 2 (Boston, 1929). The Papers of Spring Rice's successor, Lord Reading, are in FO 800. Also in FO 800 are the Papers of the Ambassador to France, Lord Bertie of Thame. Of special importance are the Papers of the chief of British intelligence operations in the United States, Sir William Wiseman, in the Yale University Library, New Haven, Connecticut, but these have been exploited effectively by Wilton B. Fowler in his dissertation entitled "Sir William Wiseman and the Anglo-American War Partnership, 1917–1918," Ph. D. diss., Yale University, 1966, published in microfilm by University Microfilms, No. 66–14, 982. A revised version has appeared in print entitled *British-American Relations, 1917–1918: The Role of Sir William Wiseman* (Princeton, 1969), one of the most important contributions to the history of

Anglo-American relations for this period. Some information on the activities of British statesmen is found in Frederick B. Maurice, *Lessons of Allied Co-operation: Naval, Military, and Air, 1914–1918* (New York, 1942); Lord (Maurice) Hankey, *The Supreme Command: 1914–1918* (London, 1956); and Arthur Willert, *The Road to Safety: A Study in Anglo-American Relations* (London, 1952).

For British naval leaders, in addition to the voluminous information available in the general files of the Admiralty, there are collections for the officer who served as First Sea Lord in 1917, Admiral Sir John Jellicoe, in the British Museum, and for the First Lord of the Admiralty, Sir Eric Geddes, in ADM 116, books 1804–1810. Useful information about military activity is in the Records of the British Section of the Supreme War Council found in the Cabinet Papers, CAB 25, and in the following publications: Henry Newbolt, *History of the Great War on Official Documents by Direction of the Historical Section of the Committee of Imperial Defense: Naval Operations*, vols. 4–5 (London, 1928–1931), 5 vols.; C. E. Callwell, *Field-Marshal Sir Henry Wilson: His Life and Diaries*, vol. 2 (London, 1927), 2 vols.

The most important recent contribution to the naval history of World War I is the magisterial work on the Royal Navy in five volumes by Arthur J. Marder, *From the Dreadnought to Scapa Flow: The Royal Navy in the Fisher Era, 1904–1919*. Vol. 4, entitled *1917: Year of Crisis* (London, 1969), and vol. 5, entitled *Victory and Aftermath (January 1918–June 1919)* (London, 1970), cover the period of this study. The author's assiduous pursuit of materials and his balanced judgment place all future scholars of World War I in his debt. As it happens Marder's special preoccupation with the Royal Navy led him to concentrate for the most part on subject matter other than that taken up in this study. Readers who wish to explore British naval activity in depth as an aspect of Anglo-American relations will find in Marder's last two volumes detailed treatment of events which are given only limited space in this study, such as the shifting leadership of the British Admiralty during 1917–1918, the details of convoy operations, and fleet activity.

FRANCE

The only archival materials open for scholarly study in France while this research was in progress were certain records of the French Ministry of Marine, held by the Service Historique de la Marine, Paris, France. The materials there of greatest import for this study are in the Es series, which includes the Papers of the Naval Staff (État-Major General) secretariat. Some records of the French Section of the Allied Naval Council are located in this collection, useful principally for the study of Mediterranean questions. For detailed information on French naval activity, consult the multivolume work by Capt. Adolphe Laurens, *La Guerre Sous-marine* (n.p., n.d.), a publication of the Service Historique de l'État-major de la Marine, a set of which is in the library of the Service Historique. Laurens published a one-volume summation of his work on the submarine war entitled *Histoire de la Guerre Sous-marine Allemande (1914–1918)* (Paris, 1930). Some reference is made to naval-political questions in the memoir of the Supreme Commander, Marshal Ferdinand Foch, *Mémoires pour Servir à l'Histoire de la Guerre, 1914–1918*, vol. 2 (Paris, 1928), 2 vols.

GERMANY AND AUSTRIA-HUNGARY

No truly systematic effort has been made herein to analyze German naval-political activity anew during the First World War, but certain archival collections on microfilm proved useful in developing background information on the German side of the war, particularly the Records of the German Foreign Ministry for 1917–1918, available from the National Archives, Washington, D.C., including those filmed at St. Antony's College and at Whaddon Hall. Also available in this country is the German Naval Record Collection of the U.S. Naval History Division, Washington, D.C., known as the Tambach collection. This material has now been transferred to the National Archives.

Among memoirs and diaries available for important German officials the following were of greatest utility for the present study: Admiral Reinhard Scheer, *Germany's High Sea Fleet in the World War* (London, 1920), by the commander of that force; the diaries of the Chief of the Naval Cabinet, edited by Walter Goerlitz, *The Kaiser and His Court: The Diaries, Note Books and Letters of Admiral Georg Alexander von Mueller, Chief of the Naval Cabinet, 1914–1918* (London, 1961); Admiral Albert Hopmann, *Das Kriegstagebuch eines deutschen Seeoffiziers* (Berlin, 1925); General Wilhelm Groener, *Lebenserinnerungen: Jugend; Generalstab; Weltkrieg* (Göttingen, 1957), edited by Friedrich Freiherr von Gaertringen; the recollections of the principal German commander, Gen. Erich Ludendorff, *Meine Kriegserinnerungen, 1914–1918* (Berlin, 1919); certain papers and diaries of an important civilian leader, Walther Rathenau, *Briefe*, 2 vols. (Dresden, 1926), and *Tagebuch, 1907–1922* (Duesseldorf, 1957), edited by Hartmut Pogge–v. Strandmann. Two secondary works of high quality are Klaus Epstein, *Matthias Erzberger and the Dilemma of German Democracy* (Princeton, 1959), about an important Reichstag figure, and Gerald D. Feldman, *Army, Industry, and Labor in Germany, 1914–1918* (Princeton, 1966). For a German perspective, see Gerhard Ritter, *Staatskunst und Kriegshandwerk: Das Problem des "Militarismus" in Deutschland,* vol. 3 (Munich, 1964), 4 vols.

For information on the Austro-Hungarian participation in the war consult the multivolume work edited by Edmund Glaise von Horstenau and Rudolf Kiszling, *Oesterreich-Ungarns Letzter Krieg, 1914–1918,* vols. 6–7 (Vienna, 1936–1938), 7 vols., and the extensive work on the Austro-Hungarian naval contribution by Hans Hugo Sokol, *Oesterreich-Ungarns Seekrieg, 1914–18,* 4 vols. (Vienna, 1933).

The general subject of the submarine war, considered largely from the perspective of the German Navy, has attracted a vast amount of attention from participants, scholars, official historians, publicists, and polemicists. The following lists some of these volumes, especially those of particular use for this study; others are cited in reference notes: Karl Galster, *England, Deutsche Flotte und Weltkrieg* (Kiel, 1925); R. H. Gibson and Maurice Prendergast, *The German Submarine War, 1914–1918* (London, 1931); Robert M. Grant, *U-Boats Destroyed: The Effect of Anti-Submarine War, 1914–1918* (London, 1964), and *U-Boat Intelligence, 1914–1918* (Hamden, Conn., 1969); Otto Groos, *Seekriegslehren im Lichte des Weltkrieges* (Berlin, 1929); Walther Hubatsch, *Der Admiralstab und die Obersten Marinebehoerden in Deutschland, 1848–1945* (Frankfurt, 1958); Hans Kutscher, *Der letzte Einsatz der deutschen Hochseeflotte* (Stuttgart, 1933); Andreas Michelsen, *Der U-Bootskrieg, 1914–1918* (Leipzig, 1925); E. Freiherr von Spiegel, *U-Boot im Fegefeuer: Ein Buch ueber den U-Bootkrieg, 1914–1918* (Preetz/Holstein, n.d.); Arno Spindler, *Der Handelskrieg mit U-Booten,* 4 vols. (Berlin, 1941); Arno Spindler, *Wie es zu den Entschluss zum uneingeschraenkten U-Boots-Krieg 1917 gekommen ist* (Göttingen, 1961).

LIST OF
CHARTS AND MAPS

Charts

Merchant Shipping Losses in Gross Tons,
     January, 1917–November 1918, *128*
World Shipbuilding Output in Gross Tons
     (excluding Central Powers), *135*
Numbers of Merchant Ships Lost to Submarines
     in the Atlantic during the Period of
     Unrestricted Submarine Warfare,
     February, 1917–October, 1918, *161*
Data on U-Boat Use, All Areas, *201*
Causes of U-Boat Losses, 1914–1918, *218*

Maps

British Waters, *155*
Mediterranean Sea, *227*

INDEX

Abbeville conference, 256

Admiralissimo plan for Mediterranean Sea: discussed in detail, 257–65; mentioned, 306

Admiralty, British: and convoy system, 71, 72, 129; criticized by Wilson, 93–94; and North Sea mine barrage, 154, 216–17; redefines grand naval strategy, 156; reasons for support of the Allied Naval Council, 177; reports to the Imperial War Cabinet on progress of the naval war, 200; and the Russian Black Sea Fleet, 252–53; summarizes views on naval policy in the Mediterranean Sea, 257–58; reports on shipping losses in the Mediterranean, 278; matures views on naval terms of the Armistice, 319–22; prepares case against freedom of the seas, 359; mentioned, 42, 53, 56, 58, 68, 84, 86, 92, 96, 98, 100, 101, 104, 113, 120, 131, 132, 134, 156, 157, 162, 163, 165, 167, 175, 181, 212, 214, 218, 243, 244, 255, 269, 298, 323. See also Operations Committee, British Admiralty; Board of Admiralty, British Admiralty

Admiralty, French, 84

Admiralty, German: admits declining success of submarines, 81; and unrestricted submarine warfare, 89, 158–60, 220–23; mentioned, 69, 70, 224, 272

Adriatic Patrol, 244

Adriatic Sea: geographic characteristics of, as they affect naval operations, 226, 237–38; mentioned, 35, 189, 224, 225, 231, 232, 233, 234, 235, 238, 239, 240, 242, 243, 263, 264, 332

Aegean mine barrage, 278

Aegean Sea, 189, 224, 252, 255, 263

Aegean squadron, 254

Albania, 232

Algeria, 260

Allenby, Gen. Edmund, 301

Allied Maritime Transport Council, 205

Allied Naval Council: founding of, 175–79; reasons for British support of, 177–78; U.S. joins, 180; does not consider ship-building questions extensively, 207; considers publication of shipping losses, 208; considers intervention in Russia and Siberia, 210–16; considers possibility of German battle cruiser raids, 219; discusses Italian questions at its first meeting, 235–36; and plan for a naval offensive in the Adriatic Sea, 246–47, 249; and the Russian Black Sea Fleet, 251–53; discusses proposal for naval redistribution in the Mediterranean at its third meeting, 255; considers Mediterranean matters during an emergency meeting, 258–59; designated as supervisory authority for the proposed admiralissimo in the Mediterranean, 261; fails to break deadlock over Mediterranean questions at its fourth meeting, 265;

and convoy and barrage operations in the Mediterranean, 274–
77; sets up subcommittee to plan
pooling of naval repair facilities
in the Mediterranean, 276; refuses to adopt the mid-Adriatic
barrage, 280; discusses naval
terms of the Armistice, 315, 332,
334, 343; and surrender of the
German High Sea Fleet, 345,
347, 348, 356; failure of, to settle Mediterranean problems, 362;
mentioned, 27, 224, 230, 243,
245, 254, 257, 264, 279, 305,
330, 333, 349
"Amalgamation" of American
troops, 183–84, 206, 208
American Expeditionary Forces,
202
Anglo-Japanese Alliance: relation
of, to secret Anglo-American naval understanding, 106–7; mentioned, 109, 117, 286
Archangel, 208, 210, 211, 212, 213,
216
Argentina, 44, 222
Armed neutrality, 44, 46, 91
Armistice, November 11, 1918: naval terms of, discussed in detail,
313–55; mentioned, 217, 308
Asia Minor, 229
Australia, 109
Austria-Hungary: reaction of, to
unrestricted submarine warfare,
225; and naval capability, 225–
61; U.S. declares war against,
231; inaugurates peace correspondence with Wilson, 303–4;
mentioned, 81, 144, 152, 230,
233, 237, 272, 286, 334, 337,
354
Azores, 153, 287

B

Baker, Secretary of War Newton
D.: comes under domestic criti-

cism, 184; summarizes U.S. position on armistice terms in message
to Pershing, 328; mentioned,
173, 342
Balfour, Foreign Secretary Arthur
James: expresses views on American intervention, 38; expresses
interest in dispatch of an American admiral to Britain, 54; develops plan for Anglo-American
naval cooperation, 56–57; de-
meanor of, during visit to U.S.,
74–75; reports to Lloyd George
on situation in the U.S., 75; urges
dispatch of American antisubmarine craft to Europe, 92; discusses secret treaties with Wilson,
105–6; and the proposed secret
naval treaty, 77, 105, 111, 115,
116–18, 122–23; discusses Japan
with Breckinridge Long, 112;
and shipping, 129, 170; urges
U.S. representation at inter-
Allied conference scheduled for
July, 1917, 143–44; denies U.S.
accusations of lack of frankness,
168; approves the Geddes mission to U.S., 296–97; counsels
concessions in certain economic
disputes with the U.S., 306; and
the pre-Armistice negotiations,
315, 323, 325, 340; mentioned,
41, 52, 59, 72, 86, 87, 109, 114,
124, 140, 142, 147, 171, 172,
191, 268, 281, 295, 315, 316,
324. See also Balfour mission to
the U.S.
Balfour mission to the U.S., 74–76,
103–4, 156
Baltic Sea, 35, 36, 188, 209, 332
Barclay, Colville, 318
Barclay, Richard, 55
Barrere, Ambassador (French Ambassador to Italy): reports on
Roosevelt's activities in Rome,
269; seeks permission to block
appointment of an admiralissimo,
271; mentioned, 262

Bastedo, Lt. P.H.: brings confidential message from Grayson to Sims, 162

Batocki-Bledau, Adolf Tortilowicz von, 34

Battle cruiser raid by Germany: considered by Allied Naval Council, 218–19

Bayly, Adm. Sir Lewis, 82, 130, 149, 182, 236, 244, 353

Beatty, Adm. Sir David: advocates close-in mining of German ports, 38; comments on the mission of the Grand Fleet, 190; insists that naval armistice terms be as close as possible to final peace terms, 323; criticizes naval terms of armistice, 349; mentioned, 71, 257, 302

Beaverbrook, Lord, 72

Belgium, 132

Belknap, Captain: supports dispatch of American capital ships to Europe to enhance naval prestige, 164

Benedict XV: urges that Wilson arrange peace negotiations, 318

Benson, Adm. William S.: develops detailed views on proper naval policy in February, 1917, 47–49; defends his advice to Sims, 55; advocates close-in blockade of German ports, 64–65; comments of R.R.M. Emmet on, 85; takes steps to protect American coast, 89; views described by Northcliffe, 95; opposes North Sea mine barrage, 154; inaugurates personal correspondence with Sims, 163; accepts Sims's recommendation for creation of a planning section, 165–66; approves recommendations of Sims when in Europe with House mission, 175; defends freedom of the seas in conversation with British officials, 178; discusses inter-Allied naval questions with British officials in London, 178; submits report on trip to Europe with House mission, 181–82; on need for shipping, 182; asks Sims for assistance in countering congressional criticism, 184; opposes appointment of Sims and himself to Board of Admiralty, 193–94; informs Sims that he must clear policy initiatives with Washington, 198; cables reprimand to Sims, 197; and the proposed Adriatic offensive, 243–45; and the pre-Armistice negotiations, 332, 334, 335, 344, 345, 347, 353–54; reasons why his choice as Chief of Naval Operations was unfortunate, 361; mentioned, 44, 58, 64, 76, 84, 92, 97, 99, 103, 136, 162, 164, 166, 168, 169, 171, 173, 176, 180, 211, 219, 239, 256, 260, 267, 296, 330, 346, 348, 352

Bernstorff, Count Johann: opposes unrestricted submarine warfare, 31; mentioned, 44

Bertie of Thame, Lord (British Ambassador to France): notes antipathy toward Italy in France, 229; mentioned, 61, 62, 149

Bethmann-Hollweg, Chancellor Theobald von: and unrestricted submarine warfare, 31, 81, 82; mentioned, 59

Black Sea. See Black Sea Fleet, Russian

Black Sea Fleet, Russian: discussed at second meeting of Allied Naval Council, 252; intelligence reports indicate German intention to employ, 254; history of, during 1918, 271–73; mentioned, 250, 251, 255, 257, 259, 262

Black War Plan against Germany: described, 44–45

Bliss, Gen. Tasker H.: appointed Permanent Military Representative to the Supreme War Council,

176; favors "amalgamation," 206; avoids participation in inter-Allied meeting on armistice terms, 315; expresses views on the terms of the Armistice, 317; mentioned, 357

Blockade: Wilson comments on, 340; mentioned, 74, 89, 158, 160, 330–31, 338, 356

Board of Admiralty, British Admiralty: approves Allied Naval Council, 177; expresses concern about maintenance of the British navy's preeminence, 192; wishes to appoint Sims as honorary member, 193; and the naval terms of the Armistice, 326, 346, 348–49; mentioned, 165, 291, 300

Bolshevik Revolution. See Russian Revolution

Bon, Adm. Ferdinand-Jean-Jacques de (Chief of French naval staff): proposes that the U.S. send old battleships to the Mediterranean for convoy duty, 152; opposes operations in North Russia, 214, 215; summarizes French naval interests in the Mediterranean, 260; favors surrender of the German fleet, 344, 347–48; mentioned, 236, 244, 246, 264, 266, 280, 334

Bonar Law, Andrew, 320, 322

Bremerhaven, Germany, 35

British Grand Fleet. See Grand Fleet, British

British mission to the U.S. See Balfour mission to the U.S.

Browning, Adm. Sir Montague E., 55, 62–64

Building program of Royal Navy: War Cabinet plans for, 79; plans for 1918, 115, 192; Geddes proposes reductions in, 298–99; discussed in memorandum for the Operations Committee, 359

Building Program of U.S. Navy: Benson expresses views on, 48; views of General Board on, 58; early discussions of, 102–3; Jellicoe comments on, 110–11; views of War Cabinet on, 111; U.S. postpones capital-ship construction, 115–16; General Board reports on, for 1919, 139; Daniels makes recommendations on, for 1919, 285; London Planning Section produces report on, 286–89; Geddes comments on, 293; plans of U.S. as explained to Geddes, 307; comments of Washington Planning Section and General Board on, 358–59; reasons why war interfered with "balanced" development of, 365; mentioned, 57, 70, 72, 95, 97, 105, 120, 310

Bulgaria, 144, 259

Bunsen, Sir Maurice de: leads trade mission to Latin America, 284

Bureau of Ordnance, Navy Department: suggests North Sea barrage, 88

Bureau of Personnel, Navy Department, 199

C

Cape Bon, 277

Cape Verde Islands, 287

Capelle, Adm. Eduard von: justifies unrestricted submarine warfare before the Reichstag, 32–33

Caporetto: Italian defeat at, 230

Caribbean Sea, 286, 288

Carson, Sir Edward (First Lord of the Admiralty), 72, 100

Cattaro: American plans for raid on, 242; mentioned, 35, 225, 241, 243, 246

Cecil, Sir Robert: advises Balfour on the secret naval understanding, 108–9; contemplates public call for economy because of the shipping crisis, 311; comments on European dislike of Wilson, 315–16; mentioned, 70, 106, 109

Cellere, Count Macchi di (Italian Ambassador to the U.S.), 232

Chair, Adm. Sir Dudley R. de: gives opinions on the submarine war, 75; prepares plan for operations of the projected naval mission to U.S., 86–87; mentioned, 111

Chamberlain, Austen, 191, 319, 324, 325

Chesapeake Bay, 46

Chile, 222

China, 107, 112

Chiozza Money, Sir Leo: complains about slowness of American merchant ship construction, 70–71; mentioned, 294

Chocheprat, Adm., 76

Churchill, Winston (American author): reports on the Navy Department to Wilson, 93, 137; urges combined Anglo-American planning staff, 165

Clemenceau, Georges (Premier of France): becomes premier, 175; and the proposal for an admiralissimo in the Mediterranean, 260–62, 266–67; resists British efforts to control the occupation of the Dardanelles, 271; and the naval armistice terms, 345; mentioned, 255, 258, 259, 269, 315, 333, 336, 337, 343, 348

Close-in offensives against Germany: Page speculates on, 78; discussed by Sims and Navy Department, 87–88; proposed by Jellicoe, against Heligoland Bight, 150; mentioned, 67, 95, 132, 133

Coastal defense of the U.S.: stressed early in emergency, 49; Sims opposes efforts to develop, 89; mentioned, 57

Cobb, Frank: helps prepare gloss on the Fourteen Points to clarify their meaning, 337–38; mentioned, 104

Colby, Bainbridge, 178, 205

Columbo, Ceylon, 107

Conference, Inter-Allied Naval, London, January, 1917, 37

Conference, Inter-Allied Naval, September, 1917: proceedings of, 150–53; offers plans to counteract U-cruisers, 219; mentioned, 143, 149, 157, 209

Congress, U.S.: declares war against Austria-Hungary, 231; mentioned, 46, 142, 233

Constantinople, 251, 252, 263

Convoy system, Allied: reasons why the British Admiralty opposed it in 1917, 67–68, 71; Admiralty decision to adopt, 71–72; nature of, 72–73; supported by Wilson, 73; Sims comments on its success, 79–80; reasons for success, 73, 78; German comments on, 73, 80–81; German attempts to counteract, 81–82; discussed by Wilson and Wiseman, 97; Sims speculates on whether Germany would employ large submarine cruisers to disrupt, 120–30; discussed at naval conference, 152; endorsed by the Admiralty, 156; German efforts to frustrate, 158; destruction of Allied, 158; efforts to develop in Mediterranean discussed, 274–81; Planning Section comments on, 189; mentioned, 46, 91, 120, 151, 205, 282

Corfu, 252, 254, 255, 256, 257, 258, 260, 262, 265

Cravath, Paul, 359

Crosby, Oscar, 191

Cuba, 49

Curtis, Lionel: comments to Bliss on British attitude toward American naval development, 357–58

Curzola Island, 242, 245

Curzon, Lord, 324

Czernin, 32, 69

D

Dakar, 287
Dalmatia, 228, 232, 238, 242, 282
Damatian Islands, 228, 239
Daniels, Secretary of the Navy Josephus: reports to Wilson on views of Benson, 44; and the building program, 64, 70, 96, 116, 285; requests reports on measures to be taken in the event of war with Germany, 45–46; supports Wilson's interest in armed neutrality, 46; requests intelligence information on German naval movements, 51; discusses convoy prospects with Wilson, 73; records views of the Balfour mission, 75; manifests willingness to support Sims, 86; discusses Wilson's motives in requesting confidential report from Sims, 98; reports Wilson's views on declaration of war aims, 114; informs Sims that protection of transports is a paramount duty, 131; opposes dispatch of coal-burning dreadnoughts to Britain, 136; stimulated to greater activity by criticism of the Navy Department, 138; approaches to conduct of his position, 138; dubious about North Sea mine barrage, 154; denies accusation that he was annoyed at the British, 167–68; comments on Wilson's appearance, 172; opposes appointment of Sims to the Board of Admiralty, 193–95; opposes foreign decorations for American seamen, 196; supports Sims in latter's desire to maintain integrity of his command, 198; and intervention in Russia, 209–10; summarizes Wilson's reasons for opposing intervention in Russia, 210; informs Sims of the Navy Department's support for bar-

rage operations, including the mid-Adriatic project, 279; reprimands Sims for unauthorized statement, 295; and Geddes mission, 298, 300; and pre-Armistice negotiations, 317, 342, 346; mentioned, 47, 54, 57, 59, 68, 76, 85, 89, 92, 93, 94, 95, 97, 100, 101, 132, 135, 137, 139, 146, 155, 156, 173, 180, 190, 204, 205, 213, 267, 269, 283, 296, 304, 305, 306, 310, 335, 365
Dardanelles, 245, 252, 264, 277
Denmark, 49
Department of State, United States. See State Department, U.S.
Derby, Lord (British Ambassador to France), 261
Dewey, Adm. George, 242
Dover, Straits of. See Straits of Dover
Drummond, Sir Eric: discusses secret naval agreement with House, 104–5; mentioned, 191, 284
Duff, Adm. Sir Alexander L., 72, 307

E

"Eagle" boats, 307
Egypt, 241
Emergency Fleet Corporation, U.S., 70
E.M.G. (État-Major General), Naval Staff of France: raises objections to Adriatic offensive, 245; urges naval terms almost identical to those desired by Britain, 323; mentioned, 276
Emmet, R.R.M.: reports to Sims on conditions in the Navy Department, 85
English Channel, 35, 90, 132, 277
Erzberger, Matthias, 32, 81
État-Major General, Naval Staff of France. See E.M.G.

F

Farragut, Adm. David, 242
Finnish White Guard, 214
Fisher, Lord, 121
Flanders, 273, 313
Foch, Gen. (later Marshal) Ferdinand: expresses desire to receive American troops, 130; wants inter-Allied conference to settle shipping problems, 170; assumes offensive on land, 202; concerned about diversion of troops and supplies to North Russia, 215; recommends armistice terms at the Senlis conference, 330; supports moderate naval terms of armistice, 333, 345; mentioned, 251, 261, 262, 308, 313, 322, 344, 348, 356
Foreign Office, British: anticipates break in relations between U.S. and Germany, 38–39; its Far Eastern Department produces study of proposed Anglo-American naval understanding, 106–8; denies U.S. accusations of lack of frankness, 167; mentioned, 52, 53, 70
Foreign Office, French, 269
Foreign Office, German: opposes extension of submarine warfare to American coast, 221; mentioned, 31, 59, 69, 158, 186, 272
Fourteen Points: issued by Wilson, including statement on Italian boundaries, 231; consideration of, during the pre-Armistice negotiations, 336–39, 355; mentioned, 221, 325, 331, 341, 348, 354
France: proposed as signatory of secret naval treaty, 117–19; expresses anxiety about shipment of U.S. troops to Europe, 152; circulates proposal in Allied Naval Council for intervention in North Russia, 210; attempts to

energize Italian naval policy, 228; mentioned, 29, 42, 100, 130, 141, 150, 185, 199, 205, 210, 225, 226, 249, 252, 253, 256, 258, 267, 274, 282, 304, 350, 354, 362
Frazier, Arthur Hugh, 264–65
Freedom of the seas: discussed by Geddes and Wilson, 309; discussed by the War Cabinet, 319–20; discussed by Wemyss in Admiralty memorandum, 320–21; discussed by the War Cabinet, 324–26; endorsed by planning committee in the Navy Department, 329; text of Point II of the Fourteen Points on freedom of the seas, 337; meaning of Point II clarified in Cobb-Lippmann gloss, 337–38; discussed during the pre-Armistice negotiations, 339, 341; Planning Section produces memorandum on, reiterating traditional American views, 358; mentioned, 26, 286, 308, 314, 331, 359
Funakoshi, Adm. (Japanese representative on the Allied Naval Council), 246

G

Gargano Head, 242, 245
Gaunt, Captain Guy (British naval attaché in Washington): reports unofficial proposal for Anglo-American naval discussions, 53; reports on conditions in Navy Department, 86; reports to the Admiralty on U.S. building program and fear of Japan, 104; mentioned, 52, 167
Gazza Island, 243
Geddes, Sir Eric (First Lord of the Admiralty): becomes First Lord of the Admiralty, 100; and the Mayo mission, 149, 151, 152;

denies U.S. accusations of lack
of frankness, 168; participates
in defining powers of the Allied
Naval Council, 179; proposes
temporary defensive policy for
the Grand Fleet, 190–91; explains to Board of Admiralty project to make Sims and Benson
honorary members, 193; grows
optimistic about the antisubmarine campaign, 199–200; urges
intervention in North Russia at
fourth meeting of Allied Naval
Council, 215; discusses Italian
questions with Roosevelt, 268;
and U.S. building program, 285,
291–93, 295–96, 298–300; and
the proposal for an admiralissimo
in the Mediterranean, 259–62,
264–66, 270; and problems in the
Mediterranean, 235–36, 239,
254; discusses renewed threat of
submarine warfare, 301–3; and
mission to the U.S., 207, 298,
300–312; and the pre-Armistice
negotiations, 324, 325, 326, 331–
32, 333–34, 343–45, 347–48,
349; discusses naval attitudes of
Wilson, 325, 349–50; mentioned,
147, 169, 176, 267, 275, 276,
277, 359. See also Geddes mission
to the U.S.
Geddes mission to the U.S.: discussed in detail, 283–312
General Board, United States Navy:
makes recommendations prior to
the U.S. entry into the war, 45–
46, 58; recommends antisubmarine effort in British waters, 74;
proposes Japanese contributions
to the war in Europe, 112–13;
criticized by Churchill, 137; approves North Sea mine barrage,
154; approves creation of an
inter-Allied coordinating agency,
176; and building program, 102–
3, 139, 289–90; mentioned, 59,
93, 159, 164, 192, 310

George V, King of England, 193,
194
Gerard, Amb. James W. (American
Ambassador to Germany), 32,
43, 44
German High Sea Fleet. See High
Sea Fleet, German
German offensive of 1918, 172, 192,
250
Giardino, General (Italian Perma-
nent Military Representative),
247
Gibraltar, 238, 241, 251, 277
Glory, H.M.S., 210
Goeben, 263
Goethals, Gen. George, 70
Gough-Calthorpe, Admiral (British
Naval Commander in the Medi-
terranean Sea), 274
Grand Fleet, British: mission of,
156, 190; mentioned, 37, 42, 63,
181, 189, 284, 336
Grasset, Adm. R.A.: consults with
American naval officials, 62–64;
mentioned, 54
Grassi, Admiral: opposes intern-
ment of German fleet, 344
Grayson, Adm. Cary, 162
Grayson, Mrs. Cary, 162
Greece, 229, 246, 267
Grey, Lord, 76, 359
Groener, Gen. William, 36, 159,
186
Grossa Island, 242
Guam, 288

H

Haig, Field Marshal Sir Douglas,
330, 334
Hall, Adm. William R., 149–50
Hampton Roads, Va.: conference
at, 62
Hankey, Lord (Maurice): recognizes importance of the war at
sea, 61; urges adoption of convoy, 71; comments on British

position on the proposed admiralissimo for the Mediterranean, 264; believes that Lloyd George won a great victory for the British navy during the pre-Armistice discussions, 349

Hardinge, Lord, 39, 108

Hawaii, 288

Heligoland, 38, 315, 321, 329, 356. *See also* Heligoland Bight

Heligoland Bight, 153, 188, 191

Hertling, Chancellor, 221–22

High Sea Fleet, German: mission of, 36, 188; makes surface raids in the North Sea, 158–59; pursues offensive tactics in the Baltic, 159; loses offensive momentum, 187–88; fails in effort to launch last offensive, 335–36; disposition of, discussed at pre-Armistice negotiations, 343–50; scuttled at Scapa Flow, 357; mentioned, 35, 63, 95, 139, 156, 157, 190

Hindenburg, Field Marshal Paul von: and unrestricted submarine warfare, 81, 158, 221–22; mentioned, 30, 69, 201

Hipper, Admiral (Commander of German High Sea Fleet), 336

Hobson, Richmond, 131

Hollis, Henry, 326

Holtzendorff, Adm. Henning von (Chief of German Naval Staff): and unrestricted submarine warfare, 30–31, 34, 69, 220–21; mentioned, 59, 159, 272

Honolulu, 108

Hoover, Herbert, 91, 294

Hope, Adm. G.P.W.: and pre-Armistice negotiations, 315, 345, 347

House, Colonel Edward M.: notes Wilson's interest in naval questions before entry into the war, 47; advises Wilson on preparations for war, 50; presses for dispatch of Balfour mission, 74; and negotiations concerning a secret naval treaty, 77, 104–6, 112, 118–23; nature of relationship with Wilson, 124; and mission to Europe, November–December, 1917, 173, 176, 179, 180–81; and Italy, 231, 233; praises Geddes mission in message to Balfour, 310; and the pre-Armistice negotiations, 309, 332–33, 335–43, 348, 350; mentioned, 91, 108, 114, 116, 142, 147, 168, 170, 184, 191, 296, 316, 318, 322, 330, 332, 345, 352, 354. *See also* House mission of 1917

House mission of 1917, 173–82, 193

Houston, David F. (Secretary of Agriculture), 50, 91, 112

Hurley, Edward N., 184, 298, 327

Hydrophone, 151

I

Imperial War Cabinet: considers peace settlement in 1917, 41; receives reports on progress of the sea war, 200–201; mentioned, 56, 59

India, 107

Indian Ocean, 114

Inter-Allied Council for War Purchases and Finance, 191–92

Irish Sea, 277

Italy: proposed as signatory of secret naval treaty, 117–19; opposes close-in offensive against Heligoland Bight, 150; wishes to explore purchases of destroyers from the U.S., 152; relationship to inter-Allied activities in the Mediterranean, 225–82; strategic concerns of, 237–38; mentioned, 29, 42, 141, 205, 225, 229, 235, 263, 354, 362

J

Japan: and proposed secret naval treaty, 105, 106–8, 109–10, 111–12, 117; Planning Section comments on, 286–89; mentioned, 48, 103, 104, 150, 213, 275. *See also* Anglo-Japanese Alliance
Japanese mission to the U.S., 117
Jellicoe, Adm. Sir John (First Sea Lord): views on naval policy in 1917, 38; reports projected activities of Sims, 65; decides to support principle of convoy, 72; produces memorandum for the War Cabinet comparing naval strength of U.S. and Japan, 110–11; describes plans for close-in offensive against Heligoland Bight, 150; supports North Sea mine barrage, 154; complains of American inaction, 167; denies U.S. accusations of lack of frankness, 168; expresses to War Cabinet need for Allied Naval Council, 175; and plan for an admiralissimo in the Mediterranean Sea, 258—61; mentioned, 39, 52, 68, 87, 100, 124, 167, 176, 177, 179, 200, 260, 262, 263, 270
Jusserand, Amb. Jules (French Ambassador to the United States), 50–51, 269

K

Kaiser. *See* William II, Emperor of Germany
Karl, Emperor of Austria-Hungary, 32
Kattegat, 188
Kerr, Phillip, 140
Kiel, 35, 189
Kiev, 254
Kite balloon, 151
Kola Inlet, 214

Kuehlmann, Foreign Minister Richard, 160, 220, 221

L

Lagosta, 243
Lane, Franklin K. (Secretary of the Interior), 57, 91, 101, 104
Laning, Harris: defends personnel policy of the Navy Department, 199
Lansing, Secretary of State Robert: prewar activities of, 43, 44, 50; sends invitations inviting British and French missions to visit the U.S., 74–75; recommends dispatch of an American commissioner to Europe to clarify the nature of the submarine question, with Japan, 113–14; authorizes 92; considers methods of dealing with Japan, 113–14; authorizes American participation in the naval conference, 146; informs Page that Sims could not accept appointment to the Board of Admiralty, 195; comments on the Adriatic question, 231–32; mentions, 51, 78, 91, 94, 111, 133, 144, 194, 267, 269, 342
Lansing-Ishii Agreement, 114
League of Nations, 118, 235, 284, 325, 342, 349, 353, 358, 359
Lenin, Vladimir, 209
Leygues, Georges (French Minister of Marine): and discussion of naval terms at the pre-Armistice negotiations, 331, 344; mentioned, 246, 260, 264
Lippmann, Walter: helps prepare gloss on the Fourteen Points to clarify their meaning, 337–38
Lloyd George, Prime Minister David: concern about submarine warfare in February, 1917, 37–38; discusses possible U.S. cooperation with Page, 39; forces Ad-

miralty to adopt convoy, 71–72; makes Geddes First Lord of the Admiralty, 100; discusses the secret naval treaty with Sims, 122; inaugurates attempt to hold an inter-Allied conference, 172–73; helps establish the Supreme War Council at Rapallo, 174; retains position as prime minister, 175; discusses inter-Allied naval questions with House mission in London, 178; comments on importance of Allied Naval Council, 180; quoted on importance of antisubmarine campaign, 186; reviews inter-Allied situation for Imperial War Cabinet, 200; makes statement on war aims, 231; and the plan for an admiralissimo in the Mediterranean Sea, 258, 263–64; comments on Sonnino and di Revel, 267–68; advises Geddes on statements to be made in the U.S., 308–9; and the pre-Armistice negotiations, 323–25, 341, 343, 345, 348; mentioned, 38, 75, 91, 106, 123, 149, 178, 184, 207, 233, 239, 254, 255, 261, 268, 294, 296, 297, 298, 309, 312, 315, 319, 322, 332, 336, 348, 349

Lochner, Louis P.: asks German government to rescind unrestricted submarine warfare, 33

Long, Breckinridge (Third Assistant Secretary of State): and Japan, 112–13, 210

Long, Walter (Secretary of State for the Colonies), 109–10

Ludendorff, General Erich: and unrestricted submarine warfare, 31, 33–34, 69, 82, 159, 186–87, 201, 221; agrees with Holtzendorff on need to acquire the Russian Black Sea Fleet, 272; mentioned, 36, 81, 302

Lyell, Charles, 284

M

Macedonia, 225, 251, 313

McGowan, Captain, 85

Mahan, Adm. Alfred Thayer, 27, 103, 121, 353, 363

Malta: conference on mining operations at, 279; mentioned, 278

Manchuria, 107, 108, 109

Mann-Tiechler, Adm. Ritter von, 159

Marines, U.S., 243

Maximilian of Baden, Prince (Chancellor of Germany): wishes to further Wilson's role as *arbiter mundi* in order to curb the Allies, 327; seeks relaxation of Allied blockade, 356; mentioned, 308, 328

Mayo, Adm. Henry T. (Commander of U.S. Atlantic Fleet): and mission to Europe, 146, 149–54; mentioned, 64, 133, 167, 168, 198. *See also* Mayo mission

Mayo mission, 166, 167

Mediterranean Sea: importance of, 225; inter-Allied discussion of situation in, 225–82; map of, 227; nature of naval warfare in, 250; generalization on obstacles to cooperation in, 362; mentioned, 35, 37, 112, 114, 175, 189

Mesopotamia, 200, 225, 251

Mexico, 107

Middle East, 259

Milner, Lord, 322

Minelaying, 65, 191. *See also* North Sea mine barrage; Otranto barrage; Sicily-Cape Bon barrage; Aegean mine barrage

Ministry of Marine, French, 260, 261

Ministry of Shipping, British: calculates ship construction needs, 79; proposes that U.S. produce more naval vessels, 295; mentioned, 70, 145, 294

Monroe Doctrine, 286

Morocco, 260
Murmansk, 34, 208, 210, 212, 213, 214, 215, 216
Murray, Arthur, 171
Mystery (Q) Ships, 151

N

National Union of Manufacturers (British), 296
Naval Academy, Annapolis, U.S., 103
Naval Act of 1916: provisions of, 285
Naval War College, U.S., 44, 55, 103
Navy Department, U.S.: interest in coast defense, 49; gives reasons for retaining destroyers in American waters, 77; criticism of, 85–86, 137; prepares statement of six naval principles to govern its activities, 94; and Japan, 113; and the Mayo mission, 153–54; opposes dispatch of coal-burning dreadnoughts to Europe, 164; suspects incompetence in British Admiralty, 166–67; comes under congressional criticism, 184; refuses to allow Sims to accept honorary appointment to Board of Admiralty, 193–96; opposes views of Sims on "amalgamation" and shipbuilding, 206; and intervention in Russia, 209, 211; revives mid-Adriatic mine barrage, 279; planning committee of, endorses freedom of the seas, 329; and building program, 116, 285, 358–59; relations with Sims summarized, 362–64; mentioned, 27, 39, 45, 47, 51, 52, 58, 60, 67, 68, 72, 76, 79, 85, 87, 88, 91, 93, 96, 101, 111, 127, 138, 155, 160, 162, 163, 164, 192, 196, 197, 198, 199, 211, 218, 224, 245, 248, 249, 255, 266, 276, 278, 279, 289, 295, 296, 298, 299, 305, 311, 330. See also Bureau of Ordnance, Navy Department; Bureau of Personnel, Navy Department
New Zealand, 109
Nikolaev, 271, 272
Nitti, Francesco, 268
Nivelle offensive, 131
North Sea mine barrage: considered by Sims, 87–88, 151; Mayo mission's proposal to build it approved by Navy Department, 153; given consideration by the Navy Department, 154; supported by Jellicoe, 154; approved by the General Board, 154; Daniels doubts its effectiveness, 154; development of, 216–18; mentioned, 95, 181, 191, 243, 251
Northcliffe, Lord: reports American opinion on naval matters, 91, 95; gives views on how to deal with Americans, 140; mentioned, 167
Norway, 158, 217
Novorossisk, 271, 272
Nuova Point, 242

O

Olympia, U.S.S., 214
Open Door Policy, 286
Operations Committee, British Admiralty: notes decline in effectiveness of antisubmarine warfare, 301; considers memorandum on the British building program, 359; mentioned, 193, 298, 300
Orlando, Premier Vittorio E.: visits London to obtain more explicit support of Italian war aims, 234; notifies French Ambassador in Rome that Italy could not accept the redistribution proposal, 262; withdraws acceptance of Jellicoe's appointment as admiralissimo, 263–64; mentioned, 255, 256, 258, 267, 348

Ostend, 78, 133
Otranto barrage: efforts to develop discussed, 274–81; mentioned, 236, 241, 243, 245, 246, 251, 265
Otranto patrol, 254
Ottoman Empire, 259

P

Page, Amb. Thomas Nelson (U.S. Ambassador to Italy): reports to Wilson on Italian reaction to the German-American crisis, 229; warns Wilson of Italian sensitivities, 229; urges declaration of war against Austria-Hungary, 230; calls for increased aid to Italy, 231; reports unfavorable Italian reaction to the Fourteen Points, 232; continues to report Italian desires for territory, 233; reports on Italian concerns about the Mediterranean, 267
Page, Amb. Walter Hines (U.S. Ambassador to Great Britain): reports lack of information on U.S. policy in February, 1917, 38; errs in estimate of Wilson, 51; approaches British Government about naval cooperation, 53–54; urges friends to lobby for naval assistance, 57; reports on good Anglo-American relations, 83; approves dispatch of the British naval mission to Washington, 86; calls for reinforcement against the submarine, 66–67, 78–79, 92; and secret naval treaty, 118, 122; reports to Daniels on the gloomy mood of London, 135; and Inter-Allied conference, July, 1917, 143–44; reports to Wilson on conditions in Europe, 148; reports to Wilson on reception of Mayo in Britain, 149; transmits British denials of lack of frank-ness concerning naval questions, 168; reports on British fears of the League of Nations, 284; urges that Sims be appointed to the Board of Admiralty, 194; mentioned, 39, 54, 56, 58, 77, 87, 94, 121, 133, 146, 160, 185
Palestine, 200, 225, 251
Palmer, Rear Adm. L. C., 158
Panama Canal, 286
Paris Conference, 1917, 172, 174–75. See also House mission
Paris Peace Conference, 1919–1920, 26, 172, 359, 365
Pelagosa Island, 243
Permanent Military Representatives: established as advisers to the Supreme War Council, 175; and intervention in North Russia, 212–13; and the proposed Adriatic offensive, 247–48; hold meeting with the Allied Naval Council to discuss armistice terms, 315; mentioned, 216, 259, 345
Pershing, Gen. John J. (Commander-in-Chief of the A.E.F.): reports on feasibility of making demands for aggressive action in Europe, 148–49; and commitment to an independent American army, 182–83; and "amalgamation," 206–7; opposes diversion of troops to Italy, 231; participates in the Senlis conference, 330; accepts fundamental Entente strategy, 360; mentioned, 202, 203, 204, 328
Pétain, Gen. Philippe, 231
Philippines, 107, 120, 286, 287
Phillimore report, 310
"Plan of 1776," 358
Planning Section, London Headquarters: established, 165–66; provides estimate of naval situation for 1918, 188–90; and proposed Adriatic offensive, 240–42, 244; prepares memorandum on Mediterranean problems, propos-

ing negotiated peace with Turkey, 252–53; and the naval terms of the Armistice, 329, 350–52; reiterates traditional American views on freedom of the seas, 358; mentioned, 259

Planning Section, Washington: issues memorandum on the building program, 358

Pless, Germany, 31

Pola, 35, 225, 237, 242

Polk, Frank L. (Counsellor of the State Department), 53, 118, 144, 169, 209

Pratt, Captain William V. (Assistant Chief of Naval Operations): made Assistant Chief of Naval Operations, 84; comments on feeling that home forces were being left out of the war, 84; effect of his appointment on Navy Department, 86; and the building program, 96, 115–16, 285–86; considers intervention in Siberia to frustrate Japanese ambitions, 213; reports to Sims on anti-British feeling in U.S., 284; draws Daniels's attention to discrepancies between Wilson and the Allied Naval Council over naval terms of Armistice, 335; proposes a navy for the League of Nations, 358; mentioned, 83, 87, 90, 113, 121, 132, 134, 136, 137, 138, 163, 164, 171, 173, 177, 179, 183, 223, 289, 297

Pre-Armistice agreement: accepted by the Supreme War Council, 341

Pre-Armistice negotiations: summarized, 354–55; mentioned, 27, 207, 280, 308, 314

Provisional Government of Russia, 208

Q

Queenstown, Ireland, 65, 68, 82

R

Rapallo, Italy, 174

Rapallo Conference, November 7, 1917, 175

Rathenau, Walther, 33, 81, 222

Ratyé, Admiral (French Commander in the Mediterranean Sea), 244

Rawlinson, Gen. Henry S., 247

Reading, Marquess of (British Ambassador to the U.S.): considered as successor to Spring Rice, 167; criticizes U.S. requests for British shipping, 207; presses Wilson to support intervention at Vladivostok, 212; advises that U.S. would not accept increase in shipbuilding program beyond given level, 295; notes problems of U.S. cooperation in the War Cabinet, 306; defends Wilson's negotiations with the Central Powers, 320; supports Smuts's view that further warfare would strengthen U.S. position, 324; points out House's interest in freedom of the seas, 325; expresses hope that the war would end in 1919, 313; mentioned, 168, 169, 211, 296, 297, 300, 303, 325, 333

Reichstag, 82, 101

Reuter, Vice Adm. Ludwig von: orders scuttling of the High Sea Fleet at Scapa Flow, 357

Revel, Adm. Thaon di (Commander of the Italian Navy and Chief of Staff): defends Italian naval viewpoints, 237–38; opposes American plan for an offensive in Adriatic, 246; opposes proposal for redistribution of ships in the Mediterranean, 255; restates his views on naval operations in the Adriatic, 256–57; comments on convoy requirements in the Mediterranean, 274, 275; mentioned, 235, 243, 247, 258, 262, 263, 265, 266, 267, 280, 281, 332

Ribot, Alexandre, Premier of France, 62

Robertson, Gen. Sir William (Chief of the Imperial General Staff), 39, 52, 167, 178

Rodd, Sir Rennell (British Ambassador to Italy): reports to Balfour on Sonnino's views, 229; receives views of Sonnino on Italian territorial aspirations, 234; approaches Orlando on question of an admiralissimo, 258; argues that Italians were justified in their naval policies, 281; reports on di Revel, 267; attempts to continue negotiations to appoint an admiralissimo, 270; mentioned, 265

Rome, Naval conference at, 248–49

Roosevelt, Franklin D. (Assistant Secretary of the Navy): exerts pressure for active naval measures prior to entry into the war, 47; urges production of submarine chasers, 51; secretly proposes naval discussions with Britain, 53; proposed to head special naval mission to Europe by Willert, 147; favors North Sea mine barrage, 154–56; fails in efforts to head mission to Europe, 166; granted wish to visit Europe, 268; and visit to Italy, 268–69; writes to Daniels about British interest in coordinating shipbuilding programs, 291; informs Daniels of Geddes's purposes in visiting U.S., 304–5; mentioned, 58, 64, 85, 270, 293, 295, 296, 298, 299, 331

Roosevelt, Theodore, 33, 47, 64

Root, Elihu, 47

Rumania, 34

Russia: Allied intervention in, 208–16; mentioned, 34, 56, 65, 100, 112, 117–19, 144, 150, 157, 159, 172, 200, 209, 215, 230, 251, 329, 331. See also Russian Revolution

Russian Revolution, 157, 174, 208, 216

S

Sabbioncello Peninsula, 242

St. Thomas, Virgin Islands, 288

Salonika, 152, 260

Samana Bay, 287, 288

Scheer, Adm. Reinhard (Commander of the German High Sea Fleet and later Chief of the Naval Staff): assumes command of the German Navy, 200–201; opposes extension of submarine warfare to American waters, 223; orders a naval raid on British coast in order to force engagement with the Grand Fleet, 336; mentioned, 159

Secret naval treaty, 1917: discussed, 103–25; proposed text of, 115; mentioned, 95, 101

Senlis conference, October 25, 1918, 330

Sevastopol, 271, 272

Shantung peninsula, 108, 109

Sharp, Amb. William G. (U.S. Ambassador to France): comments on maritime losses, 61; calls for reinforcements against submarine, 78; reports on conditions in France, 148; comments on need for inter-Allied unity, 175; mentioned, 133

Shipping: early recognition of need for, 50–51; Balfour views on, April, 1917, 56; losses of, 68–69, 128, 159–61, 235, 278, 302; efforts of Wilson to stimulate production, 70; adverse effect of merchant ship construction on naval building program, 70; British mission secures commitments for, in U.S., 76; British Ministry of Shipping calculates need for, 78; Sims considers possibility of arming merchant ships, 87–89; Secretary Lane's views on, 104; Balfour comments on need for, 129; British estimates of rate of sinkings, 134; needed levels of production recommended by Britain, 140; report on, by Graeme Thomson, at Paris conference, July, 1917, 145; losses considered by U.S. and Britain, 169–71; discussed by House mission with British officials in London, 178; need for, in 1918, 182; comments on importance of, by Colby, 205; British recommendations on construction needs and other matters, 205–6; not taken up by Allied Naval Council because of work by other agencies, 207; U.S. fails to meet production quotas of, 207; Allied Naval Council considers whether to publish statistics on losses of, 208; Britain continues to press U.S. to produce, 184; German estimates of sinkings expected in 1918, 186–87; Wiseman comments on slowness of U.S. production, 191; interest of inter-Allied organizations in, 205; coordination of construction program discussed by Geddes and Roosevelt, 291; Geddes compares U.S. and British shipbuilding programs, 292–93; discussed by special committee of the War Cabinet, 294–95; Geddes criticizes low production level of, in U.S., 303; mentioned, 81, 200, 213, 299

Siberia, 209, 210, 212

Sicily, 277

Sicily-Cape Bon mine barrage, 277, 278

Sims, Adm. William Sowden (U.S. Force Commander in European Waters): ordered to Britain to provide naval liaison, 55; adumbrates basic views, 66; urges dispatch of antisubmarine craft to Europe, 65–66, 67–68, 77, 79, 91–92, 160–61; and Anglophilism, 67, 100; and the convoy system, 72, 79–80; establishes friendship with Bayly, 82; works to insure good relations with the Allies, 82–84; and relations with the Navy Department, 84–86, 138, 185, 196–98; favors improving rather than changing British methods, 85; gives views on dispatch of battle fleet to European waters, 87, 90; discusses possibility of German submarine operations in American waters, 87, 89–90; and North Sea mine barrage, 87–88, 154, 156, 217; and merchant shipping, 87–89, 171–72, 182, 187, 208; and Wilson, 94, 96–97, 120; and the development of his staff, 99–100, 198–99; gives views to Daniels on naval policy, 98–99; discounts fear of Japan, 113; and the proposed secret naval treaty, 121–22; sustains early views on proper naval policy, 127; annoyed by Pratt's assumption that Britain could win the war without U.S. assistance, 127–29; wonders whether Germany would employ large submarine cruisers, 129–30; raises problems of troop transport with Pratt, 130; opposes close-in offensives against German ports, 132; asks Page to forward his views on the submarine war to Wilson, 133–34; defends his sympathies for the Entente cause, 134; opposes argument that dispatch of light craft would destroy the symmetry of the U.S. fleet, 136; and dispatch of coal-burning dreadnoughts to Europe, 136; promoted to vice admiral and made Force Commander of U.S. Navy in European waters, 137; wishes to clarify his powers and authority, 138; recommends that U.S. observers visit in Europe to discover nature of problems there, 138; opposes dispatch of special British naval mission to U.S., 141; proposes that Wilson visit Europe, 141, 173; attends inter-Allied conference in Paris as unofficial observer, 144–45; urges closer cooperation with the Allies, 145–46; and Mayo mission, 146, 149, 153; reports to Benson on Bastedo message, 162–63; defines mission in manner calculated to win confidence of Benson and others, 163–64; replaces Captain McDougall as naval attaché in London, 164; and Planning Section, 164–66; retains position as highest ranking naval official in Europe, 166; summarizes composition and procedure of Allied Naval Council, 177; discusses Benson recommendations with Bayly, 179; designated a member of the Allied Naval Council, 180; favors "amalgamation," 183; provides Benson with statement to counteract congressional criticism, 184–85; and appointment to the Board of Admiralty, 165, 193–96; recommends award of British decorations to American seamen, 196; responds to Benson's reprimand, 197–98; encourages visits from Washington but opposes proposals that he visit

at home, 198; informs Wilson of improvement in antisubmarine campaign, 202; develops good relations with Pershing, 202–3; informs Daniels of U.S. share of sea war, 204; approves of "amalgamation" and all efforts to expand merchant-ship construction, 206; and intervention in North Russia, 208–9, 211, 214; considers possible battle cruiser raid by Germany, 219; considers U-cruiser raids, 219; gives reasons why submarines did not sink troopships, 223; proved correct in his recommendations concerning submarine warfare, 224; and proposed naval offensive in the Adriatic Sea, 236, 239, 240, 242–44, 246–50; considers other Mediterranean questions more important than the threat of the Russian Black Sea Fleet, 253; reports to Navy Department on di Revel's opposition to naval redistribution in the Mediterranean, 255; and Italy, 256, 265–67, 282; opposes Allied Naval Council endorsement of proposal to declare war against Turkey and Bulgaria, 259; concerned about possible French opposition to Anglo-American plans for the Mediterranean, 260; defines proposed powers of Jellicoe as admiralissimo, 261–62; recommends that Allied Naval Council determine assignments of American submarine chasers, 275; and mining operations in the Mediterranean Sea, 276–81; receives reprimand for making unauthorized statements, 295; concerned about possibility of postwar trade rivalry with Britain, 297–98; and the building program, 289, 298–99; doubts that Germany could sustain renewed submarine warfare for any length of time, 302; summarizes outcome of Geddes mission, 311; and the pre-Armistice negotiations, 316–18, 328, 345–46, 352; comments on possibility of action by the German High Sea Fleet, 335; accepts fundamental naval policies of Britain, 360; achieves distinction as Force Commander, 361; summarizes naval accomplishments during World War I, 362–63; relations with Navy Department summarized, 362–64; relations with British government summarized, 364; engages in controversy with Daniels, 365; mentioned, 71, 74, 77, 86, 93, 95, 101, 124, 131, 154, 157, 158, 168, 175, 176, 181, 192, 224, 230, 273, 277, 330, 345

Singapore, 107

Smuts, Gen. Jan: initiates discussion in Imperial War Cabinet concerning peace settlement in 1917, 41; expresses desire to end war in order to curb growth of U.S. power, 324; mentioned, 325

Sonnino, Sydney (Foreign Minister of Italy): expresses suspicion of American motives, 229–30; defends Italian territorial aspirations to Rodd, 234; mentioned, 233, 246, 263, 267, 316, 336

Spa, 201

Spanish-American War, 131

Special Conference of the Allies, October 7, 1918: draws up principles to govern negotiation of armistices with the Central Powers, 314–15

Spring Rice, Amb. Sir Cecil (British Ambassador to the U.S.): reports U.S. opposition to consultation about joint measures of defense, 39; reports on German penetration of the Navy Department, 39; analyzes Wilson's reasons for avoiding Anglo-American discussions in February 1917, 40; comments on U.S. fear of Japanese-German-Russian combination, 40; analyzes Wilson's motives, 40–41; gives views on Balfour mission, 76–77; opposes dispatch of special naval mission to America, 87, 140; explains why Wilson opposed dispatch of special emissaries and missions, 142–43; reports on growing sense of power developing in Washington, 144; praises Mayo mission, 153; reports on U.S. criticisms of British naval effort, 167–68; reports on reasons for Wilson's reserve, 168; reports that U.S. naval leaders had expressed full confidence in Britain, 168; reports on American belief that U.S. would assume commercial and political leadership of world after the war, 170; writes to Balfour to complain about Catholics, Socialists, and Jews, 172; summarizes reasons for dispatch of House mission, 174; mentioned, 51, 56, 64, 111, 129, 142, 143, 169

State Department, U.S., 38, 53, 66, 75, 195, 267

Straits of Dover, 38, 136, 156, 179, 181, 190, 191

Straits of Otranto, 280

Strategy: relation to policy discussed, 29; General Board proposes naval, 45–46; reasons why U.S. accepted Entente views on, 360–61; generalizations on relation between, and policy, 364

Submarine chasers: role in Mediterranean Sea discussed, 275–80

Submarines, German. See U-boats

Suez, 107, 238, 251, 252

Suez Canal: effect of submarine warfare on, 281; mentioned, 251

Supreme War Council: founded, 174; calls upon Italy to agree to naval redistribution in the Mediterranean, 256; discusses proposal to make Jellicoe admiralissimo in the Mediterranean, 263–65; and the pre-Armistice negotiations, 341, 345, 347–48; mentioned, 175, 205, 213, 216, 230, 245, 247, 249, 254, 257, 261, 262, 270, 279, 312, 314, 345

Sweden, 36

Switzerland, 80

T

Taranto, 257

Tardieu, André, 169–70

Thomson, Graeme, 145

Train, Comdr. C. R.: reports on probable Italian opposition to Adriatic offensive, 244; criticizes di Revel in message to Sims, 258; mentioned, 267, 353

Trans-Caucasian Railroad, 113

Treaty of London, April 26, 1915: terms described, 228; mentioned, 233–35

Trentino, 233

Triangi, Admiral, 265, 267

Trieste, 233, 241

Trotsky, Leon, 209

Turkey, 32, 144, 252, 253, 259, 272

Tyrrhenian Sea, 238

U

U-boats: numbers of, operating during 1917–1918, 35–36; sinkings of, 65, 81, 218, 281; possible operations of, in U.S. waters, 65–66, 87, 89–90, 223; efforts to expand production of, in Germany, 69; reason why not deployed in groups, 158; difficulties in 1918, 201; construction of, in 1918, 187; reasons for ineffectiveness against troopships, 223; operations in Mediterranean Sea, 226; effect of Otranto barrage on, 281; apparent recovery of efficiency of, 302; Germany concentrates ship construction on production of, 302; evacuate bases in Flanders, 313; surrender of, discussed at Senlis conference, 330; surrendered to Allies, 356; mentioned, 30, 33

U-Boat Office, German: established, 159

U-cruisers: Sims speculates on possible use of, 129–30; Sims suggests methods of protecting against, 130; means of combatting, 152; discounted as danger by Sims, 219–20; operations in American waters, 223; mentioned, 35, 188

Ukraine, 271

Unrestricted submarine warfare: planned by Germany, 30–32; Admiralty estimate of its possible impact in 1917, 42; reaction to, in U.S., 43; German faith in, 61; success of, 65; Balfour's fears of, 74; German comments on success of, 80–81; course of, April–July 1917, 81; defended by Ludendorff and Bethmann-Hollweg, 82; reasons why Germany did not launch it on the American coast in 1917, 90; tactics used against, 99; Germany sustains commitment to, 158, 186–87, 302; failure of, in 1918, 187, 223–24; German efforts to improve efficiency of, 220–23; decision to extend to Mediterranean, 225; Geddes comments on, during mission to U.S., 306; end of, 313; mentioned, 101, 112, 185

V

Valona, 228
Venezuela, 287
Venice, 238
Versailles, Treaty of, 357
Virgin Islands, 49

W

War Cabinet, British: authorizes exploration of possible areas of Anglo-American cooperation, 52; authorizes Lloyd George to press Admiralty for adoption of convoy, 72; plans British naval building program, 79; and secret naval treaty, 110, 115–17; notes importance of containing the submarine, 129; decides to inform Wilson of British efforts, 140; expresses need for American naval assistance, 140; develops plan to invite a congressional delegation to Europe, 142; considers recall of Spring Rice and replacement by Lord Reading, 167; and merchant shipping, 170–71, 207, 294–95; discusses need for Allied Naval Council, 175–76; accepts Geddes recommendations for the Grand Fleet, 191; takes position on naval aid to Russia, 209; gives Geddes permission to continue negotiations for an admiralissimo, 270; proposes that Geddes negotiate shipping matters in Britain rather than U.S., 298; grants Geddes permission to visit the U.S., 300; and the naval armistice terms, 322–23, 324–26, 346, 348; and freedom of the seas, 319, 324, 340; mentioned, 37, 55, 56, 87, 108, 120, 122, 167, 184, 245, 254, 283, 291, 295, 298, 301, 303, 306, 307, 323, 334

War Department, U.S., 184
War Trade Board, U.S., 184
Washington Naval Conference, 1921–1922, 26, 124, 359, 365
Wei Hai Wei, 107
Wemyss, Adm. Wester (First Sea Lord): reports to Imperial War Cabinet, 200–201; reports to Allied Naval Council on naval activity in North Russia, 210; complains about Italian naval thought, 239; reports on German threat to utilize the Russian Black Sea Fleet, 254; supports proposal to declare war on Bulgaria and Turkey, 259; comments on weakness in British position concerning Mediterranean questions, 270–71; prepares memorandum on freedom of the seas, 320–21; and the pre-Armistice negotiations, 322–23, 344–45; mentioned, 235, 266, 275, 276, 277, 280, 291
White Sea, 208, 209, 214, 215
Wilhelmshaven, Germany, 189
Willert, Arthur: transmits Roosevelt's interest in heading an American mission to Europe to Wiseman, 147
William II, Emperor of Germany: supports unrestricted submarine warfare, 31; proves unwilling to authorize submarine operations off U.S. coast, 70, 222; mediates conflicts in the naval high command, 159; mentioned, 34, 35, 59, 221, 308, 336, 357
Williams, Sen. John Sharp, 327
Wilson, Gen. Sir Henry (Chief of the Imperial General Staff), 322
Wilson, President Woodrow: delays decision for war, 43; breaks diplomatic relations with Germany, 44; manifests interest in naval questions prior to intervention, 46–47; makes decision to ask for declaration of war, 49–51; asks

Congress to declare war against Germany, 51; orders expansion of the Navy, 51; opposes prewar consultations with the Allies, 52; complains about the Anglophilism of W. H. Page, 54; proposes confidential naval discussions with Britain, 54–55; commits himself wholeheartedly to goal of victory, 60; attempts to stimulate production of merchant shipping, 70; and convoy, 73, 97; nurses suspicions of British naval competence, 73, 131; intervenes in activities of the Navy Department, 90–100; calls for independent naval activity by U.S., 92–93; prepares telegram for Sims requesting confidential report on naval policy, 93–94, 98; addresses officers of Atlantic Fleet, 98, 131–32; expresses distrust of Japan, 112; defines his basic diplomatic posture during wartime, 114, 126; opposes public declaration of war aims, 114; and the proposed secret naval treaty, 116, 119–20, 123–24; and Sims, 120, 203; informs House that U.S. aims differed from those of the Entente, 126; works hard to set up machinery for conduct of the war, 126–27; discusses need for naval offensives with Daniels and naval officers, 131–33; reasons for opposing American representation at inter-Allied conferences, 144; and the Mayo mission, 146–47; decides to send House to Europe for inter-Allied conference, 173; and the Paris Conference, 1917, 174; approves plan for the Supreme War Council, 176; opposes appointment of Sims to the Board of Admiralty, 193–95; informs Daniels that he would veto legislation authorizing American servicemen to ac-

cept foreign decorations, 196; and intervention in Russia, 210, 212, 213, 216; issues the Fourteen Points, including statement on Italian boundaries, 231; and Italy, 232, 267, 282; expresses distrust of Britain, 283–84; begins exchange of notes with Austria-Hungary and Germany, 303–4; expresses criticism of statements by Geddes, 305; discusses possible peace terms with Geddes, including freedom of the seas, 309–10; demurs on large building program proposed by General Board, 310; tells Daniels of desire to back diplomacy with weapons at the peace conference, 310; prepares to complete war time grand design during pre-Armistice negotiations, 318; concludes negotiations with Central Powers, 323–24, 326; expresses to Geddes belief that time was ripe for peace, 327; expresses to Geddes fear of Bolshevik revolution in Europe, 327; notifies Prince Maximilian that he would refer correspondence on peace settlement to an inter-Allied meeting, 328; and the pre-Armistice negotiations, 327–28, 330–31, 334, 338–40, 342, 346, 354–55; proves unwilling to condone military enterprises that endangered his peace plans, 360–61; mentioned, 25, 34, 39, 40, 41, 59, 60, 62, 71, 78, 97, 113, 134, 143, 148, 149, 154, 162, 165, 168, 170, 172, 184, 191, 202, 212, 221, 233, 234, 239, 240, 250, 284, 285, 296, 308, 314, 315, 316, 320, 321, 322, 324, 329, 332, 333, 339, 341, 343

Wiseman, Sir William: discusses convoy with Wilson, 97; discusses proposed naval treaty with Wilson, 119–20; reports to War

Cabinet on state of Anglo-American relations, 141–42; advises Drummond on U.S. failure to meet shipping quotas, 191; reports to London on Wilson's desire to be informed on Orlando's visit to London, 234–35; comments on Anglo-American differerences, particularly over trade policy, 297; reports Wilson's annoyance at bellicose speech by Lloyd George, 296; comments on possibility of postwar friction between the U.S. and Britain, 314; mentioned, 74, 333
Wood, Gen. Leonard, 47
World War II, 26

Y

Yarnell, Captain Harry E., 248

Z

Zeebrugge, 35, 78, 95, 113, 189
Zimmermann, Arthur W. (Foreign Ministry of Germany): announces unresricted submarine warfare, 32; explains reasons for unrestricted submarine warfare, 43–44; opposes unnecessary provocation of U.S., 70; informs Hindenburg that Japan would make only limited contributions to the war in Europe, 114; mentioned, 35, 69